The Trial of Tom Horn

The Trial of Tom Horn

John W. Davis

University of Oklahoma Press : Norman

Library of Congress Cataloging-in-Publication Data

Davis, John W., 1943– author.
    The trial of Tom Horn / John W. Davis.
        pages cm
    Includes bibliographical references and index.
    ISBN 978-0-8061-5218-9 (hardcover : alk. paper)
1. Horn, Tom, 1860–1903—Trials, litigation, etc. 2. Trials (Murder)—
Wyoming—History—20th century.   I. Title.
    KF223.H63D38 2016
    345.787'025230978719—dc23

                                                            2015028035

The paper in this book meets the guidelines for permanence and dur-
ability of the Committee on Production Guidelines for Book Longevity
of the Council on Library Resources, Inc. ∞

1 2 3 4 5 6 7 8 9 10

In memory of Dr. David L. Freeman

Contents

Illustrations

MAPS

The Trial of Tom Horn

CHAPTER ONE

"Willie Is Murdered"

Early in the morning of July 18, 1901, Willie Nickell rode to a gate about three-quarters of a mile west of his parents' homestead. The homestead was in an area of southeastern Wyoming known as Iron Mountain, which sits along the eastern edge of the Laramie Mountains, a long chain of highlands extending from near the Colorado-Wyoming border northward for more than a hundred miles. Willie's father, Kels Nickell, had told his son to ride the twelve miles to the tiny hamlet of Iron Mountain to find a man who might be hired as a sheepherder, and shortly before 7:00 A.M., Willie saddled a horse and rode up the draw leading southwest from his home.

The Iron Mountain area was well settled in the early twentieth century, and most of the inhabitants made their livings raising cattle.[1] The settlers included Willie Nickell's parents—his father and mother, Mary. Kels Nickell was born and grew up in Kentucky and had enlisted in the army in 1875; he served in Wyoming and Montana and was discharged in 1880. In 1881 he married Mary Mahoney in Cheyenne; she was born in County Cork, Ireland. In 1885 the Nickells took up their homestead in southeastern Wyoming, and by 1901 they had nine children. Willie was the third child born to them.[2]

The land Willie Nickell rode through on July 18 was not the majestic mountain country found in much of Wyoming, but rolling, rugged hills, spotted with aspen, sumac, and limber and ponderosa pines. Sagebrush filled the substantial spaces between larger vegetation. Where the road lifted out of the draw, Willie rode into a ponderosa pine stand, open woods of bushy

pines among rock outcroppings, and at this opening Willie encountered a wire gate he knew well.[3]

Willie Nickell was fourteen, a quiet, well-behaved boy of average height
for his age but stockier than normal. He was wearing overalls, a little vest,
a light hat, and a shirt, and he was riding his father's horse. Willie dis-
mounted at the gate, opened it, and then led the horse through. He had
apparently closed the gate and resumed his journey when he saw something, or someone, that alarmed him, and he returned to the gate and
started to reopen it.[4]

When a bullet suddenly slammed into his body, he must have been
profoundly stunned and confused. That bullet hit him just a few inches
below his left armpit and blew out through his sternum. He froze in that
position until a second bullet hit Willie's left side just below the first bullet
and went through part of his intestines and his aorta, coming out just
above his right hip. The boy ran when the second bullet struck, like a deer
shot through the heart. Adrenaline surged through his body, compelling
him to flee frantically, but he did not get far. Willie ran back toward his
home, but collapsed within about twenty yards, falling on his face.[5]

The killer emerged, walked to the boy's body, and turned him on his
back. He pulled back Willie's shirt, apparently to check his handiwork. The
killer also placed a small rock under the boy's head. About a mile and a
half away, Kels Nickell, the boy's father, heard three shots but was not
alarmed by them, assuming someone was hunting.

The body lay on the ground undiscovered all that day. His parents, sitting at home that evening, observed that Willie had not returned and
were concerned, but they assumed their boy had not been able to catch
up to the man he had gone looking for and so had stayed overnight in
Iron Mountain.

The next morning, Freddie, Willie's ten-year-old brother, was sent on
a chore along the same road Willie had traveled the day before. He returned
in a few minutes, riding up to the ranch house, crying. His mother, standing
at the door, asked, "What is the matter?"

"Willie is murdered," sobbed Fred.[6]

Stunning though this news may have been, the people in the Nickell
house acted quickly. Kels directed his brother-in-law, William Mahoney, to
hitch up a wagon and drive Mary to the gate. Other members of the
family accompanied the two. Kels and J. A. B. Apperson, a civil engineer

and surveyor who was at the Nickells's ranch to do a survey, walked directly to the gate and arrived there first.[7]

They found Willie lying on his back with his head toward the Nickell house (to the east), his hands to his sides, and his body on the road. Willie's bloody shirt had stiffened, but it was open, exposing his wounds. The two men noted a rock about two inches in diameter under the left side of the boy's head, and Kels observed that the stone did not seem to lie there naturally as there were very few rocks in the road.[8] Apperson traced a trail of blood back to the gate, which was open and dropped at the posts. He concluded that Willie had been turned onto his back.[9]

After the wagon arrived, they placed Willie's body in the wagon and Mahoney drove it back to the house.[10] Kels Nickell and Apperson then began a cursory examination around the gate. They looked for tracks, a task made difficult because of the rough ground and because cattle had come through the area.[11] Each day the Nickell family put their milk cattle into a pasture near the gate, and shortly before Willie had arrived there on July 18, his brother Fred had taken the animals to this pasture.[12] With the gate down, the cattle had moved through it, though it was not clear if the small herd had passed through the area around the gate once or twice. The area was rough and broken, so that even without the cattle's obliterating wanderings, tracks were hard to discern. Nickell and Apperson found just one track, probably belonging to Willie.[13] They also looked for cartridges but found none, and they confirmed as well that Willie had not been carrying a firearm.[14]

Kels Nickell felt he knew who had killed his son. "Considerable trouble" between Kels and his neighbor Jim Miller—ugly, long-standing, sometimes violent disputes—not surprisingly led him to immediately suspect members of the Miller family. The fathers' clashes had drawn in the male children of the two large families. Nickell went directly to a schoolhouse located near the Miller ranch house, taking along his neighbor Joe Reed. His intent was to interrogate the schoolmarm, one Glendolene Myrtle Kimmell, who boarded with the Millers.[15]

Arriving at the school, Nickell found Miss Kimmell, as she was known, and demanded to know whether Jim Miller and his two sons, Gus and Victor, had been present at breakfast the day before. Miss Kimmell was apparently taken aback, and knowing of the trouble between the two families and not wanting to carry "news between them to keep it up," evaded

Nickell's questions. When told of the murder, she seemed more responsive but still did not satisfy Nickell with her answers.[16]

Wyomingites have always been quick to help each other in a crisis, especially in rural areas, and that afternoon neighbors came to call at the Nickells' home. The family had little time to be comforted, however. A coroner's inquest would be convened in their parlor the very next day.[17]

CHAPTER TWO

The Coronoer's Inquest Convenes

Sometime Friday, July 19, Kels Nickell sent a message to authorities in Cheyenne, the Laramie County seat about forty miles to the southeast, telling of the murder of his son.[1] Thomas Murray, the Laramie County coroner in 1901, was empowered to convene an inquest regarding any death in the county in which a person died by "unlawful means" or "by violence." Remarkably, Murray and two companions were on a fishing trip near Iron Mountain when Willie Nickell's body was found. Wyoming statutes allowed Murray to select any three citizens of the county for a coroner's jury, and he selected his fishing friends Tunis Joseph Fisher, the Laramie County district court clerk, and George Gregory, the county assessor, as well as a local resident, Hiram G. Davidson. The only men who had to travel from Cheyenne to the Nickell ranch were Deputy Sheriff Peter Warlamount and court stenographer Robert C. Morris.[2]

Rarely used today, a coroner's inquest was frequently employed over a hundred years ago. It served not only to learn the cause of a person's death but also, if a crime was suspected, to ferret out the guilty parties.[3] The coroner, by statute, exercised the powers and duties of the county sheriff. People could be subpoenaed to testify under oath and prosecutors could thereby interrogate all persons with potential knowledge of the circumstances of the death. Testimony was taken down and transcribed, so that if a witness was later charged, the testimony could be used by the prosecution. A coroner's inquest, when used well by a county attorney, was an excellent means for obtaining what modern attorneys would call "discovery"—the uncovering of evidence relevant to the commission of a crime.[4] At the same time, the process could be untidy. A coroner's inquest was an investigation usually begun with insufficient information. Unlike a trial, which was typically more focused, it meant a lot of flailing about in the dark.

Only three witnesses were called to testify at the Nickell home the next day. The first was Fred Nickell, who told of finding his big brother's body the day before. His testimony was brief, but it must have been a sad few minutes as this ten-year-old boy recounted what had to be the worst episode of his young life.[5]

Joseph E. Reed was then called. Reed testified about his visit, with Kels Nickell, to the schoolhouse where Glendolene Kimmell taught. Reed no doubt did his best to describe the interview of Miss Kimmell, but it was obviously an ambiguous interlude. Reed spoke of how they asked Kimmell a number of questions, but he could not remember all of them. He stated that Miss Kimmell first said that neither Mr. Miller nor his oldest son Gus had been at home around seven the morning of April 18, but then she said that Mr. Miller had been there but that Gus ("Gussie") had not. She avoided answering to a certain extent, saying that it was not her duty to answer such questions about the Millers' private affairs. When told of the murder, however, she said she was ready and willing to answer questions, Reed said, but still did not seem to give any satisfaction.[6]

Willie Nickell's younger sister Catherine (the fourth Nickell child) was called, and her testimony was precise. When asked to fix the time when Willie left the house, she said, "It was about four minutes after Papa left; he left about seven o'clock on Thursday morning." She also said that Willie went on horseback and that he "was all alone by himself." Catherine was the last witness in that abbreviated session, and the coroner's inquest adjourned until Monday morning, July 22, "for further hearing at the County Court House, Cheyenne, Wyoming."[7]

In 1901, Cheyenne was the largest town in Wyoming, the seat of the most populous county (Laramie), and the state capital. These superlatives were impressive only within the tiny population of Wyoming, however. The state then had fewer than 100,000 people (92,531 according to the 1900 census). Laramie County, which included what would become Platte and Goshen Counties, had 20,181 citizens, of whom 14,087 lived in Cheyenne.[8] Still, Cheyenne residents had reasons to be proud of their little city on the Wyoming plains. Created in 1867 when the Union Pacific Railroad arrived at Crow Creek in what would become far southern Wyoming, it was first known as a "hell on wheels" town, as a small army of saloon keepers, gamblers, prostitutes, and assorted ne'er-do-wells descended when the railroad arrived.[9] Most of these people did not stay long, however, but followed the transcontinental railroad caravan when the UP continued its manic charge to the west. In a short time Cheyenne, named for the Indian tribe, settled into a more staid existence, in which ambitious go-getters started building a community. By the first years of the twentieth century, Cheyenne could boast of a number of handsome two- and three-story buildings along streets paralleling the UP track, as well as "468 business entities, . . . three railroads, four newspapers, 18 restaurants, 14 grocery stores, four churches [at least eight others were unlisted], seven pool table rooms, two banks, two plumbers and one library."[10] In addition to a UP roundhouse, Cheyenne was the site of an army post, Fort D. A. Russell, a large post office and federal building, the Cheyenne Opera House, and a magnificent railroad depot.[11]

On July 22, 1901, when the coroner's inquest convened in Cheyenne, city residents were aroused and alarmed about the killing of Willie Nickell. An article in the *Cheyenne Daily Leader* stated, "Excitement over the killing is intense." A newspaper in Denver, a hundred miles to the south, predicted a lynching when the murderer was found.[12] Willie Nickell's funeral had taken place the day before, at the Cheyenne Methodist church, and Kels Nickell had created a sensation when he barged his way to the gravesite where he kneeled and "prayed heaven for strength to slay the murderer of his son."[13]

The first business at the July 22 courthouse proceedings was the testimony of three physicians who had examined Willie's body. Conducting their examinations was Walter R. Stoll, Laramie county attorney. It was Stoll's first appearance in the Willie Nickell murder proceedings, a case in which he would become a central figure. Stoll conducted most of the questioning of witnesses before the coroner's jury and no doubt decided who would be called to testify. He had arrived in Wyoming as a West Point graduate in 1880. Lieutenant Stoll had been assigned first to Fort McKinney (near Buffalo, Wyoming) and then to Fort D. A. Russell, but he resigned his commission in 1884 to study for the bar and entered the Wyoming state bar in 1886.[14] Stoll did remarkably well as an attorney. An 1892 article in the *Cheyenne Sun* said he had a clientage "the largest and most influential of any lawyer in Cheyenne," a questionable declaration given the presence of John W. Lacey and Willis Van Devanter.[15] Even if not up to the lofty standards of Lacey & Van Devanter, Stoll, in his third term as county attorney, had compiled a remarkable record, but he could be erratic.[16] As Democratic state party chairman at the time of the infamous Johnson County War of 1892, he had infuriated state convention delegates with an intemperate defense of the actions of the big cattlemen who had invaded Johnson County and had to resign before the state convention could throw him out.[17] Still, Stoll was undoubtedly an exceptional talent and his talent matched his ambition: he was a driven and aggressive lawyer. In the ten years before the murder of Willie Nickell, Wyoming newspapers were full of stories about Stoll's legal feats, which ranged from a brilliant defense in an 1891 murder case to his involvement in the most prominent civil cases in 1900.[18] Wyoming newspapers remarked especially on his skills as an orator and cross-examiner.[19] Stoll could not have known that his leisurely examination of three doctors in the Willie Nickell inquest would lead, in just over a year, to his greatest challenge as a cross-examiner.

The first physician called was Amos Barber, a Cheyenne doctor who came to Douglas, Wyoming, in 1885 after graduating from the University of Pennsylvania Medical School. Barber's path to Cheyenne was unusual. He was the first elected Wyoming secretary of state, and when the Wyoming legislature chose Francis E. Warren as a U.S. senator in November 1890, Barber became acting governor.[20] He was still governor of Wyoming in 1892 at the time of the Johnson County War, and he supported in every way he could the big cattlemen who carried north their list of seventy men to be shot or hanged. His stance was profoundly unpopular throughout Wyoming, except in Laramie County, and when his term as governor was completed, he made no attempt at further political office, remaining instead in Cheyenne, and resuming his practice of medicine.[21]

Stoll called Barber as a witness because the medical examination of Willie's body was a crucial first step in the murder prosecution. Willie's body had not been examined until three days after the boy was killed, when Barber and two other physicians went to Turnball's Undertaking Parlors in Cheyenne the morning of Sunday, July 21, 1901, to perform their work.[22] Barber submitted his report and explained it. Although the doctor testified that he performed an autopsy, his examination would not be considered an autopsy by modern standards because he did not enter the body but only examined its appearance.[23]

Barber testified that the two bullets hit Willie Nickell on his left side just under his arm and that each came out on his right side. Because they had taken the same slightly downward trajectory through Willie's body, he concluded that both bullets had been fired from the same position.[24] Barber also concluded, because of a staining on the inverted edges of the entry wounds, that both shots were lead bullets of a large caliber, at least three-eighths of an inch and perhaps as large as .45 of an inch.[25] Given the decomposed condition of the body, he supposed the wound had somewhat contracted.[26]

When asked the probable distance of the shooter from the victim, Barber could only say that the shots had not been fired within a few feet because the entrance wounds displayed no powder burns. The physician felt that the slight downward path of the bullet might indicate the position of the person shot and the person shooting. Stoll asked if the downward path might also indicate that the shots came from a substantial distance and were on their descent, but Barber thought that unlikely because, if so, they would have been spent bullets, without the energy to go completely through the body.[27]

Dr. Barber was followed by two other physicians, Drs. John H. Conway and George P. Johnston. Conway endorsed Barber's conclusions, saying, "It was entirely covered by him."[28] Johnston agreed with Barber's opinion that the bullets entering Willie Nickell's body were of a very large caliber proceeding at great velocity. He agreed that the bullets were probably lead, and he said the distended, bloated condition of the body did not affect the size of the entry wounds.[29] He did note, however, that the body's decomposition was so great that the epidermis was rubbed off on the upper wound so that it was not as plain as the lower wound.[30]

After the physicians completed their testimony, Stoll called J. A. B. Apperson, a particularly helpful witness because he was an engineer and surveyor. On Saturday, July 20, Apperson had returned to the gate, taken some measurements, and made a sketch of the crime scene, showing various key features.[31] Apperson said he thought the killing shot might have come from one of two points, one a clump of rocks only 72 feet away and the other from a place 195 feet away.[32]

Apperson told the coroner's jury that the Nickell house was about three-quarters of a mile east of the gate and the Miller house about three-quarters of a mile west of the gate. He said that he had come to the Nickell ranch on Tuesday and that all the Nickell children had been there except for the oldest boy, Kels, Jr., who was attending school in Hazel Green, Kentucky, and the married daughter, Julia Cook.[33] Apperson had done some surveying Wednesday afternoon and resumed surveying Thursday morning.[34]

Questioned about strangers (as were many subsequent witnesses), Apperson said the only stranger he knew of was a man who had come to the Nickell house on Tuesday looking for work as a sheepherder. Kels Nickell had told the man he already had a sheepherder, but then on Wednesday the incumbent sheepherder decided to leave so Kels sent Willie looking for the man who had just inquired about a job.[35] Apperson did not know the name of the man but said he had left in a good-natured way and was not angry.[36]

On Thursday morning, before seven, Apperson, Kels Nickell, and Nickell's brother-in-law, William Mahoney, had traveled from the Nickell house to resume surveying.[37] They were about to commence work when they heard three very loud shots. Apperson said one shot was fired and then, in about thirty seconds, two more in "quick succession." Apperson did not think the shots came from a revolver but from a Winchester or large gun.[38] In the hilly country around the Nickell ranch, the gate was obscured from the survey party, but Apperson said the shots came from the direction of the gate, about a mile and a half to a mile and three-quarters away from them. He also testified that he heard the shots about a half an hour after his surveying group left the Nickell house.[39] None of the three men were alarmed when they heard the shots, all thinking that someone was hunting. They worked through the rest of the day and returned to the Nickell place for dinner. Kels learned that during that day his son Fred had not fired his little gun (a .22 caliber). Willie was not at dinner, but he was not expected.[40]

That Thursday night, Mr. Apperson testified, dogs caused quite a ruckus, waking him up with their barking. It occurred to Apperson that somebody was about the Nickell place to cause the dogs to make such noise.[41]

The next morning, Friday, July 19, came the devastating news that Willie had been shot and killed. When Apperson and Kels went to the gate, they could not find any tracks because cattle had "tramped through there." Apperson concluded that Willie had opened the gate, taken his horse through, and then was shot while closing the gate. Although Apperson acknowledged that the cattle would obliterate any tracks in the road, he apparently did not consider the possibility that Willie had gone through, closed the gate behind him, set out, but then come back and was shot while reopening the gate.[42]

Apperson described the scene and gave grisly testimony about Willie's blood being strewn about the area. Apperson found a pool of blood about five feet from the gate post, and then followed a trail of blood at places five to ten feet apart from the gate, where Willie was shot, to the place he had collapsed.[43] Willie was on his back, but Apperson thought he "undoubtedly" had been on his face and then been turned over because of a pool of blood on the ground about three feet from the body, and the sand and gravel that had adhered to Willie's face and clothing. Willie's face and shirt were saturated with blood, and the shirt protruded out, exposing the wound, as if "someone had his finger in there and pulled it open." Dried blood had apparently kept the shirt open.[44]

Apperson explained that on Saturday, evidently after testimony was taken by the coroner, several people had gone to the murder site to make a thorough examination of the area, including all the jurors, Apperson and Kels Nickell, and Deputy Sheriff Warlamount. In searching for bullets and tracks, they thought they saw one of Willie's tracks about the middle of the gate, but it was apparently not distinct. Fisher, one of the jurymen, did find what looked like the imprint of the butt of a gun in soft sand "in the rear of the rocks."[45]

Apperson's testimony and that of all the witnesses preceding him related to the circumstances surrounding Willie Nickell's death. No testimony had been presented to show who killed Willie. That would change when Willie's father, Kels, took the stand.

CHAPTER THREE

Who Killed Willie Nickell?

Walter Stoll must have eagerly awaited Kels Nickell's testimony. The killing of Willie Nickell was obviously an assassination, meaning that the most serious charge, first-degree murder, would apply. First-degree murder carried an automatic death penalty in Wyoming in 1901.[1] Any competent prosecutor would feel challenged by such a case, even more a lawyer of Stoll's caliber. Kels Nickell was the first witness to address directly who killed his son, and Nickell thought he knew who did it.

He had barely begun his testimony when Stoll asked him if he suspected anybody of having killed his son. "I do," said Nickell. "I suspect the Millers." That included the father, Jim Miller, and his two sons, Gussie and Victor, and the stated reason for Nickell's suspicion was all the trouble one family had with the other: "Miller has chased this boy heretofor[e]."[2] Describing a previous year's incident he had been told about, Nickell said Jim Miller had chased Willie with a gun and "pulled a shotgun on him and snapped it at him."[3] No one had been hurt, but Nickell viewed the incident as a deadly threat to his son.

Kels Nickell was right: there had been a lot of trouble between the Miller and Nickell families. He did not recount all the incidents, but any citizen reading newspapers in southeastern Wyoming in 1900 and 1901 would have known of several troubling events. A June 23, 1900, article in the *Wyoming Tribune* featured a headline stating: "Feud between the Nickell-Miller Faction Again Re-opened." The story detailed how Kels Nickell had preferred charges against Gus (Gussie) and Victor Miller for "mutilating" fence around the Nickell place, and it referred to an earlier pistol duel between Nickell and Jim Miller. It was impossible to know what the outcome of this present quarrel would be, said the article, "as both sides are actuated by a feeling of enmity for his neighbor and will fight the case to the end."[4] The end for this episode was that the Miller boys were acquitted of the charges against them.[5]

Jim Miller kept his guns loaded because of the dispute with his neighbor, and in August 1900, one shotgun accidentally discharged, killing Miller's son Frank. Jim Miller blamed Kels Nickell for his son's death. Just four months later, when Miller and Nickell met in a Cheyenne restaurant, Miller stabbed Nickell in the shoulder and Nickell pulled a pistol but did not fire.[6] Following other incidents, Kels Nickell had Jim Miller arrested twice and each party had imposed peace bonds against the other. A peace bond is a procedure whereby a judge may order a person to post a bond, which is forfeited if the person fails to "keep the peace."[7]

In his defense, Jim Miller was not the only person who had difficulty getting along with Kels Nickell, who had a history of violent disputes. In July 1890, Nickell had a row with two men, John Coble and a man named Cross. All three were riding a train, apparently from Cheyenne to Iron Mountain, when Cross and Nickell quarreled. Nickell moved to another part of the train, but Coble and Cross followed him, and Nickell slashed Coble with a knife in the subsequent fracas. Coble pressed charges, but Nickell, arrested and tried, was acquitted.[8] In 1894, the *Laramie Boomerang* told of clashes between Nickell and other neighbors of his, the Waechters. Nickell pressed charges against John Waechter, claiming Waechter shot at him after Nickell trespassed on Waechter's meadow. The presiding judge dismissed that case, but Nickell then swore out a warrant against another member of the Waechter family, Chris, charging him with assault following a fistfight that Nickell lost. Chris Waechter pled guilty, but then John Waechter had Nickell arrested for cutting a barbwire fence and for "malicious trespass."[9]

In March 1900 the *Wyoming Tribune* wrote of still another violent incident, in which Kels Nickell had preferred charges against two men for assault with intent to kill. Henry A. Curtis and Ernest J. Addington had the bad luck to encounter Kels Nickell while looking for stray cattle. They rode through an open gate on Nickell's place, and, since it was open, they left it open. Nevertheless Nickell became "incensed at their effrontery and presumption" and then cursed the trespassers "in choice and elegant language that cannot be found in the dictionaries." Things escalated from there, and Nickell and the two men proceeded to fire salvos at each other from long distance. Both sides seemed equally guilty of assault, and how the case was finally resolved is unknown, but the *Tribune* noted that the incident showed "what trivial things at times will lead to quarrels, with death as a probable result."[10]

At the July 22 inquest, Nickell told of still another incident, dating from early June 1901. Willie and a friend, Harley Axford, had started off on a fishing trip when they met Jim Miller and some of his children. According to Kels Nickell, Miller demanded to know "if [Willie's] father was under bonds yet."[11] Then Miller started cursing at Willie, saying, "You God damned son of a bitch, you whip one of my boys and I will whip you," and he hit Willie over the head twice with a stick he used to drive his team. Nickell said that Miller had called Willie "all the dirty names he could speak" and pointed a six-shooter at Willie, cocking it and saying he was going to kill the boy. Jim Miller then tried to force Willie off his horse to fight Victor Miller, but Willie refused, thinking the elder Miller would catch him.[12]

Kels Nickell said that Jim Miller had always been trying to get Willie to fight the oldest Miller boy, Gussie. Insisting that Willie always got the best of Gussie, Nickell said, "For that reason I think the whole three is mixed in this thing." He said he figured that "the intention was to get me in place of the boy from what I have heard. I have heard a good deal of threats. I think the old man didn't fire the shots at all; I think he placed his boy there; my opinion now is that Victor is the one that fired the shots."[13]

Nickell gave two reasons supporting his theory. The first was that Victor had stayed at Joe Reed's place on Wednesday night, July 17, but left there Thursday morning at about seven, and then Victor showed up at the Reed ranch between ten and eleven o'clock that morning, and he had a Winchester rifle on his horse. The second reason stemmed from his interview of Miss Kimmell, the schoolteacher, wherein, Nickell said, she "never did tell who ate breakfast; she told me that neither Miller or Gussie ate breakfast with her," adding, "She hummed around a whole lot and didn't want to tell." Nickell did not ask her about Victor, because at that time he "thought it was the older boy and the old man."[14]

Nickell elaborated: "I believe that [Jim] Miller and Gussie saw this thing; I think Miller was on the rocks south of there. I believe these other two could have been on the higher place to give signals: I believe one reason Willie was killed there [is that] I was to be killed at the gate before I got through the gate. In place of that he saw it was Willie; he didn't want to kill Willie, and he went on through. I believe Miller saw this thing and that he gave the signal to shoot, and that he had to obey that signal and kill that boy. That is my belief the way the boy was killed."[15]

As a good lawyer and a perceptive human being, Walter Stoll must have noted that Nickell's observations were speculative, and he tried to tease more substance from the witness's statements. First, Stoll asked Nickell if he was saying that "Miller's boy might have been stationed behind the rocks," saying, "Miller thought the boy was you and signaled from a distance to his boy and his boy shot?"

"Yes, sir," said Nickell.

Stoll then asked Nickell if he had seen anything like this. "No, sir," answered Nickell. Did he know if anybody else had seen anything? "No, sir, I do not," Nickell said.[16]

Stoll abruptly switched topics and asked Nickell whether he had a conversation with Tom Horn in Cheyenne about Horn's coming to the Iron Mountain area. Tom Horn was then employed as a range detective by Bosler, Wyoming, cattleman, John Coble (the same man Kels Nickell had stabbed back in 1890) and had a notorious reputation. He was believed involved in the killing of several men at the instructions of his employer and other big cattlemen. Nickell testified that in May he had gone into a saloon, where Horn had grabbed him by the shoulder and said he wanted to talk to him. Horn had asked Nickell if he had heard about Horn's making threats against him. Nickell told Horn he had heard "lots of things," and Horn then launched into a long discourse. He said to Nickell, "I will tell you, Tom Horn may be a damned son of a bitch, but he says you have proved to him that you are a man of your word. You heard I was going to kill you when you got in with the sheep," said Horn. (Nickell had recently brought a large band of sheep into the Iron Mountain area). Nickell again said, "I have heard a whole lot."[17] Horn replied at length: "I will tell you, [a] damned son of a bitch the other day made the expression that Nickell was after his sheep and would soon be in here with them [but] he wouldn't last long because Tom Horn was going to kill him as soon as he got in here. That son of a bitch don't know Tom Horn." Horn told Nickell that the "damned son of a bitch" was Miller's oldest boy, Gus, and according to Nickell, Horn claimed: "Those fellows making talk like that are more in danger of Tom Horn than anybody in the country. The sheep don't bother me. I am working for two men, that is Johnny Coble and the Two Bar outfit. They are tickled because you are bringing the sheep in; they have no enmity against you for bringing the sheep in there. I am working to prevent men stealing off them or getting away with their property. We are not afraid of sheepmen going to steal our cattle. You have no danger in that direction."[18] This was an odd thing for Horn to have said. His employer, Coble, was surely concerned with more than theft. Sheep might eat grass his cattle needed.

Nickell testified that he had told Horn that if he had any business about his place, he should "come like a man." Horn had replied: "I am perfectly satisfied; I will tell you now, I will never make no sneaks; if I have business at your place, I will come there."[19]

Stoll asked Nickell whether the things he had heard "were about the killing of Lewis and Powell," and Nickell acknowledged that they were. William Lewis and Fred Powell were two small cattlemen and alleged rustlers who had spreads on Horse Creek (a few miles south of the Iron Mountain area) who had been gunned down from ambush in 1895. Vigorous efforts were made to find the killer, including the convening of a grand jury, but all efforts failed, in part because Iron Mountain residents felt intimidated and would not come forward to testify. The grand jury came close to indicting Tom Horn, but, in the end, declined because the evidence was not strong enough. The strong feeling in the Iron Mountain area, however, was that Tom Horn had gunned down two men at the bidding of big cattlemen who suspected Lewis and Powell were cattle thieves. A Denver newspaper, the *Rocky Mountain News,* expressed this opinion in a series of articles, one of which stated that in keeping with their lawless past practices (referring especially to the invasion of Johnson County to lynch seventy men), cattle barons had established themselves as "judges, jurors and executioners, . . . [with the intention of removing] all whom they may suspect of cattle stealing and who in any manner stand in the way of their complete possession of the range."[20]

Nickell also testified that he had been told that Horn had been seen around the area, "somewheres Wednesday," meaning July 17, 1901.[21] Tom Horn's presence was significant. Willie Nickell had been assassinated, and Tom Horn was widely suspected of being an assassin. At this early stage, Stoll was still casting about for a consistent thread of facts leading to the killer's identity. He would continue to inquire about strangers and track down all the evidence relating to the Millers, but Tom Horn's presence introduced an important new line of inquiry.

Kels Nickell comes across as an angry man who demanded vengeance, but his feelings were more complicated than that. Nickell was devastated by his son's death. He broke down during his testimony, and Reverend Benjamin Young, the minister who presided at Willie Nickell's funeral, said he watched Willie's distraught father invoke the wrath of heaven at the gravesite. Nickell had been having disputes with his neighbors for years, and when Willie was killed, Kels felt he had called this calamity down and just wanted to know what he could do.[22] People were not inclined to be critical of Nickell, because "the utmost sympathy is felt for the bereaved parents," according to an article in the *Cheyenne Daily Leader*.[23] Perhaps Laramie County people were also aware of Nickell's hard life and his good points, as a provider, a husband, and a father. Still, he was not easy to get along with.

When Nickell was a boy in Kentucky, his father was murdered by Confederate sympathizers and the family thrown off their farm in the late 1860s. He joined the U.S. Army in 1875 when twenty years old and served under General George Crook from 1875 to 1880. He arrived on the Custer battlefield on June 27, 1876, two days after the Little Bighorn fight. After his army service, he met Mary Mahoney in Cheyenne and they were married. Mrs. Nickell described her husband as a "handsome and kindly man," and from articles in some of the same newspapers that described Nickell as violent, it is clear that he was hard-working and resourceful—committed to building a better life for his wife and children.[24]

Nickell had just accused Jim Miller and his sons of horrendous acts, and the coroner's jury and Walter Stoll no doubt waited with great interest to hear from the next witness, Gus Miller, Jim Miller's older son. Gus's testimony is surprising. He answered the prosecuting attorney's questions directly and, seemingly, candidly. All we have of the testimony today is the transcript from the coroner's inquest, and typewritten words in a transcript are only part of the mosaic of impressions that the live presence of a human being presents. A transcript's limitations should always be borne in mind. A transcript shows only the words spoken, not the inflections given those words, the emphasis, the pauses, the variations in rate of speech and volume, not to mention countless nonverbal signals, such as eye contact, posture, evidence of comfort level, and gestures, all of which frequently carry more power than words. Still, the distinct impression from reading Gus Miller's testimony is that of a calm and polite witness trying to answer questions as best he can.

Gus told Walter Stoll that he was nineteen and had lived near Iron Mountain, "nine miles from the station," for about fifteen years, and he had known Willie Nickell "ever since he was a little boy."[25] Going to an important question before the coroner's jury, the prosecutor asked Miller whether he ever had any trouble with Willie Nickell. "No, sir, I never had any trouble with him," responded Gus. "Have you had any trouble with the other scholars of a serious nature?" asked Stoll. "No, sir," said Gus. "Did you have any feelings against Willie Nickell on account of the trouble between your father and his father." "No, sir," said Gus.[26]

Stoll then asked a question that Gus might have tried to evade. "Did your brother Victor have any trouble with him [Willie]?" Gus answered directly, while giving his own slant: "Yes, he had a sort of fight with him one time." Gus explained that when boys from each family met at a gate "at the McArthur place," three miles northeast, they found that Kels Nickell had wired the gate shut, which had been open. "Tell us about the fight," said Stoll. Gus answered: "It was not really a fight; they just kind of struck at one another and hit one another, got to quarreling and made up again." The Nickell boys told the Miller boys that they could not go through that gate anymore because Kels Nickell had made a land claim, and that started the dispute that proceeded to clinching and wrestling. In the end, the dispute was resolved when the Nickell boys agreed "to leave it [the gate] open until their father came back," and all the boys agreed, "We were going to be friends."[27]

Gus said he had met Willie every once in a while since this gate incident, and they "would ride along and talk as far as we would be going together." Gus said he had no quarrel with Willie, and neither did his brother, Victor, and Gus's mother and the Nickells "have always been friends." The last time he saw Willie, Gus said, was at a July 4 dance, when he talked with Willie a bit. When he left Willie, he had no ill feelings toward him and Willie had none toward him. Willie was "just as friendly as can be."[28]

Stoll no doubt expected Gus Miller to testify that he was not at the gate where Willie Nickell was killed on July 18. As an experienced prosecutor, Stoll also knew that if Gus presented a false alibi, the way to defeat it was through the details of Gus's story—a false alibi will almost always break down in the details. Stoll plunged into those details, asking about Gus's movements the morning of Thursday, July 18. Gus said he slept in a tent near his house (Victor was also in the tent) and described what he did from the time he awoke. Before breakfast he walked after a team of horses about a quarter mile south of his house, intending to use the horses for mowing that day.

About 7:00 A.M. he had breakfast at his house with his father, Victor, and Miss Kimmell.[29] Then, after breakfast, between about 7:30 and 7:45, he sharpened a sickle, got the team of horses in the corral, put on the harness, and went out and cut alfalfa until noon. Gus said all that morning he was at least a mile away from the gate where Willie Nickell was shot.[30]

Stoll asked about rifles, and Gus, appearing to tell everything he knew, said he owned a rifle and carried it for use against a coyote or wolf, but not when he did field work (such as on July 18) or went on a roundup. His rifle was a .30-40 Winchester, shooting a "metal patched" bullet with "a little soft lead on the end." Gus also testified that when his father needed a gun, he used Victor Miller's .30-30 rifle. Gus said Victor's .30-30 used the same kind of soft-nosed bullet as Gus's .30-40. He knew that Willie Nickell had a .22 rifle, which Willie sometimes carried and sometimes did not. Gus told Stoll that his .30-40 was a "magazine gun," and he also knew that most of the people in the locality carried magazine guns.[31]

Apparently Stoll concluded that the shots killing Willie Nickell were from a rifle using a smokeless powder cartridge, meaning they would be louder than shots fired from a cartridge using old-fashioned black powder, and he asked Gus Miller about the cartridges he used. Miller, seemingly not worried about the implications of using shells with smokeless powder, readily agreed that he shot smokeless powder cartridges, which made a sharp crack.[32]

Turning to the activities of Gus's brother, Victor, on July 18, Stoll asked Gus where Victor had been "from the time he got up in the morning until the people left (at) ten o'clock at night." Gus said that Victor first milked the cows and then after breakfast, about half past seven, rode to the McArthur place (about three miles from the Miller place) and then to Mr. Reed's. Gus said Victor took his .30-30 with him.[33]

Stoll asked about strangers. Gus said he knew of no strangers around on July 18 or the next day, but Tom Horn had been at their place on Tuesday, July 16. Horn had arrived on horseback Monday evening, stayed all day Tuesday, and left on Wednesday morning. Gus did not know why Horn had come to the Miller place but offered that he was "just visiting I guess."[34] Gus did know that Horn carried a .30-30 rifle, the same as his brother Victor's, which shot the same kind of bullets. Stoll asked what Horn was doing in that locality. Gus said Horn told him that he had been "down on the hill watching," and Horn remarked that he had seen Gus sending his dog back to the house Friday or Saturday evening (July 12 or 13). Gus understood from Horn's comment that Horn had been watching him very closely from a hill between the Nickell and McArthur places.[35]

Horn stayed in the tent with the Miller boys. Gus heard Horn tell Miss Kimmell that he was a range detective and so "supposed he was watching around any one taking any cattle." Horn had field glasses in a case (that Gus looked through—the Miller boys found them very interesting), and he had a belt in which he carried cartridges.[36]

Gus said that on Tuesday, July 16, Horn had been around the Miller house all day, fishing in the morning at a nearby pond with Gus's father. Around four in the afternoon, Horn rode up to what the Millers called their "tree claim," and returned to report that Kels Nickell's sheep were up there. Gus did not know if Horn was watching Nickell's sheep or why— he seemed to be—but Horn had not said anything else about Nickell. Horn stayed at the Miller place again that night, but left on Wednesday morning, going south toward Iron Mountain.[37]

Apparently testing Horn's reported comments to Kels Nickell, Stoll asked Gus whether he had ever made a remark to anyone that Tom Horn would kill Nickell if he brought sheep in. "No, sir," said Gus. Gus finished his testimony by saying that Horn's only horse was a black one that looked like it was a "good blooded horse," and there was no blanket rolled up behind his saddle, nor did Horn have a slicker.[38]

It might have been logical for the prosecuting attorney to then summon Gus Miller's brother, Victor, to the stand, but, unlike in a trial, witnesses at a coroner's inquest were usually called in accordance with who happened to be available. Apparently the next person available was William Mahoney, Kels Nickell's brother-in-law (Mary Nickell's brother). Mahoney was another member of the surveying party, and Mahoney said he had heard three rifle shots a little after seven on the morning of July 18. He thought the shots were made from smokeless powder because of the way the gun cracked. He also thought, contrary to the statements of J. A. B. Apperson, that there were no intervals between the shots, that they came "one right after another."[39]

Mahoney admitted he did not know who committed this crime and knew of no person who would have any reason for doing it. He disagreed with his brother-in-law, Kels Nickell, that the Millers killed Willie Nickell, agreeing with Stoll's statement that while he (Mahoney) knew there was difficulty between Jim Miller and Kels Nickell he did not think that either Miller or his boys would kill Willie as the result of it. The only threats he had ever heard against Willie were told him by Willie and Harley Axford, describing the confrontation of June 2, 1901.[40]

Harley Axford's testimony generally supported the accuracy of Kels Nickell's statements about the June incident.[41] Axford was the last witness in a long day of testimony in which no obvious suspect had been turned up. But there were many more witnesses still to question.

CHAPTER FOUR

The Coroner's Inquest Continues

The members of the coroner's jury no doubt listened closely to each of the witnesses before them. Their duty was to establish how Willie Nickell was killed and by whom. But the closest listener was surely Walter Stoll, for whom the coroner's jury report would begin a long journey. Stoll would have to decide whether to charge someone and, if so, for what criminal offense, and then begin the long process eventually leading to a trial. When Gus Miller testified before the coroner's jury, Stoll probably sized him up as a possible criminal defendant. Did the facts point to Gus Miller as a killer? Would a jury see him as a likeable, honest young man who could never be considered a killer, or did he have an edge that might persuade jurors that he possessed within his character the cruelty to murder another human being? From the transcript alone, it seems unlikely Stoll believed Gus Miller was an appropriate defendant, but new witnesses might reveal more sinister facts about Miller's character.

The first witness on July 23, 1901, was the one person at the Miller home on the day Willie Nickell was shot who was not related to the Millers and therefore not constrained by kinship. That person was the teacher, Glendolene Myrtle Kimmell, who boarded with the Millers. With Miss Kimmell, the tone of the coroner's inquest changed. The people who had testified earlier were rural people whose pace of speaking was slow and who sometimes had difficulty expressing themselves. Not Glendolene Kimmell. Well-educated, she was also well-spoken. As the *Cheyenne Daily Leader* put it, "The young lady school teacher made an intelligent and interesting witness."[1]

Miss Kimmell told prosecutor Stoll that she had come to Laramie County in January and had been teaching school near the Millers' place for two weeks. She testified that she first heard of Willie Nickell's death at half past nine on the morning of Friday, July 19, when Kels Nickell came into her school, asked her to dismiss the children, and then interrogated her about the whereabouts of the Miller family the day before.[2] She resisted his inquiries, however, not wanting to become a spy on the family she roomed with. When Nickell told her that his son had been shot and killed, she was more willing to answer his questions: "I told him that I could not say positively whether I had eaten breakfast with them or not. I felt sure they [Jim Miller and his two older sons] had been at the house; if they had not been I would have noticed their absence." She added, "I told him I could remember perfectly if I had time to think it over."[3]

In his testimony, Kels Nickell had presented Glendolene Kimmell's hesitation and carefully phrased response as a kind of cover-up. Nickell was an excitable man under the best of circumstances, however, and only two hours prior to his schoolhouse visit he had discovered the mangled body of his fourteen-year-old son. He seems to have leapt to a conclusion, neglecting to fairly weigh what Miss Kimmell was able to tell him.

Miss Kimmell testified that she had not been sure whether it was Friday or Thursday when she had breakfasted with Miller and his sons, but after thinking it over, she remembered with "the utmost distinctness."[4] She had no hesitation stating that Mr. Miller, Gus, and Victor were all at breakfast on Thursday morning. She had first seen Gus Miller between seven and seven thirty, and she said that he "ate breakfast at the table with me and was there throughout breakfast." Victor was also at the table eating breakfast. Miss Kimmell did not remember whether she saw the boys after breakfast, but she spoke with James Miller up until heading to school between 8:30 and 8:45 A.M.[5] She remembered having a dish of strawberries Thursday morning that Victor had picked for her the previous morning.[6]

When Miss Kimmell returned to the Miller house around four that afternoon, she remembered seeing Mr. Miller, Harry Whitman, Mrs. Will McDonald, and Gus and Victor Miller. Especially remarkable, she said, was the "impromptu dance" that began that evening and went on until nearly midnight. "Every one that night seemed to be having a most enjoyable time," she told Stoll. "That sort of dance was new to me; it was a country dance I looked on all evening and noticed particularly how everyone threw a great deal of energy into it. I remember Mr. Miller, Gus and Victor."

When asked if anything seemed to be preying on their minds, she answered, "Not the least, they seemed quite otherwise, cheerful and happy."[7] The next morning, she testified, Whitman and Mr. Miller left early for Cheyenne.[8] Miss Kimmell also said that Victor Miller told her where he had been that morning, which was consistent with Gus Miller's testimony about Victor's whereabouts (that Victor milked the cows before seven, then went to breakfast, to the McArthur place, and then to Mr. Reed's).[9]

When Stoll asked Kimmell if she had encountered any strangers the week of July 15, she said yes, that on Tuesday morning Tom Horn had come to the Miller house. Apparently taken with Tom Horn, she described him as tall and broad-shouldered, a man with "excellent features" and a very pleasant voice. His pronunciation, said Miss Kimmell, was "according to the best English usage." She said he rode a dark horse.[10]

Miss Kimmell testified that she broke the news of Willie Nickell's death to the Millers about eleven o'clock the morning of Friday, July 19. When she told Gus, Victor, and Mrs. Miller that Willie had been murdered, "they all seemed very much surprised, and they spoke in regretful terms of the boy." Was there any feeling of triumph or gladness about his death, Stoll asked? "Not in the least," she said, "it was just the opposite."[11] In closing her testimony, Stoll asked if there was anything else. "Well," she answered, "I can say that in my entire conversation with the Miller family since I have known them, I have never heard them make any threats so far as the Nickell family are concerned. They have always spoken tolerantly of them. Mr. Miller has said that he did not like Mr. Nickell, but he has spoken kindly of his children, and so have all of the family."[12]

Miss Kimmell's testimony powerfully contradicted the notion that Gus and Victor Miller had taken any part in Willie Nickell's murder. She firmly placed them in their home when Willie Nickell was shot over a mile away, and the circumstances she described seemed completely inconsistent with the Millers having felt any sense of guilt. Gus and Victor Miller seemed incapable of murdering a boy earlier in the day and then dancing the night away without conscience. As the *Wheatland World* concluded, Miss Kimmell's testimony had "disproved" the allegations against Victor Miller.[13]

The next witness, James Miller described in detail the chores his sons had begun before breakfast that morning and told of the breakfast itself.[14] His testimony matched that of his son Gus and of Miss Kimmell. This would have been expected, except that a person making up a story might well put forward inconsistent details. There was no such inconsistency.

Asked if his sons carried guns, Miller replied, "Nearly always," saying one had a .30-30 and the other a .30-40. He said that whenever he left the house he carried a gun.[15] Miller also said that when on Monday night, July 15, someone had ridden into his yard and called out, he had grabbed a handgun. Taking a revolver that he kept at the head of his bed, he had gone to the window where he squatted and called out to ask who it was. Miller testified: "He said Horn. I said who is that: he said Horn. I said turn your horse out and come in. He came in and had supper."[16]

In 1901 it was common for travelers to stop at local ranches, and Miller did not say why Horn had appeared at his ranch that night.[17] Miller said he had only "met him [Horn] to know him" twice before. Horn ate breakfast with the Millers the next morning. Miller said Horn seemed to be trying to make an impression on Miss Kimmell, and he seemed to make a very good one.[18]

Perhaps Horn had come to the Miller ranch to meet Miss Kimmell. Several witnesses, including James Miller, testified that Horn bragged about how he watched everybody in the neighborhood from the adjacent hills.[19] If true, Horn no doubt also watched Miss Kimmell coming and going.[20]

Horn spent quite a bit of time with Miller on Tuesday, July 16, which may provide other reasons why Horn appeared at the Miller place. Miller knew the pathways his neighbor Kels Nickell frequented, and Miller may have wanted Nickell's assassination from Horn. Apparently considering the possibility, Stoll asked Glendolene Kimmell whether she had heard Horn and Miller "talk about business matters." Kimmell could not help: "All the time I was at the house when Mr. Horn was there he was in my presence, part of the time alone with him and part of the time Mr. Miller was with us."[21]

Miller did say he went shooting with Horn, but all they shot at was a buzzard and some cans. Horn, Miller testified, was not a good shot. He missed the buzzard and missed the cans a time or two. (Miller himself was reputed to be an excellent shot). The Miller boys were particularly taken with Horn's field glasses. Miller said that Horn had no slicker and no blankets of any kind. Horn told Miller that he had been watching Nickell's sheep, and about 4:00 P.M. Horn went out to locate the sheep. He returned in about three-quarters of an hour and told Miller that Nickell's sheep were right up the creek and in Miller's pasture.[22]

The presence of sheep was a serious matter to a cattleman because sheep ate grass necessary for cattle, and the economic consequences of sheep grazing a cow pasture could be devastating. Surprisingly, Miller responded that he had not driven the sheep out, nor had he complained to the herder. He said he did not act because "I thought it was worse than useless," that "it would do no good." Miller said that he and Nickell had had a good deal of trouble, and he was trying to avoid more.[23] As for Horn, he immediately went back to the Miller house where he spent the rest of the evening—until sometime between nine and ten—talking with the schoolmarm. The next morning, Wednesday, Horn left the Miller place about ten and headed southeast toward Iron Mountain.[24]

Miller recalled Horn talking of a fight with mail robbers, apparently referring to Horn's work on the famous Wilcox train robbery. Horn said he had killed three men and wounded others—a complete fable. But, according to Miller, Horn made no threats against Nickell, although he did say Nickell's bringing in sheep was a very mean trick.[25]

When Stoll asked Miller for his version of the June 2, 1901, incident with Willie Nickell, Miller downplayed its seriousness, saying he had only struck at (but had not hit) Willie with a willow switch. He said he had not threatened to shoot Willie with a pistol, only that he would shoot Willie's horse if he tried to run over Victor.[26] Miller emphasized that this came about after Kels Nickell had struck Victor and repeatedly threatened him.[27] Miller also harshly criticized Willie's friend Harley Axford, who had been with Willie that day, saying that Axford "bears the name of being a liar and a thief" and that he was "not considered a reliable man."[28]

In his testimony, Miller showed that he and his family felt besieged by Kels Nickell. Miller had instructed his boys to keep away from Nickell, but, if Nickell followed them, to shoot him. That was the reason the boys carried their guns whenever they went far from the house. At the same time, Miller said that Willie Nickell was not quarrelsome, that the only thing he (Miller) had heard about was "that little spat with me" and another "little jangle."[29]

Both Miller and Nickell were emotional, belligerent, aggressive men, and Miller was not the kind to back down. Someone may have told Miller to avoid Nickell, and he may have been trying to do so, but it grated on him. Miller also may have been slanting his testimony to discredit what he expected Axford to tell the inquest about Miller's conduct toward Willie Nickell on June 2.

When Eva Miller, James and Dora Miller's teenage daughter, followed her father to the stand, she generally supported his version of the June 2 incident involving Willie, but she was more candid. Careful to admit it if she did not know something, she concurred with what Glendolene Kimmell had said, although she provided additional details, such as Victor Miller feeding the dog after breakfast on Thursday morning and that people at the Miller house that night had not only danced and eaten but had also made ice cream.[30] Eva confirmed that Tom Horn and Miss Kimmell had talked together a good deal and that Horn had shown the teacher a horsehair rope he was making.[31]

Stoll then called Harry Whitman, the twenty-six-year-old son of A. F. Whitman, who confirmed the whereabouts of all Miller family members after he arrived at the Miller place about a quarter to one on Thursday.[32] He testified he had seen nothing unusual about Jim Miller, his sons, or other members of the Miller family that night. Stoll asked him if there seemed to be any "excitement or suppressed emotion, or feeling or anything of that sort," and Whitman replied, "No, sir."[33]

Whitman said he knew of no ill feeling between the Miller and Nickell boys, and he had never heard Gus, Victor, or their father make any threats against Willie or any of the Nickell family. When asked directly about threats against Kels Nickell, however, Whitman said that Miller had said "he was prepared to defend himself at any time." Paraphrasing Whitman, Stoll asked if he was saying that "he didn't want any trouble with Nickells [sic] but if Nickells forced himself upon him he would resent it?" Whitman replied: "That is what I inferred."[34]

A. F. Whitman was the coroner's jury's last witness on July 23, 1901. Whitman said he had observed nothing unusual at the Miller place on Thursday afternoon. The Millers were "cheerful as usual," with nothing weighing on their minds, no reticence, and no forced efforts trying to be pleasant.[35] When Stoll asked about John Coble, Whitman said Coble had gone east within the last ten days. It may not have seemed important at the time, but the information was probably significant to Stoll. Earlier, Miller had noted that Horn made his headquarters at Coble's ranch. When Stoll asked about the neighborhood attitude toward Kels Nickell's introduction of sheep into the area, Whitman said he had heard a good deal of talk opposing Nickell bringing sheep into the country. People thought it was "unwise." Whitman denied any knowledge of threats of harm to Nickell, however, and said he did not know of any enemies of Willie Nickell in the neighborhood, although he had heard Jim Miller express hatred of Kels Nickell.

He quoted Miller as saying he would kill Nickell if attacked, but Miller had also said he would try to escape from Nickell, putting up with annoyances, rather than have trouble.[36]

When the coroner's jury adjourned on July 23, subject to later call, Walter Stoll had a poor case against any of the Millers. All he had was Kels Nickell's speculative accusations and the general conflict between the two families. Stoll, who had the best of seats for the testimony of James Miller and his sons, apparently did not believe he could convince a jury that the Millers were lying murderers. Other observers, as well, saw little evidence of a viable case against Miller and his sons. On July 23 the *Cheyenne Daily Leader* concluded, "Up to the present date not a single definite clue has been obtained that might lead to the apprehension of the murderer."[37]

Other events would change the agenda of the coroner's inquest.

CHAPTER FIVE

Another Shooting

On August 5, 1901, the *Cheyenne Daily Leader* carried a sensational headline: EXTERMINATION OF WHOLE FAMILY. A subhead explained: KELS NICKELL, FATHER OF WILL NICKELL, WHO WAS MURDERED A SHORT TIME AGO, THE OBJECT OF A THRILLING ATTEMPT TO KILL BY TWO HIDDEN SLAYERS— LEFT ARM BROKEN IN AN ASSAULT NEAR HIS RANCH—TWELVE SHOTS FIRED FROM AMBUSH.[1]

"Yesterday morning," the paper said, "twelve shots were fired from magazine guns by two men in ambush at Kels Nickell within three [hundred] yards of his ranch."[2] When Nickell had gone out to milk his cows about six on Sunday morning, he was said to have encountered two men lying in ambush. The shots came from two to three hundred yards away, and one hit him in his left elbow. Grabbing his left arm, Nickell ran back to his house, as the men fired at him "in rapid succession." "Bullets," Nickell said, "struck the ground all around me," and one "ploughed across my right hip but it made only a stinging and smarting sensation." Still another bullet hit Nickell in the back, but "was a glancing blow." Despite his wounds, Nickell escaped to his home, and from there he was taken to Cheyenne. Nickell said he saw both men and, of their identities, added, "there is no doubt about it this time" but declined to tell the newspaper who they were.[3] When he talked later to Laramie County authorities, he declared that he recognized the men who shot at him as Jim Miller and one of his sons.[4]

One day later, the coroner's inquest reconvened in Cheyenne and took evidence throughout the following week. Testimony focused on the Kels Nickell shooting but revisited the shooting of his son Willie and the antagonism in the Iron Mountain area toward sheep owners. Miller and his sons were arrested but still testified. Tom Horn, a looming background presence throughout the earlier proceedings, came forward and testified at length.

The testimony of several witnesses showed that on the Sunday morning that Kels Nickell was shot, the Nickell house was full of family members, including Julia Nickell Cook (who had been there since learning that her brother Willie had been killed), William Mahoney, Harley Nickell (Kels's brother), and all the younger Nickell children. Kels had gotten up early and left the house to milk his cows. Will Mahoney was up and about the house when he heard a shot, and then another, and Kels "commenced to holler." Mahoney heard six shots all told. When he realized that Kels was being attacked, he woke up everybody in the house.[5] The Nickell family poured outside and encountered Kels fleeing back to the house. He was just east of the house, in what they referred to as the potato patch.[6]

Julia, deeply concerned about her father, pushed ahead of the people walking to the potato patch. She may have been an older, married woman, but to Julia her father was still "my papa."[7] There were no further shots, and the family took Kels back to the house. Because the men in the house were afraid to go to a nearby pasture and get a team of horses, Julia got them. Then the men refused to harness the horses, and Julia rode to Joe Reed's (about four miles from the Nickell house) and brought him back to hitch the horses to the wagon. It was after ten o'clock before a wagon finally left the Nickell homestead to take Kels to Cheyenne for medical treatment.[8]

Julia testified that her father "never told us who shot him," and Will Mahoney backed her up, saying that at no time did Kels tell who shot him. Nickell's wife, Mary, testified similarly.[9]

That same Sunday morning, Victor Miller went to the home of neighbors Mary McDonald and her husband, William McDonald, and told them that "Mr. Nickell was shot."[10] Stoll and the coroner's jury wanted to know how Victor had learned so quickly of the shooting of Kels Nickell, but the suspicion against Victor was quickly cleared up. Julia testified that when she rode to Joe Reed's place about "twenty minutes of seven" on August 4, she told him that her father had been shot. Then when Joe Reed rode to the Nickell place, he met Gus Miller and told him about the shooting, and Gus went back to the Miller ranch and there, about eight thirty, told his family, including Victor, what he had learned from Reed. Victor testified that his brother's statement was the source of his information when he talked with Mary McDonald.[11]

Stoll questioned Victor in depth, and Victor's testimony conveys the same impression as that of his brother, of a polite, well-behaved, forthcoming young man. As with Gus's testimony, the limitations of a written transcript should be kept in mind, but other witnesses supported this picture of Victor. William McDonald said Gus and Victor were "good boys" who wouldn't kill Willie Nickell or any boys, and two of Victor's former teachers testified that Victor and Willie had always been on friendly terms at school, that they never quarreled.[12]

The coroner's jury heard additional evidence relating to James Miller and his sons. Shortly after Kels was shot, two of the Nickell girls, Beatrix and Maggie, saw two horsemen riding by the Nickell house. Beatrix (Trixie) said that the horses being ridden looked like Millers' horses that she had seen before, one an iron gray horse and the other a bay. She couldn't say that the riders were Jim Miller and his son (she didn't know who they were), but they were riding fast and one looked like a man, while the other looked like a boy. They rode in the direction of the Miller house.[13] Fred Nickell had also seen two men, saying they had been on foot, but Fred could provide little detail.[14]

This information seemed to have promise but was considerably weakened when Joe Reed took the stand a second time and said he had tried to confirm the girls' statements but found no horse tracks where the men were supposed to have ridden. Reed had then gone to a horse pasture gate, through which the men should have passed, but he testified: "There was nothing in the shape of man or beast went out of that gate that morning."[15] Further, nobody else in the Nickell house saw the men or the horses they rode. Worst of all, Trixie was only nine and Maggie had just turned seven. In 1901 whether a Wyoming district judge would have deemed either of them competent to testify in a trial was questionable.[16]

Reed provided the most damaging blow to the cases against James Miller and his sons. Perhaps it troubled the members of the jury that Kels Nickell had never identified the Millers until after he was taken to Cheyenne and pondered the episode for more than a day. If so, Reed's testimony would have convinced them they could not rely on Nickell's statements. Reed appears to have been a no-nonsense man, one who looked at the world calmly and was not swept away by emotion. Reed's credibility was probably heightened because he had immediately responded to Julia Cook's request that he help her father, brushing aside concerns for his own safety. Subsequent actions of the members of the coroner's jury show that they gave weight to Reed's testimony. He must have come across in person much as he appears in the transcript.

Reed said he had talked with Nickell that Sunday morning after the shooting, and he testified that Nickell had told him "he saw nobody," although Nickell added that the children had seen two men running away. Nickell did not say who the children saw, nor did he say that he had seen Miller's horses.[17]

Just as he had concerning the day Willie Nickell was killed, Stoll explored where James Miller and his sons were on Sunday, August 4. He questioned several people who were at the Miller household on Sunday morning—Miller, his wife (Dora), and Glendolene Kimmell—and he recalled Victor Miller to the stand for more questions. Dora said that her husband and Victor had been about the house on that Sunday morning and that Gus went to the McArthur place after breakfast but then returned about nine thirty to tell the family what he had just learned from Joe Reed about the shooting of Kels Nickell. All the witnesses questioned gave testimony consistent with this statement, and none seemed evasive. Whenever Stoll wanted more detail, they readily supplied it.[18]

Stoll also called several people who had seen Miller or one of his sons on Sunday, including Reed (who had seen Victor early in the morning), as well as William and Mary McDonald, Louis Dorman, and Elizabeth Stein. The McDonalds had seen Victor Sunday morning and then had gone to the Miller house later in the day. Dorman and Stein had come to the Miller home between eleven and noon. Stoll asked all of them about the demeanor of Miller and of his sons, proceeding from the commonsense notion that a person who has just attempted a murder will manifest excitement, anxiety, or at least peculiarity. Reed said that when he told Gus about Kels Nickell being shot, Gus acknowledged this but did not seem peculiar, excited, or nervous. Reed said he "couldn't tell any difference at all."[19] Mary McDonald testified that when she saw Victor about ten o'clock in the morning, he had not seemed excited, anxious, or uneasy.[20] Louis Dorman said that when Victor told him about the shooting of Kels Nickell, he had not appeared excited: "I didn't see any difference, he was the same as always."[21]

Apparently tracking down the viability of rumors, Stoll confronted Dorman, telling him: "It is reported to us that he [Miller] said to you on that occasion he would give $500.00 if somebody would kill Nichol [sic]." Dorman immediately responded: "That is false, he didn't say that; Mr. Miller never said that." Dorman denied that he had ever heard Miller make such a statement to anybody.[22] E. W. Whitman was asked if Miller had offered him five hundred or a thousand dollars to kill Kels Nickell and asked whether he had told Bill Edwards that. Whitman denied that he had ever said such a thing, to Edwards or anyone else. So Stoll called Edwards as a witness. Edwards said that Whitman had asked him once, as they were "walking and joshing together," if he (Edwards) would kill Nickell for a thousand dollars. But he testified that Whitman had not said that Miller had offered him a thousand dollars, nor was there ever any other talk about getting rid of Nickell.[23]

Stoll also questioned a man identified in the transcript only as "Mr. Jordan" about topics loosely tied to the shootings of Willie and Kels Nickell. When Stoll asked Jordan if he knew of Miss Kimmell "riding around the country horse back," he responded that he did not know of such a thing. He was asked whether he had heard that one of the Miller boys was afraid to "go home because his father would whip him and beat him." Jordan replied, "No sir, he didn't say anything of that kind." Asked if he knew a man named H. T. Shipley or a man named Schrader, in each case he said he did not.[24]

All this casting about was tedious, but it was necessary for Stoll to fully explore all leads, especially since the evidence did not point clearly to the guilt of anyone. One object of casting about was sheep. Kels Nickell had some three thousand sheep brought from Loveland, Colorado, to his ranch in May 1901.[25] Worse, he had then made provocative statements to his neighbors, and his actions and words had caused a big stir.

In 1901 there was great conflict between sheepmen and cattlemen in Wyoming. Cattlemen, who had first brought their animals to the Wyoming range, felt they had a prior claim to the grass. They asserted, with good cause, that sheep destroyed the grazing for cattle. Sheepmen responded that they had as much right to the grass on the public domain as did cattlemen, which was legally correct. By 1901, cowboys and cattle ranchers in Wyoming had killed sheep and destroyed property in several raids, although it is not clear whether any sheepmen had been killed (many had been killed elsewhere in the West).[26] In Wyoming, nine men would be shot and

killed in cowmen's raids in the next several years, culminating in the 1909
Spring Creek raid, when seven raiders gunned down three sheepmen at
their camp just south of Ten Sleep in the Big Horn Basin of northern
Wyoming. Sheep and dogs were also shot, wagons and equipment burned,
and two men kidnapped. Only after the successful criminal prosecution
of the perpetrators of the Spring Creek raid was the scourge of sheep raids
finally suppressed in Wyoming. But that was years after Kels Nickell introduced sheep to a predominantly cattle range in the Iron Mountain region.
In 1901, Nickell's introduction of sheep meant big trouble and explains
why someone was gunning for him and members of his family.[27]

Several witnesses knew of these sheep troubles. John Scroder, the herder
who drove Nickell's sheep from Colorado, testified that as he had traveled
west of Laramie, a man had come up to him and "kicked" because he was
going through with sheep. Another man had warned him that there would
be trouble. Then, as Scroder was going by, a man in a wagon said, referring to Nickell, "I don't believe he will live until 1902 if them sheep goes
in there."[28] Witnesses before the coroner's jury generally acknowledged
that people were unhappy about sheep being brought into the Iron Mountain area, but all denied that any threats were made to Nickell.[29] Such testimony is not surprising. People caught in the middle of fights between
sheepmen and cattlemen generally tried to avoid the fray. Of the dozens
of witnesses before the grand jury following the Spring Creek raid, only
one man would acknowledge the profound troubles in the Big Horn Basin
that had resulted in the deaths of four men and thousands of sheep in the
several years prior to the raid.[30]

Testifying after John Scroder, George Diedrick told of the existence of
a "protective association" in the Sybille Creek area, which would include
Iron Mountain. This organization of cattlemen had produced a small book
listing all its members. Diedrick denied that the organization was created
to prevent sheep from coming into the area, but coroner's jury members
were skeptical. Elsewhere in Wyoming and the West, cattle owners' for-
mation of a "protective association" had been the first step toward violent sheep raids.[31]

Kels Nickell's vindictive and intemperate remarks to his neighbors were
common knowledge in the Iron Mountain area, and they had made the
situation much worse. Nickell was said to have told people he was going
to eat up his neighbors' pasture and that by the time his sheep got done
"there wouldn't be enough grass to feed a grasshopper." Tom Horn quoted

Nickell as saying "every damned son of a bitch has given me dirt, and I will eat them out of house and home. I will make their asses pop out of the saddle."[32] Sheep were certainly a good instrument to accomplish Nickell's purpose. They crop grass more closely than cattle do, so that after sheep finish with a pasture it is useless for cattle until after more rain falls—sometimes a long wait in arid Wyoming.[33]

More specifically, Nickell's introduction of sheep to Iron Mountain presented problems to the Miller family. Kels Nickell's sheep had come onto the Millers' land even before the killing of his son Willie. Tom Horn reported the presence of sheep at the Millers' "tree claim," that is, in the Millers' pasture, on Tuesday, July 16, two days before Willie was killed. Surprisingly, James Miller had not tried to drive them out or even complain to the sheepherder. The problem of sheep became even more acute to Miller on Saturday, August 3—one day before Kels Nickell was attacked—when Nickell's sheep invaded Miller's homestead. That morning, the Miller family discovered sheep coming almost to their garden. The pasture they identified as theirs was government land they had fenced, but the area around the Miller home, including their garden, was deeded land.[34]

Nickell's sheepherder, Vingenjo Biango, who used the English name "Jim White," testified at the coroner's inquest. Biango, who had come from Italy in 1892 and did not speak English well, said he had only started working for Nickell about July 30, apparently as John Scroder's replacement.[35] In describing the events of August 3, he said coyotes had scattered his band and some sheep had drifted down to the Miller place. Then he had seen a woman, a man, and a boy. When the males approached him carrying rifles, the man called out, "Get out of here you son of a bitch, we don't want you around here, this is my place."[36] Biango quoted the man as saying, "The son of a bitch sent the sheep across to my house, I will fix the son of a bitch before daylight."[37]

From the testimony of James Miller and Glendolene Kimmell, the man was clearly Miller and the woman was Kimmell.[38] Miller testified, however, that he did not curse and had only told the sheepherder that he should get his sheep off Miller's land, admitting that he had said it firmly three times. This seems surprisingly moderate in light of Nickell's sheep coming almost to Miller's doorstep.[39] Miller said that the sheepherder had responded that the sheep had a right to be there, but in his testimony Biango said that when he discovered where the sheep had gone, he had sent the dog to bring them back. At the time the two men were about two hundred yards apart, and at that distance, with Biango's difficulty with English, one can understand differing versions of the event.[40] Regardless of whose version was correct, the sheep were brought back to the main herd and the sheepherder left the area.[41] The next day, however, the day Kels Nickell was shot, there was an even sharper clash.

Biango testified that he had talked with his employer after Nickell had been shot, about 11:00 A.M., as Nickell was about to be taken to Cheyenne, and that Nickell had left him a rifle and ten dollars.[42] Two hours later, Biango said, he was approached by a man and two boys, and when they came within about thirty yards, he became frightened and went downhill to hide behind a big rock. Biango claimed that the three males then started shooting in his direction, firing about thirty times.[43] When asked whether he would recognize these three if he saw them again, Biango said he did not "notice them sufficiently to see." He did not know if they were the same ones he had seen the day before.[44] It seems implausible that Biango would not be able to recognize men who came within thirty yards of him. Perhaps he was trying to avoid being a witness in a case against the three. From the questions Walter Stoll asked the sheepherder, it also appears that Biango told a different story to a deputy, saying that the three men had pointed guns at him and told him to leave the country but did not fire at him. When asked whether the three had killed sheep, Biango said he didn't know, that he was afraid for his life.[45] The sheepherder's apparent inconsistencies and his problems expressing himself in English did not augur well for his usefulness as a witness.

There was no question, however, that someone shot and killed a number of sheep that Sunday. Biango may not have known anything about this, but other witnesses testified to finding dead sheep.[46] About five that Sunday afternoon, Joe Reed traveled with Julia Cook to the sheep herd, and there he found sheep crippled and killed. Reed said that he had found sheep "strung here and there, some with their legs broke and some with their guts dragging on the prairie." He said that you could find sheep "any where you might go, some shot through their body and some with their legs broke, dead ones and crippled ones." Reed said that he counted about 50 or 60, but "there might have been 80."[47] A few days later, when lawman Joe LeFors came to the Nickell ranch, he found some "25 or 30 carcasses" of sheep that had been shot.[48]

As to the killing of Willie Nickell, Stoll sought more evidence about who might have committed the crime. He first tried to confirm Kels

Nickell's testimony that Victor Miller had stayed at Joe Reed's place the night of Wednesday, July 17, and had then left about seven the next morning, the morning Willie was killed. Reed denied these statements, however, saying that he had not seen Victor until later in the morning, perhaps nine thirty on Thursday, July 18, when Victor was in a meadow near the McArthur place, an area Victor visited almost every day. Stoll was obviously surprised at Reed's statements and delved into the matter in some depth, but Reed did not change his testimony. He also testified that when he saw Victor that Thursday morning there was nothing about Victor's manner that was unusual.[49]

Stoll also asked Reed more questions about Kels Nickell's July 19 interview of Glendolene Kimmell. Most significantly, Reed said he did not interpret Miss Kimmell's responses to Nickell's questions as suspicious, noting that she had consistently said she did not see it as honorable to convey information about the Millers to Nickell. Reed thought she was "right in a way." Even after she was told of Willie Nickell's death, she seemed to be uncomfortable telling Kels Nickell about the Millers' business.[50]

Elizabeth Stein, another area teacher, testified that the shooting of Kels Nickell was "not unexpected." When Stoll asked her why she used that expression, she said, "Everyone I suppose thought that the boy was meant for the father the first time, and that they meant to get him [Kels] sometime." Miss Stein retreated when Stoll pushed her to state that neighbors thought someone would probably shoot Nickell.[51] Still, her comment that "the boy was meant for the father" shows a widespread assumption, and it would affect the investigation.

The coroner's jury had questioned most of the witnesses they wanted to hear from and had received scant reward for their efforts. There were some tantalizing hints, but no line of evidence clearly pointed to the guilt of anyone for killing Willie Nickell and wounding Kels Nickell. The coroner's jury had a few more witnesses to question, however, including Tom Horn.

CHAPTER SIX

Tom Horn Appears

Of all the witnesses to testify in the second session of the coroner's inquest, Tom Horn was surely the most fascinating. In 1901, Horn was already a fabled and well-known character in Wyoming (one newspaper referred to him as "the famous army scout and Indian fighter," adding that he was well known in Laramie and "throughout the state").[1] Much written about Horn's life must be taken cautiously, tested against probability and verified knowledge. His autobiography paradoxically contains the most helpful and the most suspect information about him. Horn's life was complicated, and many times it was not in his interest to tell the truth. Combine this with his inclination to brag, and Horn's reliability is difficult to pin down.

Tom Horn was born in Scotland County, Missouri, in 1860, and left home in his middle teens. His father objected to his son's early departure from the family farm and beat Tom so savagely, Horn wrote in his autobiography, that he was confined to bed for a week before he could leave.[2] He went to Arizona in the late 1870s, may have taken an Apache woman as his wife, and, according to a recent biographer, became "somewhat Indianized."[3] Horn claimed that he was fluent in Apache as well as Spanish, although this boast was probably more accurate as to Spanish. One thing Horn surely borrowed from the Apaches, however, was his affinity for braiding with horsehair. In Arizona, he was seen as likeable, handsome, tall, and well-built, but with a tendency to boast.[4] In the 1880s, he made a name for himself as a scout and mule-packer. Horn was even involved in an international incident in which he was wounded and his commanding officer killed by Mexican forces, and Horn received favorable national press coverage.[5] During much of his time in Arizona, from 1882 to 1885, Horn was under the tutelage of Al Sieber, an older man who was a legend in his own lifetime and was known as the greatest of all the scouts.[6]

Horn drifted to the Tonto Basin in east central Arizona in 1887 and became involved in the Pleasant Valley War (1888–89), a particularly vicious clash between sheepmen and cattlemen. He probably participated in some vigilante raids, and, for a few years after leaving the Tonto Basin, worked for the Pinkerton Detective Agency .[7] He traveled to Johnson County, Wyoming, in May 1892 while still an employee of Pinkerton.[8]

During most of the 1890s Horn acted as a stock detective working out of southeastern Wyoming. He arrested five people for livestock theft in November 1893 in the so-called Langhoff case involving four men and a woman, Eva Langhoff. Horn said he tracked the Langhoff gang north of the Iron Mountain area in the Laramie Mountains for two months before he and several others, including a Horn admirer named Otto Plaga, surprised the gang in a barn as they were butchering stock. Horn had no arrest warrants in hand, so he took the gang to Cheyenne, where he got the paperwork he needed, and then escorted them to Laramie to stand trial. Except for one gang member sentenced to eighteen months in prison, the other gang members went free. The unsuccessful prosecutions were said to have soured Horn on the efficacy of legal proceedings against cattle thieves from then on, and Horn circulated the rumor that he would no longer depend on the law to defend his employers' interests but instead would "take things into his own hands."[9]

Horn's employers were a few of Wyoming's big cattlemen, who, after the Johnson County fiasco of 1892, still sought to suppress range theft by extralegal means. Between 1889 and 1892, Wyoming cattle barons killed many men (and one woman) based on questionable charges of rustling cattle.[10] By 1895, most Wyoming cattlemen had foresworn using violence, but a few, including John Coble, comprised a radical element that pre- ferred violent extralegal means of controlling cattle rustling. Frequently "rustlers" had committed the unpardonable sin of filing a legal homestead claim on a part of the public domain claimed by a big rancher as his range.[11] The split between cattlemen supposedly came into the open during the 1895 Wyoming Stock Growers Association in Cheyenne. Horn was said to have strolled into the room and declared: "Men, I have a system that never fails, when everything else has. Yours has!" Horn's huckstering offended most of the stockmen present, but not all.[12] Some decided to control the range less ostentatiously than they had in 1892 and instead attack alleged rustlers one by one. Their instrument for doing so would become stock detectives—and sometime assassins—like Tom Horn.

In July 1895, a little more than a year after the Langhoff acquittals, Billy Lewis, a small-time cattleman from Horse Creek in the Iron Mountain area with a record of arrests for cattle theft, was shot down while standing in his own corral.[13] Then, on September 10, 1895, Fred Powell, another small cattlemen from Horse Creek with a bad reputation, was shot just outside his home. The killer fired from an ambush site about 250 feet away, hitting Powell in the heart, and then walked to the body, apparently to examine it. In so doing, he left a "size 8 boot print" and revealed that he was a "rather heavy man."[14] The talk in Cheyenne and Laramie City was that John Coble was the money man and Tom Horn the assassin, and officials convened a grand jury and heard a great deal of hearsay evidence implicating Horn, but nothing justified an arrest.[15] Powell had received a threatening letter (as would Kels Nickell in 1901) and, while it is not known whether similar letters were sent to Powell's neighbors, several families fled the Horse Creek region.[16]

Homesteaders were not the only people who left southeastern Wyoming in the fall of 1895. The killings of Lewis and Powell created such a furor that W. C. (Billy) Irvine, one of the leaders of the murderous Johnson County Invasion, played the surprising role of mediator by advising Horn's principal (not identified, but probably John Coble) to "pull Horn off." Indeed, Tom Horn suddenly left southeastern Wyoming in November 1895.[17]

He went to Arizona, where he still enjoyed a good reputation, participating in battles against Apaches in 1896.[18] He continued to work in Arizona until late 1897 or early 1898, when he signed on with General William Shafter's Fifth U.S. Army Corps, as a mule pack master. As with so much of Horn's life story, it is hard to be sure exactly what he did contribute, but it is probably not an exaggeration to say that his service in Cuba—where the provisions Horn's mules carried were important to Teddy Roosevelt's assault on San Juan Hill—was one of the high points of Horn's life.[19] Discharged in September 1898, Horn returned to Wyoming. Having contracted yellow fever, he recuperated at John Coble's Iron Mountain ranch. It took Horn several months to regain his health, but in the latter half of 1899 he was able to pursue the robbers who committed the Wilcox train robbery.

This robbery took place on June 2, 1899, when several men associated with Butch Cassidy stopped a Union Pacific train near Wilcox, Wyoming, blew up a safe in the express car, and escaped with $50,000 in cash.[20] Horn, working for the UP, pursued several members of the gang for months but never made an arrest, contrary to some of the tall tales he told to Glendolene Kimmell at Jim Miller's house in July 1901.[21] Horn was involved in killings around this time, however.

Toward the end of January 1900, newspaper stories out of Denver told of a double killing forty miles west of Jackson Hole. The *Denver News* quoted Horn saying that about three weeks ago, he and another man had come across the camp of two train robbers and shot them down, leaving their bodies on the ground. They had then traveled to Denver to meet Union Pacific officials and secure a reward. The *Laramie Republican* carried this *Denver News* story but beneath it printed another story (from the *Cheyenne Sun-Leader*) headlined, "IT ISN'T TRUE," in which Horn denied the whole event.[22] Other Wyoming newspapers repeated some versions of this story (either saying it was true or not true), but then a new story appeared, first published in the Lincoln, Nebraska, *Evening News* on February 6.[23] This story had Horn and his compatriot (identified as a "half-breed" named Tewksbury) taking the bodies of the two men they'd shot to "a nearby village," where they were buried. Horn and Tewksbury supposedly reported the encounter to local authorities, who did not choose to detain them.[24] This Nebraska version of events, picked up by Wyoming papers, contained a further wrinkle: that "Colonel Horn" (as he was strangely referred to) had ministered to one of the bandits who was still alive, and this man ("Tex" Blair) denied being part of the train robbery but admitted that he was a cattle rustler. Horn appeared to be the only source for this story, so it is entirely possible that he and his companion had gunned down two men guilty of nothing.[25] Historian Larry Ball suspects that Union Pacific officials may have concocted this second version to place its detective "in a more law abiding light." Whatever the case, this double killing spawned a public furor at a time when Horn was still considered a "person of interest" in the 1895 Lewis and Powell murders.[26]

A few months later, Horn was associated with another double killing. John Coble was a close business associate of cattleman Ora Haley, and Haley believed there were big problems with cattle rustling in the Brown's Park area of northern Colorado, just south of the Wyoming border. Calling himself Thomas Hicks, Tom Horn headed to Brown's Park, arriving in early April 1900. While Horn was there, two small cattlemen, Matt Rash and Isom Dart, were shot down in obvious assassinations, Rash in July and Dart in October. They had received threatening letters but had ignored them.[27] After Dart was killed, Horn returned home to Wyoming, and after being delayed by a Baggs, Wyoming, barroom brawl in which Horn was badly cut in the neck, Horn remarkably gave an interview to the *Wyoming Tribune* about the situation in Brown's Park.[28] Cheyenne newspapers were known for their editorial policies favoring big cattlemen and their violence toward those they called rustlers. But it is still surprising that Horn would call attention to his presence in Browns Park, Colorado, where murders— of a kind many Wyomingites attributed to him—had just taken place.

In the *Tribune* article "Colonel Tom Horn" told of the terrible problems with cattle theft in northern Colorado and how two thieves had been shot. Horn declared that he knew well the two men, Rash and Dart, and "two more notorious rustlers never infested the Rocky Mountain country." Horn went on at length about how the two "bandits" had gone into partnership, stolen hundreds of head of cattle and horses, and established ranches from their ill-gotten gains. All these allegations were questionable and smacked of the kinds of concocted and convenient charges big cattlemen made against the people of Johnson County in 1892 before the cattlemen marched north on their mission to slaughter seventy men. Of course, Rash and Dart were no longer alive to respond to any of Horn's tales.[29]

Two other things were generally known about Tom Horn. One is that his drinking had become more notable after he returned from Cuba. As an adult, Horn frequently engaged in binge drinking, but by 1899 and 1900 his binges had become colossal benders. When not drinking, he was usually "quiet, inoffensive and even shy." But when he started drinking, Horn became a different person. His notorious drinking bouts would last seven to fourteen days, and during them he would exhibit "drunken bluster and braggadocio" before eventually passing out.[30] Also, Horn had high artistic and athletic abilities. His horsehair braiding and leather working took much of his free time and were done with great skill. A friend, someone Horn had taught rope making, said Horn was "the best rawhide and leather worker I ever saw." He possessed remarkable talent with a lariat, used the ropes he created, and his horse-breaking was said to be "first class." Horn "easily" won first honors in the riding and roping contests at the 1901 Cheyenne Frontier Days, which even over a century ago was a top national rodeo.[31]

When Tom Horn came to the stand, the tone of the coroner's inquest changed, as it had with Glendolene Kimmel. When under pressure and sober, Horn was a cool character. (One newspaper referred to Horn's "customary equanimity" and another to his "nonchalance.") But Horn was a flawed witness.[32] He spoke slowly, which seemed to be an attempt to control the dialogue, and he responded too frequently in elaborate speeches.[33] Any competent criminal attorney would have advised Horn to keep his answers short and to the point, to *only* answer the question asked. Instead, Horn, seemingly driven by an inner fear, went on and on. When Walter Stoll asked Horn if he knew what day Willie Nickell had been killed, for example, Horn said he did not. Stoll then said that he was killed on Thursday the eighteenth day of July, a comment requiring no answer beyond possibly a nod of the head. Instead Horn said:

> Now, I will tell you I don't know about the dates, but I know Monday of the week on which he was killed, on Monday morning, whatever date that was, I left Billy Clay's or come there the evening before, and I went over to Miller's ranch this Monday morning. I went to the head of hay valley this Monday and went there to Miller's ranch Monday night. I was there all day Tuesday, and on Tuesday I went up to the head of the creek that Miller lives on. Passed down to where Nickells [*sic*] had his sheep in Johnny Coble's pasture. I went up there and found they hadn't [gone on Coble land] and my business was ended. I went back to the Miller's ranch and staid [*sic*] there again that night; that was Tuesday night; I left there Wednesday morning.[34]

Perhaps Horn believed he was helping himself with such testimony, but its only effects were to provide the questioning attorney with many new subjects to inquire into more deeply, as well as useful ammunition to impeach Horn at a later time. Regardless, Horn's method of responding to interrogation was seemingly deeply ingrained and continued throughout his questioning.

When Stoll asked Horn, "Thursday, where were you?," Horn gave a strange answer: "I guess I was out on this divide between the head of the Chug and the Sabylle [*sic*]." Following a brief Stoll question ("In the cabin?"), Horn said: "I know I was in there Friday; I must have went in there; I am under the impression that I went in there Thursday night."[35] In his previous

replies about earlier days on the range, Horn was quite precise as to his whereabouts. But when asked about Thursday, July 18, the day Willie Nickell was
gunned down (then only three weeks earlier), Horn suddenly became vague.
Horn's responses seem like a studied effort to appear unconcerned about
Thursday, July 18.

Horn testified that he had left the area on Saturday, June 20, arriving
at the Coble ranch at eleven o'clock, where he ate dinner and then went
to Laramie. He said that during his time out on the range all he'd had to
eat was a piece of bacon and bread. Horn also said that on Thursday for
most of the day he was "within seven or ten miles" from the Nickells'
place and that all day he was never more than a dozen miles away.[36]

Stoll mentioned sheep troubles and then played on Horn's vanity, first
asking him whether Horn knew any facts that might help discover who
did the killing, and then saying, "You are a pretty good judge of those things
are you not?" Stoll's questions earned him another long soliloquy:

A. Just what I have heard; I don't know anything, Walter, not a thing
in the world, but I heard so cursed much from Nickells [sic] and
Miller, I don't think anything I would say would throw any lights.
I said to Miller, There is sheep right in your dooryard, Miller. He
said the sons-of-bitches or something of that kind. That is all the
remark he made. In the spring when he was over on the Plains he
cursed about them, the whole lot. I have heard Nick say he was going
to do this and do that. It isn't never anything, just what they tell you,
what they tell you, it don't amount to a great deal. Neither of them
are reconed [sic] a very high class of citizens, never have been.

Q. A source of a good deal of trouble and annoyance in that country?

A. Always have been since I have been in the country between them.
They go to the other neighbors with their troubles and tell what
kind of onery [sic] people they are. They are both the same kind of
people. I maybe [sic] mistaken entirely, neither one has good reputation, on the contrary they are reconed [sic] as being the worst kind
of people. As far as I understand it that is the standing they have.[37]

Horn added that he had heard from a man he called Otto Plagar (Otto
Plaga) that Miller had offered a five-hundred-dollar diamond to anyone
who would kill Nickell, but then Horn offered his opinion that Plaga was
"about as unreliable as Miller or Nickell" and that no one who knew Plaga

considered him reliable.[38] Horn also recounted Nickell's various comments about how his sheep were going to ruin all his neighbors and remarked that Nickell had said of Miller: "I left the sheep in his dooryard. I wonder what he will say about it?" Horn said there was a time when both Miller and Nickell were "pretty pronounced thieves," supposed to have rustled cattle, but that within the past five or six years they had been honest.[39]

Horn closed his testimony saying he had heard a great deal of talk by cattlemen that Nickell's bringing sheep into the Iron Mountain area was not right, and that they had said so in the strongest terms, criticizing bringing sheep in for no other reason than to do neighbors "dirt and damage and ruin them if he could, and boast of it then." Horn said he knew what the sentiment among cattlemen was, "that a man that would do as Nickell has could only do so, being the kind of man Nickell is, troublesome and quarrelsome, [a] turblent [sic] man without character or principle." Horn denied, however, that he had heard stockmen say how they would get the sheep out of there.[40]

Horn's testimony was followed by Glendolene Kimmell's second appearance. She opened up more than before and gave her opinions about the volatile people she had been around for the last month. Describing herself as a student of human nature, she said she took a great deal of interest in the Miller-Nickell feud. She was told all about it before she had gone there to teach, and although her school employers did not want to send her there because of the trouble, "I insisted upon having it." She explained that her experiences would add to her knowledge of life and of human nature.[41]

Miss Kimmell observed that through a strange combination of circumstances, Nickell and Miller "were thrown together [as] nearest neighbors to each other whose natures were respectively such [that] they could not get along." Miller, she said, was an obstinate man, and Nickell was a hotheaded man, and because they were very similar in their social and financial character they could not possibly get along. They might have overlooked each other's faults, but "the two men being of the same character and same plain [sic] of living, of course, they had trouble."[42]

Asked who was at fault regarding the shooting of Nickell the previous few days ago, Miss Kimmell said it was unquestionably Nickell, because he had brought sheep onto Miller's deeded land. She said she would have used force against the sheep. She was unequivocal about it, saying not only that Miller would have been justified using force against the sheep but also against the sheepherder. "I can say that if I owned it [the land] legally and had paid for it and some man drove his sheep or other stock on it and I ordered him three times to take it off I would use force, because out there if you wait for the officers to come you will wait several days, or many hours at any rate."

Stoll asked:"At the time you would not have hesitated to shoot the man?"

Kimmell answered:"If it was my land and I ordered him three times to take his sheep off, I would have shot him."[43]

She confirmed that Miller and his sons had been around his house on August 4 (the day Kels Nickell was shot). She remembered hearing Miller singing, as he was prone to do, and agreed that he was something of a religious crank.[44] Miss Kimmell also said that Miller had pointed his gun at the sheepherder, and that he was a crack shot.[45] She testified that on Sunday morning she saw two men on horseback about a quarter past ten. One was a small man and the other a good-sized man, and they passed through Miller's property, searching for horses, and they also said they would ride over to Nickell's place and see if they could render any assistance.[46] No other witness seemed to have noticed these two riders, but their presence may have explained what Trixie and Maggie Nickell saw that morning.

Joe LeFors was the last witness called. Already well-known in Wyoming, LeFors had a reputation as a capable detective.[47] Born in Texas in 1865, shortly before his family moved to the Choctaw Nation, Indian Territory, LeFors grew up in what was to become Oklahoma, one of the roughest remnants of frontier America. At an early age he learned well some valuable lessons, chief among them to keep a low profile and to stay calm, no matter the provocation.[48] He worked as a kind of pony express rider when only fifteen, and in 1885, when LeFors turned twenty, he helped to drive a cattle herd north to Wyoming, arriving at Rock Creek, four miles north of Buffalo, Wyoming.[49] Sometime in 1895, LeFors became a livestock inspector, and he was very active, with his work including an 1897 shootout in the "Hole-in-the-Wall" country of southern Johnson County.[50] Following the 1899 Wilcox robbery, LeFors, an exceptional tracker, led one of the two posses chasing the robbers.[51]

The U.S. marshal's office hired LeFors in 1900, and the next year Laramie County authorities asked for LeFors to assist in the investigation of the killing of Willie Nickell, apparently because of his reputation as a peace officer.[52] LeFors first went to the Nickells' home on August 6 (two days after Kels Nickell was shot).[53] He found Mrs. Nickell barricaded in her home, frightened to death. After some coaxing, she opened the door to him and LeFors described what he saw: "The poor woman opened the door with tears streaming down her cheeks. She was a dear, motherly middle-aged woman with three little children hanging on her skirts and all crying. A more pitiful sight I never saw."[54] Mrs. Nickell told LeFors that she did not know who had done the shooting, but was quite sure it was done "on account of their sheep" because of the threatening letter Kels had received and because the same day Kels was shot the sheepherder was run off and the sheep shot.[55] LeFors left Mrs. Nickell and examined the places where the sheep were shot and where the man or men who fired at Kels Nickell had probably been.

In his questioning, Stoll focused on what LeFors had found in the way of tracks. When he examined the shooter's location on an overlooking hill, LeFors said he found one footprint and one set of horse tracks.[56] The track was size "8 or 9," about the same size as the print found near Fred Powell's body (8).[57] LeFors followed the horse tracks through a rain, but after the tracks went through a gate about a mile away into a sandy road, he said he abandoned the trail. LeFors did establish, however, that the rider did not turn back toward the Millers' ranch but headed in the direction of the property of Joe Reed and, beyond, that of William L. Clay.[58]

After Joe LeFors, the interrogation of witnesses in the coroner's inquest was completed. The results of the inquiry were unsatisfactory to Stoll, and he said as much to several witnesses, imploring them to come forward and help the authorities solve the murder of Willie Nickell. He even made general threats: that if people had not told the whole truth he would have to prosecute them.[59] Stoll concluded that he did not have a viable case against the Millers. Their stories held up, and they must have come across well. People watching a witness can recognize immediately whether that witness is being open and honest or evasive and begrudging.

The shooting of Kels Nickell seemed to reopen the case against the Millers, but that case completely fell apart during the new testimony. Although the Millers had been arrested, the testimony of Joe Reed under-cut Nickell's claims. The *Cheyenne Daily Leader* acknowledged this, commenting that Kels Nickell's statement to Reed that he did not know who shot him meant that the charges against the Millers would be dropped.[60] Knowing of Nickell's extreme dislike of James Miller, Nickell's initial statements had already met skepticism, and no witness supported Nickell's version of the event.[61] His statement of the number of assailants was not even correct, as shown by Joe LeFors's examination of tracks, which showed there was only one assailant, not two or three.

Who killed all those sheep on Sunday, August 4, remained a mystery. Vingenjo Biango's testimony was believable when he said that on Saturday a man confronted him, almost certainly Jim Miller, who said, "Get out of here, you son of a bitch." Even the most peaceable cowman would be enraged by a neighbor whose sheep came onto his land without the slightest right and proceeded to eat one of his most precious assets, grass for his cattle. The sheepherder's description of events on Sunday seemed to fit Miller and his sons, and it would be understandable that the Millers would strike back at the invading animals. In the past, Miller had used violence against Kels Nickell, all the more so against his sheep. But again the evidence against the Millers was weak to nonexistent. Biango's testimony was of little help because he could not or would not identify the men who had accosted him on Sunday, August 4, nor could he say that these men had shot sheep. He would have been a poor witness in any event, given his difficulties with English and the inconsistencies in his testimony. The testimony of several witnesses supported the Millers, including that of Glendolene Kimmell, Joe Reed, William and Mary McDonald, and Louis Dorman.[62]

Even if it had been shown that the Millers had killed some of Nickell's sheep, that alone would not establish that one of them shot at Nickell. It is a different thing to shoot sheep that have illegally trespassed than to lie in wait and try to assassinate a neighbor.

Summarizing these results, the *Cheyenne Daily Leader* said "MYSTERY UNSOLVED." The coroner's inquest had brought out "absolutely no evidence," the newspaper concluded, and the "impenetrable mystery which surrounds the killing of little Willie Nickell at Iron Mountain several weeks ago gives promise of remaining a mystery forever." The coroner's jury had sought some clue, some scrap of evidence, but the "weary labor of examining over thirty witnesses" had left the authorities "as much in the dark as ever." The paper announced that the charges against Miller and his sons would be withdrawn and the cases against them dismissed. It also speculated that Miller would "institute proceedings against Nickell for damages and also against the county of Laramie for false imprisonment in the sum of $100,000."[63]

The results from the coroner's jury must have profoundly frustrated all the law enforcement people involved with the Willie Nickell case. It looked like the hunt for Willie's killer and Kels Nickell's assailant was about to become very cold and very stale. To give authorities the opportunity to obtain more evidence, the jury delayed its final report, but finally, on December 26, 1901, the jury issued a forlorn but standard statement: "We the jury empanelled to inquire into the death of Willie Nickell, find that the deceased came to his death on July 18th, from a gunshot wound inflicted by a party or parties unknown."[64]

Only eighteen days later, however, on January 13, 1902, authorities arrested Tom Horn for the murder of Willie Nickell.

CHAPTER SEVEN

The Arrest and Preliminary Hearing of Tom Horn

When arrested, Tom Horn was sitting in Cheyenne's Inter Ocean Hotel. As Sheriff E. J. Smalley and Deputy Richard Proctor approached Horn, the sheriff reached out his hand, saying "Good morning, Tom," and when Horn lifted his hand to the sheriff, Smalley reached down and snatched Horn's revolver, "sticking down inside his pants."[1] The sheriff did not know whether Horn would resist arrest but was taking no chances. The officers told Horn they had a warrant for his arrest on the charge of murder and marched him to the Laramie County jail. Horn said nothing more than "all right" and did not resist.[2]

Horn's arrest caused a sensation in southeastern Wyoming. The "startling news passed from mouth to mouth on the streets" of Laramie, reported the *Laramie Boomerang,* "and created as great excitement as did the foul murder of Willie Nickell six months ago."[3] In Cheyenne, word of the arrest was also a sensation, "the principal topic of news on the streets last night," it was reported the next day.[4] Cheyenne citizens were indignant. The *Daily Leader,* while insisting that it had nothing to say about Horn's guilt or innocence, nevertheless declared: "The man who shot and killed that boy, if he can be found, should swing for it before the grass grows again on the Wyoming plains."[5] The news quickly spread across the state. Articles appeared in Cody, Saratoga, Newcastle, Wheatland, and Buffalo newspapers within a week.[6] The *Buffalo Voice,* reflecting satisfaction among the people of Johnson County, who had waged a successful but frustrating battle with the power of big cattlemen just nine years earlier, said: "Chickens will come home to roost."[7]

Soon the newspapers turned from the sensational news of Horn's arrest to the case against him. Observing that Horn had been suspected in many cases but never convicted, the *Boomerang* noted that Horn was backed by friends "whose aggregate wealth is something like two millions and they will spend a good part of it in the effort to get the cattle detective free." Officers working the case had very strong evidence that might implicate other persons connected to Iron Mountain murders, the *Boomerang* added, discussing the violent deaths of Bob Burnett, Powell and Lewis, Isom Dart, and Matt Rash. The paper provided a kind of biography of Horn, part of which was inaccurate (covering family history and involvement in the Johnson County War) and part of which was generally correct (entailing Horn's work in Arizona and Cuba).[8] In the following days, the *Cheyenne Daily Leader* reported that five attorneys—T. Blake Kennedy, Roderick N. Matson, Judge J. W. Lacey, U.S. attorney Timothy F. Burke, and Burke's partner E. T. Clark)—had been retained on Horn's behalf, and that "the sum of $6,000 has been paid out by friends of Tom Horn for his defense and that this will be only a small portion of the aggregate amount expended for this purpose."[9] Six thousand dollars was a huge sum in 1901, equivalent to about $157,000 in 2012.[10]

The preliminary hearing was set quickly for January 23. The *Daily Leader* noted that the hearing would be held at the "court house," in the larger district courtroom, to accommodate the expected large attendance of "morbidly curious" people. The *Leader* also said, "The nature of the evidence the prosecution has against the cattle detective is still a profound secret to all except the officers of the court, who have not allowed anything to leak out, and the public is as much in the dark in this regard as it was before Horn was arrested."[11]

The prosecution's key evidence presented at the preliminary hearing dropped "like a thunderbolt," wrote the *Leader*. It was so unexpected that the large audience "rose to their feet in their excitement." The *Leader's* headline showed what stunned these people: TOM HORN CONFESSES.[12]

The hearing began at 10:00 A.M., and the crowd was very large. At first the case "dragged along all too slowly," as the prosecution presented well-known evidence. Several witnesses were called, including Kels Nickell, who told of hearing three shots the morning of Thursday, July 18, and of discovering his son's body the next day. J. A. B. Apperson testified as he had at the inquest, and the three examining physicians told of examining the body, concluding, among other things, that because of decomposition, the bullet holes would be enlarged, "as the skin is elastic and would be extended by the swollen bodies [*sic*]." (Dr. Barber moved away from his statement at the coroner's inquest that the size of the bullets striking Willie Nickell was at least three-eighths of an inch.)[13]

Until Joe LeFors took the stand in the afternoon, none of the courtroom spectators conceived that the prosecution "would explode a bomb of this nature in the ranks of the defense." LeFors's testimony even startled Tom Horn. Normally a stoic, Horn "lost his customary equanimity," the *Daily Leader* observed, "and could not hide the startled look which crept into his eyes when a full realization of the evidence the officers had came over him." Even Horn's attorneys "shifted in their seats and leaned forward as the details of the 'coup d'etat' were brought out."[14] "As for the prisoner himself," the *Saratoga Sun* reported, "he simply sat still, his blanched cheeks and staring eyes showing plainly the tumult that was raging within him as the witnesses repeated the words of his own confession of the awful murder of little Willie Nickell."[15]

Deputy U.S. Marshall LeFors testified to having approached Tom Horn and telling him he had secured a position for him in Montana that might require some shooting. During the ensuing conversation (which took place in Cheyenne), Horn surprisingly seems to have quickly accepted LeFors as a kindred spirit and told him startling things. "Little by little Horn's confession was wormed out," said the *Daily Leader* the next day, "until every detail connected with the murder of Willie Nickell was brought to light." Horn had told LeFors that he had taken his boots off and so had not left a trail, and he said that he had left his horse a good distance from the scene so that he could not be trailed by his horse. LeFors said that Horn had declared he never left a job like this "until I get my man." He had used a .30-30 rifle and made his shots at about three hundred yards. Horn also said: "It was the best shot I ever made and the dirtiest trick I ever done."[16]

Nor was it just the Nickell murder that Horn had admitted to LeFors. "The sensation created by the statement that Horn had confessed the Nickell murder," the *Leader* said, "was equaled by the one occasioned when it was brought out that Horn had confessed to other murders." Horn had told LeFors that he had killed a Mexican lieutenant, and that he got $600 each for the killing of Lewis and Powell and $500 for Nickell. Horn crowed: "Killing men is my specialty, I look at it as a business proposition." Of leaving a rock under Willie Nickell's head, Horn said: "That is the way I hang out my sign and the way I collect my money."[17]

Bad as were all these admissions, there were more, but all had not been caught by a newspaper reporter no doubt frantically scribbling notes. There was worse news for Horn. His statements to LeFors had all been overheard by Deputy Sheriff Les Snow and court stenographer Charles Ohnhaus, who had sat silently in an adjacent room, listened, and put Horn's comments down in writing. Horn could not deny that he had said everything LeFors testified he said.[18]

The next day, January 24, the *Cheyenne Daily Leader*, probably animated by intense public interest and apparently having obtained the notes of the court reporter at the preliminary hearing, set out the Horn admission testimony to LeFors at length. The *Leader*'s story filled most of eight columns, taking up the majority of two pages in the newspaper's tightly packed matrix.[19]

The story filled in many details. Shortly after 11:00 A.M., January 12, 1902, Horn and LeFors had gone to the U.S. marshal's office at the suggestion of Horn, who told LeFors that he did not want to talk in the Inner Ocean Hotel because they would be noticed and interrupted. LeFors readily accepted Horn's proposal, because he had earlier made arrangements for Snow and Ohnhaus to secretly station themselves in an adjacent room to overhear LeFors's conversation with Horn.

Once at the office, LeFors presented Horn a letter of introduction from W. G. Prewitt of Helena, Montana, who had some work for Horn. Horn asked if these Montana people were afraid of shooting, and LeFors assured him they were not. Horn then said, "There is one thing about me, I shoot too damned much; you've got to protect your employers, but I've never gotten my employers into trouble yet." Perceiving an opening to start Horn talking about Willie Nickell, LeFors told Horn he was the best man to cover up his trail LeFors had ever seen and that "in the killing of Willie Nickell I never could find any trail." Horn took the bait. He responded that he had gone "bare footed" and had left his horse a "damn long way off" from the gate. When LeFors asked why Willie Nickell had been shot, Horn replied: "I think it was this way. Supposing there was a man in the big draw to the right of the gate . . . , and the kid came up from this way and saw this party, and then run off in a southern direction as indicated and swinging around to get through the gate the party who saw him there . . . ran across and shot him as he went through the gate. That is my opinion of it." Willie Nickell was shot, said Horn, "for fear that he would get down to the house and raise a h[ell] of a muss or commotion." When LeFors asked him if running "bare footed" didn't hurt his feet, Horn replied that he had ten days "to rest up after a job of this kind."

LeFors asked Horn about reports, and Horn expressed his disdain for them. "I don't want to be making reports all the time. I will simply have one report to make and that will be my final report. If a man has to make reports all the time they would catch the wisest s__ of a b_____ on earth."

Horn brought up the "schoolmarm" and told LeFors that "she [Glendolene Kimmell] was smooth people; she had written me a letter after the testimony at the coroner's inquest as long as the governor's message." Horn said that Kimmell told him everything that had occurred in the investigation, and this information let him plan a strategy: "Stoll thought I would prove an alibi, but I fooled him." Miss Kimmell also told Horn to "look out for Joe LeFors. He is not all right." Horn had difficulty stating dates when discussing his dealings with Kimmell, and said, "everything dates from the killing of the kid. I don't remember dates. D_____ if I want to remember them."

Horn told LeFors that nobody carried him any food when he was out on the range, causing LeFors to ask Horn how "a big man like you, weighing over two hundred pounds, can do that?" Horn acknowledged that he got hungry, so hungry "I could kill my mother for grub," but he didn't quit until he got his man. When the two men discussed Horn's rifle, Horn said he thought the .30-40 would hold up better than a .30-30, but he "liked to get close to his man, the closer the better." LeFors asked Horn whether he carried his spent shells away with him, and Horn said: "You bet your G__ d_____ life I did."   When LeFors asked Horn to tell him about the killing of Willie Nickell, Horn replied, "I will tell you all about it when I come back from Montana, it is too fresh or too new yet."

The two men then left the marshal's office but came together again about two thirty that afternoon, when they spoke for another hour and a half to two hours. When asked about other conversations, LeFors testified, "We had conversations about various things, mostly about killing people; among them was an instance spoken of where he killed a lieutenant in the army in old Mexico at a dance." Then Horn told LeFors that he was paid $2,100 for killing three men and shooting at one five times. LeFors surprised Horn when he told him that he knew Horn had been paid on a train between Cheyenne and Denver for killing Lewis and Powell. The deputy marshal said Horn had received two hundred-dollar bills and the rest in gold, and Horn admitted that was true. Horn told LeFors that when he shot Lewis, "[he] was the scaredest G__ d_____ s__ of a b____ you ever saw." Horn declared to LeFors, regarding killing people, "I think I have a corner on the market." He told LeFors that none of his dealings were in writing and that he did all his business through John Coble. Horn bragged that he never had any trouble collecting his money, because "I would kill a man if he beat me out of ten cents that I earned." In closing, LeFors said that during these sessions Horn had been "perfectly sober as far as I could tell."

In the testimony of stenographer Charles Ohnhaus, Ohnaus showed how close he and Deputy Sheriff Snow had been to Horn. Ohnaus said that when Horn was leaning back in his chair, "he was not more than three feet from the door where I was." He said that he and Snow were on a buffalo overcoat on the floor. "We were both lying on the floor with our heads close to the threshold of the door." Ohnaus further noted that there was an inch-wide crack at the top of the door where the door didn't close tightly. "We could hear very distinctly."

Following the hearing, Judge Samuel Becker bound Horn over for trial upon the charge of first-degree murder.[20] One of Horn's attorneys dissented, telling the *Cheyenne Daily Leader* that "Horn had a good defense and was guiltless of the crime charged against him." Horn's defense team put up a vigorous fight to obtain bail, so Horn could be released pending the trial. The applicable Wyoming law stated, "All persons shall be bailable by sufficient securities, except for capital offenses when the proof is evident and the presumption great." Horn's lawyers made long arguments to "secure the liberty of Tom Horn," but Walter Stoll countered them with equally lengthy arguments. Ruling that the proof against Horn was evident and the presumption great, Judge Becker "committed the prisoner without bail."

CHAPTER EIGHT

Prologue to Trial

Most of the credit for the stunning turnaround from the depressing last days of the coroner's inquest to Tom Horn's arrest went to deputy U.S. marshal Joe LeFors. When LeFors traveled to Iron Mountain in August 1901 (as a favor to the dying Sheriff Shaver of Laramie County), he quickly reached some conclusions. From the day he arrived, LeFors saw the shooting of Kels Nickell and the murder of Nickell's son as sheep cases, arising out of Kels Nickell's introduction of the woolly critters cattlemen hated. The assassination and attempted assassination, thought LeFors, were intended to send a message and drive sheep out of the Iron Mountain region.[1]

When LeFors returned to Cheyenne from Iron Mountain, Sam Corson, chairman of the Laramie County commissioners, sought him out, asking his opinion about who was behind the assaults on the Nickell family. LeFors told Corson that "the finger of guilt pointed to the few cattle companies who were using that particular range." Corson volunteered to try to get the consent of LeFors's chief at the U.S. marshal's office for LeFors to work on the cases, and he was successful. Assigned to the Nickell cases, LeFors worked quietly in the background until his dramatic appearance at the preliminary hearing.[2]

At first LeFors made little progress in his investigation. Several trips to Iron Mountain rendered no clues. Then, on August 14, 1901, he met Tom Horn (for the first time) at a saddle shop in Cheyenne. The two men "had quite a visit" about guns, and LeFors noted that Horn was "rather inclined to brag." LeFors must have suspected Horn in the Nickell shootings (a reasonable surmise given the nature of the Willie Nickell killing and the fact that Horn had been in the area), and he boldly asked Horn how he came to let the old man get away. Remarkably, Horn replied that "the sun was not shining on the sights of the gun or else it would have been different," and "you ought to have seen him run and yell like a Comanche Indian."[3] The conversation apparently then moved elsewhere, but Horn's comments led LeFors to believe that the stock detective was a prime suspect in the killing of Willie Nickell.

LeFors decided to delve deeply into Horn's past, hoping to find information he might use in future meetings with Horn. Convinced that Horn was the gunman who had shot Lewis and Powell six years earlier, LeFors took trips all over Wyoming putting together information relating to the two killings.[4]

LeFors learned other information about Horn as well. Only a few days after his August conversation with Horn, LeFors heard that "in a drunken orgy" Horn had commented to the effect that he sometimes "got too handy with a Winchester." Making friends with a man and woman having an illicit affair in Cheyenne, LeFors, who did not care about the man, found the woman of interest because her husband, back at Iron Mountain, would sometimes put Horn up.[5]

During this time, LeFors was in conference with Walter Stoll nearly every day, but if Stoll was absent, LeFors still dictated his evidence to Mrs. Kitzmiller, Stoll's secretary, who made a record of the evidence LeFors gathered. When Stoll returned to his office, he could read that record.[6]

During late September and early October 1901, Horn spent time in Denver. He arrived there about September 28, with the intent of enjoying the yearly Denver Carnival. Horn fell in with three young men the evening of September 29. They all drank heavily and about five the next morning an argument began that ended in a physical altercation. Horn was beaten severely (he was an inept fighter when drunk) and his jaw was broken in two places, although it is not clear whether fists (possibly augmented with brass knuckles) or a cane caused the fractures. Horn spent a couple of weeks in a Denver hospital.[7] During this time, it was rumored that Kels Nickell was coming to Denver to confront Horn, perhaps to kill him. Nickell had the time to go to Denver because he had just sold his Iron Mountain place and was moving to Cheyenne. His shattered elbow had healed and amputation was not required, but Nickell wanted to leave Iron Mountain "on account of the threats that had been made against him."[8]

Newspapers in Wyoming told all about Horn's Denver excursion, and, if Horn's escapades were not colorful enough, they made up, or at least accepted, yarns. The *Laramie Boomerang* referred to Horn as "the best known scout in the United States," saying that his father was also a scout and that Tom was born among the Indians. His father, said the *Boomerang,* "went down from a bullet from the gun of an Indian," but Tom had extracted his revenge, killing "thirty of the redskins."[9] None of these statements was remotely true (Tom Horn's father fled Missouri, a fugitive from justice, and moved to British Columbia, apparently dying there in 1891), but newspapers seemed to prefer the romance of a storied figure to a more pedestrian reality.[10] Newspapers also seemed to relish the drama of a confrontation between Horn and Nickell. That said, Horn was hardly trying to avoid a dispute with Nickell, telling the *Denver Republican* that Nickell brought sheep into the country and then attended a school board meeting where, at his first opportunity, he jumped up and told his neighbors that he "intended to keep them [the sheep] there no matter what people said or thought." Horn blasted people like Nickell: "There is no man who is big bad good or tough enough to bring sheep into a cattle country."[11] Despite Horn's incendiary comments, Nickell never went to Denver to find him."[12]

Back in Cheyenne, LeFors put together a plan to induce Horn to make candid admissions. His plan, and a lucky meeting on a train, led to the biggest break in the case. LeFors wrote to Montanans he had known (W. D. Smith, chief livestock inspector for the state, and W. G. Prewitt of Helena), saying he knew of a first-rate cattle detective for whom he wanted to secure a job. Smith replied, saying that the Montana Live Stock Association was looking for a detective.[13] As the *Cheyenne Daily Leader* later reported, "This correspondence was carried on for some time, the Montana people being conscientious in the matter and unacquainted with the plan of LeFors." LeFors succeeded in obtaining an offer for a position for Horn in Montana with W. G. Prewitt, and even while Horn was in Denver LeFors corresponded with Horn about the proposed Montana job.[14]

In November 1901, after taking a man to the penitentiary in Rawlins, Wyoming, LeFors traveled eastward back to Cheyenne, and he noticed that George Prentiss got on the train at Bosler Station. LeFors later referred to Prentiss as "one of the bosses at the Bosler Ranch," probably meaning one of the foremen who worked for John Coble (recall that Horn made his headquarters at Coble's ranch). Prentiss was not, in fact, a Coble employee but was probably an employee of the Swan Livestock Company.[15] For LeFors's purposes, however, it did not matter who employed Prentiss, only that he was knowledgeable about the arrangements behind Willie Nickell's murder. If LeFors was right—that Tom Horn was the killer of Willie Nickell and a group of cattlemen had hired him—several top men would have known about the deal and would be extremely sensitive about Horn's conduct.

Seeing his opportunity, LeFors formulated an audacious plan and then acted on it. After boarding the train, he sat down next to Prentiss and "brought up the killing of little Willie Nickell." LeFors said to Prentiss: "George, what are all the Pinkertons doing around Cheyenne? I saw three there in the last three days. One time I saw them following Tom Horn around. Tom was drinking and[,] I understood, talking about the Nickell case. Why don't you send him out of the country? Horn is going to get someone in trouble yet by his talk."[16]

LeFors was stretching the truth to present to Prentiss a picture of Tom Horn dangerously out of control [certainly plausible], hoping that Prentiss would see LeFors as a friend and open up to him. Prentiss responded exactly as LeFors hoped. He replied, apparently with alarm, that if Horn talked too much, they would have to "bump him off" themselves. This comment must have thrilled LeFors. As he wrote later, "This was my first real information that I could rely on—that Tom Horn was guilty of the killing of little Willie Nickell."[17]

Prentiss made more startling admissions. He told LeFors that he had not paid for the "last killing," but had paid Horn in gold and paper money while on a train between Cheyenne and Denver for "jobs committed" earlier, a telling phrase. LeFors assumed that Prentiss's reference to "jobs committed before" was to the killings of Powell and Lewis.[18] These admissions assured LeFors that he was on the right track, but they did more. Prentiss's assumption that LeFors was a friend opened a clear path to carry out the rest of the deputy marshal's plan. LeFors told Prentiss that he had a letter from W. D. Smith, chief livestock inspector of Montana, asking LeFors to send him a man for detective work. LeFors suggested to Prentiss, "This [Montana] might be a good place to get Horn out of sight for a while."[19]

Prentiss jumped at LeFors's suggestion. After reading the letter from W. D. Smith, which indicated that "they wanted a man who had plenty of backbone and was entirely unknown," Prentiss said that "it was just the thing to get Horn out of the country." Prentiss volunteered to see

John Coble and discuss the matter with him. Prentiss said that even if Horn did not want the job, they "would make him take it whether he wanted it or not."[20]

Soon after, Coble came to Cheyenne to visit LeFors at his office. Coble asked to see the Smith letter and then requested it to take back to Bosler. LeFors gave Coble the letter but urged the cattleman to have Horn respond quickly, saying that he (LeFors) would have to do something soon. Shortly after this, LeFors received a letter from Horn, who said he was coming to Cheyenne from Bosler. The contents of this letter surely pleased LeFors. Anxious to establish his credentials for the Montana job, Horn made some highly imprudent disclosures. Saying he wanted the Montana position, Horn wrote: "I feel sure I can give Mr. Smith satisfaction." "I don't care how big or bad his men are or how many of them there are, I can handle them. They can scarcely be any worse than the Brown's Hole Gang, and I stopped cow stealing there in one summer." "You may write Mr. Smith for me that I can handle his work and can do it for less expense in the shape of lawyer and witness fees than any man in the business."[21] The letter was practically a confession that Horn had killed Matt Rash and Isom Dart.

The parties continued to correspond, including a January 7, 1902, letter in which Horn told LeFors, "I will get the men sure, for I have never yet let a cow thief get away from me unless he got up and jumped clean out of the country." As well, LeFors received a letter from W. D. Smith providing Horn with final instructions upon reporting to Helena.[22]

On January 11, 1902, LeFors sent a telegram to Horn, telling him to come to Cheyenne, saying that upon his arrival he (LeFors) would give Horn a letter of introduction to his Montana employers. LeFors met Horn, who arrived by the train that night, and next morning, a Sunday, January 12, 1902, he met Horn again for a drink at the Inter Ocean Hotel. Then he excused himself, saying he had to run an errand and would meet Horn later at the U.S. marshal's office.

LeFors's errand was to make final arrangements with Leslie Snow and Charles Ohnhaus. When LeFors first laid out his plan for eliciting a confession from Horn, Walter Stoll instructed him to implant reliable witnesses to the conversation so there would be no question about the accuracy of Horn's admissions and so that no defense attorney could discredit them. LeFors then contacted Snow and Ohnhaus and made the arrangements whereby these two men could secretly overhear everything said between Horn and LeFors.[23] As soon as Horn left his afternoon meeting with LeFors,

Ohnaus immediately began to transcribe his shorthand notes of the conversation between Horn and LeFors, and the next day, January 13, a warrant was issued for Horn's arrest.[24]

Throughout, Horn gave LeFors, a U.S. deputy marshal, remarkable trust, so much so that after he was arrested, Horn asked to see LeFors, whom he asked for help.[25] A big part of the shock Horn apparently felt when LeFors testified at the preliminary hearing no doubt came from Horn's realization of the monumental error he had made in treating LeFors as a buddy.

After bail was refused, Horn resided at the Laramie County jail, and his incarceration was not pleasant. There were eleven prisoners in the jail, including Horn.[26] From the beginning, though, Horn was segregated, kept under strict confinement, and "excluded from the outside world in his cell in the heart of the city as if he were 1,000 miles from civilization."[27] He was not allowed any visitors (not even his brother and niece), except for his attorneys, who were permitted to talk with him by order of the district court.[28] Horn's cell had once held Kinch McKinney, a "noted cattle thief" who for fourteen hours held the jail captive while blazing away with a rifle his attorney provided. Made of crisscrossed steel strips, the cell's ceiling was of "chilled steel" and its steel floor formed the roof of "the common prisoners' quarters beneath."[29] Not until June 11 was Horn allowed to leave his cell and get some fresh air (accompanied closely by a deputy sheriff). Newspapers reported that he was getting nervous and was not eating well, although the *Cheyenne Daily Leader* hastened to add that this was not evidence of his guilt.[30]

As the trial approached (it was thought the case would be tried in May), local newspapers kept up a continuous chatter about all things relating to Horn and the charges against him. At one point, the *Cheyenne Daily Leader* complained that only the Laramie County sheriff and his deputies declined to talk about the Horn case.[31] Interest did not stop at the state line. Indeed, local newspapers seemed to take pride in the fact that such important national publications as the *Police Gazette* and the *New York Sunday World* ran articles about Horn.[32] After Horn's trial began, the *Daily Leader* wrote, "This case has become one of almost national interest."[33]

Not long after Horn's arrest, the *Daily Leader* noted that Laramie County citizens were making a great many "hasty if not unwise comments" about the Horn case. Such comments, said the *Leader,* might make it difficult to select a jury, and citizens should refrain from speaking "in unqualified terms about the guilt or innocence of a prisoner." The *Leader* hastened to note, however, that it was the right of a newspaper to publish "all the facts about the transaction that can be obtained" and said that opinions expressed by newspapers about the guilt or innocence of a defendant did not particularly influence people.[34]

Indeed, newspapers did not hesitate to speculate about the fine details of the prosecution and defense tactics. On March 13, 1902, the *Daily Leader* carried two stories about the case, one declaring that Horn's lawyers would try to establish an alibi and contend that Horn's talk to LeFors was just "braggadocio."[35] The other was a story that Duncan Clark, foreman of John Coble's Bosler Ranch, had quit because Coble wanted him and his men to swear in favor of Horn. Clark denied the charge and said he was leaving because he was setting up his own operation.[36] Discussing defense tactics in greater detail, the *Weekly Boomerang* said that the attorneys for the defense and prosecution were working diligently and that local attorneys were predicting the legal battle would be "one of the most bitter and hardest fought in the history of Wyoming." A big focus of the case would be whether Tom Horn was drunk when he made his statements to Joe LeFors. The defense would not seek a change of venue, however, because even if successful, not much would be gained and the defense would lose advantages it had in Laramie County.[37] The article did not mention it, but Laramie County had been the only place in Wyoming to support the Johnson County invasion. Although attitudes had changed, Laramie County was where most of the remaining diehard Wyoming cattlemen (and their employees) resided.

Bill Barlow wrote a bitter editorial for the Douglas, Wyoming, *Budget* (subsequently picked up and run by other Wyoming newspapers), which fairly expressed the disgust and anger the public felt about the Horn revelations.[38] Barlow characterized Horn as "a type of the bravo of the middle ages whose dagger thrust was an article of commerce at so much per prod, but whom civilization was presumed to have long since eliminated from modern society." Barlow could not resist bringing up Glendolene Kimmell, saying, "Gentle dalliance with a school-marm appears in the evidence, and as the gentleman himself volunteers the information that she was 'sure smooth people' it is presumed that she was—affording an agreeable diversion, doubtless, from his arduous duties of pulling his pop on cowardly cattle thieves, and shooting little boys in the back."[39]

Barlow was not the only newspaperman intrigued by Kimmell. The *Cheyenne Daily Leader* declared that Horn had been warned by his "sweetheart" but had failed to heed the warning, and as a result "he is now languishing in the county jail charged with the crime of murder." The

Leader said, "Miss G. M. Kimball [*sic*] is a petite, vivacious piece of femininity, less than five feet in height, but possessing an education extraordinary in a young lady of such an age." The *Leader* stated that when Kimmell came to Cheyenne to testify at the coroner's inquest, Horn met her at the depot and "paid her every attention."[40]

Horn and Kimmell seem to have been infatuated with each other, but it was an exaggeration to call her Horn's sweetheart. It is true that the two had met at the Cheyenne train depot and that they had then walked from the depot, with Miss Kimmell on Horn's arm, but the meeting at the depot was apparently their only other contact after their time together at the Miller Ranch.[41]

Newspapers' comments about the killings of Matt Rash and Isom Dart in Brown's Hole, Colorado, were especially unwelcome to Horn and his supporters. Wyoming newspapers early raised the suspicion that Horn had killed Rash and Dart, and on February 3, 1902, the *Denver Post* openly charged Horn with their murders.[42] About a month later, two Wyoming newspapers reported that Colorado wanted Horn, and that if acquitted of the Willie Nickell killing, he would probably be charged in Colorado for the killings of Rash and Dart.[43]

The public attitude toward Horn and his big cattlemen supporters was unambiguous. The vast majority of Wyomingites saw Horn as a craven assassin employed by cattlemen who were as guilty as he was. Newspapers openly charged cattlemen with hiring Horn to assassinate, and they opined (or at least hoped) that several cattlemen would be charged with murder as a result of the Horn prosecution.[44] Even Colonel Edward Slack of the *Cheyenne Daily Leader* condemned murder, although Buffalo newspapers quickly pointed out his hypocrisy. Back in 1891 and 1892, Slack was one of the strongest supporters of the big cattlemen who invaded Johnson County.[45]

In truth, some Wyoming newspapers pulled their punches when writing the history of the shameful conduct of big cattlemen in Wyoming, but not so Colorado newspapers. On March 2, 1902, the *Denver Post* blared a series of front-page articles by the well-known reporter Polly Pry (a pen name for Mrs. Leonel Campbell Ross O'Bryan).[46] Pry was a skilled writer, but, more important to the Horn case, she was brash and unafraid to declare some harsh truths.

The headline to several Pry articles read "Wyoming's Appalling Record of Rustler Assassinations Brought to Light of Day," and her first target was Wyoming's senior senator, Francis E. Warren.[47] Her story spoke of "What a Federal Senator Can Do," and she blasted Warren as a man who had driven thirty to forty families off public land that he controlled. "And it is this sort of despotism," she concluded, "that has brought about conditions which make it possible for men like Tom Horn to live in a supposedly law-abiding community." Then she launched into a long article about Willie Nickell, whose murder had devastated the Nickell family, Tom Horn's long history as an assassin, and his confession to Joe LeFors.

Pry's longest piece in this group was headlined "Long Record of Murder." She had obviously spoken with Wyoming people who had told her of the murderous history of the state's cattle barons. She wrote about the 1889 killings of Ellen Watson and James Averill and numerous other assassinations. Pry obtained a copy of Asa Mercer's 1894 book, *The Banditti of the Plains (The Crowning Infamy of the Ages)*, and presented Mercer's flaming indictment of Wyoming cattlemen for the Johnson County invasion. Pry concluded that by 1892, the big cattlemen "had rolled up a record of fifteen cowardly and brutal murders and the small farmers throughout the commonwealth were in a state of terror."[48] She concluded with an intrepid declaration of what was at stake in the trial of Tom Horn:

> If Horn were alone concerned, he would hang tomorrow.
>
> But—holding the good name and honor of so many men of wealth and prominence in his blood-stained hands—he still sees a fighting chance for himself.
>
> The coming May term of court will determine whether the people of Wyoming will again stand aside and see a few men— who have deliberately appropriated vast tracts of the public domain and enriched themselves at the expense of the state, and who stand for nothing except their own interests—to openly defeat the ends of justice, and by the expenditure of their ill-gotten gains, again turn an unnatural monster loose among the people. Or, whether the public has now arrived at that point where they will demand that the axe be applied to the very root of the evil and let the chips fall where they may.

Another issue further delayed the Horn trial. The Wyoming legislature had passed a new jury law in 1899, but there were technical problems with the new act. If it was declared invalid, then prosecutions under it, such as

State v. Horn, might be set aside. Wyoming newspapers discussed the problem as early as February 1902.[49] Walter Stoll challenged the jury law, seeking to have it declared valid (or not) before the Horn trial. There were mixed feelings about Stoll's actions. The *Wheatland World* praised Stoll, saying that Laramie County should not risk the great cost of a second trial for Tom Horn. There was grumbling in early September, however, when the Wyoming Supreme Court had rendered no decision and the appeal backed up trials for fifty men kept in local jails.[50]

Of all the participants in the expected trial, Horn would seem to be the one most likely to be dissatisfied with the delay. A June 1, 1902, letter to Duncan Clark (former Coble foreman), however, showed that Horn was apparently not downcast and had certainly not lost his sense of humor. In it, Horn tells Clark that he will do some leatherwork for Clark and then closes: "I am as well and hearty and as well treated as any one could possibly be. My only objection to living in jail is that I can't attend church regular."[51] As an adult Horn rarely, if ever, attended church.

Finally, on September 12, 1902, the *Cheyenne Daily Leader* said that a Wyoming Supreme Court decision had upheld the jury law, meaning that the Horn case could proceed.[52] Three days later the *Daily Leader* announced that the Horn trial would start on October 10.

The Laramie County Courthouse in Cheyenne, described in the *Denver Post* as "old fashioned," was probably a typical facility in the early twentieth century. It was a "square red brick structure," containing a district courtroom, the same courtroom where Tom Horn's preliminary hearing was held, and the place where lawyers, judges, witnesses, and spectators would gather on October 10. The room was large and filled with sturdy wooden furniture (probably oak). Ornate bronze figures held asbestos lights. The walls were decorated with flower-pattern wallpaper and the ceiling was vaulted. A "high, rusty stove with a pipe extending half across the room" heated the chamber, and jury seats sat behind a "thin, highly polished railing." The judge's bench sat to the left of jurors, and "long, green-covered" tables for the attorneys were placed in front of the bench.[53]

Public comment had abated when the trial was postponed, but when the trial date was announced on September 15, strong interest throughout the state was revived. On September 28, the *Sheridan Post,* 325 miles from Cheyenne, ran the comments of "Sauntering Silas," showing that the people of a town on the opposite side of Wyoming from Cheyenne had discussed the case of *State v. Horn* in depth.[54] The writer described Horn as a "beast possessed of destroying elements, which, if used, would cause many a fireside to contain a vacant chair, and many a heart to ache at the untimely end of a loved one." Wheatland, Wyoming, was the town closest to the Iron Mountain area where Willie Nickell was killed, and the *Wheatland World* quoted the *Cheyenne Daily Leader,* which said: "A chain of evidence has been forged around Tom Horn so strong that any jury which could be drawn in the state would convict the cattle detective."[55] Other newspaper articles commenting about different aspects of the Horn case appeared in other Wyoming newspapers, including pieces from Sundance, Cheyenne, Buffalo, and Laramie.[56]

The general attitude toward Horn was distinctly negative, but Horn did have his supporters. As might be expected, they came from the ranching community, people who saw Horn as protecting their way of life. The *Denver Times* even ran an article saying that Horn's Iron Mountain friends were "standing by him nobly." The article presented surprisingly candid remarks from people around Sybille Creek who supported Horn. They talked of earlier plans to lure Kels Nickell out of his house and to lynch him. When a half-dozen men had approached Nickell's house, however, they had found Nickell sitting inside his door with a Winchester across his knee, and that discouraged the delegation. But these cattle ranchers declared that "the annihilation of Kels Nickell and of his sheep was to have been a benefit to the community." They talked of how important it was to have a cattle detective and how damaging was the presence of sheep; they felt besieged by sheep interests. The boy was killed by mistake, said Horn's friends, and none of them would have sanctioned it had they been there.[57] Said one woman during the trial: "The people who trapped Horn into a confession are a thousand times worse than Horn, and when he gets out their skins will be like sieves."[58]

People thought the Horn trial would be long and arduous. The *Cheyenne Daily Leader* predicted the case would be "the longest in the history of the state." Walter Stoll himself said it would take three weeks to select a jury, three weeks to introduce testimony, and another week before the jury returned with a verdict.[59] Wyoming people deeply believed that Horn was guilty, not only of the killing of Willie Nickell but also of Powell, Lewis, Rash, and Dart, but they worried that Stoll would be outnumbered, outspent, and outgunned. "Although a man of signal ability, great force of character and a thorough knowledge of the law," Stoll was only one man against eight excellent lawyers hired by big cattlemen (Lacey, Burke, Edward Clark, Gibson Clark, Matson, Kennedy, Burdick, and Breckons).[60]

Although the trial was scheduled to begin on October 10, groundwork had to be laid. On September 23, an initial group of jury candidates (called a "venire") was selected. Anticipating difficulty selecting a jury, thirty-six names were drawn, rather than the usual twenty-four."[61] The venire was selected out of one thousand names placed in a box. Remarkably, only three were from Cheyenne (a city with about 70 percent of the Laramie County population), but twelve were from Wheatland (with less than 5 percent of the Laramie County population). Even more remarkably, the panel contained many ranchmen Horn knew.[62] This initial selection must have pleased the defense and worried the prosecution. Laramie county cattlemen would not have much sympathy for Kels Nickell, the man who brought sheep onto a cattle range.

October 10, 1902, was a Friday, and from the beginning of that week, the town assumed "a gala appearance, as if a festival of its own was about to be rung up." Cheyenne started filling with people, including subpoenaed witnesses, spectators, and a lot of newspaper reporters.[63] So anxious were some Denver newspaper people for the beginning of the trial that a large group of writers, staff artists, and staff photographers came to Cheyenne on Sunday night, apparently thinking that the trial would start on Monday.[64] They had to return home, but although the trial was not scheduled to convene until Friday, some preliminary legal steps were taken on Thursday, when at least some prospective jurors were examined as to general qualifications. Four were disqualified and District Judge Scott had twenty more names drawn. This second venire produced what the *Cheyenne Daily Leader* called a "strange feature." Kels Nickell, father of the murder victim in the Horn case, was selected for the jury. The *Leader* assured its readers that Nickell would "of course, be disqualified from service."[65] On that same day, Nickell was issued an order to show cause why he should not be held in contempt of court. On Wednesday, October 8, Walter Stoll asserted, Nickell had pulled a knife and threatened a prospective juror, accusing him of having been bribed to acquit Horn. The *Denver Post* speculated that the only explanation was that Nickell had become "crazed" over the loss of his son.[66]

On Friday, October 10, 1902, the full weight of the case of *State v. Horn* descended upon Cheyenne.

CHAPTER NINE

The Trial Begins

Well before the Horn trial began at 10:00 A.M., crowds converged upon the Laramie County Courthouse. By nine, the courtroom was full. One newspaper described the gathering as immense, and another said that the courtroom was "crowded to its utter capacity all day and every foot of standing room was occupied."[1] The presence of all these avid spectators certainly supported the comment of the *Laramie Boomerang* that the case had aroused people "to a degree not reached since the cattlemen's invasion" of Johnson County a decade earlier.[2]

The large contingent of newspaper people in Cheyenne also testified to the strong public interest in the case. Three tables were set aside for newspaper people "inside the railing," the trial area normally reserved for the judge, witness stand, attorneys' tables, and defendant's seating.[3] Present were correspondents, artists, special writers, and photographers from all the major Denver newspapers—the *Times, Post, Rocky Mountain News, Denver News,* and *Republican*—as well as reporters from Chicago, Kansas City, and St. Louis.[4] All these newspapers profiled the key actors at length.

The presiding judge was Richard H. Scott, whom the *Denver Times* described in glowing terms, calling him "the personification of dignity and determination" and saying: "There will be no back talk nor frivolling in the district court of the First District of Wyoming while Judge Richard H. Scott is on the bench. Judge Scott has a comfortable, portly frame, a soft, persuasive face, and dark brown eyes that are kindly disposed up to a certain point, but beyond that point the face takes on a keen, cold look, and the eyes a warning glitter. The magistrate supersedes the man and neighbor."

There was more to Scott than the *Times* portrayed, however. He had been the presiding judge in the 1893 trial in which big cattlemen were charged with murder and arson committed when Johnson County was invaded. The judge had made questionable rulings in favor of the big cattlemen, resulting in the complete acquittal of men undoubtedly guilty of murder.[5] Observers of the Horn case must have wondered whether Scott would favor the interests of big cattlemen in this case and lean in favor of the defendant.

Press reports also described in detail the lead attorneys for the prosecution and defense. Walter Stoll was said to be a "medium sized man, inclined to portliness, bald and wearing eye-glasses." He was not impressive physically, but when speaking, he "was not only graceful, but the earnestness, the great desire of the man in his professional pride, made him the only figure in the room."[6]

John W. Lacey, Horn's lead attorney, had a reputation as "one of the most brilliant criminal lawyers in the western country."[7] Lacey came to Cheyenne in 1884 after President Chester A. Arthur appointed him chief justice of the Wyoming Supreme Court. He was soon followed to the state by his brother-in-law, Willis Van Devanter, and by 1892 the two men had established Lacey & Van Devanter, which gained the reputation as the best law firm in Wyoming. Van Devanter went on to a seat on the U.S. Supreme Court, but Lacey remained in Cheyenne.[8]

The character most awaited, of course, was the defendant, Tom Horn. At 9:30 A.M., Judge Scott told the sheriff to bring Horn into the courtroom. When Horn entered, he assumed his part in a trial that, according to the *Denver Post,* promised to be "the most famous case in the history of Wyoming criminal courts." The *Post* characterized Horn as "rather pale" and stooped at the shoulders but otherwise none the worse after several months in jail. He wore a dark suit with a corduroy vest and was said to have "a restless, bright eye," to twirl his mustache "nervously," and to look "like an inoffensive man and not the hero of dime novels." The *Post* described his countenance in great detail: "a peculiarly shaped head, a small brow, sloping abruptly to the cranium, devoid of hair for half the distance along the top, until it grows short and black, but not thick. His nose is the prominent feature and is as straight as a line drawn with a ruler, his eyes deep set and brilliantly sharp, his ears large and setting out from the head."[9]

Horn had also been present in the courtroom the day before, on October 9, before the crowds had arrived, when Kels Nickell was selected as a prospective juror. "Then it was," said the *Denver Post,* "that for a moment, the father of the murdered boy, and the man accused of that murder, looked at each other. There was not the slightest twitch of a muscle to change Horn's expression. He coolly looked at Nickell while the latter, entering the jury box, encountered his gaze. Nickell dropped his eyes and looked away. Horn continued to pierce Nickell with his steady gaze; it was a confident, contemptuous, half-amused look, and the jurors were plainly annoyed."[10]

The next day the judge would address Nickell's October 8 assault of a prospective juror, calling Nickell into his chambers. Not surprisingly, Scott went easy on Willie Nickell's father, though he gave him a severe lecture. Nickell promised to behave, and the judge apparently decided to drop the matter if Nickell kept his promise. Nickell's friends and family remained critical of Nickell, saying that he "does more to hurt the case than any other factor."[11]

Some of the Denver newspapers noted what they perceived to be the trial's broader context. "This is an isolated instance of the warfare between cattlemen and sheepmen," said the *Times.* "The Horn trial is the entering wedge of the sheepmen into universal rights in the grazing rights of Wyoming."[12] Taking a different slant, the *Post* noted how the trial was "of such vital interest to stockmen, cattlemen and sheepmen. Tom Horn was in the service of cattlemen in the warfare against the small ranchmen. But more than the telling of the actual tragedy is expected during the progress of the trial. Much of the dark history of the range may now come to the light of day."[13]

Courtroom spectators, whatever their philosophies, were intensely interested in the proceedings. The *Post* said that "every word uttered by the court or attorneys[,] and every move of the famous prisoner, is watched with the keenness that shows the almost unparalleled interest taken in this case."[14] And what they watched that first day was the selection of jurors.

Many thought jury selection would take perhaps three weeks, and spectators were surprised how the exercise turned out. As the *Cheyenne Daily Leader* said: "It slowly dawned upon those present that . . . from all indications this afternoon a jury will be selected in a day or two."[15] Many predicted that numerous prospective jurors would be excused for having formed an opinion of Horn's guilt or innocence. In fact, as many jurors were disqualified because of their stated unwillingness to convict for murder based upon circumstantial evidence than for having formed an opinion.[16]

The two sides whittled down an initial pool of eighty-six jurors to thirty-six men. Attorneys questioned these survivors in depth and then passed or challenged.[17] The *Denver Post* described this proceeding in detail:

> Mr. Sullivan (a prospective juror) had formed an opinion and evidently didn't desire to serve. He was finally excused. Henry Hoffman was also excused on the same ground. H. W. Yoder had formed an opinion from reading the newspapers. Tolson had also formed an opinion. The challenge of the prosecution to Charles Stamm was overruled. While he had formed an opinion, had heard of and discussed the case, he did not doubt his ability to go into the trial presuming the defendant to be innocent until proven guilty. McDavin was excused. O. V. Seaborn, H. W. Thomas, William Taylor, George P. Knight, H. J. Northrup, A. J. Peterson, and R. A. Walker were called by the clerk. Northrup stated he had a personal feeling against Horn. On the challenge by the defense he was excused.
>
> Attorney Stoll passed R. A. Walker. Attorney questioned Tolson and Thomas. George P. Knight, who keeps a candy and laundry store in Cheyenne, and is a man of strong views, occupied much time of the defense.[18]

And then, remarkably, at 3:30 P.M., a jury was secured, after only three hours. The *Cheyenne Daily Leader* announced the jury to its readers: "J. E. Barns, H. M. Yoder, C. H. Tolson (colored), Charles Stamm, O. E. Seaborn, H. W. Thomas, G. H. Whitman, E. C. Metcalf, F. F. Simon, E. R. Babbitt, Amos Southmore, and Homer Payne."[19]

Indications that the jury's makeup would be skewed in favor of Laramie County ranchmen were borne out, producing a jury composition that surely delighted the defense. The prosecution would have preferred jurors who were from Cheyenne and not part of the ranching community, but although fourteen thousand of the twenty thousand people in Laramie County lived in Cheyenne, only two of the twelve selected jurors—Tolson, a porter, and Barnes, a butcher—were from Cheyenne. Another man, Metcalf, was a blacksmith from Wheatland. The remaining nine jurors were described as follows: "O. E. Seaburn, ranchman in Goshen Hole country;

Homer Payne, cowboy employed by the Two Bar outfit (Chugwater); F. F. Simon, foreman of White ranch on Little Horse Creek; H. W. Thomas, ranchman residing near Lagrange; T. R. Babbit, a ranchman near Lagrange; Amos Harbaugh, foreman of Two Bar ranch; G. W. Whiteman, ranchman residing near Uva; Charles Stamm, ranchman on Wheatland flats; . . . H. W. Yoder, a Goshen Hole ranchman."[20]

The jury selected represented an auspicious beginning for the defense, and bad as the appearance of this jury was for the prosecution, the reality was worse. When the jury panel was first chosen, one of Horn's attorneys, T. Blake Kennedy (later to become a federal district judge in Wyoming), went to the Laramie County jail and discussed the jury list with his client. Kennedy told Horn that the list contained "quite a number of ranchmen in the County whom [he] might possibly know." Horn and the young lawyer went over the list very thoroughly and Horn marked those he would find acceptable as jurors. As Judge Kennedy reported many years later, "strange as it may seem, six of those on the original panel were selected."[21] Not only did Horn know and approve of several jurors, one of them, Homer Payne, was actually a friend of his.[22]

The *Laramie Boomerang* found the rapid selection of the jury to be suspicious: "Men of affairs predicted that the delay in getting a jury would wear out the patience of everybody concerned, and that it would be a material aid to the defense. On the contrary the defense made as few challenges and as little trouble as possible. They have some trump up their sleeves, which in their own minds is capable of taking any trick that may turn up."[23] The defense attorneys made "as little trouble as possible" because they probably recognized they had fallen into a remarkably favorable panel and did not want to force the selection of additional panel members not likely to be as sympathetic to Horn.

A long recess was taken, and, at first, it seemed that testimony would be heard that afternoon. There were certainly a lot of witnesses to hear from; the prosecution had issued subpoenas to seventy-five people and the defense to ten.[24] But then other matters were addressed, including swearing the jury in and giving the jury some initial, general instructions. Most importantly, Walter Stoll would present the prosecution's opening statement.

Stoll was known as a great orator, but his opening statement was short. In a "clear and concise" presentation, the Laramie County prosecuting attorney confined himself to a close recitation of the facts he intended to present to the jury.[25] Those following the case already knew well what information had been revealed, and the newspapers reporting the trial would focus on new information that Stoll might present.

In fact, Stoll brought to light several items not known previously. Providing the jury with the Iron Mountain setting, and using maps that had been specially prepared, Stoll told the jury of the morning of July 18, when Willie Nickell was given his instructions to find a sheepherder and mysterious shots were heard, as well as July 19, when Willie Nickell's body was found. But then he informed the jury of a blood-stained sweater that had been brought to a Laramie shoe store shortly after the killing of Willie Nickell by a man identified as Tom Horn.[26] Stoll revealed more new facts when he said that Horn had arrived in Laramie about eleven o'clock on the morning of July 18 (the morning Willie was shot). Horn was then riding a different horse than the one he had been riding in the Iron Mountain area for the previous few days, and the new horse was covered with foam. Stoll said the distance between the gate where Willie Nickell was killed and the city of Laramie could be covered in only a few hours by hard riding.[27] Stoll also told the jury he would present the testimony of three men from Denver, witnesses previously unknown to the public, and each would testify about incriminating statements Horn had made to him.[28]

Stoll's opening statement would normally have been followed by an opening statement from the defense, but, surprisingly, John Lacey asked to reserve his opening statement until after the prosecution had completed its case. With Lacey's declaration, the first day of Tom Horn's trial came to a close. The next morning (Saturday, October 11) the jury would hear live witnesses, and the public could not wait to learn what these people would say. As the *Laramie Boomerang* commented, "The interest in the case is intense and there are many expressions of opinion as to the outcome."[29] One common opinion was expressed by a man identified only as "a politician and lawmaker of Wyoming." He confidently proclaimed: "They will never do anything to Tom Horn—you mark my word! They may have a farce of a trial, taking a few days or a few weeks, but that needn't worry Horn."[30]

CHAPTER TEN

The Testimony Begins

The weather was "dark, drizzly and gloomy" on Saturday morning, October 11, 1902, but the courtroom was filled to standing room only, and the presence of "a large number of ladies" was noted.[1]

The first witnesses showed the jury the setting of the crime. William S. Ingham, a surveyor and civil engineer, provided three maps he had made. Ingham's maps were on a scale of one inch per two miles and covered a relatively large area.[2] G. W. Zorn, a Cheyenne civil engineer, provided three maps showing smaller areas. One covered the ground within a radius of two miles from the point where Willie Nickell was killed, and another showed a similar area but only for a mile by a mile and a half.[3] William Walker, a Cheyenne photographer, testified about eleven photographs showing the gate, the bluff in back of it, and a panoramic view looking south from the top of a pile of rocks near the gate.[4]

Ingham and Zorn's testimony was more than just a prosaic explanation of map details, however. The two also provided information that would have real weight throughout the trial. Ingham was familiar with the territory between Iron Mountain and Laramie City. Having worked for eight years for the Iron Mountain Land and Cattle Company, he had ridden over virtually every trail and road in the area.[5] The country was easy to ride through on a horse without being detected, he told the jury, and if a horse was ridden fast, it took about three hours to ride the thirty-two miles from the site of the gate to Laramie.[6] Because the defense never contradicted

Ingham's testimony, his estimate of three hours from the gate to Laramie would stand to the end of the trial.

In addition to his maps, Zorn had also prepared a list of twenty-six places from which the gate could be seen, and he showed on one of his maps where each of these points lay.[7] Zorn's list demonstrated twenty-six examples of a direct line of flight for a rifle bullet to the gate, showing that an assassin could have fired from any one of these twenty-six spots.

Walker was the last witness offered by the prosecution during the morning of September 11. One newspaper said that the morning's testimony "lacked somewhat in interest at times" but described the afternoon proceedings as "all absorbing."[8]

The first witness that afternoon was E. D. Titus, who provided important testimony supporting the charges against Horn. In his testimony before the coroner's jury, Horn said he had remained in the Iron Mountain area until Saturday, July 20, and did not come to Laramie until that afternoon.[9] Titus contradicted Horn, saying he saw Horn during the evening of Friday, July 19, at the Custer House bar. He was sure of the date because the next day after he saw Horn he heard of the killing of Willie Nickell. (Later testimony would show that this news was first reported in Laramie newspapers in the evening edition of the Friday, July 19, *Laramie Republican*).[10] Titus said that he and Horn had a drink together between 8:00 and 9:00 P.M.[11]

Titus's testimony was significant for another reason. It prompted the first clash between John Lacey and Walter Stoll—combat that would, in the end, determine Horn's fate. An astute attorney, Lacey must have immediately recognized the importance of Titus's testimony. It undercut Horn's alibi, his assertion that he was elsewhere than at that fatal gate early the morning of Thursday, July 18, 1901. Horn had said that while he had been in the general area of the gate he was drifting to the northwest, away from the gate, and that he had not returned to the Coble ranch until Saturday and had not arrived in Laramie until Saturday afternoon. Titus's testimony produced the trial's first unfriendly cross-examination. But Lacey had a problem: he did not have much ammunition against Titus. What Lacey did, therefore, was to impugn Titus's memory as selective, implying that Titus had a hidden bias to remember in a carefully unfair way.

Lacey asked Titus first whether he remembered anyone else in the bar the night he'd had a drink with Horn. That night was more than a year previous, however, and Titus remembered only a few details about the presence of other men. Then Lacey went on to test the witness's memory of his activities around July 19. Titus said that he spent that time in and around Laramie trying to hire men to do haying. Titus's memory regarding when he came to Laramie, other than on Friday, July 19, and when he conducted haying operations, was even more vague. Titus aided Lacey's objective—to question why Titus remembered details of his meeting with Horn so distinctly—when Titus became defensive about his memory. Titus insisted, "It is not very faulty. I recollect the occurrence as I have stated it." Then Lacey asked questions intimating that Titus had drunk quite a bit when he was with Horn, and Titus responded that it would be impossible to say "how many times I did drink." Titus did manage to point out that the death of Willie Nickell was an unusual event and may have caused things to stay in his memory. He said that he knew his encounter with Horn was Friday night because he did not hear of the Willie Nickell killing until Saturday.[12]

Upon redirect examination, Stoll had only one question, going to the heart of why Titus remembered the day of his conversation with Tom Horn: "Do I understand you to say that the facts to which you referred was the fact that people were talking Saturday about the killing of Willie Nickell?" "Yes, sir," was Titus's response.[13]

This little battle would seem a standoff between Lacey and Stoll, but we cannot know how the jury perceived Titus. If he came across as an honest man trying to tell what he knew as best he could, Lacey's cross-examination would have no effect, and Titus's highly important recollection would stand. But if Titus seemed evasive or to hold a grudge against Horn, then the cross-examination might have been effective to cast doubt upon the witness's veracity.

Next, using members of the Nickell family, Walter Stoll presented testimony directly relating to the killing of Willie Nickell. First called was William Mahoney, Willie's maternal uncle, who testified that he had last seen Willie just before leaving with Kels Nickell and J. B. Apperson to undertake some surveying. Willie was saddling his horse to go find a sheepherder. When the survey team was about a mile and a half from the Nickell house, about 7:00 A.M., they heard three shots "one after the other," which, from the way the gun cracked, sounded like smokeless powder to Mahoney. He thought they came from the place where they later found Willie. It was assumed at the time that someone was hunting wild game.[14]

Mahoney said he saw Willie's body lying on its back the next morning, about eight thirty or nine. He observed blood near the gate and saw that Willie's shirt was saturated with blood and that there was gravel on his vest, face, and shirt. Mahoney concluded that Willie's body must have been turned over, because "I don't see how it (gravel) could get on any other way." After taking care of the body, Mahoney said he returned to the scene in the afternoon and examined it but found no tracks. He had also found no firearms.[15]

Mrs. Mary Nickell, Willie's mother, was next called to the stand. Her testimony was not long and essentially corroborated other witness's versions of the time spent at the Nickells' home on July 18, 1902, just before Willie rode off on his last journey. But what Mrs. Nickell said was not nearly as important as who she was and what she had suffered. The prosecution wanted the jury to remember the terrible loss to the family when Willie was killed. The *Denver Post* wrote: "The mother, whose hair is beginning to turn gray, and whose features, still hinting of the comeliness of her earlier days, wore an air of pathetic sadness, in a calm, subdued voice, gave her testimony. Horn did not embarrass her with the steady gaze he had directed at the other witnesses. Instead, during the greater portion of her testimony, he talked in a whisper with one of his attorneys."[16] Surprisingly, John Lacey chose to cross-examine Mrs. Nickell. It is hard to guess Lacey's purpose, because he simply went over seemingly well-established details. The cross-examination was brief, however, and appears from the transcript to have been undertaken in a quiet way.[17]

Mary Nickell's husband, Kels, followed his wife to the stand. This was something of a surprise, because it had been speculated that Kels, given his volatile nature, would not be used as a witness.[18] Nickell verified all the information about the events of July 18, which by then were well known. When he cross-examined Nickell, however, Lacey ignored what Kels had just testified to. Lacey's first question heralded a major effort by the defense. "Did the boy ever have trouble in that vicinity?" asked Lacey. "Yes, sir," replied Nickell. Nickell then admitted that Willie had "quite a bit of trouble with the Miller family." Lacey pushed hard into this subject, asking how serious and how frequent the trouble had been, whether anyone was carrying guns, and whether he (Kels Nickell) was present at any of these disagreements. Nickell's response was that he had not been present and that the trouble was not frequent; he referred to "little rows" between the boys.[19]

Lacey then moved away from the disputes between the boys and asked Kels whether there had been trouble between him and James Miller. This question earned Lacey the prosecution's objection that the question was not a proper matter for cross-examination. Judge Scott ruled, "I think the objection is well taken and will be sustained."[20]

Scott's ruling, probably disappointing to the defense, was not surprising. The defense wanted to try the Miller family for the murder of Willie Nickell, but Lacey and his defense team had a problem. While in 1902 it was well established legally that a defendant could present testimony showing that someone else had killed a murder victim, it was also well established that testimony showing only opportunity and a motive to kill a victim was not admissible. Courts had declared that it was only speculation that a person with a motive had acted upon it, generating a "mere suspicion."[21] And the Horn defense had no evidence to show that any of the Millers had acted to bring about the death of Willie Nickell.

John Lacey was surely aware of the state of the law but pushed hard anyway to bring before the jury evidence relating to the Millers. (Lacey left the topic for a few minutes, but then asked whether the Miller boys generally carried a gun. The prosecution's objection again cut him off.[22]) The arrest of the Millers for the attempted murder of Kels Nickell had been well publicized, and the vast majority of adults in Laramie County surely knew that the Millers had been arrested (but then let go), and Lacey probably felt that he need only remind the jury of the troubles between the Millers and Nickells for them to consider an alternate murderer.

Eleven year-old Freddie Nickell followed his father to the stand. His testimony takes only eleven lines in the trial transcript, but it was intensely and sadly dramatic, described as a "little mosaic of tragedy in the dark structure of the trial." When Stoll asked Freddie questions about finding his older brother's body, the boy provided direct, succinct answers. Stoll then asked Fred what he had done as soon as he saw the body. Fred started sobbing violently and wailed, "I went home." The boy then slid off the witness stand "crying bitterly" and "groped his way to his father, whose arms were outstretched and who sat on a window sill. Father and son sat together, Nickell awkwardly patting the little man until his tears ceased falling." Stoll asked no further questions and the defense declined to cross-examine.[23]

Little Freddie Nickell obviously needed his father at that moment in his life, but it was odd that Kels was present. Judge Scott had excluded all prosecution and defense witnesses from the courtroom, but Kels had made a plea to remain, saying to Judge Scott: "There's no one with a better right than I to listen to this case. If I violate any rule of the court, then put me out."[24] The judge's decision to allow Nickell to stay in the courtroom allowed him to be there when his son broke down.

J. B. Apperson, the civil engineer who testified at the coroner's inquest, was next called at the trial, and, with one notable exception, testified substantially as he had previously. Apperson spoke of what he had heard and seen on July 18 and July 19, telling of various distances he had measured, including a distance of sixty-six feet from the gate eastward to where Willie's body was found and three hundred yards less fourteen feet from a downed tree to the gate.[25] Apperson found horse tracks about forty feet from the gate, where reins had dropped to the ground. These tracks were almost surely those of Willie's horse, which had wandered down the fence line on the west side.[26]

Apperson told the jury of footprints he had found west of the gate close to a pool of blood. His direct testimony regarding these footprints became a point of contention later in the trial:

Q. [by Walter Stoll] These foot prints you saw, how many of them were there?

A. I could not say, probably four or five. Cattle had passed through that gate in the meantime and had obliterated the horse tracks and the foot prints.

Q. These tracks, were they not the tracks of a boy, or small in size?

A. I didn't pay particular attention to that, as well as I remember now they were probably of a boy who wore [size] 6 or 7 shoes.

Q. They were at the west of the gate?

A. Yes Sir.

Q. Close to the pool of blood?

A. Just on the edge of the road.

Q. Were they close to the marks made by the reins of the horse?

A. Yes Sir.

Q. Did you find more than one horse[']s track there?

A. No, I did not.[27]

Despite Apperson's clear testimony, the *Denver Post* reported that on cross-examination Apperson had said he had seen four or five size-seven boot prints near the body. This report was inaccurate. The trial transcript shows no such statements on cross-examination, and no witness testified to seeing "no. 7" footprints near the body.[28] The *Post* article is interesting, however, because the defense was later to make the same erroneous statements found in the article.

Laramie County coroner Thomas Murray was next called to the stand, and his testimony primarily related to his visit to the scene on Saturday, July 20. His observations were consistent with those of other witnesses but of limited use because by the time Murray came to the scene other people had gone over the ground.[29] Murray reported seeing footprints around the place where the body was found, but he provided no further details. Murray also spoke of the "quite distinct" imprint of the butt of a rifle in some rocks about sixty-five to seventy yards from the place the body was found.[30]

Shifting gears, the prosecution then called Amos Barber. Ordinarily, Dr. Barber would have been a notable and distinguished witness. He was a graduate of the University of Pennsylvania College of Medicine, but, even more significant, he had held high offices in Wyoming, serving as secretary of state and governor. Unfortunately for Barber, however, he had been the acting governor of Wyoming during the April 1892 cattlemen's invasion of Johnson County, and his actions during that crisis were deeply unpopular in the state. Ordinarily, an acting governor such as Barber would have considered running for governor in the general election following his elevation from secretary of state, but Barber apparently had not considered it. Instead, Edward Ivinson of Laramie was selected as the Republican candidate for governor. As it was, Ivinson was drubbed, losing to Democrat John Osborne 9,290 votes to 7,509, a shocking result in normally heavily Republican Wyoming.[31]

Dr. Barber repeated his autopsy report given at the coroner's inquest, testifying that when he first saw the body it was in a "high state of decomposition" and was "bloated and swollen." Barber used Waldo Moore, an attorney hired by Kels Nickell who was assisting Walter Stoll, as a living mannequin. Moore made, according to the *Denver Post*, "an excellent, if animated, blackboard."[32] Barber gave his opinion that both shots had been inflicted while Willie Nickell was standing at the gate (because two bullets had gone exactly the same direction through the body). He presumed that the body had fallen facedown and that it had been turned over.[33]

To that point Barber was testifying as Walter Stoll expected him to. But then the doctor said something that may have been unexpected. He testified that the bullets hitting Willie Nickell were from a weapon of .38 to .45

caliber (.38 of an inch to .45 of an inch), moving away from his preliminary examination position and back to his testimony at the coroner's inquest.[34]

Stoll may not have been surprised by this turn, however. He knew of Barber's initial testimony (that the bullets were from .38 to .45 caliber), and he probably knew of the doctor's strong support of the violent actions of big cattlemen during 1892. Cheyenne was a small enough place that if Barber had let slip his change of position it likely would have gotten back to the prosecuting attorney. Whether Stoll knew of or suspected Barber's shift, he certainly responded quickly and appropriately to the doctor's new testimony.

Stoll first asked Barber if he remembered stating at the preliminary hearing that he couldn't "state anything with certainty as to the size of the caliber." Lacey promptly objected, as Stoll by asking this question seemed to be challenging his own witness, thereby committing an evidentiary violation lawyers refer to as "impeaching your own witness." Judge Scott ruled that the objection was "preliminary," and Stoll plunged on, as shown by the trial transcript:

Q. I will ask you to recall this question being asked you on the pre-liminary hearing: "Could you tell anything as to the size of the projectile?" To which you answered "No sir." Then this question "What could you say on that subject" to which you replied "I could not testify accurately on account of the decomposition of the body." What effect would decomposition of the body produce both as to its exit and entrance to which you replied "It would be difficult to state just what effect it would produce; I think decom-position of the body owing to the swelling of the tissues have a tendency to contract a bullet wound as far as muscular tissues are concerned, in the skin I have the opinion that it would enlarge that point for this reason, the skin is an elastic covering; in this particular case where there was advanced decomposition the gas was swelling the skin and stretching the elastic tissues. If you take a thin piece of rubber and make a small puncture in it I think the puncture would be larger than otherwise." Then this question "The stretching force could be the cause of stretching the skin in all directions?" and your answer "Yes the gas tending to escape would extend the skin in all directions." Do you recall those questions and answers?

A. I do.[35]

John Lacey objected to this whole line of questioning, saying that it was "leading and in the nature of cross examination," but Judge Scott ruled against Lacey, reasoning that if Dr. Barber wanted to correct his testimony, Stoll had the right to call it to his attention. Stoll and Barber then bickered about whether Barber was being inconsistent.[36]

In his cross-examination, Lacey probably had high expectations that he would be able to turn this prosecution witness into a witness for the defense. He would not be disappointed.[37] Lacey asked Barber whether anyone had represented Tom Horn at the coroner's inquest. The answer, of course, was that no one did. More damaging, however, was Barber's insistence that staining around the wounds indicated that the bullets striking Willie Nickell were lead (consistent with bullets used in the old-style black powder rounds, not the new smokeless powder rounds such as the .30-30 Horn used, which shot steel-jacketed bullets with a lead point). And Lacey had Barber repeat the details of all the points he had made at the coroner's inquest, showing, according to the doctor, that the caliber of the killing bullets was between .38 and .45.[38]

Allowed redirect examination, Stoll scored some points. Barber insisted that his testimony at the coroner's inquest and the preliminary hearing were consistent and that he had no desire to correct his preliminary hearing testimony. The doctor gave long, not wholly convincing answers to the prosecutor's questions, and although he insisted he had nothing to correct, said that since the preliminary hearing he had reviewed "a great many authorities" and they were consistent with his earlier position.[39]

Reporting newspapers generally concluded that Barber's testimony was good for the defense, but they also noted that the witness was "slightly mixed."[40] Barber was the last witness presented on Saturday, October 11, 1902, and the court recessed until Monday morning.[41]

The *Denver Post* reported that Dr. Barber's testimony "is not regarded by the prosecution with anything else than disgust." It was also observed that Barber's "sudden change of memory may be accounted for by a little ancient history," referring to the doctor's role in the Johnson County War.[42]

Nevertheless, the defense had undeniably scored with Barber's testimony, so what was Walter Stoll to do? His principal medical witness had just declared that the *lead* bullets hitting Willie Nickell had been at least .075 of an inch bigger than the bullet shot by Tom Horn's .30-30 rifle. If that testimony stood, Horn must be acquitted. Perhaps Barber's testimony was the reason Horn was described as "relaxed" at the end of the October 11 testimony, "laughing and talking with his lawyers."[43]

CHAPTER ELEVEN

The Trial Continues

The trial resumed Monday morning, October 13. Walter Stoll was determined to counter the gains the defense had made from the testimony of Amos Barber, but first he had to do some housekeeping. Stoll presented witnesses who had carefully examined the ground around the gate for bullets and shells and had found nothing. Alfred Cook, the sheriff of Albany County (seated in Laramie City), testified that Tom Horn had left a large, dark brown horse at the Elkhorn Bar in Laramie shortly after the murder of Willie Nickell, described the brand found on the horse, and related his July 21, 1901, discussion with Horn, who told the sheriff he had come to Laramie the afternoon before. T. F. Cook, locomotive fireman and husband of Julia Nickell Cook (but apparently not related to Sheriff Cook), testified about his trip to the Nickell ranch on July 20, 1901, to look after the family's sheep.[1]

Mr. and Mrs. Nickell were called and asked to identify the clothing Willie had been wearing when he was killed. Willie's father said that the clothing he was shown had been taken from Willie's body after it was brought back to the house. He had turned the clothes over to the sheriff, and they had been put into evidence.[2]

Jury members were struck by Willie's clothes. The *Cheyenne Daily Leader* said, "The clothes were . . . handed to the jury to inspect and the bloody garments were fingered gingerly by the jurors. They looked at the bullet holes and slowly turned the shirt, which was one mass of blood, over and over."[3]

Stoll then began his assault on the testimony of Dr. Barber by calling a glamour witness, Peter Bergerson, a gunsmith from Cheyenne, described by the *Denver Post* as the "champion rifle shot of the world at 200 yards."[4] Bergerson was qualified as an expert witness on the subjects of ammunition, guns, and gunshot wounds. Shown the vest of Willie Nickell, he was asked the "probable caliber of the bullet that made the hole." "It looks about a 32 or 30 something like that," he promptly responded. The size of the hole was affected by what clothing it passed through first, Bergerson explained, and whether the shells had been held in a tubular magazine or a box magazine. In a tubular magazine, such as a .30-30 Winchester, a bullet, even in the course of a day, was "considerably flattened," meaning that it would tear a bigger hole. When asked a hypothetical question, whether the bullets striking Willie Nickell were fired by smokeless powder or black powder, Bergerson responded, "That would be hard to say, because high pressure [smokeless powder] tears generally larger holes."[5]

Defense attorney Lacey pushed Bergerson, in a "very rigid" cross-examination, to agree that the hole in a body is a little smaller than the bullet as a rule. Bergerson would not agree with Lacey's proposition, but said, "If the bullet is sharp—it will make a hole smaller than the bullet," adding that the hole made by a bullet is "usually a little smaller instead of larger."[6] Bergerson was recalled by Stoll a few minutes later, and the prosecuting attorney showed him several kinds of rifle shells that were put into evidence. The defense scored a point on cross-examination when Bergerson said he did not believe he could tell the difference between the sound of a gun shooting black powder and one using smokeless powder from a distance of two and one-half miles. Bergerson thereby cast doubt on the witness statements that the shots they heard on July 18, 1901, were from smokeless powder.[7]

Presenting the testimony of three Cheyenne physicians, the prosecution first called Dr. H. J. Maynard. The *Denver Post* said the doctor was "of precise speech, a nervous manner and a veteran of the civil war, where he had seen many gunshot wounds causing death." Referring to Maynard's "full face, deeply lined and crowned with a sweep to one side of iron grey hair," the *Post* said the doctor "wore an expression of deep concern" as he provided explanations to the jury.[8] Maynard had practiced medicine for forty-three years and was said to have had "very extensive" experience with gunshot wounds and their effects on the human body during the Civil

War.[9] As was the practice in 1902, Stoll asked Maynard a long hypothetical question (that takes up a full transcript page) about what could be told, after three days had passed, about the caliber of a bullet that had struck Willie Nickell's body. The key consideration for Maynard was that three days passing meant that no determination of the diameter of a bullet could be made within .10 of an inch to .25 of an inch.[10]

As with Bergerson, John Lacey tried to push Maynard into a blanket statement that the wound was always smaller than the diameter of the bullet. All Maynard would agree to, however, was that this would be true until tissue had sloughed away, but he pointed out that tissue changes within a two-, three- or four-day span after death. The witness did not see how the measurement could determine the caliber of the bullet under such circumstances.[11]

Dr. L. P. Desmond, the youngest of the three doctors to testify, was experienced with the effects of bullet wounds from modern cartridges. A medical school graduate at a time when not all people calling themselves doctors were, he had practiced for about five years. Again Stoll asked a long hypothetical question, after setting out all the circumstances of the Willie Nickell shooting, regarding what the witness could determine as to the probable caliber of the bullets that struck Willie. Dr. Desmond declined to make any estimate of the caliber, reasoning that "the wound of entrance and exit has to do with a hundred and one different causes." The doctor detailed some of these, including what the bullet struck, the kind of bullet, whether it mushroomed, the tissue it went through, and the point of exit.[12]

John Lacey, in his cross-examination, tried to get Desmond to agree with him that stains on the victim's skin showed that an old-style bullet had been used, but Desmond would only say that such stains might demonstrate a greater likelihood of that. When Lacey tried to get Desmond to agree with his general proposition that the size of a bullet would be at least as large as the hole created, Desmond would only say the proposition was true under limited circumstances.[13] On redirect examination, Desmond concluded that "it is merely guesswork as to the caliber of the bullet."[14]

Dr. Desmond was a confident witness, and Lacey apparently believed that he was an effective one, because his cross-examination was rigorous, said to be "warm and emphatic," but he was not able to shake Desmond's testimony. Desmond "was positive in all his statements and proved as good a witness for the prosecution as he proved a bad one for the defense," sum-marized the *Denver Post*. "His testimony tore large holes in the statements made by Dr. Barber on Saturday."[15]

The final physician called by the prosecution was Dr. M. C. Barkwell. As with the other two physicians, Barkwell was affirmative, declaring, "No man could tell the caliber of a bullet under such circumstances." In explain-ing his reasons in detail, he emphasized the explosive effects of new, high-pressure cartridges. On cross-examination, Lacey "read from authorities to prove his theory that the wound at the point of exit was smaller than the caliber of the bullet." As the *Denver Post* saw it, however, Lacey "tried to shake the witness's testimony, but failed."[16] The cross-examination and subsequent redirect examination of Dr. Barkwell were much longer than those of Desmond and Maynard, and it went deeply into the question of marks left around the skin by lead- or steel-jacketed bullets, but as the examination dragged on, Barkwell's testimony became abstruse and "dis-interesting" to spectators.[17]

If Dr. Barkwell's testimony about stains around the wounds was only effective to obscure the issue for both parties, the prosecution benefited. The defense had hoped to establish that it was impossible for Tom Horn to have committed the crime because he carried a .30-30 and Willie Nick-ell's wounds had been caused, said the defense, by a rifle with a larger cali-ber. Unless the defense could firmly establish impossibility, however, other evidence against Horn, such as his confession to LeFors, would be a more deciding factor. The *Cheyenne Daily Leader* may have summarized how the jurors regarded the medical testimony when it said: "The substance of the testimony of the different physicians seems to show that it is impossible to tell with any degree of certainty, from the size of a wound, what the caliber of the bullet was that made it, although many things can be taken into consideration to give some idea of this."[18]

The witnesses called to counter Dr. Barber's testimony indicate that Stoll knew before the trial began that Barber was not going to hold to the testi-mony he gave at the preliminary hearing. Arrangements for the testimony of physicians and other busy men could not be effected on a day or two days' notice.

As part of its coverage of the Horn case, the *Denver Post* interviewed Denver men with special knowledge of gunshot wounds. One, a physi-cian who had "testified in every murder trial in Denver within the last ten years," stated that if a body is decomposed, "it is extremely difficult to base any conclusions on the size of the bullet by the appearance of the wound." He also noted that the bullet used in killing the boy was almost surely a steel bullet with a lead tip, rather than a steel–jacketed bullet, and a lead–tipped bullet mushrooms upon impact. Another man interviewed by the *Post*, an attorney who was also an authority on bullet wounds, said that "it will be very difficult, if not impossible ... to prove by the appearance of the wounds alone what kind and what caliber of weapon was used in the murder of Willie Nickell."[19]

The battle over the caliber of the bullets that had killed Willie Nickell was the big fight during the court's October 13 session. Both prosecution and defense knew this struggle had the potential to decide the case in favor of Tom Horn. Oddly enough, both sides pronounced themselves "highly pleased" with the testimony presented. An attorney for the defense even declared, "We had it all our way this morning; it would have been better for the state if these physicians had not been called."[20]

When a major issue is addressed, attorneys expend a great deal of effort and emotion, and their tendency is to relax after the big dispute is over. In reality, trial attorneys are not finished until the judge adjourns the trial for the day, usually not until 5:00 P.M. Thus, there was more work to be done on October 13. Every long trial has its star witnesses and its key exhibits, but each also has its bit players, people seen as necessary to testify about only one point, to bolster the testimony of another witness, or to provide foundation (authenticity) for the admission of evidence. The lawyers in charge of a case have to consider such witnesses and employ them when necessary. Testimony relating to matters other than the caliber of the gun that killed Willie Nickell resumed at 3:00 P.M. that day.[21]

James Mathewson, publisher of the *Laramie Republican,* testified that his newspaper, an evening paper, had run an article on July 19, 1901, about Willie Nickell's death, but printed no further articles about it on July 20, 21, or 22. The defense objected to Mathewson's testimony, but Stoll said he was trying to fix the date when the death of Willie Nickell became generally known in Laramie, and Judge Scott allowed the question.[22] This evidence was intended to bolster the testimony of E. D. Titus, that he'd had a drink with Horn the evening of July 19, the day before everyone started talking about the murder of Willie Nickell.

When the prosecution called W. C. Eagan, manager of the Pacific Hotel in Laramie, Eagan presented pages from the hotel's cash book and register for July 17, 18, and 19 (the date that Horn allegedly arrived in Laramie), and explained how it could be determined when a person came to the hotel and when he left. Three pages of documents (exhibits 22, 23, and 24) were marked for identification but not offered into evidence, meaning the jury could not consider them unless they were put in evidence later.[23]

Pete Warlamount, a Laramie County sheriff's deputy, presented a paper prepared by Albany County Sheriff Cook regarding the brand of the horse Horn had left in the stable in Laramie. Warlamount got the paper on July 28, 1901.[24] This testimony was a follow-up to Sheriff Cook's earlier testimony about a good-sized, dark brown horse that Horn had left in Laramie and a paper showing its brand, which Cook had drawn and given to Warlamount.

Walter Stoll then called Duncan Clark, the previous foreman of John Coble's Bosler Ranch. Stoll could not have expected Clark to be helpful, so he drew from this reluctant witness only that Horn had left the ranch before July 18, 1901, and that Clark had seen Horn in Laramie the afternoon of Saturday, July 20.[25]

Stoll next called John Ryan, a man who had worked as a cook at Bosler Ranch. Ryan testified that Horn was not at the ranch on July 18 or July 19, 1902, but had been there for two or three hours on July 20, when he ate the midday dinner there. After changing his clothes, Horn left for Laramie, Ryan said.[26]

T. F. Burke, another of Horn's attorneys, and the U.S. attorney for the state of Wyoming, was not pleased with Ryan's testimony. His first question to Ryan, intended to impeach the witness, demanded that Ryan admit that he told the coroner's jury that Horn rode in on his "little black horse" but then left on a bay.[27] The defense wanted to establish this testimony because it undercut the prosecution's position that Horn had arrived in Laramie on July 18 on a bay horse. Surprisingly, Ryan did not support his former employer. Referring to his testimony at the coroner's inquest, he said: "I think it was a mistake." When Burke pushed the witness to admit he had made a statement about a black horse, Ryan said he didn't remember and didn't think he had testified to that. Burke then read Ryan a large portion of his coroner's inquest testimony, insisting that he had so testified. But Ryan would not be pushed in the direction Burke so obviously wanted him to go, saying he did not remember having so testified and that he did not "positively recall it at present" when Burke asked him if Horn did not come to the ranch on a black horse on July 20.[28]

In his redirect examination, Stoll, seeing that the witness might be confusing memories, asked Ryan when he had last seen Tom Horn. Ryan said July 27, and Horn was then riding a bay horse. Under Stoll's questioning, Ryan drew off entirely from his coroner's inquest statement that Horn had come to the Coble ranch on a black horse on July 20 and left on a bay. Instead, he testified that he did not see Horn when Horn rode up to the ranch on July 20, and that he was positive he saw Horn on a bay on July 27, but "that is the only recollection I have of the bay horse at present."[29]

The defense lawyers chewed on Ryan for a good while longer but were not able to change the overall tenor of his testimony.[30] This promising witness, who might have bolstered Horn's expected testimony that he first came to Laramie on a bay on July 20, contributed nothing to the defense.

Hiram Davidson, another John Coble employee, tried to be more helpful to the defense. Davidson said he was a mail carrier, but in 1901 he had supervised three ranches "on Chugwater" for Coble, places that straddled the line between Laramie County and Albany County (and thus were close to the Nickell property). Davidson said that Horn was not at any of the three ranches under his supervision during the week of July 15, 1901. After Stoll asked Davidson about pastures on the various ranches under his control and Davidson told of several, including two in which horses were kept, Davidson admitted that he only rode these pastures once a week. His duty, he said, was to see in a general way that the place was kept intact, and he said (most significantly), that if a horse was put in or taken out of a pasture, he would not be apt to notice it.[31] On Lacey's cross-examination, Davidson tried to strengthen his direct examination testimony, saying that he had not noticed any riding horses in the big pasture, and, besides, the horses in that pasture "were wild and not riding horses."[32] Most of the jurors probably knew a great deal about how a horse might be left in a pasture and how a change could be arranged, so the significance of Davidson's testimony rested in the experience of the jurors.

William L. Clay, the last witness of the day, was another person Horn counted on, but Clay's testimony never ventured into controversy and so was a quiet end to the day's work. Clay said that Horn had stayed at his place (not an uncommon event) the night of Sunday, July 14, and left Monday morning riding a "brown black" horse weighing 750–800 pounds and with a roached mane, and carried a .30-30 rifle.[33]

Other than the testimony of the witnesses addressing the caliber of the bullets that struck Willie Nickell, the newspapers saw nothing of great interest during the October 13 trial proceedings, so they talked of evidence and testimony to come, focusing especially on Glendolene Kimmell. Kimmell had been subpoenaed, was in Cheyenne, and would take the stand, the *Denver Post* observed. The *Cheyenne Daily Leader* asked in a headline: "Will Tom Horn's Sweetheart Turn State's Evidence?"[34] The *Leader* surmised: "The greatest sensation of the case will be sprung when the petite little school teacher is placed on the stand." Kimmell had been the teacher "at the little school house near the ranches of Kels Nickell and James Miller," the *Leader* noted, and during the inquest she was said to have kept Horn posted on all developments. According to Horn, the paper said, Kimmell was "half Corean [*sic*], one-quarter Japanese and the rest German." A remarkable linguist, she spoke half a dozen languages fluently. She had met Horn while living at the Miller ranch, become infatuated with him, and thus "played quite an important part in the subsequent developments." Supposedly Horn had said some things about Miss Kimmell that she could not forgive, and "she intended to tell all she knew."[35]

This development, if true, would indeed be sensational. The *Daily Leader* also announced that George A. Matlock, a shoemaker from Laramie, was prepared to testify that Tom Horn had left a bloody sweater in Laramie shortly after the Willie Nickell murder. Matlock, the paper said, could "positively identify" Horn as the man who had left the sweater. "The strength of this evidence cannot be over-estimated." Indeed, Horn would have a lot of explaining to do if he left a bloody sweater in Laramie just after Willie Nickell was killed.[36] The *Daily Leader* added that a man from Denver had arrived in Laramie who was going to testify that he heard Horn say in a Denver saloon that he "was the main guy" in the Willie Nickell killing.[37]

Not all the supposed upcoming testimony was seen as going against Horn. The *Daily Leader* predicted testimony from Otto Plaga, a young man who was a friend of Horn's and had competed along with him at Cheyenne Frontier Days. Supposedly, Plaga would testify that he had seen Horn at a place thirty miles from the gate where Willie Nickell was killed an hour after the killing had occurred. The presentation of alibi testimony was logical, said the paper, because "no other theory [than an alibi] could be consistent with the facts that are known and proven."[38] This newspaper story proved helpful to the prosecution because Plaga had not testified at either of the two earlier proceedings and so could have been called to the witness stand as a surprise witness, with the prosecution unprepared to rebut his testimony. With the publication of this story, however, Walter Stoll could ready his cross-examination and look for some contrary witnesses.

Still more tantalizing information arose when the *Denver Post* said that two Iron Mountain ranchmen were going to be called as eyewitnesses to the shooting of Willie Nickell, men who "happened to be out at the early hour of the murder." Their identity was being carefully protected, however, "for obvious reasons." The *Post* then referred to the murder of Matt Rash, who, along with Isom Dart, was killed in the Browns Park area of northern Colorado. Horn had supposedly admitted to killing Rash, telling this to, of all people, Rash's father.[39] Returning to the trial in Cheyenne, the *Post* remarked that John Coble was in the courtroom for the first time, identifying Coble as Horn's friend. Coble, the *Post* said, was "frequently mentioned as one of the men furnishing funds for Horn's defense."[40]

As for Horn himself, his mood seemed to have steadied after the beginning of the trial. "Now that the case is under way [Horn] has recovered his nerve, and is the same cool, indifferent stoic as before," reported the *Daily Leader.* "He seems to view with calm indifference the proceedings upon the outcome of which hangs his fate, and aside from an occasional consultation with his attorneys, lolls back in his chair and takes things easy. He chews tobacco incessantly and leans over toward Sheriff Smalley to expectorate in a cuspidor near his chair."[41]

CHAPTER TWELVE

A Bad Day for Tom Horn

Walter Stoll presented fourteen witnesses during the fourth day of the trial, and when his day's work was done, Tom Horn's story of his whereabouts on the day of Willie Nickell's murder was cast in serious doubt. Stoll's witnesses showed that just thirteen hours before Willie Nickell died, Horn had been four to five miles from the scene of the killing, and that four hours after Willie died, he had ridden into Laramie City. Horn, said one of the witnesses, was carrying a bundle of clothes with him when he arrived in town.[1]

Willie's brother Freddie, who had broken down in earlier testimony, was the first witness of the day. This time Freddie contained his emotions, and the eleven-year-old boy, the youngest person to testify, was deemed "one of the best witnesses introduced so far on the trial."[2] Freddie told the court and jury that about two weeks (maybe three or four) after his brother was killed, he had found a .30-30 cartridge at a gate two miles from the gate where his brother had been shot, and he had then given it to his mother. He referred to the gate where he found the cartridge as the "Coble gate," one leading to Iron Mountain. John Lacey cross-examined Freddie very gently. Freddie told Lacey the cartridge was on the ground with nothing over it, "just like it fell out of a belt or something, been laying there." When Lacey asked about Willie's horse, Freddie said they had found it, still with the saddle on, a week after they found Willie.[3]

Later that day Freddie's father was recalled to the stand to support his son's testimony. Kels Nickell pointed out on a map the location of the Coble gate, and the lawyers bickered over the amount of traffic on the road going through the gate. Nickell said that the road was "not what you would consider a public highway traveled by many people" and agreed with the suggestion that "if they wanted to travel very much they would get tired of opening gates."[4] Stoll's next witness, Freddie's mother, said she had delivered the cartridge found by Freddie to Deputy Sheriff Peter Warlamount. Warlamount, soon presented as a witness, identified the .30-30 cartridge. Lacey objected to admission of the cartridge because it was "remote," but Judge Scott allowed it, saying the jury could "give it such weight as [they] think advisable."[5]

Victor Miller had followed Freddie Nickell to the stand. Stoll's decision to use Victor as a witness was surprising because Stoll knew Lacey was trying to pin Willie Nickell's killing on the Miller boys. Stoll may have wanted the jury to see and hear Victor and Gus Miller rather than hide them while Lacey demonized the two young men. Perhaps Stoll wanted the jury to see what it was about these boys that had persuaded him they were not murderers.

Victor testified that he was eighteen years old and that he had seen Tom Horn at the family ranch on Monday, July 15. While there, Horn went shooting and fishing and watched Nickell's sheep to see whether they got off deeded land. Victor said Horn had stayed at his family's home Tuesday night, that he carried a .30-30 rifle, and that he was riding a black horse with a roached mane.[6]

From the transcript, Victor seems a polite, well-mannered young man, and he seems to have remained so when Lacey cross-examined him. Lacey asked Victor whether he had seen a sweater (Victor had not) and whether he had heard Horn's tall tale about killing five of the Wilcox train robbers (he had).[7]

Then, predictably, Lacey started asking questions he knew would draw objections from Stoll. He asked Victor Miller whether there wasn't "a great deal of trouble in that neighborhood between Nickell and his neighbors," whether Victor had personally had trouble with Willie Nickell, and whether, in June 1901, Victor had not "offered to fight him [Willie], and your father told you to fight him. And Willie run you down with a horse and your father pulled a pistol and told him if he did that he would shoot the horse." Stoll objected and the judge sustained the prosecution in all its objections. Lacey's tactic—to put improper evidence before a jury by asking detailed questions setting out forbidden information—was not uncommon for the time.[8] In modern trial practice, a prosecutor fearing this strategy would probably submit a pleading called a "motion in limine," seeking to have the trial judge instruct a defense attorney not to employ such questions. In 1902, however, such motions were not part of the prosecution's arsenal, and defense counsel routinely presented improper information to the jury by asking questions they knew would be objected to.

Lacey also asked Victor whether anything "in the world was said about killing Willie Nickell while Tom Horn was at the Miller ranch." This question was proper under 1902 rules and there was no objection. Victor replied, "No, sir."[9] Lacey then established that both Victor and his brother had .30 caliber guns.[10]

Victor's brother followed on the stand. Gus, who had turned twenty in March, was asked most of the same questions as his brother. His answers were substantially the same except that Gus particularly remembered Horn's field glasses because he had looked through them. Gus did not recall a sweater but thought that Horn might have had a coat tied to his saddle. Lacey did not repeat the offending questions he had asked Victor, but he did ask Gus whether he had heard any conversation about killing Willie Nickell. As had his brother, Victor replied, "No, sir."[11] It was a safe question for Lacey because if Gus had overheard any conversation by Horn about killing, it would likely not have been about Willie but rather about Willie's father, Kels.

Dora Miller, Gus and Victor's mother, testified in a generally similar way to her sons, as did Eva Miller, Gus and Victor's sister. Eva's testimony was hardly crucial to the case, yet she earned special mention by the *Cheyenne Daily Leader* and a photograph in the *Denver Post*. That "special mention" shows why the stark presentation of words in a trial transcript sometimes fails to catch the human impact of a witness's appearance. Underneath the sub-headline "A Rural Belle," the *Daily Leader* wrote: "Miss Eva Miller, a rosy cheeked girl of eighteen summers, with a wealth of chestnut hair, was the next witness, and corroborated the testimony of her mother who preceded her. Her striking beauty made her an important witness in the eyes of the spectators."[12]

John M. Bray was the first of two important witnesses to tell the jury of Tom Horn's whereabouts on Wednesday, July 17, and Thursday, July 18, 1901 (the day Willie was killed). Bray testified that he had seen Horn Monday morning, July 15, at William (Billy) Clay's ranch. Bray had seen Horn again on Wednesday "in the evening after work," meaning after his work for Billy Clay, which finished at 6:00 P.M. Horn was on a ridge in the open, Bray said, looking "as if he was holding his hands over his eyes or had his field glasses." Bray did not speak to Horn but just passed him by. Later that evening, however, at a place about four to five miles from the Nickell ranch, Bray said he saw Horn moving northwest.[13]

Because Bray was the witness who had last seen Horn on July 17, he established the opening bracket around Tom Horn's whereabouts on Thursday, July 18. Frank C. Irwin, an Albany County rancher, would establish the closing bracket. Irwin said he had seen Horn about eleven o'clock "in the forenoon" of July 18. Horn, said Irwin, was riding "just on the outskirts of Laramie on the north of the city," proceeding toward Laramie City.[14]

Irwin also testified that he knew the black horse branded CAP that Horn frequently rode but that the horse he saw Horn on that Thursday morning was a larger, dark bay horse. Irwin said he just happened to be in that area of Laramie because "I had lost our milk cow"—he was looking for it. The horse Horn was riding was "very warm" and "looked very tired when I met him," he said. "He was lathered and sweated a good deal." Noting a good many details about Horn and his horse, Irwin testified that Horn had a small bundle tied behind him that he supposed was a coat, although he didn't know for certain, and he saw a six-shooter. Irwin remembered the time because he could trace his activities that morning just before the midday dinner hour. Irwin had also seen Horn on other occasions that day, including that evening at Allen's saloon. Most significantly, Irwin saw Horn just after his initial 11:00 A.M. sighting, when Horn rode up the street to the Elkhorn barn. Irwin was then only about a half block from Horn and he watched Horn ride into the barn. Irwin said he was sure the date was July 18 because the next day he saw an article in the *Laramie Republican* about the Nickell boy being killed. He identified the article when shown the July 19, 1901, issue of the *Republican*. He said he was reading the paper and when he came across the article he remarked to two companions that "I bet Horn did this." When Lacey objected to Irwin's statement, Judge Scott struck it from the record.[15]

Lacey must have undertaken his cross-examination of Frank Irwin with a strong sense of purpose because Irwin's testimony bristled with convincing detail. If believed, it would completely undercut Horn's story. According to the *Denver Republican,* the defense attorney asked questions "for nearly an hour in an attempt to tangle him [Irwin] up, but finally excused the witness, having failed to shake him in the slightest degree."

Admitting to an earlier disagreement he'd had with Horn in which "hot words" were spoken, Irwin said, "I have no particular love for him [Horn]."[16] In his redirect examination, Walter Stoll asked Irwin if his "difficulty" with Horn would cause him to "color" the facts. Irwin said it would not, saying he had been reluctant to testify at all.[17]

Bray's and Irwin's testimony was crucial to the prosecution's case because these two men so thoroughly undercut Horn's story about his actions between Wednesday, July 17, and Saturday, July 20. Stoll wanted to make sure the jurors were fully aware of Tom Horn's expected testimony while Bray's statements were fresh in their minds, so he had called to the stand Robert C. Morris, the official stenographer at the 1901 coroner's inquest, between the testimony of Bray and Irwin. Through Morris, Stoll presented large sections of inquest evidence. His purpose was clear: to showcase Horn's coroner's inquest testimony about his whereabouts during the days around the murder. Horn, Morris said, had told the coroner's inquest that on Wednesday, July 17, he had "pulled across the hills over on the head of the Sybille" and the rest of Wednesday was "perhaps eight or nine miles" from the Nickell house, in two pastures.[18] At the coroner's inquest Horn had also said that on the next day, Thursday, July 18, he had been "out on the divide between the head of Chugwater and the Sybille," and that late that evening he had seen John Bray "coming down from Billy Clay's." (Bray had testified that he saw Horn when he rode from Billy Clay's place early the previous evening, on Wednesday, not Thursday.) Horn had noted, "I don't suppose all day Thursday at any time I was as much as a dozen miles from there [the Nickell place]."[19] On Friday (when E. D. Titus testified he had seen Horn in Laramie), Horn said he had been "over around Fitz-morris's place" all day and had returned to the Coble ranch about ten on Saturday morning, July 20, and that afternoon, about two or three, had left for Laramie City.[20]

Given Irwin's testimony that Horn had ridden his horse into the Elk-horn barn on July 18, this stable became an important focus of the trial. Charles H. Miller, then one of the stable's proprietors, was called and testi-fied that in early July 1901, Horn had left a black horse with a roached mane (branded CAP) in his stable. Not long after, the next time Horn came into the establishment, he had brought in a larger horse, a bay without a roached mane.[21]

Miller said the bay horse was "pretty warm, pretty tired," and when he mentioned this to Horn, Horn replied that the horse couldn't be tired because he had just come in from the ranch. After the animal had rested up, Miller observed that it was "a pretty good looking horse." Miller could not swear to the date Horn had brought the horse in, but it was either a day or two after he heard of Willie Nickell's being killed or a day or two before. Miller observed that Horn had a six-shooter but was pretty sure he had no other firearms.[22]

Taking the witness in hand, Lacey tried to get Miller to move away from earlier statements, but Miller remained firm. He acknowledged that the bay horse had stayed in his stable until a few days later, when Frank Stone rode the horse away. When Lacey pushed Miller about how long the horse had remained there, all Miller could say was that the horse was there for at least several days, adding, "It might have been a week and it might have been two." Lacey asked if the account book might refresh Miller's recollection as to when Horn came there, and gained a small success when Miller said, "I think it would."[23] Lacey boldly pushed forward, asking Miller to find the account book and bring it to the court. Miller said his partner John Wallace had it and that he was "here now." Lacey then asked that a deputy sheriff contact Wallace and continued with Miller, establishing that Horn had not again taken the horse out of the stable, that during that time Horn had no other horse there, and that when Miller took the saddle off he had noticed a scabbard but no rifle.[24]

The short testimony of two other witnesses interceded, and then Miller resumed his place on the stand, saying he now had the account book in hand. "What do you find there?" Lacey asked. Miller answered: "Tom Horn, July 20th to 30th, ten days."

Lacey cinched down this highly favorable response: "Does that refresh your recollection as to when the horse was brought?" "Yes, sir," responded Miller. Lacey asked the witness when the horse had been brought there and was told, "July 20th the book says."[25]

Lacey's persistence had paid off in a big way. As the *Cheyenne Daily Leader* commented, "This was quite a victory for the defense as the 20th was the day Tom Horn swore he reached Laramie, while John Braae [sic] testified that Horn reached Laramie on the morning of July 18th, the day of the murder. This book entry will go far towards convincing the jury that Horn's statement was correct, although contradicted by other evidence."[26]

When Stoll stood to cross-examine the witness, he knew his case had just taken a blow and that unless he found a way to blunt the force of Miller's testimony the whole prosecution would be threatened. Stoll first established that outside of the entry, Miller had "nothing to fix the time as July 20th." He then elicited from Miller that he had not made the entries but that Miller's partner, Wallace, had made them. Stoll noted that entries were not made when a customer came in, but when the horse left the stable. So, Stoll submitted to the witness, the entries "necessarily had to be made from recollection?" "Yes, sir," said Miller. "And that was when that was done?" "Yes, sir," answered Miller.[27] Stoll then submitted four pages from the account book, including not only the Horn entry but also more than a hundred other entries over several days.[28]

This seemingly innocuous series of questions enabled Stoll to shift the focus from a virtually certain memorial that Horn's horse was placed in the stable from July 20 to July 30 to a question of the accuracy of a ten-or-more-day memory in a busy establishment. As the *Denver Post* put it, in the redirect examination Stoll, "with a sly manner as if he was going to take the court room into his confidence, . . . developed . . . the fact that in the peculiar system of bookkeeping in the stable, the accounts of 'boarders' were kept backwards, so to speak, that only the date when the bill was paid was entered." Still, the *Post* observed, "the fact July 20 was in black and white was an impression that was hard to remove."[29]

Stoll had just dodged a bullet. If the account entry had been presented to the jury without challenge, it would have been a strong basis for reasonable doubt. Miller's testimony was still harmful, but Stoll's examination had prevented it from destroying the state's case.

Stoll next called Mortimer N. Grant, Laramie justice of the peace (and a cousin to Ulysses S. Grant). Grant was asked to testify about a July 1901 conversation that had taken place in the Elkhorn stable between stable employees about Tom Horn "having just come in the barn," as Stoll put it, "on a tired, played out horse." Stoll seemed to be using some of Lacey's tactics, putting information before the jury that the judge was not likely to admit. When Lacey objected to the questions to Grant as hearsay, however, Judge Scott put off a decision, saying, "I am not clear on the proposition; I would like some authorities on it."[30] The judge would not rule on Lacey's objection until the next day; meanwhile, Stoll's question must have lingered in the jurors' minds.

George A. Matlock, Laramie shoe merchant, came to the stand next, the same man who, according to the *Cheyenne Daily Leader*, could "positively identify" Horn as the man who had left a blood-stained sweater with him in Laramie. Stoll quickly dispensed with preliminary questions and went to the heart of Matlock's expected testimony, asking whether Matlock had seen Horn at any time in July 1901. None of the newspapers reporting the trial tell of the moments before Matlock's answer, whether he gave an ominous sign, such as a long pause before answering. Still, Matlock's answer must have been a shock to the prosecution: "I saw a man who resembled him very much."[31]

Seeing Matlock backing off previous statements, Stoll started asking leading questions, to which Lacey predictably objected. In one such question, Stoll said, "I will call your attention to an occasion when a package was left at your establishment. I will ask you to state whether to the best of your opinion and belief the man that left that there was this defendant?" Lacey objected to any answer because "the defendant is not identified." Judge Scott helped the prosecution here by ruling that the question was acceptable because the witness's statement (that "the man resembled the defendant very much") was sufficient, and the jury could weigh for themselves whether the identification was satisfactory or not. The ruling did the prosecution little good, however, as the witness just repeated his statement that the man he saw resembled Horn very much.[32] The situation did not improve. When Stoll asked Matlock about "spots," the only thing the witness would say is that he saw some spots on the sweater that "resembled blood very much." Matlock did say that the man he saw was tall and raw-boned, with stooped shoulders, and that when the man came in asking to leave the package, he had told the man to take it back to the shoe shop.[33]

On cross-examination, Lacey induced the witness to say he was not positive that the man he saw was Tom Horn or that the sweater had blood spots on it. Matlock also agreed that the stains might be a good many other things than blood. Lacey could not push Matlock further, however, and Matlock repeated his favored phrase that the man he saw "resembled" Tom Horn and the substance on the sweater "resembled" blood.

Stoll directly challenged the witness in his redirect examination, asking Matlock if he did not make a statement after he had seen Horn that Horn was the man, but Judge Scott sustained Lacey's objection to the question.[34]

It is not uncommon for a witness to lose nerve in a trial and seek refuge in less positive testimony, but it is always maddening to a questioning attorney. When Matlock left the stand, Stoll must have been boiling with frustration.

The next witness, George Powell, a shoemaker employed by George Matlock, gave Stoll an opportunity to tighten the connection between

Horn and the sweater. Powell said that on a July 1901 afternoon, a gentleman had brought in a package and that he, Powell, had then "looked up
and glanced at the man." The "gentleman" had left the package, saying he
would come back in a short time, but he had never returned. The package
had lain in the shop for two or three months before Powell opened it.
When he did, he found a dark blue, "filthy dirty" sweater, containing "considerable fiber of some kind" and with stains on it. He took the stains to
be blood stains.[35]

When asked to identify the man who brought in the sweater, Powell
said, "From resemblance I think he [the defendant, Horn] is the man."
Powell could not say positively that Horn was the man he saw, however.
Under cross-examination, Powell said "the man was a big man, tall, and I
noticed the gait of the man; I could be more positive if I could get that
man to walk across the floor."[36] The *Laramie Boomerang* reported that "the
defense would not let their client walk across the room," which probably
did not sit well with the jury. Powell's statements grew stronger as the cross-
examination proceeded (the *Boomerang* said his testimony was "more positive" than Matlock's).[37] Powell testified that "I would not swear he is the
man, but I am satisfied he is the man" and that even though he would not
swear the stains he saw were blood, "I feel pretty near confident that it was
blood" (the witness said that he looked at the sweater "a good deal").[38]

Powell said the sweater was in the shop for another month. He then
had it laundered and wore it on fishing and hunting trips. Finally, he sent
the sweater to Tom Horn in Cheyenne at the request of Laramie County
sheriff E. J. Smalley.

The next day of the trial (October 15, 1902), Sheriff Smalley and Deputy
Proctor testified that Horn was shown the sweater and admitted it was his
("I guess that is my sweater, all right"). Proctor said that when he showed
Horn George Powell's letter, Horn at first said that he did not have a
sweater, but after looking at it he said it was his.[39] On cross-examination,
Lacey tried to put words in Proctor's mouth, asking him to agree that Horn
had said, "All sweaters look alike to me. I will claim this one." But Proctor
refused to accept the suggestion, stating, "That conversation didn't take
place."[40] The two law enforcement officers' testimony was particularly important to the prosecution, because it made Matlock and Powell's tepid testimony less significant.

Roy Campbell, one of three Denver men who were supposed to testify
to incriminating comments Horn had made in Denver, was called to the

stand. Campbell said he was a telephone man, and, when asked if he had ever seen the defendant, said, "Once only, Carnival Week, a year ago." When asked to fix the date, he said he could not.[41] Campbell said he and a friend had dropped into a saloon near Seventeenth and Blake in Denver and there met a third friend, and this man had made mention of detective work. At that, another man at the bar said, "I am a stock detective, Tom Horn is my name." One of Campbell's friends, Frank Mulock, then told Horn: "If you are a Wyoming detective, it seems to me that you would be up there and getting some of that [reward] money from the Willie Nickell killing. According to Campbell, Horn had replied, "Why, that is all right, I am the main guy in that case. . . . I know all about it."[42]

Campbell had taken this comment as "a drunken cowboy's talk," adding that Horn was "very much intoxicated." Then Horn had fished for some money in his pockets to buy drinks, Campbell recalled, but when unable to find any had pulled out a piece of white paper, apparently a check. He had said, "I have plenty of it," and he had then unsuccessfully tried to cash the check. Campbell said Horn had then come to their table and stated, "That Nickell shot was the best I ever made in my life."[43] With this startling testimony, Stoll turned the witness over to the defense.

When T. F. Burke conducted his cross-examination, one of his first questions was: "This was during the Carnival Week, you are positive about that?" Campbell answered, "Yes, about that time, the exact date I cannot say." Then Burke asked several questions, pushing Campbell to say whether he had noticed "any wounds there." Campbell had not, nor had Horn carried a crutch or a cane, nor had Horn conducted himself as if disabled.[44] These seemingly innocuous questions would be the center of a great dispute before the trial was over.

Campbell said he had not taken Horn seriously, but about a month later, in early November, Frank Mulock brought up the Willie Nickell killing, and Campbell and Mulock discussed Horn as being "the man we seen down there." Burke pushed Campbell to say that he had read an article reporting Horn under arrest, but Campbell did not agree, saying that he (Campbell) had read articles, but they were "discussing the fact he was interested in the deal."[45] (Horn had not been arrested until January 1902, two months after Campbell testified that he and Mulock had discussed Horn in connection with a newspaper article or articles. In October 1901, however, the *Denver Republican* had run an article about Horn, in which the paper interviewed Horn at a Denver hospital, where he was recovering from his broken jaw, and the newspaper provided some background, including a general comment about the finding of "the dead body of Willie Nickell" and noting that "the identity of his slayer has never been revealed.")[46]

The prosecution had begun to deliver on its pledge to present the testimony of three Denver men who had heard Tom Horn make incriminating statements. One promising witness who apparently would *not* testify, however, was Glendolene Kimmell. The *Denver Republican* said that the elaborate story about her expected testimony had been "manufactured out of whole cloth." She was now residing in a small town in southwestern Missouri, as was known to Wyoming officials, had not been subpoenaed (but would appear if she was), and she was not angry at Tom Horn.[47]

The prosecution presented a document showing that a dark brown horse with two white feet was branded with "lazy T Y." The last witness called on October 14 was Dallas R. Cowhick, the Laramie County clerk, who presented a portion of a book showing the record of brands. T. L. Coble was shown to be the owner of the Lazy TY brand.[48] The apparent purpose of this evidence was to show that the horse ridden into Laramie by Horn after Willie Nickell was killed was owned by the Coble ranch.

It had been a good day for the prosecution. Walter Stoll had succeeded in confining Horn within a seventeen-hour time frame between Wednesday evening, when seen by John Bray, and eleven on Thursday morning, when Frank Irwin testified to having seen Horn ride into Laramie. Evidence about the navy blue sweater, though shaky in parts, showed the probability that Horn had possessed a blood-stained item of clothing at a time very near the murder of Willie Nickell. Worst, from Horn's standpoint, was his admission to Sheriff Smalley and Deputy Proctor that the navy blue sweater was his, which in turn solidly linked him to that shoe shop in Laramie. And at the end of the day the prosecution had presented Campbell, with still another damning Horn admission. The defense had its moments that day, but, all in all, the *Cheyenne Daily Leader's* headline, "FORGING STRONG CHAIN OF EVIDENCE AROUND TOM HORN," seemed quite appropriate.[49]

CHAPTER THIRTEEN

Joe LeFors

Of the many people caught in the vortex of the Tom Horn trial, the witnesses may have suffered the worst fate. Banished from the courtroom, they had to wait outside until called to testify. But a man with a merry fiddle changed their time from deadly boredom to fun. Edward "Doc" Moore lived about fourteen miles northwest of the Nickell place and played at all the big dances held in the Iron Mountain area. On October 15, 1902, he started playing his violin outside the courtroom. As people danced to his music, the mood invaded the courtroom. And "as the strains of a waltz or an old-fashioned quadrille, played only as the artist who officiates at the barn dances can do," said a *Denver Post* reporter, "there was a gentle tapping of feet on the part of many" inside the courtroom "as they kept time with the music." Some even left the courtroom to join the group down below, and judges and attorneys "flocked to the window" to hear the music.[1]

Those still in the courtroom remained deadly serious about the trial, however. This crowd, the *Denver Post* declared, "could not be duplicated in any other court room in the country. The audience is the result of conditions peculiar to the range, the life in the great, unsettled stretches of country, where the small ranchman and the cattle baron are at war and where life is shed to preserve the range of the great herds of cattle held by the large owners."[2]

Cowboys, the *Post* wrote, were "very much in evidence" at the trial despite the belief that cowboys had followed the buffalo into extinction.

"Tall young ranchmen line the walls" of the courtroom, including "two men of the range, with high cheek bones and evidently of Norse birth, in their splendid strength transported Vikings of the plains."[3]

The *Post* also noted the large number of women present, saying that their faces "excite[d] speculation." "One in a brown dress occupies a seat on the other side of the railing behind Horn. This woman, if she were the prosecuting attorney, could have no livelier interest in the proceedings. Attorney Stoll is impassive beside her animated countenance. She looks as if she might have strong views on woman suffrage and go in for politics." None of the women "seem to evince any sympathy for Horn," the *Post* reporter observed, and "after the blood-stained shirt and other garments were shown the jury the mothers in the courts room fairly blazed at the pleasantly smiling defendant."[4]

Not all the courtroom spectators disliked Horn, however. Some were dazzled by his celebrity. "It is almost amusing the way strangers who have never seen Tom Horn size him up in the court room," said the *Cheyenne Daily Leader*. "He is pointed out at times in much the same manner as a parent would explain to a little child the wonders of a rare animal in a menagerie."[5]

Such was the courtroom setting on October 15, which began with a bright, crisp, sunny morning. It was an important day in the trial. Spectators anticipated the introduction of some sensational evidence. Indeed, the day was termed the "crisis" in the case against Horn. It would see the testimony of two more men from Denver and the presentation of the most critical evidence, the January 1902 conversations between Horn and Joe LeFors.[6] First taking up the pending matter of the testimony of Justice of the Peace M. N. Grant, Judge Scott ruled that he would sustain the defense objection to Grant's testimony as hearsay.[7]

The prosecution then called Frank W. Mulock, the second man who had encountered Horn in Denver in the fall of 1901. Mulock testified that he lived in Denver and worked in the state Republican headquarters there. He said he had seen Tom Horn "during the week of the Carnival, 1901, in Denver."[8]

Detailing his encounter with Horn, Mulock said he had gone to a saloon, the Scandinavian House, sometime after 11:00 P.M., and there engaged in a conversation about his work as a detective "for the Burlington." After Tom Horn spoke up and said, "I am a detective in Wyoming," Mulock had replied, "If you are from Wyoming and a stock detective, I think you would go and find out and get that reward for the man that killed Willie Nickell." Mulock testified that Horn had hesitated and then said, "I am the main guy in that Nickell case."[9]

Horn's subsequent comments, Mulock said, left no doubt what he was saying. Horn had been "pretty drunk" and described more particularly his role in the Willie Nickell case, stating, "That was the best God damned shot I ever made" and "that is the dirtiest trick I ever done." Mulock testified that he just said yes to Horn's comments and told Horn he did not want to drink any more, but Horn kept talking about the Willie Nickell case, saying, "There is a lot of people mixed up in it in Cheyenne, and they had better keep their noses out of it." The next day, Mulock testified, Horn had spoken to him and said he was feeling "pretty rocky" and asked Mulock if he had done any "loud talking." Mulock replied, "Yes, you did." Horn then asked Mulock if he would "say nothing about it," and Mulock said "no." Horn then walked off. Mulock testified, "This is the last I ever seen him." Stoll asked Mulock whether this conversation "occurred before or after he was hurt in Denver." Mulock answered, "It must have occurred before because he was all right that night; there was nothing the matter with him. I afterwards read of having trouble some place in a saloon."[10]

Under T. F. Burke's cross-examination, Mulock acknowledged that when he first saw Horn in Denver, Horn was "very drunk," staggering when he walked up the street, and that he was bragging. Attorney and witness bantered about when the witness had contacted LeFors, with Mulock first saying that he did not know whether Horn had then been arrested or not but that he thought LeFors had sworn out a warrant against Horn. He said he knew it was winter when he contacted LeFors. Burke asked Mulock on what day he had met Horn. Mulock's replies would become important, and the trial transcript shows exactly what he stated:

A. I don't know positively what day, it was carnival week.
Q. The Carnival had already commenced?
A. Yes, sir.
Q. It was not before the Carnival?
A. No, sir.[11]

The final Denver witness, Robert G. Cowsley, followed Mulock to the stand. Cowsley said he was a civil engineer and told Stoll that he had met the defendant once, "during the Carnival last year, the first week of October."

Cowsley said he was with a friend, Roy Campbell, who belonged to the same national guard troop. He and Campbell had gone to the Scandinavian House and a friend (Mulock) came in with a stranger he did not know.[12]

Cowsley told the court that the stranger had introduced himself as Tom Horn. Cowsley then recounted the conversation earlier testified to by Mulock and Campbell, saying he "naturally supposed he [Horn] was a detective working on the case." Cowsley said Horn soon disabused him of this notion when he came over to the table where Cowsley was sitting, struck the table with his hand, and said, "That Nickell business was the God damned best shot I ever made."[13]

Horn had tried to cash a check at the Scandinavian House, but the bartender returned it, saying it was too big to cash. Then, said Cowsley, there was "a little argument" about where the check could be cashed, and "pretty soon Mulock and Horn left." That was the last Cowsley saw of them.[14]

Again, Burke cross-examined, and again he pushed the witness to agree that Horn was drunk and "full of braggadocio." Cowsley agreed. Burke asked Cowsley when he first made this incident known to Wyoming officers. Cowsley said he had told Stoll of the incident about two weeks earlier. As he had done with the other Denver men, Burke asked Cowsley what day he had met Horn. Cowsley said, "I can't say the day. It was the first week in October I remember." Burke asked what was going on in the carnival that day. Cowsley did not remember but said, "I had taken part in two or three parades in which the National Guard turned out." Burke seized this opportunity and tried to induce Cowsley to say that he had already taken part in three parades. But Cowsley told Burke that he didn't remember how many he had been in at that time.[15]

Walter Stoll shifted from Denver in October 1901 to Cheyenne in January 1902. The prosecutor presented several witnesses who testified about the sobriety of Tom Horn on January 12, the day Horn and LeFors had their long conversations. The testimony began with a Cheyenne police officer, A. D. McNeil, who said he had seen Horn at 10:00 A.M., January 12, going up a hallway leading to the U.S. marshal's office. "I am quite intimately acquainted with Mr. Horn," said McNeil. "I noticed he was quite talkative. I could not hear the conversation, any more than they were talking; that drawed my attention to the fact. I could not state positively. I could not say he was under the influence of liquor, but I would say he was drinking."[16]

Bartender Vincent McGwire testified he had seen Horn frequently and saw him at the Tivoli Bar in Cheyenne about 2:00 P.M. that day. "He was sober as far as I could judge."[17] E. S. Robinson also testified that he had seen

Horn at the Tivoli around two, adding: "To the best of my knowledge he was sober." Burke challenged Robinson, wanting to know how he could have remembered this one encounter, then over a year and a half previous. Robinson replied that he remembered Horn saying to him, "How do you do there," and he especially noticed Horn's being accompanied by LeFors: "I thought they were a funny pair of fellows together."[18]

Louis M. Hall, employed by a wholesale liquor house, said he had known Horn for six or seven years. He said he saw him with LeFors on a stairway "that leads up to the U.S. Marshal's office." Hall said that he could not state positively, but "I would swear very near positively that he was not [under the influence of alcohol] at that time."[19]

Finally, Paul Bailey, chief deputy U.S. marshal, who knew Horn, testi-fied that he had been in the marshal's office for a short time, about 12:15 P.M. on January 12, and had seen Horn with LeFors. Bailey said that he took no particular notice of Horn but "did not see or hear anything that would indicate to me that he was other than sober."[20]

Having concluded his presentation about Horn's sobriety on that day, Stoll moved on to the dramatic moment all the spectators had been wait-ing for, calling Joe LeFors to the stand. When LeFors took the witness chair, he and Horn looked at one another, said the *Denver Post,* and it was not a friendly moment. These were two men, "who, their friends say, will begin shooting as soon as one is free." Horn "scowled and never moved his eyes, black almost, with the lids narrowed and the mouth under the mustache in one straight line. The face, with this expression, was an ugly one. His right hand supported it, three fingers reaching up the cheek and hiding the jagged scar on the throat." Word had gone out that LeFors was to testify, so the courtroom was packed, "more crowded than at any time since the trial began." Despite the numbers of people, the *Post* reported an "intense silence" settling over the courtroom.[21]

Stoll laid what lawyer's call "foundation" for presentation of a conver-sation, having LeFors tell where and when he talked with Horn and who was present. LeFors said he had spoken twice with Horn on January 12, 1902, the first in the morning in the second-floor office of the U.S. marshal.[22] Then Stoll asked LeFors to provide "the commencement of the conver-sation."[23] The defense made no objection to the question. Under the law in 1902, there was no legitimate basis for objection.[24]

LeFors's answer was meandering, drifting from a letter of introduction to reports of shooting. LeFors ended his statement saying, "The next word spoken, I forgotten just what it were just at this time." Realizing that his witness was having trouble, Stoll asked more directed questions. He used a form of question stating that "if anything was said to you as to [breaking up a gang of thieves, covering up his trail, where his horse was, etc.], what was it?" This seemed to help LeFors, but John Lacey quickly objected to "this suggestive form."[25] Stoll modified his form of question slightly, and LeFors continued to do better, gradually telling the full story of his January 12 conversations with Horn, setting out each admission Horn had made and presenting all relevant correspondence as well. Despite LeFors's sometimes faltering presentation, the spectators hung on "every word falling from the witness."[26]

Horn's statements, as recited by LeFors, were well known by then. They were still shocking. LeFors related almost all of them: Horn said he had gone barefoot to cover up his trail. Horn had left his horse a "God damned long ways off." Horn had feared having to kill someone he did not want to kill. Horn "supposed" that Willie Nickell was killed "to keep him from making a hell of a commotion." Willie Nickell was shot at about three hundred yards and it was the "best shot he [Horn had] ever made" and "the dirtiest trick I ever done." Horn had used a .30-30 Winchester. Horn got hungry but "never quit a job until he got his man." Saying that Horn had been "sober and rational as far as I could tell," LeFors testified that Horn had told him that he got "$2100 for three dead men and another shot at five times" and that he had put a rock under Willie Nickell's head "to collect my money for a job of this kind." Horn had added, "I got that [payment for killing Willie Nickell] before the job was done." As his final statement about Horn's comments, LeFors said that Horn had told him, "Killing people is my specialty; I look at it as a business proposition and I think I have a corner of this market."[27]

Stoll then presented a string of correspondence relating to the Montana offer of a job to Horn. One was the January 1 letter to LeFors, wherein Horn wrote, "They [the Montana rustlers] can scarcely be any worse than the Brown's Hole gang and I stopped the cow stealing there in one summer."[28] Completing this presentation of correspondence, Stoll turned the witness over for cross-examination.

The thrust of Lacey's cross-examination was to accuse LeFors of telling "tall yarns" about killing people. Lacey asked LeFors, "What mention was made of your killing people?" "I never told him I killed anybody," replied LeFors. Lacey asked then whether something wasn't said "about your killing these people down in Texas?" "Not a word," said LeFors. "Didn't you tell some tall stories, not true of course, of various things of that kind?" "No, sir," answered LeFors. Lacey: "Didn't you swap tall yarns that had no foundation?" LeFors: "I don't know what you call a tall yarn—I have never seen any." LeFors did admit that he had told about fights he had been in, but they weren't yarns, "those were actual fights."[29]

Lacey and LeFors continued to joust in this manner, arguing about what were "tall yarns" and what was "legitimate work." Lacey then asked LeFors more general questions, including one about a statement made by Horn that "the kid run off south and across the road that leads up from the gate [and then swung back to the road]." Lacey then intimated that LeFors was out to get a reward, but LeFors denied that his testimony had anything to do with a reward.[30] The impression from the transcript is that LeFors had recovered his poise and was giving as good as he got. The *Denver Post* saw LeFors's testimony the same way, reporting that "attorney Lacey conducted the cross-examination fiercely, but did not succeed in weakening it."[31] When LeFors left the witness stand, however, his eyes were "dimmed with tears." The *Cheyenne Daily Leader* said it was impossible to say why, whether "under the stress of excitement, intense emotions or the hot cross fire of questions which irritated and worried him." "But certain it is," said the *Leader,* "that it does not require but very little to bring tears to the eyes of the shrewdest and most brilliant detective in the western country."[32]

Leslie Snow and Charles Ohnhaus followed LeFors to the stand. Snow, a deputy sheriff, testified about the June 12, 1902, conversations he had heard between Horn and LeFors (a two-and-a-half hour conversation in the morning and one of about an hour and a half in the afternoon). Snow summarized what he had heard from an adjacent room, covering essentially the same topics LeFors had. Snow said that he had seen Horn following the morning conversation (at about half past twelve) and that he was sober.[33] In his cross-examination, Lacey hit Snow about "the kind of stories they swapped," emphasizing that the whole conversation was a matter of LeFors asking questions and Horn answering them.[34]

Lacey's questions were intended to support one of the defense's main contentions, that LeFors got Horn sloppy drunk and then asked a lot of leading questions, putting words in Horn's mouth, followed by Horn's numb assent. Given that position, Ohnhaus's testimony became especially important. Ohnhaus, the stenographer who took notes as he heard Horn and

LeFors talk, said that he and Deputy Snow had placed themselves in "Mr. Hadsell's" private office adjacent to the U.S. marshal's private office. They were behind a door, he said, lying on a large buffalo overcoat. The marshal's office, which shared the door to Hadsell's office, was of average size with a high ceiling.[35] "The slot in the door was filed down so that it let the door drop from the top," producing an inch-and-a-half gap, Ohnhaus said. As well, there was a gap on the threshold under the door "where shoes had worn a place on the slat." So, Ohnhaus said, "the sounds from the adjoining room could be heard very distinctly."[36]

Ohnhaus presented the Horn and LeFors conversations verbatim, including the exact wording of every question. The questions can thus be evaluated to see if they were leading (the kinds of questions that instructed Horn how to answer, putting words in his mouth to be echoed back), or are open-ended (those in which Horn could explain, usually headed by words such as "who," "what," "when," "where," "how," or "why").[37]

When their first conversation began, it had actually been Horn asking LeFors questions. Horn asked LeFors if he knew anything about the nature of the work being sought by the Montanans. LeFors responded that they were good people and that Horn would "have to get right in among them and gain their confidence and show them you are all right." Horn then said that he did not want to make reports and that there would only be one report, the final one. "If a man has to make reports all the time, they will catch the wisest son of a bitch on earth," Horn said. Horn then asked LeFors whether these people were afraid of shooting, and LeFors assured him they were not.[38] Horn said, "I shoot too God damn much I know; you know me when it comes to shooting, I will protect the people I am working for, but I have never got my employers into any trouble yet over anything I have done."[39]

LeFors had then said to Horn, "You are the best man to cover up your trail I ever saw. In the Willie Nickell killing I could never find your trail and I pride myself on being a trailer." This was not a question, much less a leading question, but Horn replied to it nevertheless: "No, by God. I left no trail, the only way to cover up your trail is to go barefooted."[40]

LeFors had asked, "Where was your horse?" This was a question but an open-ended one, not a leading question. Horn had answered, "He was a God damn long ways off." LeFors said: "I would be afraid to leave my horse so far away, you might get cut off from him." Again, this was not a question, merely a comment, but again Horn responded: "You don't take much chances. These people are unorganized, and anyway I depend on this gun of mine. The only thing that I was ever afraid of was that I would be compelled to kill an officer or a man I didn't want to, but I would do everything to keep from being seen, but if he kept after me, I would certainly kill him."[41]

LeFors had said to Horn, "I never knew why Willie Nickell was killed, was it because he was one of the victims named or was it compulsory?" This might be considered a leading question, although it presented a choice to Horn. Horn selected neither of the choices LeFors presented, however, saying instead, "I think it was this way; suppose a man was in the big draw to the right of the gate, you know where it is—the draw that comes into the main creek below Nickell house where Nickell was shot. Well suppose a man was in that and the kid came riding up on him from this way, and suppose the kid started to run for the house, and the fellow headed him off at the gate and killed him to keep him from going to the house and raising a hell of a commotion. That is the way I think it occurred."[42]

LeFors had then asked: "Tom, you had your boots on when you ran cross there to cut the kid off, didn't you?" This is definitely a leading question, but Horn did not follow LeFors's suggestion. Instead, he said, "No, I was barefooted."

Horn had then resumed asking questions of LeFors, saying, "Joe, do you remember the little girl?" LeFors asked who Horn meant, and Horn started talking about "the school marm," saying that she was "sure smooth people" and that she wrote him a letter "as long as the Governor's message telling me in detail everything asked by Stoll the prosecuting attorney; Stoll thought I was going to prove an alibi, but I fooled him." LeFors asked him, "Did the school marm tell everything she knew?" This question might be construed as leading, and Horn agreed to it, but he did not simply accede to LeFors's question but elaborated on it at some length, speaking about how Miss Kimmell had warned him of Joe LeFors, telling him to look out for LeFors, saying, "he is not all right." Horn had also criticized the Millers, stating, "They are ignorant old jays, they can't even appreciate a good joke," and added, "The first time I met the girl was just before the killing of the kid, everything you know dates from the killing of the kid."[43]

LeFors had asked, "How many days was it before the killing of the kid?" This is not a leading question, and Horn did not answer it succinctly. He said, "Three or four days; maybe one day[—]damned if I want to remember the dates. She was there at this time and of course we soon paired ourselves off." LeFors asked: "What nationality was she?" This is not a leading question, but LeFors then asked a question that was leading: "Tom, didn't Jim Dixon carry you grub?" Horn, however, did not agree to LeFors's suggestion. He said, "No, by God, no one carried me grub."[44] LeFors asked, "Tom, how can a man that weighs 204 pounds go without anything to eat for so long?" This is not a leading question, and Horn told LeFors that he did manage, although sometimes he carried a little bacon. LeFors said, "You must get terribly hungry, Tom?" This might be construed as a leading question, although a point of no great significance, but as with other of the replies to LeFors, Horn did not simply agree to LeFors's words but felt he had to elaborate. Horn said, "Yes, sometimes I get so hungry that I could kill my mother for some grub, but I never quit a job until I get my man."[45]

LeFors had asked, "What kind of a gun have you got?" This is not a leading question. Horn said he had a .30–30 Winchester. LeFors asked if he thought the .30–30 would hold up as well as a .30–40. This is not a leading question and Horn once again answered the question and then elaborated, saying, "No, but I like to get close to my man, the closer the better."

LeFors had asked, "How far was Willie Nickell killed?" Again, this was not a leading question (although it assumes that Horn knew how Willie Nickell was killed), and Horn answered it with elaboration: "About 300 yards. It was the best shot that I ever made and the dirtiest trick I ever done, and I thought at one time he would get away."[46] LeFors asked, "How about the shells, did you carry them away?" This can be construed as a leading question, but it was not followed by an indifferent assent. Instead Horn said, "You bet your God damn life I did."[47]

Horn and LeFors had then made ready to depart the marshal's office, but as they did, LeFors said to Horn, "I could always see your work clear, but I want you to tell me why you killed the kid; was it a mistake?" This is not really a leading question, a moot point because Horn declined to answer it, saying, "Well I will tell you all about that when I come back from Montana, it is too new yet."[48]

When Horn and LeFors returned to the marshal's office in the afternoon, they resumed talking. Horn spoke of his life, how he had "lived about 15 ordinary lives," and how "the first man I killed was when I was only 26 years old. He was a course [sic] son of a bitch." LeFors asked Horn, "How much did you get for killing these fellows, in the Powell and Lewis case you got $600 apiece; you killed Lewis in the corral with a six-shooter, I would like to have seen the expression on his face when you shot him." These comments would not be deemed leading, and Horn responded only to LeFors's last observation, saying "he was the scaredest son of a bitch you ever saw—how did you come to know that Joe?"[49]

LeFors had replied: "I have known everything you have done Tom for a great many years, I know where you were paid this money." This is a comment, not a question, but Horn responded, "Yes, I was paid this money on the train between Cheyenne and Denver." LeFors asked, "Didn't you get two one hundred bills and the rest in gold?" This question is leading (or, as a trial attorney might say, "leading and suggestive"). Horn apparently agreed to it, but once again did not simply accept LeFors's words but added his own. The transcript seems to leave out the word "yes," but if added, Horn's reply would have been as follows: "Yes, and this is where I learned to take care of my shells there after I flashed powder in them to make them smell fresh and the damned officers never found them."[50]

LeFors had then asked Horn, "Why did you put the rock under the kid's head after you killed him, that is one of your marks, isn't it?" The second part of this question is leading, and Horn answered, "yes," but he added, "That is the way I hang out my sign to collect my money for a job of this kind." LeFors asked, "Did you ever have an agreement drawn up?" This question could be answered either "yes" or "no" but could be construed as leading. Horn said no but then added, "I do all my business through Coble he is the whitest son of a bitch in the country in a job of this kind." LeFors said, "In the Powell and Lewis case, did Coble put in towards your pay?" This might be construed as leading Horn to answer "yes," but Horn responded, "No, I wouldn't let him, he fed me and furnished me horses and had done more for me than any man in the country."[51]

LeFors had asked Horn: "Did you ever have any trouble to collect your money?" The question is not fairly construed as leading, and Horn embellished: "No, when I do a job of this kind they know they have to pay me; I would kill a man if he tried to beat me out of ten cents that I had earned." LeFors followed Horn's comment: "Have you got your money yet for the killing of Nickell?" This is perhaps a leading question, but Horn did not accept LeFors's wording and said, "I got that before I did the job." LeFors asked, "You got $500 for that why did you cut the price?" Horn did not agree that he cut the price, saying, "I got $2100," and LeFors asked, "How much is that a man?" This is not a leading question, and Tom Horn elaborated: "That is for three dead men and one man shot at five times; killing men is my specialty; I look at it as a business proposition and I think I have a corner on the market."[52]

The evaluation of each question LeFors asked shows not one example of a leading question followed by unqualified acceptance of the question as LeFors framed it. Tom Horn volunteered all the most damaging parts of his responses. The jury perhaps also noted that Horn's statements were specific to the topic and detailed.

Walter Stoll asked Ohnhaus if he had ever seen Horn, and Ohnhaus said that on a couple of occasions he looked through the keyhole and saw Horn. Ohnhaus also said that that afternoon he passed by Horn within two or three feet and concluded, "I would say that he was not what you would call an intoxicated man; I won't say that he didn't have a drink, one two or three perhaps, but I don't think he was drunk."[53]

Lacey immediately hit Ohnhaus on his failure to write down stories about killing people. Ohnhaus denied that LeFors told anything about killing people, but Lacey showed the witness a statement from the preliminary examination in which Ohnhaus seemed to accept that such stories were told.[54]

At 3:30 P.M., October 15, 1920, Walter Stoll announced that the state would rest.[55] The presentation of the case had been thorough, addressing every element of the crime of murder and seemingly all the evidence that might reasonably support the charges. Newspapers covering the trial had a great deal to say about the prosecution's presentation. One brief comment by the *Cheyenne Daily Leader* did not bode well for the defendant: "It looks very much as if Tom Horn was like the famous parrot who talked too much."[56] Indeed, the consensus among the newspapers covering the trial was that the prosecution had presented a solid case. The *Denver Republican* wrote: "On all sides are heard expressions of opinion that the state has made a strong case."[57] Said the *Cheyenne Daily Leader,* "The facts brought out by the prosecution in its efforts to convict Tom Horn of the murder of Willie Nickell were not as sensational nor convincing as was expected before the trial." The newspaper was probably referring to the rumored testimony of two eyewitnesses to the killing, which never happened. Nor did Glendolene Kimmell testify. Yet, said the *Leader,* "they undoubtedly form a strong chain of circumstantial evidence which is bound to make a powerful impression on the minds of the jury."[58] Most significant to the *Leader* was Horn's confession and Joe LeFors's testimony. "The whole strength of the case depends upon the effect of the confession or statements on the jury."[59] The *Leader* thought the confession particularly telling, saying, "One of the strongest features of this confession is that it tallies, in every detail, with the circumstances surrounding the murder. If Tom Horn did not kill Willie Nickell, he betrayed a perfect knowledge of the conditions under which the boy was killed, even to an explanation of the rock placed under the boy's head."The man who obtained that confession came in for high praise. "The deft manner in which LeFors led the defendant on to tell his story of the killing of young Nickell and other crimes shows a high order of detective skill," said the *Leader.* "It is the most adroit and masterly piece of detective work in the annals of crime."[60]

The attorneys defending Tom Horn also had to know that the state had presented persuasive evidence showing their client's guilt of murder. They were capable and confident men, however. They would begin presenting their case the next morning, October 16, 1902, and the ensuing few days would show their high skill and deep determination to fight for their client's life.

CHAPTER FOURTEEN

Of Bullets and Bullet Holes

Interest in the Horn case continued unabated. The defense would be presenting its case, and Walter Stoll would have the opportunity to cross-examine. As the *Laramie Boomerang* noted, "Stoll's reputation as a cross-examiner causes much anticipation for starting [startling] things in the next few days."[1]

So, when T. F. Burke rose to give the opening statement for Tom Horn, he had the close attention of the courtroom. Burke used this advantage immediately, declaring the prosecution's case weak. "Mr. Stoll has failed to show any motive actuating Horn in the commission of the deed," said Burke, "and we will have little trouble, I believe, in showing that Horn was having a little quiet fun with La Fors [*sic*] when he told him what they claim he did in the United States marshal's office. It is foolish to believe that Horn would be so incautious after his long experience as to permit himself to fall into any such trap or talk seriously of these matters [to LeFors]."

Such an argument had to be presented carefully. Burke seemed to be contending that Horn, an experienced assassin, who knew all the ins and outs of how to make his profession work, would never have been candid with a deputy U.S. marshal. "It is scarcely possible to believe, too, that Horn would travel in his bare feet over this disintegrated granite ground," Burke continued, "so hard that the hoof of a horse makes little impression, in order to cover tracks that could not be made."[2]

The defense, through R. N. Matson, first presented several witnesses addressing Horn's sobriety—or lack of it—on January 12, 1902. Grover Reis, a bellboy at the Inter Ocean Hotel, had seen Tom Horn at the Inter Ocean bar early that morning (about 12:30 or 1:30 A.M.) and, from his previous contacts with Horn, judged him "about half shot."[3] Al Leslie, a Cheyenne bartender, said he saw Horn on January 12 until about 6:00 A.M., first drinking at the Hynds bar and then at Kerrigan's, another Cheyenne bar. "Before I left him," Leslie said, Horn "was drunk," adding that Horn was bragging about the Wilcox train robbery and "was talking like any other drunken man would talk." Stoll's cross-examination showed that although Leslie had matched Horn drink for drink, Leslie still felt he could accurately judge Horn's state of sobriety.[4] Stoll intended to point out that either Leslie was not drunk (and, therefore, by implication, Horn would not have been drunk either), or that Leslie was drunk, meaning that his testimony about Horn's sobriety was not reliable.

Andrew Nelson, bartender at the Inter Ocean Hotel, testified that he had seen Tom Horn at the bar beginning about 7:00 A.M., January 12, that Horn had about a half dozen drinks, and that he was drunk. But Nelson also said, in response to Stoll's cross-examination, that he'd only seen Horn for a half hour at the Inter Ocean bar, leaving the question of whether Horn had drunk all half dozen of his drinks in the witnessed half hour.[5] The defense next presented Frank Kerrigan, "bartender of the Arcade Saloon, Phil Kerrigan, Cheyenne," to tell of Horn's January 12 state of sobriety. Kerrigan said he saw Horn between five and ten o'clock, and that Horn was drinking (maybe a half dozen drinks). Horn was also talking freely, telling the well-known story of how "a regiment of Spanish Mexican soldiers were shooting at him" but he still got away. Kerrigan said he did not see Horn walk, so he did not know if Horn was drunk, but he did know that Horn did not stagger.[6] John Fullerton, Inter Ocean Hotel, the final witness regarding Horn's sobriety that Sunday morning, said he saw Horn once at about one o'clock (apparently meaning 1:00 P.M.) and that Horn was talking and bragging, as he was wont to do when drinking. Fullerton said when he saw Horn he was "pretty well loaded."[7]

The *Denver Post's* lack of respect for this testimony is instructive. The paper quoted a "delighted spectator" who referred to the testimony as "evidence of booze and bragadaccio [*sic*] from men who might be called experts of jags." And the *Post* said that "the majority of the men in the court room could not bring themselves to look upon the testimony seriously."[8]

To begin the defense of Tom Horn with witnesses asserting his drunken state on January 12 seems odd. In the first place, under 1902 law, statements given by a defendant when drunk were not inadmissible for that reason alone. The fact of intoxication was only a factor for the jury to consider in giving weight to the confession. The law was clearly established that jury members were the ultimate judges whether a defendant was under the influence of alcohol at the time a confession was made, and also to what degree the accused was under the influence.[9] More than this, however, as perhaps indicated by the comments of the *Denver Post,* there was a serious question whether proving Horn drunk would help his defense or hurt it. People have long felt that drink promotes truth rather than deception. Indeed, there is an axiom with ancient roots, said to have been coined by Pliny the Elder: "In vino, veritas": in wine, there is truth.[10] The worst weakness in such evidence, however, was that its significance could be overridden by the content of Horn's remarks in his confession. If Horn seemed to speak coherently, it would be hard for the defense to assert successfully that he was so drunk that all his statements should be disregarded.

Why, then, would the defense have begun its case with such faulty evidence? The answer is probably found in the fundamental reality that John Lacey and his co-counsel could not choose their facts. Lacey could push hard to have the facts construed in favorable ways, and certainly did, but there is an irreducible minimum beyond which no attorney can safely go. Lacey had to present his case with the hand he had been dealt, and if the cards in that hand were weak, there was only so much he could do. Even if the odds of prevailing under a theory of drunkenness were remote, Horn's attorneys could have felt that, given the stakes, they had to take this chance.

The testimony of the five men who observed Tom Horn on January 12 did not take long, and the defense moved to another topic: the caliber of the bullets striking Willie Nickell. Perhaps Stoll hoped his previous efforts had stifled the defense contention that Tom Horn's .30-30 rifle could not have caused the wounds suffered by Willie Nickell, but the defense attorneys were nothing if not tenacious, and they presented four more doctors to further advance their contention.

The first such physician was Dr. George P. Johnston, one of the three Cheyenne physicians who examined Willie Nickell's body on July 21, 1901 and testified at the coroner's inquest. Johnston "takes himself with much seriousness," the *Denver Post* observed. "He is a handsome man of 40 or thereabouts, with iron-gray hair, a haughty manner and a positive voice."[11] Dr. Johnston was an affirmative witness on direct examination. He told of his twelve years' experience practicing medicine and surgery after his studies at a medical college in Ohio. He also had considerable experience in gunshot wounds and had studied them "pertaining to my work as a surgeon."[12]

Johnston said he had carefully examined the body, and, "in every respect," he concurred in the report made by Amos Barber for the coroner's inquest. The examining physicians found two wounds in Willie Nickell's body and Dr. Johnston said that two bullets "must have struck the body almost at right angles," because they made "clear, circular" holes. Dr. Barber, said Johnston, used a scientific instrument intended for this purpose and determined that the two entry wounds were three-eighths of an inch in diameter and that the exit wounds were one-half inch and one inch, respectively.[13]

Johnston gave his opinion that "the missile must have been at least 3/8 of an inch in diameter." "It might have been considerably larger," said the doctor, "but it could not have been smaller, according to all evidence we have on gunshot wounds." Johnston said that his impression was that the wounds had not only been made with large-caliber bullets but also that the bullets had been made of lead.[14]

Defense attorney Burke then made a striking demonstration that must have impressed the jury. He produced three bullets, a .30-30 soft-nosed bullet, a .38 caliber bullet, and a .45 caliber bullet. Dr. Johnston looked at all these and declared that he did not think the wounds he had examined could have been made with the .30 caliber bullet, that they could have been made by the .38 caliber, but that he thought they had probably been made with a bullet about the .45 caliber size. He said the bullet holes made in Willie Nickell's body would not be larger than the bullets striking him and that if the bullets were not deformed, the bullet holes would probably be smaller. The "perfect circle" made by the bullet, however, showed "that the bullet was in its natural shape and undeformed."[15]

Johnston told the jury that he had also considered the "explosive effect" of a bullet. From his study, he concluded there was no such effect at the point of entrance of a bullet. In response to Burke's question, Johnston

assured the jury that this proposition had been "scientifically demonstrated."
"Every authority I have consulted has been unanimous on this point
without exception."[16]

Johnston also addressed the gravel that had adhered to Willie Nickell's
body and clothes. From this evidence and his analysis of blood flow, Johnston said the body when found had been turned over at least three and a
half hours after the shooting and that it more likely had been ten to twelve
hours and perhaps as many as twenty or twenty-four hours.[17] The physician added in conclusion that he had been subpoenaed by the prosecution
but not called as a witness, leaving the implication that the prosecution
had decided his testimony would be adverse and so chose not to use him as
a witness.[18]

Stoll once again faced a challenge. How would he deal with this confident and apparently effective witness? Stoll's technique as a cross-examiner
was to question a witness cautiously and politely, rarely raising his voice,
and the trial transcript seems to bear out this quiet approach.[19] Stoll first
established that when Dr. Johnston saw the body, Willie Nickell's clothes
were not present. Johnston had not otherwise looked at them, and he had
only examined the appearance of the body. Stoll said to Johnston, "And
as far as your knowledge of the appearance of the body, where the blood
was upon the clothes, and so on is concerned, you have nothing to base
any conjecture upon except as it was stated in Mr. Burke's question, have
you?" Johnston replied, "I have not."[20]

Stoll moved on to other topics but soon returned to the clothing Willie
Nickell had been wearing when he was shot. "Now as a fact recognized
by physicians and surgeons," Stoll asked, "is it not true that when a bullet
goes through clothing, or strikes some other object previous to striking
the body, then results are obtained which do not correspond with the theoretical results, that is the result which we obtain by the simply firing at
the body itself?" Johnston admitted this proposition, and Stoll continued.
"And as a scientific fact you are willing to say to this jury are you not
that a projectile, assuming the projectile to have what we call a soft nose,
the same projectile will make a different wound, depending upon the character of the nose of that projectile?" (Stoll's emphasis on the standard .30–30
soft-nosed bullet was understandable given the makeup of the jury; western
ranchmen knew guns. It was a virtual certainty that several of these 1902
jurors knew all about the popular new .30–30, including the bullets it shot
and its ballistics. A Winchester rifle was an everyday tool used by men on

the range. Even today, Wyoming men know guns.[21]) Dr. Johnston conceded that the bullet would make a different wound.[22]

Stoll's next question, a logical extension of his earlier ones, asked the physician to concede that a wound made by a new bullet would be smaller than if the nose had been flattened. Johnston apparently did not like the direction of the questioning because he began to equivocate, asserting he had never seen any authority supporting that. Stoll could have argued with Dr. Johnston about this statement, but instead he employed the doctor's answer to push Johnston into agreeing that this was a subject in which he lacked knowledge. Soon Johnston took refuge in the contention that all possibilities in this area were conjectural (even "very deceptive"), depending upon many varying circumstances.[23] This was exactly the point Stoll wished to make regarding the determination of the caliber of a bullet from the hole it made in a body.

Stoll noted that the three physicians who examined Willie Nickell's body had only looked at the surface of the body and did not actually conduct an autopsy. When Dr. Johnston challenged the prosecuting attorney's statement, Stoll replied: "Probably I don't understand what that means? May I obtain that information from you? When we speak of autopsy, what do you understand by that generally?" Witness and attorney sparred some more, and it became clear that Johnston's objection was not with the use of the word "autopsy" but the implication that failure to penetrate the body cavity and trace the course of the bullet meant that, in Stoll's words, "you cannot tell much about the course of a projectile." Attorney and doctor sparred further, but Johnston's position was not strong here. Eventually Stoll backed the doctor into a corner from which he could not escape when Stoll asked: "You do not pretend to say to the jury that you could be accurate in determining the nature of a projectile without tracing its course through the body?" Johnston replied, "To a certain degree I could." Stoll came back: "Only relative is all you wish to be understood, approximately?" Answer: "Yes."

Dr. Johnston seemed to retreat from the firm statements he had made on direct examination on other points as well. When Stoll and Johnston began to discuss the "axis of the flight" of a bullet, Stoll's training as a soldier gave him special insight. Stoll asked Johnston a long, hypothetical question: "It [the bullet] keeps a rotary movement if the projectile is moving in a horizontal or a line of a parabola? There is a rotary movement around that axis of its flight, and if something deviates that projectile from its ordinary course, so that instead of its flying through the air in a straight way it took another position, it would still be revolving about its axis of flight and the projectile be of such a form that it might make a somewhat circular wound, would it not?"

"That would depend upon the circumstance," answered Johnston.

"Yes, certainly; you do not wish to be understood that it could not be?" Johnston answered, "We judge simply from the appearance presented to us."[24] Once again, Stoll had pushed the doctor to soften his previous testimony.

Johnston also seemed to pull away from his hard position regarding the kind of bullets that had struck Willie Nickell. Stoll asked, "Now in the matter of the bullet, you would not say that this was simply a lead bullet? You would say also it might be a case bullet or soft nose bullet?" Dr. Johnston replied, "It might have been a case bullet, I can't say accurately as to that."[25]

Inquiring about decomposition of Willie Nickell's body and the rubbing off of the epidermis, Stoll followed with a more general question: "In the same connection on this point, that you necessarily eliminated matters concerning which you know nothing, not knowing the circumstances under which the shots were fired, not knowing how far off the party was who did the firing, being left simply the body before us, eliminating the clothing and matters of that kind, were you present at the time that Dr. Barber testified on the preliminary hearing of this case?" Johnston said he was, and Stoll reminded the doctor that he had confirmed Barber's testimony. But Johnston surprisingly now pulled away from such an affirmation, saying that he had confirmed the facts but not Barber's theories. Perhaps Johnston anticipated this cross-examination question, as his response seems disingenuous. In his direct examination he had said he concurred with Barber's coroner's inquest report "in every respect," but regarding Barber's preliminary examination testimony he made careful distinctions. Johnston was apparently trying to avoid Barber's preliminary examination statement that because of the decomposition of the body, he (Barber) could not testify regarding the caliber of bullets that had struck Willie Nickell.[26]

Whatever the case, the effectiveness of Johnston's testimony depended greatly on his response to Stoll's cross-examination. If jury members thought he was shading his testimony to favor the defense, they would devalue his statements. On the other hand, if they believed he was trying to present his opinions without regard to whom they favored, then his evidence would carry real weight.

Comments from the newspapers covering the trial on Johnston's testimony lend insight. The *Denver Post* said that Johnston "was positive when he was right and even more sure when he was wrong." The *Cheyenne Daily Leader* wrote: "The cross examination of Dr. George P. Johnston relative to gunshot wounds proved to be par excellence, the best exhibition of this kind in the progress of the trial. For probably an hour the sharp wits of one were arrayed against the wits of the other and some of the most abstruse problems in ordnance were gone into in the minutest details and every question was replete with technical words such as 'trajectory, parabola, axis of rotation and axis of flight.'" In general, the *Leader* concluded that the medical expert evidence was "greatly shaken by the rigid and shrewd cross examination to which they were subjected by Prosecuting Attorney Stoll."[27] Offering a different take, the *Denver Times* said Dr. Johnston "was a good witness and the wonderful cross-examiner, Stoll, had a hard time with him."[28]

The next witness was Dr. William F. Lewis, a surgeon at Fort D.A. Russell (now Francis E. Warren Air Force Base), but before Dr. Lewis took the stand, Judge Scott addressed the matter of newspaper artists, "stationed at various positions in the court room, sketching attorneys, witnesses and jurors," who were distracting the jury from the evidence presented on the witness stand. (To a modern attorney, it is surprising that the artists were allowed such freedom in the first place.) Judge Scott then ordered all the sketch artists from the courtroom. The *Cheyenne Daily Leader* told its readers that the artists were continuing their work outside the courtroom after each witness retired.[29]

Dr. Lewis, like Dr. Johnston, was a confident witness on direct examination. Newspaper comments indicate that he was probably more likable than Johnston (a "charming gentleman" and a "most agreeable companion" said the *Denver Post*), which by itself would make him a more formidable witness.[30]

Lewis told the jury that he was an army surgeon (he was "Captain Lewis") and a medical school graduate. He had seen some two hundred gunshot wounds and had read authorities on the matter. He said that about three-quarters of these wounds that he had seen were from modern, small-caliber bullets (less than .31 of an inch in diameter).[31] Lewis agreed with Johnston that the circumstances in the case showed that the bullets striking Willie Nickell were three-eighths of an inch or larger and that it was not possible they were made by a .30 caliber bullet.[32] Lewis concluded by stating that

Willie Nickell's body had been turned over after death, at least between three and six hours after death because "the blood would not have coagulated or dried sufficiently to have stuck the gravel to the shirt in less time than 3 hours so that it would adhere after the body was turned over."[33]

Stoll immediately went after Dr. Lewis's assertion that gravel and other small particles would have only adhered to Willie Nickell's clothing after three to six hours' bleeding. He first showed that Lewis's testimony was hypothetical and then said, "But Doctor, if the boy had fallen, would not the weight of the boy's body necessarily have forced gravel and especially small pieces of dirt into his face and into his clothing; would not the very impact of the blow of the body on the ground necessarily have produced that result?" Lewis defended his earlier statement at first, saying, "I should not think sufficient for the gravel to adhere unless the body had lain for some time three hours [*sic*]." But Stoll refused to let Lewis's contention rest. He asked, "Have you seen persons that have for instance fallen from horse back, their horse having stumbled, and they have plowed into the ground, now is it not a fact that the dirt and gravel adhere to their faces and hands and clothes for a long time and immediately after they get up?" Begrudgingly, Lewis answered: "The smaller pieces of sand," but he insisted that his answer would be correct "so far as the gravel adhering to the skin is concerned." Finally, though, Stoll forced Lewis to admit that gravel "might adhere to the skin if there was sufficient force to the fall." Stoll then asked a question that brought the jury into this whole inquiry: "There is nothing very mysterious about little experiences of this kind, in our lives every day, Doctor?" "No Sir," replied Dr. Lewis. Underlining his point, Stoll said, "There would be nothing about the condition of the clothes of the body that would require any special knowledge, any expert knowledge, but rather the appearance could be accounted for by our own common experience in daily life?" "I should think so," said the doctor.[34]

Taking after Lewis as Stoll did was not surprising. Indeed, it was surprising that Stoll had not challenged Dr. Johnston more vigorously on this contention. Perhaps Stoll had been surprised by Johnston's testimony and was not prepared to challenge it, but Dr. Lewis's testimony gave him a second chance to attack the defense on this point. In doing so, Stoll applied good cross-examination technique. If a cross-examiner detects a weakness in an otherwise strong witness, blasting that witness on his clear mistake can serve to taint everything else the witness says. Stoll not only had an excellent opportunity to do that, but the tactic was even more appealing because the topic fit within the jurors' knowledge and experience. Most of the Horn jurors had worked on the range, riding horses. It was an almost universal experience that men working on the range took falls, and when they did the invariable custom was to get up and dust themselves off, cleaning sand, gravel, and grass off their clothes. So the theoretical pronouncement of a Cheyenne physician that particles only stuck to a body and clothes when blood was present for three to six hours just would not wash with this group of men. Even before Stoll started his cross-examination, many of the jurors may have been skeptical of Lewis's testimony.

In something like ten minutes, Stoll was able to cast a pall over all of Dr. Lewis's testimony and probably make allies of the jury members because he had validated their experiences. It appears also that the initial questions made Lewis more pliable in the later questioning. Stoll challenged the relevance of Lewis's experience to Willie Nickell's killing, although not in an overbearing way. Instead, he established that most of the physician's experience was with wounds upon a living body, and that he'd had "very little" opportunity to study the appearances of wounds upon dead bodies.[35] By careful half steps, Stoll took Dr. Lewis considerably closer to more damaging admissions than the doctor intended to go. Lewis agreed that "the appearance and the effects of the wounds upon the living body and upon the dead body are different." And he also agreed with Dr. Senn, a "very good authority," that the living body and the cadaver represented two "entirely different media in studying the effects upon the modern bullet." Lewis conceded that various conditions could create different effects, "and no one can speak with very much authority unless he knows all of the conditions." The doctor agreed that many conditions regarding a bullet's pathway could "vary or modify the appearance of the wound." "All you can say," Stoll continued, is that "certain conditions may have existed, but that in addition to those conditions, there may have been many others of which he knows nothing, that may also have produced those same results?" Lewis said that was right, but qualified his response, adding, "unless you know the exact character of the wound that is made by the bullet." Stoll used this comment to suggest to the doctor, "You never know the exact character of the wound without proving it or tracing it on through its entire course?" Lewis responded, "No, except you can get an exact description of the wound of entrance." Stoll then asked Dr. Lewis whether it was not a well-known fact that if the bullet was followed through the body "you might find the bullet, the bullet that produced that wound of a considerably less caliber, deformed in such way . . . to produce the wound." Dr. Lewis responded: "You might find that true, but the appearance of the wound would give you some idea." Apparently the physician paused to consider what he had just said, and then he pulled back, adding, "or very certain idea." Thereafter, Lewis insisted that if he saw a wound of entrance, he could "form a pretty safe conclusion as to the form and caliber of the bullet."[36]

Stoll shifted his point of inquiry and asked Lewis if it was possible that a bullet might be deformed so as to preserve its original shape, presenting "an entirely regular surface, and yet be larger than it was originally?" Dr. Lewis agreed. Lewis also agreed that a soft-nosed bullet could be so battered that it would make a wound with a diameter different from an intact bullet, and still it would be more or less regular.[37]

Stoll shifted his focus again and asked the doctor about another limitation to his expertise. Lewis agreed that his experience had been more with solid steel or nickel-coated army cartridges, which are not soft-nosed bullets. Stoll asked the witness whether he "would expect a wound made by an army bullet . . . to be smaller than one of the same caliber made by a bullet which is soft nosed and which may have been battered down?" Dr. Johnston had balked at a very similar question, but Lewis answered affirmatively: "If it has been battered down," he said.

The culmination of all of Stoll's patient probing and pushing came when Stoll asked Dr. Lewis: "So that as a professional and scientific man, you would state as a matter of fact, if a soft nose bullet had been battered down, so that it was larger than when originally made, and if the conditions were such that forces operated upon it in such a way as to produce something outside of the ordinary results which you obtained, it would not be altogether improbable or impossible for a wound as large as 3/8 of an inch to be made by a .30-30 caliber?"

Lewis said, "A soft nose bullet, yes sir."[38]

It was a key moment in the trial. Dr. Lewis had just undercut Horn's principal defense, that his rifle could not have fired the shots killing Willie Nickell. The *Laramie Boomerang* reported that the witness "got provoked at the questions and finally said the wound might have been caused by a .30-30 soft nose bullet."[39] Provoked or not, Lewis had just made an admission devastating to the defense.

In redirect examination, Lacey worked to rehabilitate his witness, having him qualify his answers to Stoll's cross-examination. Dr. Lewis insisted that for a .30 caliber bullet to make a hole .38 of an inch it would have to be .38 of an inch in diameter. The jury surely detected, however, that this was damage control and inconsistent with what Lewis had just testified to.

The last witness of October 16 was Dr. John Conway, the third physician who had viewed the body of Willie Nickell on July 21, 1901. His testimony was not successful. One newspaper reported that Conway's testimony "was about the same as the [other] physicians. When he was cross questioned he got fearfully mixed up in his statements and after two and one-half hours of Stoll's questions he became badly tangled up." More than this, Conway made at least one admission that compromised his testimony. When asked by Coroner Murray at the inquest whether the bloated condition of the body made any difference in the condition of the wound of the hole caused by the bullet, Dr. Conway had answered, "It would of course; those wounds were comparatively large."[40]

Conway's speaking voice further hindered his testimony. The doctor "adopted a whispered and sibilant tone on the stand," the *Denver Post* observed, "which drove the reporters and the court stenographer to deep but not loud profanity, and had every juryman sitting up straight with his hand behind his ear listening with strained attention to the wee, small voice of the distinguished doctor."[41]

Probably a worse factor for Dr. Conway was that the court and jury were fatigued by all the technicalities. Indeed, the defense must have been discouraged by press comments about the attention of the people in the courtroom on October 16. The *Denver Post* reported that the "first day of the defense [October 16] was very slow and monotonous."[42] The *Laramie Boomerang* said the crowd that gathered on that day to hear exciting developments was disappointed. Referring to all the technical testimony, the *Boomerang* said, "The day was very tiresome. The witnesses are weary waiting to be called and those called are tired of the rigid examinations."[43]

Had the defense clearly shown that Tom Horn's .30-30 could not have fired the bullets that killed Willie Nickell, the *Boomerang* would surely have deemed it an "exciting development." Too, if the jury shared the view of the *Boomerang* and saw the day as "very tiresome," it did not augur well for the defense.

CHAPTER FIFTEEN

The Defense Continues

As the trial of Tom Horn began its second week on Friday, October 17, 1902, many people in Cheyenne viewed the case as an extravaganza. The *Cheyenne Daily Leader* characterized the week of the trial as "remarkable," noting that the "famous Tom Horn Trial" drew "big crowds every day and a cloud of witnesses and correspondents." The week must have been wearisome to the participants, however, especially for Horn. The *Denver Post* observed that Horn's mood changed as the case proceeded. At first, he showed "supreme confidence and nerve," but as the prosecution presented evidence and one damaging blow after another fell, his nerve failed him, said the *Post*. As the parade of witnesses began, Horn had fastened a beady eye on his tormentors as if "he had the power to confuse the person on the stand," but this power failed him when Deputy Sheriff Snow and the stenographer Ohnhaus took the stand. When Ohnhaus told of Horn's declaration that killing men was his specialty, "the prisoner grew pale. He was nervous and his hands twitched continuously and he moved around in his chair." But then Walter Stoll announced that the state rested and, perhaps, said the *Post,* Horn would know some welcome relief from the man "who has been prosecuting him with such relentless energy."[1] There were moments in the first day of the defense presentation that may have encouraged Horn, but a realistic appraisal could not have inspired much optimism. The defense still had more to offer, however, including some sensational charges then unknown to the prosecution. And Horn may have taken heart because soon he would mount the witness stand himself and talk to the jurors directly.

Dr. W. A. Burgess, a Cheyenne surgeon, was the first witness of the day for the defense that Friday. As with the previous physicians presented by Horn's legal team, Burgess was a well-qualified witness, and he testified to exactly the same points as had all the previous defense medical witnesses—that the bullets had been lead, that they had to have been three-eighths of an inch in diameter or more (reciting the stated standard rule that the bullet hole was always smaller than the missile), and that the body had been turned over but only after several hours (as shown by the adherence of what the doctor referred to as gravel).[2]

If the jury did not see this testimony as tedious and repetitious, it may have seen it as too consistent, as if the witnesses were reading from the same script. Such testimony was certainly advantageous to Walter Stoll. After Dr. Johnston's testimony, he was not surprised by anything the following physicians said.

Stoll quickly moved Dr. Burgess away from his position regarding the adherence of gravel, first having him agree that the whole question was one of "common experience." Then Stoll said, "In your experience haven't you observed this to be generally the rule, a man is shot [and] killed instantly and he falls heavily on his face or back and he is picked up with his clothes and hands covered with dirt, in case he falls upon the ground if he was turned over, do not they adhere, don't they remain there?" "Probably does," answered Burgess.[3] Then Stoll showed how this witness's experience and opportunity to be aware of relevant facts were limited. Because Burgess had never seen the body, he could only assume a set of facts, and he had never taken modern projectiles (such as a .30-30 slug) out of a human body.[4] He had never hunted Wyoming's large game and thus had never observed "entirely different" wounds from the same caliber of bullet. Dr. Burgess agreed further that "you might have quite a large wound made by a comparatively small projectile" because of a bullet's deformity caused by going through clothing. The doctor also agreed that it was "laid down in the books" that often very large projectiles made very small wounds and that very small projectiles made large wounds.[5] It was impeccable cross-examination by Walter Stoll.

The defense attorneys did a good job rehabilitating Burgess on redirect examination, but their situation was similar to what it had been with Dr. Lewis. The jury had just heard the witness say exactly opposite things.

The *Denver Post* bluntly concluded: "Dr. W. A. Burgess proved a poor witness on cross-examination."[6] Burgess seems a particularly unfortunate choice for the final medical witness, the physician whose words would probably be remembered best. The defense attorneys had probably believed Burgess would do better than he did. It appears that during his cross-examination Stoll detected that the doctor was not doing well, and so kept piling on questions producing admissions inconsistent with the testimony of previous physicians. Whatever the reasons for Burgess's poor performance, his testimony probably sealed the fate of the defense contention that .30-30 bullets could not have been the ones that struck Willie Nickell. Indeed, a *Post* sub-headline read, "But Most Observers Doubt That the Caliber of the Bullet Has Been Determined."[7]

Following Dr. Burgess was another physician but not one from Wyoming. Dr. W. L. Davis introduced himself to the jury as a physician and surgeon from Denver and said that at 5:30 A.M., Monday, September 30, 1901, he had treated one "T. Horn" for a fracture of the lower jaw.[8] Davis said that as a result of his treatment, Tom Horn could not speak but could only communicate in writing, a condition that endured for two weeks.[9] John Lacey's final question was to ask when the carnival began in Denver. "It began on the first of October," said the doctor.[10]

Dr. Davis's testimony seemed like a coup for the defense. Frank Mulock had testified that he had seen Tom Horn during the week of the carnival, that the carnival had already commenced, and the incident was not before the carnival). Robert Cowsley, another of the Denver witnesses, said he had seen Horn during the carnival, "the first week of October."[11] And Roy Campbell had testified that he had seen Horn "about that time" (during the carnival week), although he couldn't say the exact date.[12] The defense obviously intended Dr. Davis's testimony to support a declaration in final argument that the testimony of the three Denver witnesses could not possibly be correct because Horn could not have spoken to them during carnival week.

Yet again Walter Stoll faced a defense witness who appeared to have seriously undercut his case, but he was well prepared for this witness. Perhaps he had grown suspicious when the defense had so persistently asked the Denver witnesses whether the encounter with Tom Horn took place during carnival week. Producing a *Denver Post* newspaper dated September 30, 1901 (containing an account of the official program), Stoll asked the doctor to review it, with an idea toward refreshing his recollection. The defense immediately and forcefully objected to this tactic, but Judge Scott allowed the prosecutor to ask questions relating to dates. Stoll asked Davis if the carnival ceremonies began on Monday night (September 30). The doctor said he could not say, but then Stoll said to Davis, "Carnival week was understood as the week beginning September 29, 1901?" Evidently looking at the *Denver Post* just shown him, the doctor said, "That would be the first day of the week."[13] Davis's response was a bit ambiguous, but, surprisingly, Lacey made no redirect examination, perhaps sensing he could only make the situation worse.

By his cross-examination, Stoll had formed a plausible chronology mostly fitting the testimony of the three Denver men. Stoll could fairly argue that these three men had met Horn the night of Saturday, September 28, on the eve of the carnival, which began on September 29, and that during the next evening, September 29, Horn had his unfortunate encounter leading to his broken jaw that had to be treated the morning of September 30. It was in fact established that Horn came to Denver on September 28, 1902.[14] Still, Lacey could argue that the alleged meeting with the three Denver men could not have happened during carnival week as the three witnesses had testified.

Closely observing this testimony, the *Denver Post* noted: "The witness (Dr. Davis) was forced to admit that he had made a mistake when he said the carnival began Tuesday, October 1."[15] This was not exactly correct, although the *Post* correspondent did have the advantage of watching the witness testify and Davis may well have presented his testimony—by such things as pauses or voice inflections not appearing in the transcript—so that the *Post* comment was accurate. The *Post* also said that the Denver men had testified to the date of their meeting with Tom Horn, when, in fact, none of them was sure of the date of their meeting with him. It appears that the reporter was not directly following the actual testimony but constructing a plausible scenario from the testimony. The position of the *Denver Post* as to the impact of Davis's testimony was certainly clear. The paper's headline read: "Denver Testimony Worthless in Defense of Tom Horn and Coble's Effort Was in Vain." Stoll's cross-examination had once again weakened what seemed to be a deadly assault by the defense, but to what extent would only be known when the jury rendered its verdict.

The defense then called John Wallace, the former partner of Charles Miller in the Elkhorn stable. Miller had earlier testified that Tom Horn had brought a large bay horse into the stable in July 1901. After Lacey pushed Miller to produce an account book, Miller had read a book entry saying, "Tom Horn, July 20th to July 30th, ten days." On cross-examination, though,

Miller had said the entry had not been made when the horse was brought in but when the horse had been taken out. Thus, the entry had been made from memory. Miller also said that his partner Wallace had made the entry.[16]

Wallace testified that the handwriting on the Horn entry was his, but when Lacey asked him if this entry refreshed his memory, Wallace said, "I cannot say more than the book shows it." He added that he and his partner had talked it over and "figured it was ten days." They concluded, said Wallace, that "we spoke of it as being a week ago Saturday." Wallace said he was positive he had heard about the killing of Willie Nickell before Horn brought the horse in.[17]

Stoll, apparently surprised when Charles Miller read the "Tom Horn, July 20th—July 30th" entry, was not surprised by Wallace's testimony. The prosecutor first established that Miller and Wallace had just taken over the Elkhorn stable in early July. "Things were somewhat at 6's and 7's for some time?" asked Stoll. Wallace replied, "The business was a little new to us yes." "And a horse brought there by anybody was not entered at the time it came in?" asked Stoll. "No, sir," replied Wallace.[18]

Stoll then pursued a short string of questions that undercut the benefit of Wallace's testimony to the defense.

Q. So far as that is concerned, your entry may have been so far as the facts are concerned, a day or two out of the way, is that right?
A. I don't think it is possible to be two days out of the way.
Q. It might have been a day, as a matter of fact might have come there on the 19th? You don't think you would have a mistake of 2 days?
A. I do not think we made a mistake at all, but [it] is possible that we made a mistake."[19]

The *Laramie Boomerang* probably summarized the overall effect of Wallace's testimony best when it said: "On cross examination he (Wallace) admitted that the books were badly mixed up and he couldn't tell much by them."[20]

The defense then called Willard S. Carpenter, who said he was in the ranching and stock business. Carpenter told the jury that on July 18, 1901, he had gone to John Coble's Bosler Ranch to "run a hay gang." He had been there the morning of July 20, when he saw Tom Horn riding a black horse with a roached mane. Horn, said Carpenter, was looking for a horse that he could ride to Laramie, and he selected a large, dark bay horse "from out of the pasture." The horse looked fresh to Carpenter, who said it "had not been rode lately."[21]

Surprisingly, Stoll's cross-examination was not extensive, and the reporting newspapers did not single out Carpenter's testimony as significant. This testimony, however, would seem to have strongly supported Horn's statements that he did not ride the large bay horse into Laramie until July 20. It is possible that the bay horse was taken out of the Elkhorn stable after being put there on July 18, but this possibility seems to conflict with Carpenter's testimony that the horse was fresh on the morning of July 20.

The defense next called Duncan Clark, the former superintendent of the Iron Mountain Ranch Company, which included Coble's Bosler Ranch and two other Iron Mountain ranches. Clark lent support to Willard Carpenter's testimony.[22] He told of a large dark bay horse called Pacer owned by John Coble, with the Lazy TY brand. Clark said the horse had been at the ranch on Friday, July 19, 1901, and had been put in a pasture. Clark also said that he had gone into Laramie on July 20 and had met Tom Horn there, although he (Clark) had not seen the horse Pacer then. Clark testified that Pacer was "very seldom rode, he was fat" and that if "he was rode very fast, he would sweat considerably."[23]

Lacey then asked Clark about sweaters worn by Horn. Clark said he was quite familiar with Horn's clothes, but the only sweater he had ever seen Horn wear was a dun-colored sweater.[24]

Prosecutor Stoll immediately pointed out that Clark had been a "superintendent" for John Coble, obviously to demonstrate that Clark might still be deeply aligned with Coble, Tom Horn's good friend and sponsor, the man who handled all of Horn's business dealings. Most of the jury probably already knew that, but it is rarely prudent for an attorney to make assumptions about what a jury knows. Stoll pointed out that in his coroner's inquest testimony, Clark had testified that he "had no particular reason to observe what particular article of clothing he (Horn) had." Clark acknowledged that he "never paid much attention." Stoll also noted that other horses were branded with the Lazy TY brand, although Clark said, "not a great many."[25] With this last area of inquiry, Stoll finished his cross-examination. Once again, Stoll did not mount a strong challenge to a defense witness whose testimony seemed very favorable to the defendant.

John Lacey then called Alfred Cook, the sheriff of Albany County, to the stand. Lacey had Cook testify that in his investigation relating to the Willie Nickell murder, he had learned that the horse Tom Horn had left in the Elkhorn stable was "Mr. Coble's private saddle horse, the horse he calls Pacer." Lacey pushed Cook to state what he had learned about when Horn's horse had arrived in Laramie, but the prosecution objected on the grounds that the question sought hearsay, and its objection was sustained.[26]

Sheriff Cook was followed to the stand by T. F. Burke, the defense attorney, called by his co-counsel. Burke said that when he had visited the scene of the homicide he had found that the ground was "disintegrated granite ... of a coarse type" and that there was quite a bit of cactus, with "very little vegetation in connection with the soil." Burke gave his opinion that going across this soil in bare feet "would be utterly impossible unless it would be right in the road where the wheel tracks are." Burke also spoke of rocks sticking up and said he thought it impossible for anyone to see a person in the draw from the road.[27] T. Blake Kennedy followed Burke to the stand and said that he had examined the ground and his testimony was "the same" as Burke's.[28]

To a modern lawyer, this seems a strange exercise. Stoll did not bother to cross-examine either of these defense attorneys, probably trusting the jury to recognize that their representation of Tom Horn made them deeply biased witnesses.[29]

Frank Stone took the stand and testified that on July 21, 1901, he had come to Laramie "for some hay hands," and while there had met Tom Horn. The two had gone drinking and that evening roomed together. Horn was "pretty well intoxicated," said Stone, and Stone had to help him get into bed. He took off Horn's shoes and stockings and did not notice anything about his feet. Stone assured defense attorney Burke that if Horn's feet had been cut or bleeding, he "undoubtedly" would have noticed that, but they were not. Stone also testified that he had never seen Horn wearing a blue sweater and he had never known of his having one.[30]

In his cross-examination, Stoll challenged the witness about an event that took place in the office of Mortimer N. Grant, the Laramie justice of the peace. Stoll asked Stone if he had not been in the offices of Grant and, in the presence of two other men, if he had admitted that it was July 19, 1901, when he had spent the evening drinking with Tom Horn. Stone admitted he had spoken to Grant but denied that he had said he was in Laramie with Horn on July 19.[31]

Otto Plaga followed Frank Stone to the stand. The *Denver Times* described Plaga as a "dapper, dandy sort of a cowboy," and the *Denver Post* character-ized the witness as a "lean, lanky boy; black-eyed and considered a great flirt with the girls of the Iron Mountain Country."[32] Like Horn, Plaga was a successful rodeo competitor. He was reported to have shined in Cheyenne's 1901 Frontier Days—"first money in the 'breaking contest.'" It was also written that Frank Stone rode an "outlaw horse" in the same competition, and that Duncan Clark "did fine work in the fancy cattle roping."[33] Plaga was to play a key role as the principal support of an alibi for Horn.

Plaga testified that he was twenty-four, had known Tom Horn since 1894, and that on July 18, 1901, he was "up in the hills," about eight miles from where he lived in the Iron Mountain area, a spot that was about twenty-five miles "in a westerly direction" from the Nickell place. He was there in the morning, about eight o'clock, "gathering cattle and prospecting."[34]

Plaga told the jury he had seen Horn riding along. He knew Horn's horse, a "black brown horse" weighing about nine hundred pounds, with the brand CAP and a roached mane, and he recognized the horse when he saw it. Plaga said he was only about 150 yards from Horn, and he could tell that the horse was very fresh. Horn didn't speak to him or see him, said the witness. Plaga was higher than Horn, he testified, and during the time he saw Horn he (Plaga) was "cracking quartz rock." Plaga watched Horn for two to three minutes and later mentioned to his stepfather that he had seen Horn.[35]

In his cross-examination, Stoll asked several questions about the "prospecting" that Plaga said he had been doing. Plaga said he intended to make a mining claim, but there was no claim on record when he was working on quartz rock, and he did not make a claim later. But Plaga still said he went to the place where he saw Horn both to prospect and get some cattle. Stoll could not get the witness to modify the time or the day he had seen Horn. Stoll asked Plaga to show on a map where he was, but Plaga said he could not read the map. Stoll did get Plaga to admit that he was "very friendly" with Horn for a long time and that they had ridden together a great deal. So, Stoll asked, "why didn't you call to him, or say something to him as he was passing by?" Plaga replied that he "was cracking this quartz" and "wanted to keep that to myself."[36]

When he completed his testimony, Otto Plaga left the impression that he was one more effective witness who Stoll had not seriously challenged. As the *Denver Republican* remarked, Plaga's alibi testimony "appeared to be convincing."[37] It is hard to say why Stoll did not cross-examine Duncan Clark, Frank Stone, or Otto Plaga as aggressively as he had some of the earlier witnesses. All were close friends of Tom Horn, having known him since Horn first came to Wyoming, having ridden the range with him, and having competed in Frontier Days with him. During the time Horn's friends testified, the *Denver Post* interviewed a number of Iron Mountain men, who, the *Post* said, talked freely in Horn's favor. Even after Kels Nickell's boy was murdered, the paper said, "the feeling of the ranchmen and others from the Iron Mountain country against [Kels] Nickell is still of the bitterest kind." One man declared: "Show me a man, woman or child in that country [Iron Mountain] that does not stand up for Tom Horn, and I will show you a cattle thief."[38] Horn's friends would not be less supportive and surely tried to testify as favorably as they could in Horn's favor, possibly even to the point of perjury. Perhaps Stoll felt he could not make much headway against such men and he depended upon the jury's general knowledge as to who was close to Tom Horn, and thus, whose testimony might be suspect. Still, such a tactic was risky. Stoll had to have been concerned that the members of the jury shared the Iron Mountain attitudes and were not skeptical at all of the testimony of Horn's friends.

Raymond Hencke followed Plaga to the stand and supported his stepson's statement that on July 18, 1901, Otto told him he had just seen Tom Horn. Hencke added that Deputy Warlamount had come to his house shortly after Willie Nickell was killed, and that, after Warlamount left, Tom Horn was mentioned in connection with the boy's killing.[39] Stoll's first question was whether Hencke's stepson had told Warlamount anything about seeing Horn. Hencke said he did not "know anything about that." Stoll asked Hencke why he had not said anything to Warlamount about Otto's having seen Horn the morning of Willie Nickell's murder. Hencke said he did not know about the Tom Horn connection until Warlamount was gone, but he also admitted that he had not later written to Warlamount or otherwise contacted him.[40] This was an effective line of questions from the prosecutor. Everybody in the Iron Mountain country knew that Horn was charged with the murder of Willie Nickell in January 1902. If Otto Plaga and Raymond Hencke were aware of evidence apparently exonerating Tom Horn, why had they not come to the authorities with it?

The defense then called A. F. Whitman for the purpose of testifying about feuds between the Nickell family and other people in the Iron Mountain area. Stoll successfully objected to such evidence, but Lacey used the opportunity to announce (apparently in the presence of the jury) that he desired to prove that there were feuds "not with one but with two or three immediate neighbors that resided there in the vicinity and the character of the feuds and that there had been threats of killing on both sides, and that both Mr. Nickell and Miller had been bound over to keep the peace to one another."[41]

Whitman was an interesting choice to forward this evidence because he certainly had disagreements with Kels Nickell. At one time, a meeting had been held at Whitman's home at which "it was proposed to hang Nickell." Also, during the night of October 14, 1902, Whitman had attempted to cut across railroad yards over which Kels Nickell was watching. Nickell had seen him and attacked him, injuring Whitman.[42] During the coroner's inquest after Willie Nickell's death, Whitman had acknowledged a good deal of talk against Kels Nickell because of his bringing sheep into the area (that it was an "unwise" thing to do), but he had agreed that in the talk among neighbors he had never heard anybody speak of intending to inflict an injury upon Kels.[43] Whitman's testimony to the coroner's jury was obviously inconsistent with his knowledge of the true attitude against Nickell.

Then, at 3:44 P.M., October 17, 1902, the defense called the defendant, Tom Horn, to the stand.[44] Horn's testimony had not been expected that day, and the crowd "had dwindled away at the afternoon recess." Nevertheless, "a ripple of excitement passed over the courtroom" when Lacey called out the name "Tom Horn." With that, "The cattle detective walked to the defense stand amid a deathlike silence," took his seat, and faced the jury.[45]

Willie Nickell (*Denver Post*, October 7, 1902)

Kels and Mary Nickell (*Denver Post*, October 13, 1902)

Fred Nickell and Julie Nickell Cook (*Denver Post*, October 15, 1902)

Glendolene Kimmell (courtesy American Heritage Center, University of Wyoming)

Walter Stoll (*Denver Times*, October 10, 1902)

Amos Barber (courtesy Wyoming State Archives)

John Coble (courtesy American Heritage Center, University of Wyoming)

Early photograph of Tom Horn (courtesy American Heritage Center, University of Wyoming)

Joe LeFors (courtesy American Heritage Center, University of Wyoming)

Deputy R. A. Proctor and Sheriff E. J. Smalley (*Denver Post*, October 11, 1902)

John W. Lacey (*Denver Times*, October 10, 1902)

Polly Pry (*Denver Post*, October 15, 1902)

The Laramie County district courtroom where the case of
State v. Horn was tried (*Denver Post*, October 15, 1902)

Judge Richard Scott (*Denver Post*, October 17,
1902)

The *State v. Horn* jury (*Denver Post*, October 12, 1902)

148

Peter Bergerson (*Denver Republican*, October 14, 1902)

Photograph of an 1894 Winchester .30-30 rifle in the same configuration as Tom Horn's 1894 Winchester .30-30 (courtesy of Washakie Museum and Cultural Center)

Edward "Doc" Moore, country fiddler, and others (*Denver Post*, October 16, 1902)

"Dawn in Wyoming!" (*Denver Post*, October 26, 1902)

Laramie County jail, about November 20, 1903, the date of Horn's execution (courtesy American Heritage Center, University of Wyoming)

Tom Horn, with men escorting him back to jail, August 9, 1903 (courtesy Wyoming State Archives, [Meyers, Neg. 625])

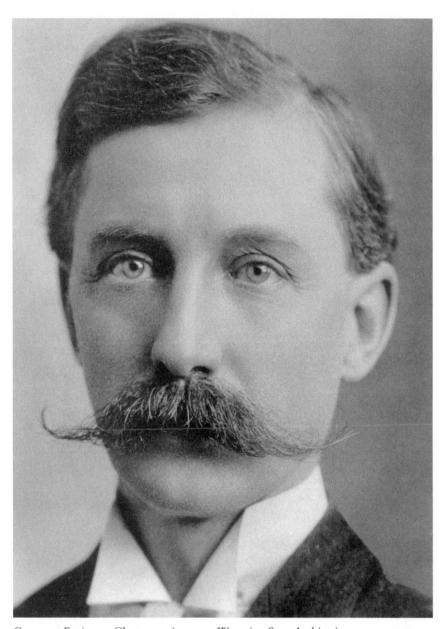

Governor Fenimore Chatterton (courtesy Wyoming State Archives)

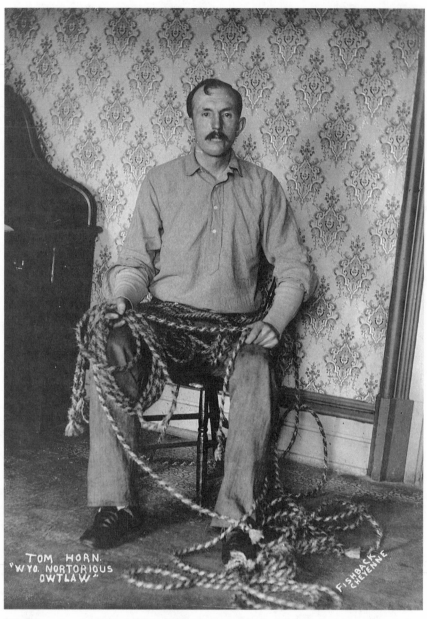

Tom Horn, in what historian Larry Ball refers to as the last photo before Horn's execution (courtesy Robert G. McCubbin, Santa Fe, N.Mex.)

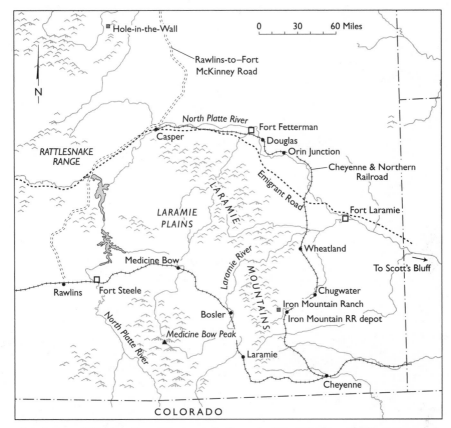

Southeastern Wyoming (showing present-day Laramie, Albany, Goshen, and Platte Counties).
Cartography by Bill Nelson. Copyright © 2016 by the University of Oklahoma Press.

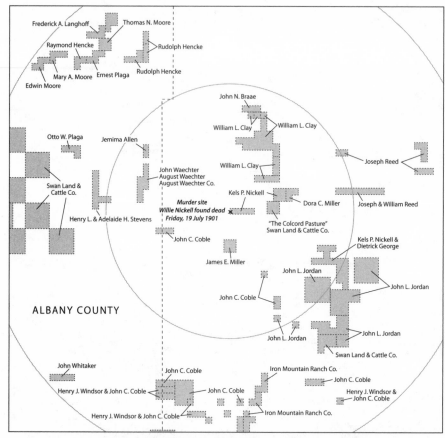

Nickell property in 1901, Iron Mountain region, with surrounding ownerships. Cartography by Bill Nelson. Copyright © 2016 by the University of Oklahoma Press.

Tom Horn Takes the Stand

When Tom Horn was suddenly called to the witness chair, he "responded with fierce promptitude and smiled at the excitement."[1] When he sat, he appeared to be completely comfortable. Horn crossed one leg over the other and "rolled a quid of tobacco from one side of his mouth to the other." And when he spoke, the *Cheyenne Daily Leader* said, Horn "gave his answers in clear, distinct tones, with a well-modulated voice."[2]

Horn declared his residence as "the county jail" but said that before July 1901, he had made his home at Coble's ranch, working for the Iron Mountain Ranch Company. His business, said Horn, was to "ride on the range alone and look after the interests of the company." He said he was "reconned [*sic*] . . . by the people in general as a stock detective." The purpose of his work, he said, was, "as closely as I possible [*sic*] can to shove all the cows and calves that I found—you understand this country is all fenced—wherever I found cows and calves belonging to the company in any one else's pasture, I drove them home to brand them—that is the nature of the work. I also keep as good track of the people in the country as I can that are killing and marketing beef; everything of that nature that will have a tendency to protect the interests of the company."[3]

Horn recounted all his movements from about the middle of July 1901, when he stopped at Billy Clay's on a Sunday evening (July 14). He said he had spent that night and part of the next day at Clay's and then in the afternoon gone to Clay's pasture, then through Nickell's pasture to Coble's north pasture. That night he had gone to Jim Miller's ranch and stopped there, Horn said, because Miller had told him that "if [I] ever come in his neighborhood to be sure and call."[4]

The next day, Horn said, he "didn't do anything in particular." He said he "laid around and went fishing in the front part of the day; laid around and went up the creek to see where Mr. Nickell's sheep were located." The reason he went to look at Nickell's sheep was to see if they were in Coble's pasture. He found they were not, so he went back to Miller's where he stayed the night. Horn acknowledged that while at Miller's he talked mostly with "a young lady by the name of Miss Kimmell."[5] As he pronounced these words, he did so with a sly grin that, commented one correspondent, "would have made Miss Kimmell turn state's evidence on the spot had she been there to see it."[6] The next morning (Wednesday, July 17, 1901), he said, he had departed the Miller place shortly after Miss Kimmell had left to teach school.[7]

Horn testified that he was riding a horse branded CAP on the shoulder (and named CAP), a small, very dark brown or black horse with a roached mane. The only firearm he was carrying was a .30-30 Winchester, and he carried nothing else but field glasses. He could not recall what he was wearing. Horn said he never had a sweater. "Sweaters are worn in the winter time. This was the middle of summer."[8]

When he left the Miller ranch, Horn said, he had headed directly away from Nickell's ranch. He "swung around and crossed the South Chug [the south fork of Chugwater Creek] below Nickell's ranch." His purpose, Horn said, was to check out a pasture called "the Colcord Place" and see if Nickell had any sheep there, but he found "not a sign of sheep there." So then Horn had proceeded back toward the Laramie Plains, going through Nickell's pasture and then over Clay's pasture (Clay's land was generally due north of Nickell's). Horn said that at no time was he going "toward this gate [where] Willie Nickell was killed." He said he was going in the opposite direction from the Nickell's house.[9]

That evening (Wednesday), Horn said, he saw Johnny Bray "somewhere about sundown." Horn supposed that Bray was going home, but he only watched him for a minute. Horn acknowledged that he had been in plain sight, "but it occurred to me that he (Bray) didn't see me." The cattle detective said he wanted to get "on the other side of the branch of the Sabylle [Sybille]." He explained that there was a "continuous line of settlements on the Sabylle," meaning there were several pastures he had to work. Horn said he did not want the owners of these pastures to see him looking the pastures over, because they "might be disposed to shove cattle" elsewhere before he came along. That night, Horn said, he had slept on one of the short tributaries of Sabylle Creek.[10] His purpose, he said, was to head into the upper Sabylle country, which was, in general, many miles west and north of the Nickell place.[11]

When John Lacey asked him about his investigations Horn replied: "I don't have any particular place to go, or any particular time. I don't work under any particular instructions at any time. I am supposed to go when I please and where I please, and how I please. The boss or foreman of the ranch, the manager of the ranch leaves that entirely to myself." The morning of Thursday, July 18, 1901 (when Willie Nickell was shot), Horn said he chose to work through pastures and work "on back towards the Coble Ranch."[12]

Horn testified that on that Thursday morning he was in the vicinity of Marble Top Mountain. "I was all day all around there on some of the forks of the Sabylle, and even up as far as the Divide, at some of the heads of Chug I was in that country all day." It was all rough country, said Horn, although "if a man wants to ride rapidly, he can ride rapidly." Horn described his actions as going back and forth. "I naturally go all over the country, or else I would not know what is going on." Horn said that on Thursday night he had slept at some spring, which he could only describe as "a little spring that is really one of the very headwaters of the Sabylle." He said he had intended to work himself to the Fitzmorris place and then back home.[13]

On Friday morning, July 19, Horn said, he "went down close to the Fitzmorris place." He did not see Fitzmorris but with his field glasses did see a man from a distance of about one-half mile. Horn testified that he first saw the man from nine to ten o'clock. "I saw this man all that day off and on."[14]

Horn said that on Friday night he was "still on the Sabylle," on the tributary of another fork, about ten to twelve miles from the home ranch, Bosler. Saturday morning, Horn said, he went to the home ranch, arriving there "somewhere around the middle of the forenoon."[15] When he arrived he found Jack Ryan and his wife in the house, and Carpenter putting up hay.[16]

During the entire time of his excursion, proceeding from the home place to the Miller place, and back to the home place, Horn said he rode his black horse CAP and never changed horses. Horn said that after he arrived at the ranch, he wanted to go to Laramie where he had an appointment, and he talked with Carpenter about this. Carpenter told him that the only horse at the ranch that was any good was John Coble's horse, Pacer. Pacer, said Horn, was a "big, fat snorty horse," branded Lazy TY. Horn described the horse as a handsome, very dark bay horse with "a little touch of the weed, as we call it." Horn first had something to eat and then on that Saturday, the same day he got into the ranch, he rode Pacer to Laramie and took the horse to the Elkhorn barn.[17]

Lacey asked Horn if he took the horse out again for the next week. Horn replied that he had not taken the horse out, that it was Frank Stone who took the horse out. Horn said he did not leave Laramie from July 20 to July 30, and that, when he afterward did, it was on a two-wheeled cart when he went up the Little Laramie with Frank Stone.[18]

Lacey then proceeded to counter every aspect of the state's case, asking about Horn's talk with LeFors, and "what it was that you and LeFors were doing." "We were just joshing one another," Horn said, "throwing bouquets at one another you might call it." When asked whether he intended to seriously admit he had killed Willie Nickell, Horn said, "I never had anything to do with the killing of Willie Nickell; I never had any cause to kill him. And I never killed him. He (LeFors) was joshing me about it and I did not object." Horn added, "There was nothing serious about the talk at all; it was all a josh all the way through. There was no concealment. If they [Les Snow and Charlie Ohnhaus] were there at the table I would probably have gone on all the same, I don't think that would have made any difference."[19]

Lacey asked about the men who had testified "as to some talk you had during the first week of October as they put it, the festival week in Denver"? Horn said the talk never took place, because during the first week of October he was in St. Luke's Hospital in Denver with a broken jaw and couldn't speak. He could only communicate by writing.[20]

Horn denied that the blue sweater was his. When it was first presented to him he said he was asked whether it was his and he had said, "I suppose it is that sweater they wrote me about. . . . I said all sweaters look alike to me." "I said to the jailer if that is mine, you had better have it washed; I never saw it before or I never seen it since."[21]

When asked the truth about his being in Laramie on July 18 (as told by Frank Irwin), Horn said: "I was not there." When Lacey asked him about the testimony of Ed Titus that he drank with Horn the night of July 19, Horn said, "He did not drink with me on the night of the 19th—I did not go into Laramie until the 20th."[22]

With that the direct testimony of Tom Horn concluded. Unquestionably Horn did himself a great deal of good by his testimony. The unanimous opinion of the covering newspapers was that Horn had done well, casting grave doubt on the prosecution's case. The *Cheyenne Daily Leader* said Horn had given a "clear, convincing story explaining his every act" and asserted that the story Horn told "was a straightforward tale that carried conviction to the minds of all who heard it." The newspaper acknowledged that the tale of a man accused of a crime "must be taken with grains of allowance." "Yet," said the *Leader*, "Horn's story dovetails perfectly with the other evidence brought out not only by the defense but with many material facts established by the prosecution."[23] The *Denver Republican* said Horn established "an almost perfect alibi." His testimony "changed the aspect of the case in favor of the accused man" and "appeared to be convincing."[24] The *Republican's* reporter cited bystander remarks to the effect that Horn did not reach Laramie until July 20, that Willie Nickell's wounds were caused by a weapon larger than Horn's .30-30, and that Horn didn't make the comments in Denver attributed to him. Readers were also told, however, that if Horn was acquitted in Cheyenne, Colorado authorities stood ready to charge him with the killings in Routt County (Brown's Hole).[25] The *Rocky Mountain News* said that putting Horn on the stand was a "masterstroke with but one or two lapses." The "lapses," said the paper, occurred when Horn made attempts at humor. "The occasion is too grave a one for jesting."[26] Even the *Denver Post,* which had viewed the prosecution's efforts in a favorable light, said that now "the belief is general that the jury ... will report a disagreement."[27]

Horn completed his direct testimony just a few minutes before five o'clock, and the court was adjourned until the next morning, when he would face cross-examination by Stoll. Horn's direct testimony, "under the friendly auspices of his counsel," had gone well. But the "crisis of the trial," said the *Denver Post*, "is how the accused man will sustain his cross-examination."[28]

CHAPTER SEVENTEEN

Cross-Examination

When Tom Horn was called to the stand in the late afternoon of October 17, the move surprised the few remaining spectators in the courtroom. There had only been rumors that he would be called. The next day, when it was well known that Horn would testify and be cross-examined by Walter Stoll, the courtroom was crowded. People began arriving at 8:00 A.M., standing in line at the courthouse doors, and "every inch of space in the room was occupied."[1] The *Laramie Boomerang* said hundreds of people had to be turned away.[2] Those who did get in must have been disappointed at first, because the day did not begin with Horn's cross-examination. Instead the defense called Robert D. Stockton, a hotelkeeper from Denver, to impugn Frank Muloch, one of the three Denver men who testified to Horn's having made incriminating statements.

Stockton, who had been a deputy sheriff, testified that he had known Muloch for ten to twelve years and knew Muloch's generally poor reputation in Denver for truth and veracity ("It is very bad," he said). When the witness offered comments on Muloch's general moral character, Stoll objected. Judge Scott ruled the objection proper, because impeachment was limited to truth and veracity (meaning that the defense could present evidence showing only that Muloch could not be trusted to tell the truth, and *not* that his general moral character was bad).[3]

When Stoll tried to show that two factions in Denver had been battling for the past eight or nine years and that Muloch, as part of one of the factions, had been arrested by the other, Stockton grew feisty. Resisting Stoll's suggestions, he found ways to interject comments such as "The only thing I know, he was wearing a star and grafting on the prostitutes; he was arrested for that and fined," and "He has been in so many disreputable things I am satisfied it was not all factions, at all." Stockton even declared that he had a copy of Muloch's arrests taken from the police court, but Stoll refused to let him present this paper. Stoll did manage to push Stockton to admit that Muloch may have been a deputy sheriff of one of the factions and that he (Stockton) did not know the cause of Muloch's arrests.[4] However effective Stoll's questioning, Stockton was clearly a dangerous witness, one of the few Stoll did not best on cross-examination. Those in the courtroom may have overlooked the fine points of Stockton's testimony, however, because his appearance as a witness, though brief, delayed Tom Horn's testimony, and it was Horn's cross-examination that the audience wanted to hear.

Horn came to the stand about 9:25 A.M. that Saturday, October 19, 1902. When Stoll began asking questions, his examination was "listened to with a silence that was remarkable in such a crowd."[5] Questions and answers were "conducted without sensational features." That was not Stoll's way. Instead, the prosecuting attorney "talked to Horn as if he was holding a personal conversation."[6] Although not "sensational," Stoll's examination was deadly earnest, described as "long, minute and searching."[7]

Stoll immediately hit Horn with one of Horn's statements to Joe LeFors in a January 1, 1902 letter, in which Horn said, "I do not care how big or how bad his men are, I can handle them, they can scarcely be any worse than the Brown's (Hole) gang, and I stopped the cow stealing there in one summer." Stoll asked Horn whether this statement referred to "the well known fact that there were two men killed down in Brown's hole while you were there and in this way cow stealing was stopped?" Defense counsel immediately objected to the question "as it makes assumption to men being killed." Judge Scott agreed with the objection and Stoll rephrased his question, omitting the references to the two men being killed and just asking what Horn's statement referred to. Horn told Stoll that his answer would "necessarily need somewhat of an explanation to the first question that you asked me," and Stoll invited him to finish his answer.[8] Horn replied:

You asked me in the first place, if my work was more than that of the ordinary stock detective's work, I said it was[;] the reason I said it was this—Ordinarily a man out handling stock in all manner of shape and form in connection with their detective work, the ordinary detective as I understand them are men who go around and put up jobs on this man and that man and some other man, and that is something I never have done. I have got out where the stealing was going on and remained continuously in the country where it is a matter of stealing calves, I associate myself so directly with the neighborhood that stealing cannot go on without my being present; if they steal I will catch them in the act of stealing on account of being there[;] consequently if a man is caught stealing he gets out of it the best way he can.[9]

Horn embellished on his answer and in doing so announced his method when answering questions: "Some of those questions in the answering yes or no would reflect considerably on me, where an explanation would give a better understanding."[10] Horn proceeded to give elaborate explanations time and again throughout his testimony. Reporters closely noted Horn's testimonial methods. "In his replies Horn uses a vast amount of verbiage and often makes long explanations of his statements," noted the *Cheyenne Daily Leader.* "He has a peculiar habit of elevating his eyebrows in talking, that wrinkles his forehead as if he were worried, but this is a habit that means nothing."[11] Said the *Denver Post:* "His testimony did not come spontaneously. He had too many explanations that he was always willing to offer. His manner was scarcely natural." Horn's answers, the *Post* added, "were slowly put in speech; he was only too anxious to explain anything that might be in doubt, but he took his time in doing so."[12]

Walter Stoll did not push Horn to shorten his answers. It seemed, rather, that Stoll wanted Horn to elaborate, and Horn certainly obliged. Stoll inquired further about the "character of your business." He questioned whether Horn filed complaints, reported the commission of crimes, and had people tried or "avoided that and avoided the matter of witness fees." Horn replied by referring to the 1893 Langhoff case, saying, "I can give you an illustration of what I have done in this country of which you are familiar, that of catching one of the most notorious cow gangs in the country, the Langhoff outfit; they were five of them if I remember distinctly engaged in the killing of cattle, calves, and I caught them directly in the act at 9 o'clock at night and just gathered them in myself and took them off to jail; that was all there was to them; there was no expense to the county or the people that hired me."[13]

Stoll wanted to know whether Horn had arrested men since the Lang-hoff case and brought them to trial in Cheyenne. Horn evaded the question but eventually had to admit that since the Langhoff matter, there had been no complaints and no arrests. Horn said that when he found people stealing, he took cattle away from them and turned the cattle back to his employers but had not had anyone prosecuted. The defendant said he "would like to tell why." Horn than went on at great length (most of a full page in the transcript) explaining about the reputation of the Lang-hoff outfit, that he caught them and had eleven witnesses, but of the six people tried, only one was convicted and he was soon pardoned. Since the Langhoff business, Horn explained, his method had been simply to frustrate theft by his presence ("identifying myself with the country"), which "would have a tendency preventing him [a thief from] stealing any more and it would also save that calf in question."[14]

Stoll asked Horn what the purpose of his visit to the Miller's ranch had been, "to see whether somebody had stolen calves, or was it to ride in among the people there and inspire terror by your presence and actions?" Horn ignored the reference to "terror" and told Stoll that he was in the area because "Nickell had moved a bunch of sheep into that country and I heard rumors of considerable kick and growl in that country." He said he had wanted to satisfy himself that Nickell had not been trespassing on Coble's ground. Then Horn qualified his answer, saying that he had only spent two hours "looking after Nickell's sheep," while for ten days he had looked over pastures, meaning investigating theft or misplacement of cattle.[15]

Stoll asked Horn whether he had looked over the pastures of William Clay, the man with whom Horn always stayed when he was in the area (and a friend of Horn's). Stoll's apparent purpose was to illuminate the incongruity that Horn would conduct an investigation of a friend and ally such as Clay. Horn said, however, that he had ridden through Clay's pastures several times and that he was investigating Clay. The prosecutor sought to learn why Horn had gone to Miller's ranch on Wednesday. Horn at first avoided giving him an answer but finally said that he had no object in going to Miller's ranch and that this visit was his only one to Miller's place.[16]

Stoll then sought explicit detail about where Horn had gone after leaving the Miller place. The descriptions found in the trial transcript are ambiguous because the map references in the testimony are unclear, but the newspaper reports are helpful. Horn seemed to say that he had proceeded generally from the Miller place to the north and west (he zigzagged, going through Nickell's pasture at one point, where he saw no one).[17] Horn reached the "Colcord place" Wednesday evening, he said, when he saw John Bray, and then he went three or four miles and stopped.[18] Horn showed the jury on a map where he stopped, and it was apparently only a few miles west and north of the Nickell ranch, lying between the Jim Allen and Gus Waechter places. Horn said that he had first stopped at Mud Springs, about a mile or two from Bray's ranch, where he had earlier left some bacon and bread, tying it in a tree. He had then proceeded to a "little spring that runs in the Sybille."[19]

Horn testified that he got up the next morning (Thursday, July 18) "somewhere about six or seven o'clock," and got on his way without eating breakfast. His statements were rambling and, as Horn said, were a guess. Horn's testimony about his Thursday morning activity was also rambling, although he did say that he worked pastures. Horn testified that before coming to Miller's ranch, he had earlier worked pastures of the "small ranchmen," and so on Thursday morning he had only looked at the pastures of the Two Bar and John Coble. Horn said he headed in a westerly direction, "holding out towards the head of the creek's head of the Sybille entirely." He denied going far enough north to be near the Plaga, Hencke, and Moore places, however. Horn said that he killed a young jackrabbit around noon, which he ate, although perhaps not until the evening.[20]

After confirming Horn's version of his whereabouts on Wednesday and Thursday, the prosecutor confronted Horn with his coroner's inquest testimony. The current trial testimony seemed inconsistent with what Horn had earlier said. Horn vacillated when faced with the coroner's inquest testimony, at first denying what he had said, but then insisting that he was testifying the same way except that he only knew how to describe the landscape and had no skill placing it on a map. In the first part of his cross-examination, however, Horn had directly, and apparently confidently, used introduced maps to show the jury where he had been. But Horn also said that information obtained after his coroner's inquest testimony had refreshed his memory. He explained, "I really didn't have any idea what you were going to ask on that occasion as you asked a question here and there. I was beginning to place myself and to know and remember where I was; and I really didn't know when I came in the Court House (where Horn testified before the coroner's jury) until after I had talked the matter over with you in the court and I defined my route as I have stated all the way through."[21]

Horn's picture of himself as disinterested observer is inconsistent with his avid interest in Miss Kimmell's letter "as long as the governor's message" and his strategy that he would fool Stoll by not presenting an alibi. The *Cheyenne Daily Leader* declared that Horn had changed his story and that Horn's two versions conflicted. At the coroner's inquest Horn had testified that on Wednesday he was near the ranches of Hencke and Allen on the Sibylle and that on Thursday he was close to the Nickell place. But at the trial, his version was that it was Wednesday when he was close to the Nickell Ranch and on Thursday he was in the Sybille country. "That is," wrote the *Daily Leader,* "in his present tale his whereabouts on the two days are precisely reversed."[22] Horn also testified that he saw John Bray on Wednesday night; at the coroner's proceeding, he said he saw Bray on Thursday night.[23]

The *Denver Republican* thought Horn's testimony undercut Otto Plaga's attempted alibi: "In direct contradiction to this story [of Horn's] is the statement of Plaga that he saw Horn at 8 o'clock on Thursday morning near the Fitzmorris place and at a point 25 miles west of Nickell's ranch or about 15 miles west of the point where Horn claims to have been on Thursday morning."[24]

The prosecuting attorney moved on to Horn's actions on Friday, July 19. Horn testified that he had spent all that day Friday around the Fitzmorris place, examining Two Bar pastures there. That night, testified Horn, he slept in a "nice comfortable place in the canyon." Horn said he had no extra blanket or coat but did use his saddle blanket, as "even in the summer it is moderately cool."[25] From there on Saturday morning, July 20, Horn said, he rose at daylight and rode "right straight into the ranch" (meaning the Coble ranch at Bosler). He said that his ride was about twelve or thirteen miles and that he rode there on the same horse he had been using.[26] Horn then obtained Coble's big bay horse and rode it to Laramie. He said the horse "was pretty fat and I let him go."

Stoll quizzed Horn at length about people he saw during these travels, and his relentless questioning apparently started to bother Horn. The *Cheyenne Daily Leader* commented that Horn "is beginning to evidence signs of nervousness under the rapid fire of questions which Mr. Stoll has hurled at him for three solid hours." Horn acknowledged that in his entire trip he had not seen anyone except Bray and one man at a distance near the Fitzmorris place, nor had he seen anyone when riding into Laramie.[27] Stoll's purpose was to show that Horn could present no evidence to support his testimony of his whereabouts from July 17 to the morning of July 20, 1901.

When Stoll pushed Horn on the date he rode into Laramie, Horn said he knew "to a certainty" that he did not arrive in Laramie until July 20. But when Stoll asked Horn whether he knew "to a certainty" that he did not go into Laramie on July 18 or July 19, Horn's response was odd: "From the evidence produced here it would be evident I would have went into Laramie it would be for the purpose of proving an alibi. Certainly would have proved it to a certainty. I was not there until Saturday evening."[28] Some attorneys may have challenged Horn about his experience creating alibis, but Stoll, perhaps believing that the jury would note this strange answer and consider it, moved on.

Stoll asked Horn if on Saturday afternoon he had seen Frank Irwin (who had testified that he had followed Horn into Laramie on Thursday), but Horn insisted he had not seen or met Irwin on Thursday, Friday, or Saturday. He said Irwin could not have seen him at the place Irwin testified to seeing him because he (Horn) had not been there.[29] It was a point of greater significance than appeared because by his testimony Horn had increased the onus of proof on himself. If Horn had testified, for example, that he had seen Irwin on Saturday, then his attorneys could have argued that Irwin just got the date wrong. By Horn's actual testimony, however, he forwarded the strong inference that Irwin made up a story—committed perjury. But perjury is much less likely than a simple mistake, which witnesses make frequently. When Frank Irwin testified in the case, he seemed to be a straightforward witness, one whose testimony was not diminished despite a rigorous, hour-long cross-examination by John Lacey. If the jurors found Irwin likeable, or at least credible, they would resist the inference that he was a perjurer. And if Frank Irwin was believed, Horn's entire story about his travels from July 17 to July 20 would collapse. Horn's testimony forced his attorneys to argue that three other witnesses had committed perjury.

Stoll asked Horn whether he had met the three Denver men who had testified about conversations with him at the Scandinavian Hotel. Horn vigorously denied that he had, saying, "It is a fact that I never met, or spoke or saw them, or heard of them. I heard of them through information. The papers, the witness papers that I had a copy of is the only way I had any idea; it is the only intimation that I had they were in existence. As far as seeing them or speaking to them I never saw or spoke to them, not any occasion in the world." Horn said he never said any of the things that Mr. Mulock testified to, or that Mr. Cowsley testified to, or that Mr. Campbell testified to—"I had no conversation with them at any time in the world."[30]

A criminal defendant who insists that multiple witnesses against him are committing perjury has an uphill climb. For each witness he has to explain why that person would come into court and bear false witness. It certainly happens, but usually a strong motivation is uncovered. Frank Irwin testified that he'd had a disagreement with Horn, but that spat did not seem enough to motivate Irwin's testimony. The jury had no doubt closely watched Irwin, and if, especially after the strong test of Lacey's cross-examination, the jurors did not see Irwin as being the kind of malicious character who would commit perjury out of spite, they were unlikely to discard his statements. The defense had succeeded in casting doubt on Frank Mulock's character, but again, that evidence would be filtered through the impression, good or bad, that Mulock otherwise made on the stand. And no negative evidence had been presented against the other Denver men, Cowsley and Campbell, who appeared to be young, upstanding people. With these witnesses also, the jury members would filter defense arguments through what they actually saw when the men were on the stand.

A second problem arises when accusations of wholesale perjury are made. Why would different people, unconnected in life (such as Frank Irwin and Roy Campbell), come forward with a series of lies against Horn? To successfully challenge the prosecution's case, the defense needed to show why these people were not simply dutiful citizens.

Stoll continued with his cross-examination, bringing up Horn's sobriety, with the apparent purpose of showing that Horn may have been so drunk that he did not remember his conversations with Mulock, Cowsley, and Campbell. When Stoll asked: "You do not wish to say you might have had a conversation of this character, but you were in such a condition you do not recall what it was?" Horn shot back: "I wish to say that I never saw, or spoke or heard of them until they took the witness stand." Politely, Stoll then asked, "At that time . . . were you in a condition to remember whether you had these conversations with these men or not?"[31]

Horn's response was stunning, probably the biggest blunder of his testimony. He said, "I remember everything that occurred to me in my life." Stoll saw his chance: "You have never been so much under the influence of liquor so as not to remember what you said?" "Not if I could talk," responded Horn.[32]

Laramie County in 1902 only had about twenty thousand citizens, and within that number there were smaller societies, such as those engaging in cattle ranching. Tom Horn's proclivities were well known in his community, including his very public displays of drunkenness in local bars. This was perhaps to Horn's benefit, because the jury might just discount what he had just testified to. But Walter Stoll would not discount it, and he had just been given a very strong argument. Horn's testimony had undercut one of the main parts of Horn's defense: that Joe LeFors, a man who knew of Horn's weakness when drunk, had taken unfair advantage of him. That defense lay in shambles, struck down by the defendant's own statements. "It is the opinion of many people in Cheyenne," said the *Laramie Boomerang,* "that Horn's testimony was in opposition to the advice of his lawyers, as it practically destroys the evidence of witnesses who tried to show that Horn was intoxicated when he made the confession to LeFors."[33]

Had the cross-examination ended there, the prosecution could have claimed a victory, but the worst was still to come for the defendant. Walter Stoll's cross-examination, although mannerly, was a matter of life and death to Tom Horn, and Stoll still had not asked about the most damning evidence of all: statements Horn had made in his confession.

CHAPTER EIGHTEEN

More Cross-Examination

Walter Stoll first set the scene for the jury. He had Tom Horn confirm the January 1902 dealings with Joe LeFors about the offer of a job in Montana. Horn agreed that as far as he knew at that time, the proffered job was "bona fide."[1]

Stoll then referred Horn to the conversation regarding making reports to an employer, and he asked if Horn had said: "If a man is compelled to make reports all the time, they would catch the wisest son of a bitch in the world."

Horn began his answer with a soliloquy:

> Don't give me too much at a time. I think I made that remark. Of course, I don't know as that is the exact language and those oaths being used; but in all probability I used them, as I am given in a natural way to profanity; I would naturally suppose I did while I don't remember the exact words that occurred during that conversation; but I would naturally use words anyhow to that effect, for the simple reason that when you go into a country where you are a stranger you want to get everything behind you. I am giving only my idea, because if you have to go out and write letters to this boss or that boss, when you are on a mission of that kind, if you are in a neighborhood they will about locate you.[2]

Given Horn's slow rate of speech when testifying, this answer must have presented a long dead spot in the trial. Stoll asked Horn whether he "knew at the time perfectly well what you were saying as you do now?" Horn answered, "I did." Stoll may have been surprised and pleased that Horn was continuing to insist upon his lucidity when talking to LeFors (he could have pulled away from these statements after talking to his lawyers), but Stoll was not about to let up. "You do not claim that you were so intoxicated that you did not know what you said?" Horn gave him an even more favorable response: "I know to a certainty I know what I was saying. I had not been to bed the night before; I had been up visiting, drinking, having a good time; I knew perfectly well what I was saying."[3]

Why Tom Horn insisted so strongly on his clear-mindedness when dealing with Joe LeFors is hard to fathom. Years later one of his lawyers referred to Horn's "passion for 'braggadocio,'" which is as good an explanation as any.[4] Perhaps Horn was thrown off when Stoll turned to the confession. He became "perceptibly restless," said the *Cheyenne Daily Leader*: "As each damaging statement was brought up Horn entered into an explanation of each one, explaining what the sentence meant, and putting a different meaning on the statements made."[5] This pattern would continue throughout Horn's testimony.

When Stoll asked Horn about the "shooting" discussion—that is, when Horn asked whether "these [Montana] people" were afraid of shooting, and commented, "I will protect the people I am working for; when it comes to shooting you know me"—Horn admitted using the quoted language. But he again felt he had to provide further explanation. "Everytime that Lefors and myself have ever met," Horn told the jury, "the conversation has generally been about shooting someone or killing someone. As a matter of fact I do not remember to have talked with Mr. Lefors about anything else more than somebody he had killed, or somebody I had killed. I think we were telling one another such stories at near every occasion we had met previous to this time."[6]

Stoll pressed Horn on the wording of his statements. Horn said his comments simply meant that "I always consider I have to protect the people I am working for" and that "a man, more especially a man like myself must be very careful, or the numerous reports that are following . . . with the reputation I have gained—I don't know why but with the reputation I have I know it necessitates my being extremely careful all the time; and I am naturally careful to protect the interests of the people I work for."[7] Horn's comments to LeFors about protecting his clients were made in the context of "shooting," however, and Horn did not explain how shooting fit with the need to protect his clients.

Stoll asked Horn if he had not said to LeFors, "I know you are the best man to cover up your trail I ever saw; in the Willie Nickell killing I could never find your trail, and I pride myself on being a trailer." Horn responded: "That is where the orange blossoms come; he commenced to throw bouquets at me; and I naturally returned the compliment; I commenced to rig myself up." Stoll jumped on Horn's comment, asking, "When he said in the Willie Nickell case [']I could never find your trail['] and [']I pride myself on being a trailer,['] you considered that a compliment?" Horn tried to change the subject, saying that his comment came from an earlier conversation with LeFors. Whereupon, Stoll asked Horn if he had not admitted in that previous conversation that he shot at Kels Nickell five times. Horn denied such a statement and reiterated that he could not have been connected to the Willie Nickell or Kels Nickell incidents because he was elsewhere. Stoll then added detail to his challenge that Horn had shot at Kels Nickell, charging that the statement had been made in Hynd's saloon on August 14. Horn again changed the subject, stating that LeFors had said to him, "Tom, if you will throw in with me we can cinch that damned outfit out there."[8]

When John Lacey objected, saying that Horn had already answered Stoll's questions two or three times, the pace of the questioning slowed, but Stoll soon regained his momentum, asking if Horn had said, "No, by God, I left no trail, the only way to cover up your trail is to go barefoot." Horn admitted he made the statement but declared that he was not there. "Notwithstanding that fact you did use this language to Mr. LeFors?" "Yes, sir," Horn replied ambiguously, "I would have used anything else." Stoll asked Horn if he was, then, "in perfect possession of your faculties at the time?" "I was," answered Horn.[9]

Stoll asked about Horn's comment that his horse "was a God damned ways off." Horn again admitted his statement but again said it really was not true, that "the horse was a long ways off at that time; and I was with the horse also." Stoll asked if Horn had said or implied to LeFors "that you and your horse were separated." "I just allowed him to draw any inferences he wanted to make," replied Horn. Horn admitted that he had said what Stoll had just read. "You knew perfectly well what you said?" asked Stoll. "I think I did," Horn answered. Stoll asked Horn about the conversation in which Horn had said he depended on his gun, that the only thing he was afraid of was that he might be compelled to kill an officer (but would do so "if he kept after me"). Horn admitted he had made these statements and was sure "I knew what I said," but he felt that the statement needed explanation. "I would have said anything else that pleased him," Horn said. "I felt very nice that morning; I felt peaceful [and] I would have told a dozen more lies if he felt inclined to think that way."[10]

Stoll continued to grill Horn about each statement in the confession. He asked if Horn had explained to LeFors why Willie Nickell was killed. (Horn had said that "the kid came riding up" on a man in the big draw to the right of the gate, that comes into the main creek below Nickell's house where Nickell was shot, the kid had started to run for the house and "the fellow headed him off at the gate and killed him to keep him from going to the house and raising a hell of a commotion"). This question prompted another long explanation. "I think I used very much that language," Horn said,

> for the simple reason that at the preliminary examination I did not know the details of the killing of the boy, I did not know he was on that road going to Iron Mountain. I supposed the circumstances of killing the boy, were, he was prowling around the hills and run on to somebody else, I got this in my mind, I never knew any of the details and he [LeFors] began to question me about that, I just told him what I had to. Had I known the boy was going to Iron Mountain, I might have told him I run on to him going to Iron Mountain, I would have told him anything that fitted the case that was sprung on me. I didn't know about the details of the killing, it didn't fit what seems to be the facts of the case. It was no fault of mine because I didn't know what the facts were in the case.[11]

Stoll pursued the details in Horn's statement. Horn insisted, however, that the details he supplied LeFors were all "imaginary facts," that he never knew any of the details but had heard rumors and newspaper comments that had given him the impression that the boy was headed off at the gate while making a break for the house and that thirteen shots had been fired at the boy. Horn repeated his contention that LeFors had expressed "a desire by him to throw in with me and help convict somebody else."[12]

Stoll asked Horn about the comment that he was barefoot when pursuing Willie Nickell. Horn admitted he made the comment, but said: "I felt at the time it was a pretty ridiculous statement to make."[13] Horn then felt he needed again to elaborate:

> He asked me I presume half a dozen times about these ten days I stopped in Laramie, he asked me several times what I done these ten days. I hadn't done anything—It occurred to me when he said you must have used your feet pretty bad, it occurred to me then that a man could not have run across there without using his feet pretty bad and I just said, a man has to lay off a week or two. I had some intimation about these ten days before, he asked me about the ten days I stopped in Laramie. I never could exactly understand why, before the developments in this trial. I did understand officers had been there, Pete Warlamount and a sheriff of our county had been making an investigation just subsequent to the killing of this boy as to the exact time when I come into Laramie; of course, I knew that investigation would develop the fact that I come in there on Saturday.[14]

Stoll asked Horn about his dealings with Miss Kimmell, including the conversation about fooling Stoll, who thought he would prove an alibi. Horn admitted saying all this, and Stoll asked him whether this was a josh. Horn explained that when the conversation with LeFors showed "he was trying to implicate me . . . I didn't want to disappoint him, I would have helped him out in any manner." Stoll asked whether these words were said under the influence of liquor, and Horn said, "I had been drinking considerably, of course, but as far as that influenced anything I had to say, I knew perfectly well what I was saying."[15]

Tom Horn was a complicated character, but there was little in his life to indicate that he harbored a deep need to accommodate people at virtually any cost or that he would go to extreme lengths to avoid disappointing such acquaintances as Joe LeFors. So again it is puzzling why Horn would so strenuously avoid the inference that drink affected his conduct when talking to LeFors. There was some plausibility to Horn's initial defense that he made statements under the influence of drink, much more than that he made statements simply to please LeFors. And this was not lost on Walter Stoll.

Stoll asked about other areas of discussion with LeFors, including the comments by "the school marm" about LeFors, that he had met Miss Kimmell just before the killing of the kid, and that "everything dates to the killing of the kid." Horn admitted that all these statements were made and that he was "thoroughly cognizant" of the language used.[16]

Horn admitted that he had told LeFors he preferred a .30-30 because "I like to get close to my man, the closer the better," as well as the statement that Willie Nickell was killed from three hundred yards and "it was the best shot and the dirtiest trick I ever done, I thought at one time he would get away." Horn said he never knew any of the details, and Stoll asked him, "Then if you never knew it, why did you say the boy was killed at a distance of 300 yards, and that it was the best shot you ever made?" "I was just bluffing," Horn replied, but he added that he never remembered the language about the shot being the best shot he ever made and the dirtiest job he ever done. It was the only statement in the confession that Horn even partially objected to. Horn quickly noted, however, that he had every reason to believe that the court stenographer (Ohnhaus) took everything down accurately and made no mistakes.[17]

Stoll brought up the last comments of Horn's morning conversation with Joe LeFors, when Horn had told LeFors that he would tell him all about it when he came back from Montana. Horn admitted this conversation, but said, "I was afraid to go any more into the details of the shooting of the boy, because I could see that he knew more about it than I did." "I thought before I went any more into the details I had better post myself more about the details of the killing of the boy[,] that is what I thought at the time."[18]

Stoll asked Horn whether in the early afternoon of his Sunday conversation with LeFors, Horn hadn't said, "We have been together about 15 minutes and ... there is some people saying what are those sons of bitches planning now, and who are they going to kill next." Horn admitted the quoted language was used, and Stoll noted that although the cattle detective said he was not a killer, Horn supposed that people would be talking about his killing somebody.[19]

When Stoll asked Horn about his conversations with LeFors, Horn said there were at least three. The question gave Horn the opportunity to repeat the persistent theme of his testimony, that LeFors had asked him to "go in with him and furnish evidence from the country to convict somebody in the country." Horn stated that LeFors said he could handle the sheriff and prosecuting attorney and could also furnish some witnesses. This plan was for the purpose of getting the thousand dollars in reward money, said Horn. Horn also said that the only other subject of their conversations was what bad men they were and how many men they had killed.[20]

Stoll asked Horn about his statements that if he got killed now he would, in his words "have the satisfaction of knowing that I have lived 15 ordinary lives; I would like somebody who saw my past and could picture it to the public; it would be the most God damn interesting reading in the country . . . the first man I killed . . . was a coarse son of a bitch." Horn admitted having used these words, and Stoll asked him whether there was anything in his past that could be used as the basis for his assertion. "There was certainly not, I never killed a man in my life." Stoll immediately hit Horn with his statements regarding the killing of Powell and Lewis (with a six-shooter). Horn admitted having used the quoted language but said, "If he would have asked me if I killed him with a double barreled gun or Gatling gun, I would have said yes." Horn asserted that he was in the Bates Hole country of Natrona County when Lewis was killed and observed that the grand jury had not indicted him.[21]

Prosecutor Stoll established that Lewis and Powell had been shot and killed, but Horn denied that it was a fact "that he got $600 apiece for shooting them," even though he had said he did. "Oh, no," said Horn, "if he (LeFors) had said I got $17,000 I would have told him yes." Stoll asked, "If you got $50.00 apiece you have told him the same?" Horn replied, "Yes, or a $1.25."[22]

Stoll also established that Horn had told LeFors he had received money while traveling on a train between Cheyenne and Denver, and that he had also said he left five .45–90 shells after he flashed powder in them, "and the damned officers never found them." Horn admitted that he had used this language, and he understood fully at the time, saying, "I think I remember very distinctly of its having been used; he was telling me how smart he was and I didn't want to look like a farmer entirely." Horn added that he had never done "anything of that kind," and that the statements about receiving money were a falsehood.[23]

Stoll asked Horn whether he had said that he put a rock under the kid's head after he killed him because, in Horn's words, "that is the way I hang out my sign to collect my money for a job of this kind." Horn admitted he had said these things and understood them fully at the time they were stated. Horn further said that not only had his mental condition not deprived him of understanding his statement, he also had a very distinct memory of that part of the conversation, and "it occurred to me that he (LeFors) knew a great deal more about the details of the killing than I did." So, said, Horn, "I had better be careful how I talked, or he would know I was lying to a certainty."[24] Horn even admitted that he knew LeFors suspected him of the Nickell murder and was trying to connect him to it.[25]

Stoll asked Horn about his conversation involving John Coble (that he did all his business through Coble, who is "the whitest son of a bitch in the country in a job of this kind, but that he [Horn] wouldn't let him put in toward his pay in the Powell and Lewis case"). Horn admitted he had fully understood his statements at the time. Horn also acknowledged that he had said and understood that "when I do a job of this kind they know they had to pay me." "I would kill a man if he tried to beat me out of ten cents that I had earned."[26]

Horn insisted, however, that he had never killed anybody or contracted to kill anybody. Stoll asked Horn if he wanted LeFors to understand that he would kill a man if that man tried to cheat him out of ten cents after Horn had done a job. Horn responded, "He knew different. LeFors is very much the same kind of a man I am for talk."[27]

Stoll asked Horn if he had told LeFors that he got his money for the killing of Nickell before he did the job. Horn admitted that he had and understood fully what he had stated, but said, "I thought I would sooner lie than disappoint him."[28]

Lastly, Walter Stoll asked about Horn's statements that he had received $2,100 for three dead men and one man shot at five times. Horn asserted that "anything that would have occurred to me I would have said," but he acknowledged he had used and fully understood the language (including the statement, "Killing men is my specialty. I look at it as a business proposition and I think I have a corner on the market"). Horn also acknowledged that the three dead men referred to were Lewis, Powell and Willie Nickell, and the man shot at five times was Kels Nickell.[29]

John Lacey's redirect examination was very brief. Lacey asked Horn why he didn't deny "insinuations" that he had killed Willie Nickell. Horn told him that Joe LeFors was the only man who said in his presence that he had anything to do with the killing, and that he (Horn) was always of a "generous disposition" and would "rather lie than disappoint him; when he said I done the killing I would have told him just the same." Lacey asked

Horn if the only men he ever did kill "were in these friendly talks with Joe and other people like that?" Horn agreed, completing his examination by saying: "As far as actual killing is concerned I never killed a man in my life or a boy either."[30]

Horn came off the stand about 4:00 P.M. and resumed his seat behind his attorneys. When he sat down, Horn "drew a long breath and stretched himself like a man who had been in a terrible tension," reported the *Rocky Mountain News.* He had made scarcely a break all day long, only towards 4 o'clock beginning to show nervousness and something like fear."[31]

In fact, most of the newspapers covering the trial thought it had been a bad day for Tom Horn. "Talked Too Much," was the *Cheyenne Daily Leader's* headline. Horn's cross-examination was the "chief topic of conversation" in Cheyenne, the paper said, and Horn's "fondness" for talking had made him an easy mark for the prosecution. Horn had "slopped over, telling all that was necessary and a great deal more. Efforts to restrain or check him were made by his attorneys without success."[32] The *Denver Republican* thought Horn had done well at first, but then he lost "some of his remarkable nerve." The turning point had come when Horn began admitting the correctness of his statements to Joe LeFors, and the paper said that both Horn and his attorneys were surprised and disappointed by Horn's performance.[33] The *Denver Post* was skeptical that Horn "was only a miserable braggart." "All day he [Horn] explained that he was a truthful man about everything but murders and his weakness was to say he committed crimes of which he was innocent."[34] Only the *Laramie Boomerang* thought Horn had done well, writing that Stoll failed to get anything from Horn that was not already brought out in direct examination. Horn, declared the Laramie paper, "never once lost his head, but replied to all questions intelligently when the attorney would try to trap him with incorrect statements Horn would correct him . . . His absolute assurance astonished the audience."[35]

The newspapers covering the trial all had interesting opinions, but in the end the only opinion that mattered was the jury's. Jurors must determine facts, including, most importantly in a criminal case, the credibility of witnesses.[36] And, if a defendant testifies, he is usually the most important witness of all. The twelve jurors no doubt listened very closely to Horn's every word. As well, although the words used by the defendant were important, perhaps as important were the nonverbal messages, the kind sent out by every human being whenever an account is given. Those messages would be processed through the filters of the jurors' experiences in life. The Horn jury possessed a wealth of knowledge with which to consider Horn's testimony. Horn was a well-known figure in southeastern Wyoming—most of the jurors knew him—and Horn's activities mostly involved cattle out on the range. All but two or three of the jurors had spent much of their lives working with cattle on the range. But no one in the courtroom could be certain of the jurors' reactions to Horn's testimony. Until the jury began deliberating, each juror probably did not even know how other jurors were leaning.

After his cross-examination, it did not look good for Horn. But was his performance a mortal wound? It all depended on how the jury judged his appearance on the stand.

CHAPTER NINETEEN

Concluding Evidence

The conclusion of Tom Horn's testimony on October 18 did not end the day. Horn's defense team had more witnesses to present. The first was Charles H. Miller, the stable owner who had earlier testified on behalf of the prosecution. This time, however, Miller was ready to help the defense. He recalled that Frank Stone had come into the livery barn the day after Horn had come in and the same day that "Colonel Bell" had arrived with a number of horses. Miller checked his account book and declared that Bell had arrived on July 21 and departed on July 22, meaning that Horn had come in on July 20.[1]

Stoll rose, perhaps wearily, to confront this resurrection of a charge he thought he had buried. Stoll first established that if the Bell entry was not correct, then Miller's conclusion was not correct. Then he showed that Miller had not made the Bell entry until after Stone left the stable, and that before seeing such an entry later on the witness stand, Miller's recollection had been that Horn had arrived just before or after the newspapers had started covering the killing of Willie Nickell.[2] Stoll also reminded the witness that he and his partner John Wallace had made no entry for a week or more after a horse was brought in and made no entry until the man went away, when they "figured back from . . . recollection." Stoll asked Miller if all he wanted to swear to was that Stone had driven a team into his barn, and Miller agreed. Stoll also showed Miller the pencil mark setting out July 22 (1901) and suggested that it was a "new mark."[3]

Defense attorney John Lacey seemed greatly concerned about this last suggestion and in redirect examination quizzed Miller at length about it (thereby perhaps giving it more significance than it deserved). Lacey asked Miller questions about the freshness of the pencil marks in the account book (indicating that the "freshness" of the marks depended upon whether the pencil had been wetted) and generally tried to rebut the suggestion that the book might have been tampered with. John Wallace, Miller's former partner, followed him to the stand and essentially repeated Miller's testimony.[4] During Wallace's examination, a juror asked a question of the witness directly and the question was answered.[5]

Two more witnesses were called briefly by the defense. One was Robert C. Morris, a court stenographer who repeated some of John D. Ryan's coroner's inquest testimony. The testimony read by Morris to the jury confirmed Ryan's earlier testimony that Horn had ridden his little black horse into the Bosler Ranch on Saturday, July 20, 1901.[6] But Ryan had effectively admitted this testimony earlier and repudiated it, so it is hard to see any substantial advantage to the defense from the court stenographer's testimony. The second witness was Tom Horn, who wanted to clarify the names of the pastures he went through on Wednesday night, July 17.[7] With this very brief appearance, the testimony for Saturday, October 18, 1902, was completed.

It was apparent that the defense had little more to present, but John Lacey did not rest the defense's case, for the obvious reason that he and his colleagues wanted the remainder of the weekend to consider whether they had overlooked favorable evidence that should be presented. The announcement that a party rests carries finality, and lawyers understandably welcome an opportunity to consider their case at leisure before resting. Such consideration no doubt took place during the time before court reconvened on Monday, October 20. But when the court convened, the first words spoken in the courtroom were the announcement: "The defense rests, your honor."[8]

According to procedural rules, the prosecution could present rebuttal testimony after the defense rested. In this most contentious of cases, few doubted that the prosecution would present rebuttal evidence. Some even thought the rebuttal evidence would take longer to present than the prosecution's case in chief.[9]

Walter Stoll's first witness was Charles Miller, the man who had just testified for the defense. Stoll showed Miller the July 17, 1901, issue of the

Laramie Republican, which stated that "Major" Bell [the "Colonel Bell" referred to earlier] had been in Laramie on July 17 hiring hay hands, but attorney and witness reached no clear resolution whether this meant that Bell may have been in Laramie for several days before July 21 and may have come into the livery barn before July 21.[10]

Prosecutor Stoll offered into evidence "the rules and measuring tape as produced by Dr. Lewis of the Army, the measuring scale showing the division of the inch into 64 parts, and the steel measure tape and the Winchester rifle." The defense objected, saying that each of these objects was "incompetent and irrelevant and not proper rebuttal," but the judge received the items in evidence.[11]

Evidence offered in rebuttal frequently seems to be nitpicking and dull. Attorneys who have been engaging in sometimes ferocious battle become so sensitive that no opportunity to score a point is declined. A trial attorney can never know when or if the client's case has been firmly established (or firmly lost) and must consider that a point not made may turn the case. But the testimony of the next witness was hardly dull: Joe LeFors's second appearance struck real sparks.

Stoll offered Joe LeFors's testimony to contradict Tom Horn's statements that LeFors had asked Horn to go in with him to pin the Willie Nickell murder on someone to gain the reward. Such testimony would seem to be directly relevant, as Horn's statements would undermine LeFors's credibility, and therefore it would be appropriate to deny them. The defense did not agree. From the beginning, John Lacey vigorously objected to any testimony about whether such a conversation had taken place. But LeFors answered, "We never had any such conversation." Lacey asserted that this statement was not competent—it is hard to see on what basis—but Judge Scott ruled it was. Stoll pushed his advantage, asking LeFors about all the variations of Horn's charges, and in each case Lacey insisted that the questions were "not proper rebuttal, not properly relevant and as seeking to impeach about matters that were brought out by the defendant, not relevant to the examination in chief of the witness Horn."[12]

Lacey tried to persuade Judge Scott that Horn had not offered his comments about the "put-up job" voluntarily but were drawn out of him by Stoll. Stoll responded that on several occasions Horn had volunteered these statements himself. The two lawyers argued strongly for several minutes, and whenever Judge Scott could get a word in edgewise, he indicated that he disagreed with Lacey's contentions. Lacey was so persistent, however, that Scott finally had the jury excused from the courtroom, declared a recess, and called on Lacey to present his authority.[13]

Stoll had apparently anticipated Lacey's contention because within a few minutes of the recess a messenger arrived from Stoll's office with an armful of books. People in the courtroom laughed when they saw "the porter coming in with a large pile of law books, reaching from his hips to his tilted-back chin—every book with paper marks showing between the covers." Lacey, on the other hand, returned to the courtroom "with only one law book in his hand." Whereupon, the two lawyers commenced to argue. The *Cheyenne Daily Leader* described the fight as "one of the most fiercely contested of the trial." Explaining the issue's significance, the *Leader* said: "If it could be proved that Horn lied about these conversations, the inference was that Horn had lied about other matters and the impeachment of the defendant would be strongly established."[14] The two attorneys argued the issue for a half an hour. At the end Judge Scott, apparently after having some of Horn's testimony read back to him, pronounced, "I am inclined to think that the question asked comes within the rule."[15] By Scott's decision, not only would LeFors's testimony denying a conversation about a "put-up job" be allowed, but LeFors could testify to what the actual topics of earlier conversations with Horn had been.

The jury returned to the courtroom, Stoll repeated his question seeking conversations between LeFors and Horn, and Lacey made one final objection, which was overruled. LeFors said that on August 14, 1901, at the Tivoli Saloon, he had asked Horn how he came to let the old man (Kels Nickell) get away. Horn replied, "Don't you think so, it was early in the morning and the sun was not shining on the sights of my gun, or else it would have been different." Horn had also said, "You ought to have saw him run and yell like a Comanche Indian." During LeFors's reply, Lacey objected twice, asking that all answers be stricken out, but again his objections were overruled.[16]

LeFors also testified to another conversation with Tom Horn, when Horn had told him that a man on the coroner's jury would tell him (Horn) "everything that has happened on there," and LeFors said that during all these conversations with Horn, Horn was "perfectly sincere." John Lacey objected to LeFors's every answer during this interval.[17]

The defense attorney, having had every one of his objections to LeFors's testimony turned away, now had the right to cross-examine, and it is safe to assume that LeFors faced an angry lawyer. Lacey directly confronted LeFors with a series of charges:

Q. [Lacey] You state that you did not talk with Tom Horn about the amount of the reward?

A. [LeFors] I did not talk with him about the amount of the reward.

Q. Did you not mention to him the fact that there was a thousand dollars reward?

A. I never talked to him about the reward at all.

Q. Did not the subject of the reward come up between you at all?

A. Yes, sir.

Q. Did you not say in that conversation by Harry Hynd's that Jim Miller could easily be convicted on the evidence you had already?

A. I did not.

Q. And that Vic. Miller could easily be convicted?

A. I didn't say anything of the kind.

Q. You did not say that in either of the conversations?

A. No.

Q. You have taken a good deal of interest in the case?

A. I have taken an interest in this way, the defendant wanted to talk with me.[18]

Lawyer and witness bickered a while longer, but soon Lacey completed his questions. LeFors's testimony appears to have been a plus for the prosecution, as LeFors addressed and contradicted all the charges against him by Tom Horn.

Leslie Snow, one of the two men who overheard the January 1902 conversation between Joe LeFors and Tom Horn, testified next. He said that he had heard the entire conversation, including the tone of Horn's voice and the manner in which Horn talked. "Horn was sincere in everything he said," Snow affirmed. "There was no joshing about it that I could see." Lacey moved to strike the answer, but Judge Scott ruled, "Let it remain in." Lacey in his cross-examination asked only two questions, establishing that Snow had not seen Horn's face or "anything about it."[19]

Stoll then presented the brief statements of six witnesses, the purpose of which was to respond to Otto Plaga's alibi testimony in favor of Tom Horn. Each stated that he knew Otto Plaga and was familiar with Plaga's reputation for truth and veracity. G. W. Faulkner "could not say that it is good."[20] Lacey's cross-examination was counter-productive, because, as the lawyer pushed the witness, Faulkner kept adding harmful detail, saying that he had heard people say that Plaga "was a kind of talker, pretty windy kind of talker," and listed several men who indicated that Plaga did not tell the truth.[21]

Charles H. Edwards, Jr., said that Plaga's reputation for truth and veracity was bad and that he would not believe him under oath. Lacey was more careful with this witness and only asked a few questions.[22] Hiram G. Davidson also testified that Plaga had a bad reputation for truth and veracity and that he would not believe him under oath. Lacey did not cross-examine.[23] Tom Moore said Plaga's reputation for truth and veracity was "tolerably bad" and that he would not believe him under oath. Again Lacey did not cross-examine.[24] Richard Fitzmorris testified as had the previous witnesses, but this time Lacey had some cross-examination questions. The witness agreed that Plaga's reputation was so notoriously bad that every-body knew it and there could be no mistake about it.[25] The cross-examination seemed unfavorable to the defense, but there was a hint that Lacey probably had some of his own "reputation" witnesses lined up and that they would show that Fitzmorris was overstating his case. John A. McArthur was the final reputation witness, and he said that Plaga's reputation "ain't very good." In his cross-examination, Lacey again pushed the witness to overstate his position and Fitzmorris obliged, indicating that practically everybody who knew Plaga thought his reputation for truth and veracity was bad.[26]

The testimony of these six men was interesting for reasons beyond their opinions of Otto Plaga's reputation for truth and veracity. At the beginning of the trial, it had seemed that people in the Iron Mountain area were intimidated and, therefore, reluctant to testify for the prosecution. As one newspaper noted, "It has been very apparent even to the most casual observer that the state has gathered its evidence with great difficulty and that it has been almost impossible to get anything out of the very persons who could, it is believed, tell a great deal if they chose to do so."[27] The reputation testimony from the six men, however, indicated that as the trial proceeded that feeling of intimidation had waned.

Stoll then called the Laramie marshal, Ernest Davies. Davies, an old-timer who had lived in Laramie since 1869, recounted a conversation he had over-heard on October 6, 1901, between Mortimer Grant and Frank Stone. Davies said that Justice of the Peace Grant had asked Stone where Stone had been on the day Willie Nickell was killed. Stone told Grant, said Davies, that he had been on the Snowy Range working for Bell, and then "had met Horn on the 19th [of July], and had a drink with him."[28]

Davies was an important witness for the prosecution because his testimony undercut Frank Stone's earlier statements that he had not met Horn in Laramie until July 21, 1901. Burke cross-examined Davies, and his questioning showed that he was aware that Davies's testimony had hurt Horn's case. Burke tried to show that the conversation about Horn had been "sprung" on Stone and that the reason for Stone's presence before Grant was a drunkenness charge. Davies responded that the discussion had just been normal conversation and that Stone had made his comments about seeing Horn on July 19 "without any hesitancy." Burke kept pushing Davies, asking him why Stone remembered the date of his meeting with Horn and whether he (Davies) had recounted all of the conversation. Davies's answer was probably not to Burke's liking: "It was probably not exactly all; he said something about being brought down here to prove an alibi, and that he was not going to come down here to prove this thing, that they couldn't get him; but I didn't pay much attention to it."[29]

Walter Stoll's redirect examination showed the prosecutor's confidence that Davies had handled the cross-examination well. Stoll merely had Davies explain that the conversation between Grant, Stone, and Davies had occurred a day after Stone was arrested and that Stone had only been drunk the day before.[30]

Stoll then called Justice M. N. Grant, former sheriff of Albany County, to confirm that on October 6, 1901, Grant had had a conversation with Frank Stone and that Stone had "said he was in Laramie on the 19th of July, 1901, and he [had] drunk with him [Horn] that evening." Conducting the cross-examination, Lacey accosted the witness: "You had Frank Stone up there and cross-examined him about this case, and about where he was after you had just fined him for being drunk?" Grant acknowledged the conversation but said that it had occurred before he fined Stone.[31]

The *Cheyenne Daily Leader* thought that Grant's and Davies's rebuttal testimony was a "strong point" for the prosecution.[32] With this testimony, Walter Stoll announced that he wanted to call two more witnesses and then rest but that the witnesses would not reach Laramie until the afternoon, and so the prosecution reserved the right to call them later.[33]

The defense immediately launched into sur-rebuttal and presented a string of witnesses to show that Otto Plaga had a *good* reputation for truth and veracity. These men included Thornton Biggs (Ora Haley's foreman), Henry Mudd, Ed Hofmann (of Cheyenne), Fred Hofmann (also from Cheyenne), Sam Moore (employed by the Swan Company), Frank Perry Williams (who lived six miles from Cheyenne), William Clay, Frank Ferguson (from Wheatland), Joe Reed, and Duncan Clark.[34]

All these men testified to essentially the same thing: that they knew Otto Plaga and that he had a good reputation. Their testimony seemed to be diminished by Stoll's cross-examination, however. Stoll showed that most of these men were personal friends of Plaga's and that they had never discussed his reputation with anyone but could say only that they had never heard it called into question. Stoll's obvious point was that such witnesses were only making assumptions about the reputation of Plaga because the question had never been addressed. In two instances (Ed and Fred Hofmann), Stoll showed that the witness had rarely visited the Iron Mountain area. One witness, Williams, although he admitted he was a personal friend of Plaga's, did seem to do Plaga's reputation for truth and veracity some good because he testified that he'd had conversations about Plaga's reputation and that at least a couple of men had said that Otto was "a good fellow."[35]

One of Horn's attorneys thought Stoll's cross-examination had not been successful, saying that the prosecutor's questions had "very materially aided them" because in every case the witness had testified that he had not heard Plaga's reputation discussed, which was, claimed the lawyer, the strongest point in favor of the witness's opinion.[36]

Duncan Clark was the last of these reputation witnesses, and the prosecution chose not to present further testimony. The *Rocky Mountain News* reported that Stoll expected a witness from Denver for the afternoon session but that he had not shown up[37]). At the completion of the questioning of Clark, the trial transcript shows a handwritten declaration: "And this was all the evidence given in the cause."[38] What remained were the final arguments to the jury.

CHAPTER TWENTY

Final Arguments

The early twentieth century was a time of oratory, especially in sensational legal cases.[1] No time restrictions were placed on final argument, and lawyers took full advantage of this opportunity. The epic arguments in *State v. Horn* lasted four days. Even in this era, however, the most effective oratory was rooted in a solid factual presentation. The jury in *State v. Horn* had seen exactly what the attorneys trying the case saw. Attempts by any lawyer to contradict the jurors' settled perceptions would lead the jury to distrust the lawyer's fancy language. The problem was that the whole case was a desperate struggle to shape facts to support each party's view of reality. Each side no doubt began the case with the intention of presenting an authoritative set of facts that would allow the lawyers to drape highly persuasive arguments over the structure of the factual presentation. But in that endeavor, only one side could succeed.

Attorneys for the prosecution and for the defense knew well the strategy of the other side. From the day of the preliminary hearing when Tom Horn's confession to Joe LeFors was revealed, that confession was the central evidence of the case. The defense wanted to keep it from deciding the case against Horn. The prosecution wanted the opposite: for the whole case to turn on the confession. Thus, Horn's legal team forwarded defenses aimed at making irrelevant the January 12, 1902, session between Horn and Joe LeFors at the U.S. marshal's office. The declaration that Horn's .30-30 rifle could not have made the wounds found upon Willie Nickell's body was the principal attack. And the alibi was forwarded to show the confession

impossible because Horn had not been the one at the gate on the morning of July 18, 1901. Walter Stoll's earnest efforts against these defenses
aimed at keeping the focus on the confession. Should their defenses fail,
Horn's lawyers did have a string of arguing points why the confession was
not really what it so strongly appeared to be. But these arguments were
ones the defense deeply hoped the jury would never feel the need to
consider. The parties' starkly differing positions were zealously forwarded
throughout the long final arguments.

The *Cheyenne Daily Leader,* fully understanding the thrust of each side's
strategy and arguments, cogently observed that "upon Tom Horn's veracity
rests his fate." The newspaper concluded: "If the jury believes he told the
truth when he made his startling confession to Joe LeFors, a verdict of murder in the first degree will be returned against him. If they believe that
he is a liar, they will acquit. If there is a division of opinion on this subject,
the jury and not the accused will hang."[2]

The morning proceedings on Tuesday, October 21, did not begin at
their usual hour because Judge Scott and the attorneys were working on
instructions to the jury (as they had the afternoon before).[3] Both parties
had forwarded proposed instructions to the judge and he decided which
ones should be presented to the jury. Each side no doubt presented reasons
why its proposed instructions were appropriate under Wyoming law.
Although the judge and attorneys were not present in the courtroom,
spectators had gathered there that morning, but the crowd was not as large
as it had been, at least at first. The Nickell family was present, including
Kels, his wife Mary, "with her sad smile of resignation," and Freddie, who
had attended every session of the trial. Mary Nickell's mother was seated
next to her daughter so that, as the *Cheyenne Daily Leader* noted, three
generations of the family were seated side by side.[4] Tom Horn was also
present, and "sat as stolid as an Indian and appeared only slightly interested
in the proceedings," according to the *Denver Post.*[5]

Judge Scott entered the courtroom at about 10:15 A.M., and five minutes
later the jury was seated. The next half hour was taken with reading the
instructions to the jury. Ordinarily, this reading is a low-key exercise, but
the *Daily Leader* found drama in it:

> Judge R. R. Scott, in delivering the instructions to the jury, was
> clear and distinct in his enunciation. His mellow voice, deepened
> by the realization of the significance of the occasion, was very

impressive, and as there fell from his lips the interpretation of the law on which the jury would weigh that evidence and arrive at their verdict the accused sat silent with eyes that seemingly looked far into the future, a sad, pensive expression that made it look as if he was listening to his own funeral oration. His cheeks were slightly flushed and he plainly showed that terrible, intense, nervous strain under which he has been laboring so long.

Murder was the topic of the first two instructions. The judge told the jurors that they could consider only first- and second-degree murder, that manslaughter (a lesser degree of homicide) was "not involved in this case." Judge Scott noted that the key distinction between first-degree murder and second-degree murder was premeditation. The judge's instruction explained that "it is not necessary that such premeditation should have existed in the mind of the defendant for any particular length of time before the killing; it is sufficient if he had deliberately formed in his mind a determination to kill and had thought over it before the shots were fired."[6]

Judge Scott gave instructions addressing the weight the jury should give the testimony of witnesses, especially that of Tom Horn. When considering credibility, the judge said that jurors should take into consideration the interest a witness might have in the result of a case, and they should treat the defendant's testimony as they would the testimony of any other witness. The jury has a right, said Scott, to consider a witness's "appearance upon the witness stand; the manner in which they gave their testimony; their intelligence or lack of intelligence, and their candor or lack of candor; . . . their relationship to the deceased or the defendant . . . ; the reasonableness or unreasonableness of their testimony"; and whether their testimony was contradicted or whether the witness had been impeached. The judge said a witness could be impeached by contrary statements made elsewhere and by showing a bad reputation for truth and veracity. Finally, the judge said, the jury could, if they believed a witness had knowingly testified falsely, disregard the "whole testimony" of the witness.[7]

Judge Scott gave two long instructions about confessions. He said, "A confession is a voluntary admission . . . in the participation of a crime, and it is legitimate and competent evidence." The judge pointed out, though, that while the defendant had not said that the confession had been extorted, Horn had asserted that the confession testified to by Lefors, Snow, and Ohnhaus had been "a mere joke, or josh," and Scott told the jurors that they must resolve whether Horn's statements had been "voluntary and sincere statements . . . admitting his guilt or participation in the killing of the deceased." The instruction went on: "It is also claimed by the defendant that he was under the influence of intoxicating liquors when making the confession." Scott's instructions about intoxication may have taken aback some supporters of Horn. "The fact that a person is intoxicated when making a confession does not render the confession inadmissible, but goes only to the weight to be given to the confession," the judge advised, adding: "It is exclusively for the jury to determine what weight they will give to the confession."[8]

This instruction might surprise some residents of the Iron Mountain area, the *Rocky Mountain News* predicted, because the defense was "said to have assured the Iron Mountain people last summer that a confession made under the influence of liquor, or obtained by an officer of the law under false pretense, would not hold good when the case came to trial." The Denver newspaper wrote: "At least it was this impression that fortified the ranchmen in stubbornly maintaining silence when deputy after deputy went through the country trying to obtain evidence."[9] In other words, Iron Mountain people were told that Tom Horn would probably be returning after his trial, significant because few men of that area wanted to have incurred the ire of a liberated Tom Horn.

In a separate instruction, Judge Scott said that "a confession must be corroborated by proof of independent facts and circumstances," which would be sufficient if "there be such extrinsic corroborative circumstances as will, when taken in connection with the facts, establish the person's guilt in the minds of the jury beyond a reasonable doubt."[10] Scott instructed the jury as to the alibi forwarded by the defense (that Horn was at a different place when the offense was committed) and regarding the burden of proof (reasonable doubt, in general).[11] The burden of proof instruction completed the thirteen instructions proposed by the prosecution.

The defense had forwarded a set of instructions that supported its theory of the case, and the next fifteen instructions Scott read had all been tendered by the defense. Tom Horn's defense team wanted to emphasize that the case against Horn was circumstantial, and so one of their instructions told the jury that "the circumstances must not only all be in harmony with the guilt of the accused," but those circumstances cannot reasonably be true and the defendant be innocent. Another said, "If there is any one single fact proved to the satisfaction of the jury by a preponderance of the evidence which is inconsistent with the defendant's guilt this is sufficient to raise a reasonable doubt and the jury should acquit the defendant."[12] Other instructions emphasized the importance of proof beyond a reasonable doubt and of the proof of a motive (if not shown, a circumstance in favor of the defendant), as well as the fair consideration of the defendant's testimony, and noted that admissions needed to be "real and genuine admissions" of guilt and not "idle vaporings and part of a mere contest in telling yarns."[13]

The remaining defense instructions underscored the need for the physical facts surrounding the killing to be consistent with the alleged confession. They also told the jury to consider the extent to which Horn may have been "under the influence of intoxicants," said that if the gun in the defendant's possession could not have caused the wounds found on Willie Nickell's body they should acquit Horn, and told the jurors what they should consider regarding Otto Plaga's testimony.[14] Judge Scott completed the instructions by adding one of his own, saying that the jury should consider the instructions "not singly" but "together and as a whole."[15]

The jurors must have found this long list of points and directives to be abstract and perhaps confusing. But the attorneys arguing for each party would carefully point out to the jurors exactly why the instructions were important and especially how certain instructions required a finding of guilt or of innocence.

When Walter Stoll stood up and addressed the jury at 10:55 A.M., the newspapermen covering the trial were impressed. The *Denver Post* said Stoll's argument was delivered in a "full, even voice, holding the attention of the jury and spectators throughout."[16] The *Cheyenne Daily Leader* said that during the hour remaining before the noon break, Stoll "poured forth his eloquence, weaving about the cattle detective the warp and woof of a skein that threatens to enmesh the man accused of a revolting crime and bring him to the gallows for the murder of a fourteen year-old boy."[17] And the *Rocky Mountain News* said Stoll's "strong and dominant personality was breathed out over the entire courtroom during his speech."[18]

"Wyoming has been afflicted with a series of assassinations," Stoll began, noting that when the news of Willie Nickell's killing was broadcast, it was followed shortly by the comment that another private assassination had occurred in Wyoming. These assassinations, Stoll said, have "retarded the development in the state."[19] By this last phrase, Stoll did not mean to confine his comments to economic development, but rather to the perception of political immaturity, in the form of "ill fame attached to the state from the horrible murders of the past."[20]

Stoll reminded the jury that "crime does not stalk by daylight, but covers up its track, and it is our [the prosecution's] duty to find the murderer and demand a full investigation." The jury has a duty also, said Stoll, being "a part of the machinery of the law impaneled to act with the officers of the county. You are just as essential a part as the judge, the prosecuting attorney or the sheriff. You have just as certain functions to perform in this work of investigation."[21]

Stoll told the jurors that they must find a verdict of murder in the first degree or an acquittal, and he told the jurors why. He said that Willie Nickell had passed through the gate and was going toward Iron Mountain when he encountered "a foe." Willie fled back to the gate, away from this foe, who was after him with a rifle and intended bodily harm. Not until Willie reached the gate, though, were the fatal shots fired. Stoll said that this narrative demonstrated premeditation, showing that "from the moment the boy first discovered his foe secreted in the rocks to the time that he felt the hot flash of the deadly missile through his vitals, that foe was intent upon taking the life of the boy, was premeditating the crime and if murder has been committed, it is murder in the first degree."[22]

As to the caliber of the bullets that struck Willie Nickell, Stoll said that no one could know what that caliber was. He pointed out that the physicians at the coroner's inquest, the preliminary hearing, and the trial all testified to different things, some presenting statements contradictory to what they had said earlier. The most authentic evidence, declared Stoll, was that of Peter Bergerson, the expert rifle shot. Stoll played to the stockmen jury when he said that a ranchman's testimony would be better than that of some of the experts. The prosecutor "bitterly arraigned" some of the physicians' testimony, and the crowd in the courtroom laughed when he said: "I would not attempt to explain this matter to them"—that of deformed bullets affecting the shape of a wound—"but I will to you." Stoll argued that when the soft-nosed bullets hit the clothing and then the body of Willie Nickell, they "mushroomed," causing the wound to be larger than the caliber of the bullet.[23]

Given how complex and confusing the physicians' testimony had been, Stoll's argument here was relatively short and direct. His comments probably reflected Stoll's confidence that in his cross-examination he had undercut the defense witnesses and that his own witnesses, who had said there was no way the size of the bullet could be determined from Willie Nickell's decomposing body, had been persuasive.

On the question of Tom Horn's purpose in the Iron Mountain area in July 1901, Stoll countered Horn's declared intention of going to Iron Mountain to check on the calves of his employer (as he had stated at the coroner's inquest). "Horn's objective point was the Nickell Ranch," Stoll said. "His course was almost a direct line to the Nickell Ranch and return, during which he did not look after a stolen calf, did not visit pastures where, according to his own statement, he might have found stolen calves, but spent days in that section without accomplishing the object for which Horn stated he went there." Stoll pointed out that "Horn ceased to work for the Two Bar outfit on July 1st, but two weeks later he visited the Colcord Place (owned by the Two Bar)." The prosecuting attorney asked rhetorically: "If he went there to look over calves, why did he inspect only 'casually' the pastures he went through on his way to Iron Mountain?" "Why did he waste ten days in that section without looking for stolen calves when 'the working season is short'?" The real object of Horn's visit, Stoll contended, "was to watch the Nickell Ranch and the Nickell family."[24] Stoll then directly addressed Horn's testimony: "I say, gentlemen, that his statement is false and unreliable."[25]

As for an alibi using the testimony of Otto Plaga, Stoll read Horn's coroner's inquest testimony, wherein Horn said he had spent Thursday near the Nickell ranch, not in the area where Plaga testified he had seen Horn. Further, Plaga was a friend of Horn's, said Stoll, and if he saw Horn riding "in that lonely place not over 150 yards away," he would have hailed him. Stoll said that Plaga testified incorrectly as to the distance from the spot he claimed to have seen Horn to the Nickell ranch, saying it was twenty-five miles, when the actual distance (apparently determined from the maps presented in evidence) was only "a fraction less than thirteen miles." Stoll concluded that the whole alibi testimony looked suspicious and was based on the statements of a man five witnesses who knew Plaga well said they would not believe under oath. (There were, of course, six witnesses who had said that Otto Plaga's testimony was worthy of belief, although the credence given by the jury to either group would probably depend more on the quality of the testimony than the numbers of men testifying.)[26]

As for Horn's statement that he had not arrived in Laramie until July 20, 1901 (and had not been there on July 18), Stoll declared: "The conclusion is clear that he was in Laramie on Thursday and Friday and went to the Bosler Ranch on Saturday."[27] Stoll's contention fit the facts somewhat, but they ignored the damaging testimony of Willard Carpenter and Duncan Clark that Horn had been seen on his black horse that day and did not take the bay, Pacer, until Saturday, July 20. The jury surely knew that Carpenter and Clark were Horn's allies, but Stoll had not given the jury any direct reason why they should slant facts in favor of their friend. Nonetheless, Stoll argued that "the alibi statements come from sources that are friendly to Horn and suspicious, and you should examine them with careful scrutiny."[28]

Stoll also addressed the sweater incident (Horn bringing a dirty, bloody sweater to a shoe shop in Laramie in July 1901) and the vagaries of the Elkhorn barn entry book.[29] The defense had vigorously attacked the evidence relating to the sweater, and in fact some parts of the described chain of events were not strong—especially the testimony of the two Laramie witnesses who could never bring themselves to say that they were sure that the man who brought in the sweater was Tom Horn. But the testimony of two Laramie County sheriff's deputies that Horn had admitted the sweater was his was an anchor to the chronology. On these points, and others, Stoll employed a refrain that he sounded time and again: "Counsel [for the defense] will say you must reject this because Horn says it is not true."[30]

After the noon recess, the court convened again at 2:00 P.M. Stoll's arguments thus far had addressed the fine points of the evidence and had not featured the soaring eloquence for which he was so noted. In the afternoon, however, Stoll hit his stride, especially when he talked of confessions.

In what one newspaper called a "brilliant per-oration," Stoll spoke of his belief in a force of nature akin to conscience that compels confessions. "I do not profess to know all of the working of the unseen laws of nature," Stoll told the jury. "There is some unseen, unknown force in human nature that invariably brings to light, through confessions, crimes which could never become known in other ways. When Willie Nickell was fleeing from his relentless, unforgiving foe, there was a force in his nature which impelled him to let all the world know of the horrible crime about to be committed. It was this force which, ... compelled the man that stood in that big draw at the right of the gate when he was speaking to Joe LeFors to confess the murder of the boy whose blood was on his hands." Stoll eloquently capped his argument: "'Now confess,' it said, and secure in the belief that he was talking with a friend and a confidante, the guilty mind, prompted by the awful resistless force of conscience, made the man speak out."[31]

Stoll declared that "no other man upon the face of the world could have described that crime as did the one who confessed to Joe LeFors." The prosecutor gave as an example Horn's knowledge that the shots were fired from three hundred yards (when "by actual measurement" the big draw in which Horn said he was stationed was just ten feet less than three hundred yards from the gate). In addition, no one but Horn knew the boy had run back to the gate or that a rock had been placed under the boy's head or that Willie Nickell had been "cut off at the gate" (only afterward, said Stoll, did it come out that a pool of blood was discovered at the gate) or that it was just before the killing of the kid that Horn had met the schoolteacher at Miller's ranch.[32]

Of the three Denver witnesses, "Let us throw aside Mulock's testimony," said Stoll, "but take into consideration the hatred, bias, malice of this man Stockton exhibited toward Mulock, and we still have the testimony of Campbell and Cowsley." And, Stoll pointed out, "in his own testimony Horn said he left Cheyenne for Denver September 28, in ample time to have met the three men and then fought with McKenna and Corbin[,] in another saloon, who fractured his jaw."[33]

Stoll also challenged the defense's contentions that Horn and LeFors had engaged in a continuing joshing contest and that Horn had been drunk when he spoke to LeFors. He noted that when LeFors met with Horn it was for the "perfectly serious" purpose of obtaining a job. He also noted, "The very fact that twice, once in Denver and again in Cheyenne, Horn had used the same words: 'It was a dirty job,' in describing the killing, made just this bit of a confession sufficient in itself." Invoking the old adage that in wine there is truth, Stoll averred: "Truth comes out when a man soaks himself with liquor, the mental decadence ensuing making him less secretive, less shrewd in his cunning."[34]

It was in his final comments, though, that the prosecuting attorney justified his reputation as an orator. In the fifth hour of Stoll's argument, the *Rocky Mountain News* reported, "everyone in the room was strung to the highest pitch by one of the climaxes for which Mr. Stoll is justly famous." Stoll spoke of the boy "in his last dreadful moment, gazing into the face of his cruel foe" and excoriated Horn as "a cruel coward" who shot down a fourteen-year-old. He closed with what the *Rocky Mountain News* referred to as "a sustained burst of eloquence": "Something always compels an assassin to confess. In this case, it was the voice of Willie Nickell, striving to tell his father who had brutally slain him."[35] Tom Horn seemed to be especially afflicted by these charges. As Stoll spoke, Horn "slouched in his chair, with his head on his hand as though he were almost ill under the strain, his face flushed but drawn, the corners of the mouth dropping and twitching as constant reference was made to the boy." And indeed, the fact that the victim was just a boy seemed to bystanders to weigh especially heavily against Horn.[36]

Horn was not the only one affected. The *Denver Post* wrote that as Stoll closed, "women were sobbing unrestrainedly. The graphic picture he has drawn of the murdered boy, his deep, full voice reaching every corner, his face alive and ringing conviction carried with him in sympathy nearly all who heard him. The jury was visibly affected, several of the twelve men leaning forward in their seats and watching every move with changing faces."[37]

It was 4:45 P.M. when Stoll completed his initial argument and the court adjourned.[38] The next morning, after brief arguments by the two lawyers assisting Stoll, the defense would unlimber its big guns and fire back at the prosecution.

CHAPTER TWENTY-ONE

The Defense Responds

The prosecution completed its first round of arguments on Wednesday, October 22, with two short presentations, one by Clyde Watts, a young attorney assisting Walter Stoll, and the other by H. Waldo Moore, an attorney hired by Kels Nickell. Both talks lasted perhaps thirty minutes each and neither was memorable. Both admitted that Stoll had covered the ground, but each added his own thoughts to some common themes—that the whole case turned on the confession, for example, and that Tom Horn had wrecked the Nickells' happy home. Moore was Stoll's opponent in the 1902 race for Laramie County attorney, and his speech was so palpably inferior to Stoll's "brilliant address" that the *Denver Post* speculated that Stoll may have set up the arrangement to demonstrate the contrast between the two lawyers and forward his election chances.[1]

At 10:05 that morning, T. F. Burke, U.S. district attorney, followed Moore. Burke was a potent member of the defense team. He spoke for over four hours and the *Laramie Boomerang* termed his speech "powerful."[2] Burke began "in a slow, clear and forceful manner and in direct contrast to the former speakers of the morning."[3] He first spoke of circumstantial evidence, emphasizing its weakness and saying, "It is necessary to bring into play every faculty of discernment and understanding." Presenting an old shibboleth of defense attorneys—that it is better that one hundred guilty men go free than that one innocent man be convicted—Burke cited instances of circumstantial evidence gone wrong.[4] As he spoke, the defense attorney "became more earnest, and as this increased in intensity he pitched his voice higher until at times it was shrill and piercing as he closed the recital of these incidents." But then Burke apparently moderated his tone and told the jury that he only wished to more clearly show the members of the jury "the great care you must exercise in a case of circumstantial evidence."[5]

Burke told the jurors he could not understand why Horn had been charged for the crime and not other people, except to note that, having thoroughly studied the evidence, "I have seen enough at this trial to see that on the part of the prosecution there is a determination to convict and not that the truth shall prevail."[6] Burke asserted, "Counsel for the prosecution admits there is no motive for the crime charged." It is hard to know the source of this allegation, because there are no indications in newspaper reports of any such statement. Clyde Watts had made some diffuse comments about motive in his final argument, and apparently they provided what Burke perceived as an opening.[7] But whether or not the prosecution had admitted there was no motive, Burke was determined to pursue the point to a conclusion satisfying for the defense: "Why should Tom Horn kill a 14 year-old boy?" asked Burke rhetorically. "Let that question ring in your ear until you can satisfactorily answer it."[8] "You cannot pick out of all the evidence introduced a single reason why. In a murder case a motive must be shown. In this case none has been shown. This is reasonable doubt No. 1. Treasure it up in your mind when you go to your jury room and do not forget it."[9]

The problem with this argument was that the jury members surely knew of Tom Horn's reputation as an assassin and that Kels Nickell was a likely target. Cattlemen around Iron Mountain were vocal about killing Kels Nickell, even asserting openly to newspapers that the murder of Nickell would be a community benefit.[10] It is a reasonable inference, therefore, that cattlemen were even more openly vocal against Nickell among themselves. Nine or ten of the jurors were cattlemen and had to have known that not only were a great many Iron Mountain people in favor of killing Nickell but that Horn was a logical man to do it. So when Horn told Joe LeFors that he shot Willie Nickell to keep him from going back to his home, raise a "hell of a commotion," and warn his father, Kels, Horn's statement would fit in the minds of the jurors. Unless the jury was determined to acquit Horn regardless of the facts (certainly a possibility), it is unlikely that the jurors would have any problem with the question of motive.

Burke talked of the three Denver witnesses. He neatly turned Stoll's point—that the similarity of language Horn used at different times and places verified each statement—against the prosecution. Burke said the similar language "suggested convincingly" that the three Denver men who said Horn made the statements had all obtained these words from newspapers. Burke did not verify his contention by referring to specific newspaper articles, however.[11]

Burke was just warming up against the Denver witnesses. Two of the men, Mulock and Cowsley, had testified that they spoke to Horn after the Denver Carnival had started. None of the three had testified unambiguously to a specific date of their encounter with Horn, however, although each had said it was during the carnival. When Burke had asked Roy Campbell if his encounter with Horn had been during carnival week, Campbell had answered, "Yes, about that time, the exact date I cannot say."[12] There was also a question as to what constituted "carnival week." Denver doctor W. L. Davis seemed to agree with Walter Stoll's assertion that carnival week began September 29.[13] But Burke was not about to credit such fine distinctions. Instead, he assailed the Denver men in scathing terms, asserting first that Horn had been in a Denver hospital at the time he supposedly spoke to Mulock, Campbell, and Cowsley, and then declaring, "If ever testimony was shown to be absolutely perjured it was the testimony of these dregs from the lowest of society." "This testimony alone is enough to spoil the whole case of the prosecution," pronounced Burke. "A case that has to be bolstered up with perjured testimony is a very poor case of circumstantial evidence." Burke sealed his point: "Here is reasonable doubt number two."[14]

Burke then turned to the testimony of the various physicians. He said that three physicians at the coroner's inquest had testified that the bullets striking Willie Nickell were larger than .30 caliber, the size of the bullets fired by Horn's rifle. But the prosecution, when it presented its case in chief, had only called as a witness Dr. Barber. Then, said the *Laramie Boomerang,* Burke became "very impressive." Walking to Walter Stoll's desk, he pounded it with his fist, "thundering out" to Stoll: "Why did you discharge the other doctors if you wanted to get at the truth? Were they false? Did they refuse to testify as you wanted them to? We called them and their testimony was not that which would hang a man—not the kind you wanted. What a desperate situation the state has gotten itself into when it has to impeach two of its own witnesses, two of our professional men."

Throughout this tirade, Stoll sat "sphinx like."[15]

Burke then turned to the confession and Horn's drinking. The defense contended that Horn had been drunk when he spoke to LeFors and that LeFors had taken advantage of Horn. But then Horn had undercut this position when he insisted, time and again in different forms, that he had known "perfectly well" what he was saying when speaking to LeFors.[16] The defense attorneys, however, were unwilling to abandon what may have been their most plausible defense. "Horn says he remembers everything he says," said Burke, "or at least the state said so, but you and I gentlemen, know otherwise. Memory is a funny thing, but when the notes had been read over and over to him, the defendant honestly admitted he might have said so." Burke then declared that a convincing array of witnesses showed that Horn really was drunk. Burke pleaded with the jury: "Why, you would not take a drunken man's life, would you?"[17]

A panel of twelve jurors is an intelligent unit, and this jury no doubt quickly grasped what T. F. Burke had just told them. Not only should they disregard all those inconvenient statements Horn had made to LeFors, but they should disregard another set of inconvenient statements: ones Horn had just made *to them*. Jurors, as with the usual run of human beings, do not like to be played for fools, and Burke's tactic seriously endangered what he had just said about the Denver confessions, that this point alone should undercut the entire case.

Burke sneered at what he described as Stoll's "brilliant peroration, the masterpiece of his career" concerning a spirit in the boy that compelled Horn to confess. Stoll's statements were not only absurd, the defense attorney declared, but sacrilegious. "There is a yellow streak of absurdity all through this case," he said of the confession. Performing "a few acrobatic tricks by way of emphasis," Burke said that Horn's story would "look well in a yellow covered novel." Burke's sarcasm, his "train of ridicule," was said to cause the audience to smile constantly. Even Horn was said to have smiled broadly at times.[18]

The confession was absurd "when compared to the facts of the case," Burke declared. It would have been impossible for a man to climb out of the draw and "cut the boy off at the gate." Burke noted that in the confession Horn said he liked to get close to his man, but the shot here was from three hundred yards away. Another absurdity to Burke was that Horn supposedly ran across to the gate in his bare feet, "a feat no living man could accomplish." It was also an absurdity that Horn was supposed to have put a rock under the boy's head to collect his money, when he also said he had already been paid. Still another "absurdity," said Burke, was that the body of Willie Nickell, according to expert testimony, could not have been turned over for at least three hours after he was killed, meaning that if Horn rode back to Laramie that morning, as the prosecution contended, he could not have turned the body over.[19]

Burke's impact on the jury could not be known. He was a man of personal force and charm (the *Denver Post* said, "like all Irishmen, [he] is a great story teller"), but Burke was also taking considerable license in his discussion of the evidence. The contention that "no living man" could traverse the ground near the gate in bare feet was questionable, and Burke ignored Stoll's cross-examination of physicians in which they had effectively withdrawn their statements that dirt and grass would only cling to Willie Nickell's body after a several-hour wait.

Burke scored when he said that the records in the books from the Elkhorn stable, even though not made until ten days after the fact, were likely more accurate than Frank Irwin's memory a year later.[20] Pulling away from his client's intimation that Irwin had willfully misrepresented what he had seen on July 18, 1901, Burke said he was only saying that Irwin was mistaken. "It is the easiest thing in the world to be mistaken as to the day when it occurred over a year ago."[21] Given Burke's usual harsh assessments of witnesses and evidence against his client, this statement might well indicate that Burke believed Frank Irwin had come across well to the jury.

Burke resumed after the lunch break, declaring that all the evidence pointed to Horn's innocence, rather than to his guilt. If Horn had a bloody sweater, he certainly would have gotten rid of it "during that long ride through unsettled and mountainous country," Burke argued, rather than leave it in a shoe store.[22] This argument is interesting for two reasons. First, it seems Burke came close to admitting that Horn did have a bloody sweater. Second, the defense counsel cherished this argument because no matter the situation, the defendant got off the hook. If an attorney's client properly covered his tracks, then there would never be an arrest or trial. But if the defendant left any clues, it was proof that he was innocent, because he never would have done such a careless and stupid thing. The truth is, however, that a great majority of those who commit crimes are neither smart nor careful. Highly competent criminals are found mostly in mystery novels.

Burke then tried to turn Tom Horn's coroner's inquest testimony to his client's favor. Because his client "frankly and candidly" admitted that he was in the vicinity of the crime when it was committed, Burke proclaimed that Horn had "told the plainest, most candid and most truthful story of any witness on the stand."[23] Here Burke was making a virtue out of his client's necessity. There was no way in the world Horn could have denied that he was in the area when the crime was committed because Miss Kimmell had seen him. So had Jim Miller, Victor Miller, Gus Miller, and Eva Miller—and they had all so testified at the coroner's inquest. John Bray was still another witness who had seen Horn near the Nickell home (the evening of Wednesday, July 17, 1902), and Bray had so testified in the trial. Not to be deterred, Burke insisted that since Bray had seen Horn, Horn must not have been wanting to commit murder, because otherwise he would have secreted himself. This creates a reasonable doubt, said Burke, "a doubt as big as a mountain peak."[24]

Still another reasonable doubt arose from Otto Plaga, who had seen Horn on the morning of Thursday, July 18, 1901, far from the gate where Willie Nickell was killed. And Plaga should be believed, Burke declared, because ten witnesses testified that they would believe Plaga, whereas only five testified they would not. The problem with this was not so much the argument but that the jurors had watched Plaga—and most probably knew him—as well as all fifteen (or sixteen) of the "truth and veracity" witnesses, and they had probably long since determined in their minds the worth of Plaga's testimony. Neither Burke's arguments (nor Stoll's) were likely to change any minds about Otto Plaga.

So too had the jury likely made its own conclusions regarding all the doctors' testimony to the caliber of the rounds that hit Willie Nickell's left side the morning of July 18, 1901. The jury had seen and heard the direct, cross-examination, redirect, and re-cross examination of the three doctors, as well as physicians presented by the prosecution who presented contrary testimony. Counsels' arguments about the veracity of witnesses the jury had watched testify were not going to make much difference at this stage.

Late that afternoon—"when the hands on the big clock on the west wall on the district court room just pointed to 4 o'clock"—Burke completed his argument and yielded to his co-counsel, John Lacey.[25] Lacey's style of argument was unlike Burke's or Stoll's, but he drew a favorable contrast between his methods and Stoll's, saying that he was not going to attempt "flights of eloquence, but just talk facts."[26] Addressing the jury, Lacey walked back and forth in front of the jury box, talking in a "convincing, quiet, easy way."[27] The jury had heard an eloquent appeal from Mr. Stoll, a man "who has a reputation for swaying juries," Lacey observed, but when the jurors carefully considered every single fact, he said, they would conclude that "not one of the state's points has been proven beyond a reasonable doubt." Then, said Lacey, "it will be to you a pleasant duty to give to life and liberty the protection allowed by law."[28]

John Lacey was known well in Cheyenne, and the *Cheyenne Daily Leader,* being a local newspaper, knew of and wrote at length of his reputation. Although Lacey was "one of the most brilliant criminal lawyers in the western country," he would not be deemed "eloquent," the *Daily Leader* said. But Lacey only lacked "flights of oratory," and his "keen, incisive statements" had just as great an effect as oratory at "swaying the opinions of men." Lacey, said the *Leader,* "is clear in enunciation, subtle in his deductions and conclusions, and withal so logical in his assumptions and plain in his sequences of thought that all can understand and follow him through the most delicate windings of arguments."[29]

The man who listened most carefully to Lacey was the defendant, Tom Horn, and he responded emotionally to Lacey's presentation. "Leaning forward, as if realizing that his happiness, his future, and in reality, his very life, depended upon the words that issued from the mouth of his counselor," the *Daily Leader* wrote, Horn listened intently. "Not a word escaped the man whose life hangs in the balance." Horn's empathy with Lacey was complete: "If the attorney told a humorous story, Horn smiled; if he portrayed the awful effects of the dastardly deed committed, a sympathetic look of sadness crept over the lineaments of the defendant; when [Lacey] dwelt on the innocence of the man charged with this awful crime, Horn's face reflected the hope that he felt." In complete opposition to Horn's moroseness when Stoll was speaking of him in "scathing terms as a criminal of an extraordinary type," Horn showed elation as Lacey presented his case to the jury.[30]

Lacey began by saying that no one deplored the murder of Willie Nickell more than he, and he added that "no one desires more earnestly to see the perpetrator of that ghastly crime brought to justice." If the jury believed Horn committed the crime, they should, "without hesitation," find him guilty of first-degree murder.[31] This last comment followed logically from Lacey's indication that he wanted truth and justice to prevail above all, and it was a point hard to deny, but it is still surprising that Lacey would risk this concession.

After virtually every point made during his argument, Lacey referred to the court's instructions and explained them to the jury.[32] On the court's instruction about burden of proof, he said the defense need not prove Tom Horn innocent, but the prosecution had to prove Horn guilty beyond a reasonable doubt and to a moral certainty. "A confession must be supplemented by a perfect chain of circumstantial evidence," he told the jury, "perfect in every link, as a flaw in the chain must necessarily give rise to the creation of a reasonable doubt."[33] This last point was generally consistent with the court's instructions, but Lacey buffed the court's instruction to a brighter sheen, for the obvious purpose of lifting the prosecution's burden of proof as high as possible.

During the taking of evidence, Lacey had done his best to accuse the Miller boys of killing Willie Nickell but was frustrated by legal rulings. In his final argument Lacey hit the point harder, although he had to be careful or Judge Scott might stop him again. Noting that John Apperson had found size-six or size-seven footprints close to the place where Willie Nickell's body was found, Lacey observed that Tom Horn obviously wore larger shoes than a six or seven and that there was only one witness with shoes of that size (Victor Miller).[34] It was not clear whether Lacey was referring to a place a few feet from the body or the area around the gate. The actual testimony from Apperson had been that the footprints had been found just west of the gate, near a pool of blood, but Lacey omitted that detail, for the obvious reason that the footprints near the gate were almost certainly Willie Nickell's.[35] Surprisingly, Lacey specifically noted that the court had shut him off from presenting the stories about friction between Willie Nickell and others, and, therefore, "it was not incumbent upon the defense to prove who committed the crime."[36] Commenting about Judge Scott's legal rulings was risky for Lacey, but by carefully couching his statement about the rulings within the context of the defense's burden of proof, Lacey probably spared himself an objection from Stoll. But there was little question in the minds of observers what Lacey was trying to do. As a *Denver Post* headline put it the next day: "The Miller Boy Accused of Slaying Willie Nickell by Horn's Chief Counsel."[37]

Lacey turned on the Denver witnesses as harshly as had Burke. Ignoring ambiguities and complexities in the testimony over exactly when the three men said they had spoken to Horn and when carnival week had begun, Lacey presented the jury with an uncluttered picture. The three Denver witnesses had unanimously agreed that Horn's admissions were made during carnival week, he said, and the first day of carnival week was Tuesday, October 1. Horn's jaw was broken, however, the early morning of Monday, September 30. Therefore, concluded Lacey, "it was an absolute impossibility for the accused to have made the statements credited to him" by the three Denver men.[38] Lacey accused Mulock of being a liar and focused on Mulock's criminal record, saying that it showed Mulock's capability of perjuring himself.[39]

Lacey next addressed Tom Horn's sobriety when Horn spoke to Joe LeFors on January 12, 1902. Lacey, like Burke, brushed aside his client's consistent statements that he knew and remembered what he was saying to LeFors. Driving his point all the way through, seemingly without regard to the actual facts presented in evidence, Lacey said that Horn had been "in that state of inebriety when every [thing] has a rosy hue and he was at peace with the world. In such state it is but natural that he should readily agree to anything LeFors suggested." In fact, said Lacey, "All the answers were in reply to leading questions." "It was a case of a sober man with a shrewd, acute mind, playing with the idle talk emanating from a dazed brain and bringing out and creating such statements as was desired. It was a case of suggestion entirely. Horn did not bring out a single new fact regarding the killing. The facts were suggested by LeFors and acceded to by Horn."[40]

This pronouncement fits the defense theory perfectly: that Tom Horn had been badly impaired from his drinking and numbly accepted all the suggestions LeFors made. As Lacey said, "All the answers were in reply to leading questions." He gave no specific examples of answers following leading questions, however. In fact, there are none to support his argument. The verbatim transcript of Tom Horn's confession is available and it is an easy matter to fully analyze the January 12, 1902, conversation between LeFors and Horn (as was done herein in chapter 13). That transcript shows that LeFors posed only a few leading questions and that there is not a single example of a leading question followed by unqualified acceptance of the question as LeFors framed it. Horn volunteered the most damaging parts of his responses to LeFors. Worse for the defense, Horn's statements were detailed and specific to the topic.[41] For his argument to be effective, Lacey had to hope that the jurors would not read the confession transcript, although Walter Stoll's long cross-examination of Horn, in which he quoted

each question and answer and elicited a response to each from Horn, probably meant that the exact nature of the questions LeFors had posed to Horn
were firmly implanted in the jurors' minds.

John Lacey had to break off his argument because of the close of court
that Wednesday, October 22, 1902. When he resumed the next morning,
only about twenty people sat in the audience. One newspaper referred
to a "deserted courtroom," and the question on the streets was, "When
is Mr. Stoll going to talk again?"[42] Lacey was surely aware that Stoll would
follow him to the lectern, but while he had the floor, Lacey was going
to forward the cause of his client vigorously.

The prosecution had misled the jury by changing Horn's testimony
to refer to the draw on the north (near the gate), Lacey said, when Horn
must have been speaking about the draw on the south. But, said Lacey,
"Horn was talking of the big draw north of the gate," demonstrating Horn's
lack of knowledge about the scene. Lacey's point was not helped when
Kels Nickell, sitting in the audience close to the front, proclaimed aloud,
"There is only one draw there, not two."[43]

Lacey spoke of how Kels Nickels had directed his son to leave Thursday
morning to go to Iron Mountain and find a sheepherder. Then, Lacey
said, somebody learned that Willie was to follow the pathway to Iron
Mountain. The defense lawyer declared that he did not know whether
that was one of the neighbors or one of the children from the school, "but
somebody found out, lay in wait, and shot him twice in quick succession."[44] By this formulation, Lacey meant to include only the Miller boys
as prospective assassins. But it was more likely that the assassin was gunning for Kels Nickell, not Willie, and that the gunman was waiting along
this road because he knew Kels Nickell frequently used it, not because
information had been learned about Willie's trip to Iron Mountain.

Lacey referred to the impression of the butt of a gun discovered behind
a pile of rocks only sixty to seventy yards from the gate. "This shows," said
Lacey, "that the person who killed Willie Nickell laid in wait and not in
any draw according to Horn's assumption. This assumption does not correspond to the material facts in the case and must give rise to a reasonable
doubt."[45] Lacey's argument might have been persuasive to the jury, but it
assumed that a gun made the imprint immediately before Willie Nickell
arrived at the gate (about 7:15 A.M.) and not at some earlier time. On
July 18, the sun rises about 4:40 A.M. (MST), so there had been about three
hours of daylight before Willie Nickell first rode up to the gate.[46] The

assassin may well have arrived at the site some time before Willie did and experimented with different places to lie in ambush, including the pile of rocks where the butt impression was found, before ensconcing himself in the draw.

Turning to the caliber of the gun used to shoot Willie, Lacey insisted that he had been shot with a large-bore rifle that used black powder. "All of the physicians, theirs and ours, agreed that the size of the wound is the same or smaller than the bullet that made it," he said, insisting that the prosecution was calling a lot of doctors liars.[47] Lacey must have been hoping that the jury had not been paying close attention to the physicians' testimony. Their actual statements were not close to Lacey's representations. Dr. Amos Barber had made different statements at different times. Dr. H. J. Maynard had said that nothing could be determined (as to the size of the bullets) after three days. Dr. L. P. Desmond had acknowledged that under limited circumstances the size of the bullets could be determined, but generally the size of the bullet could not be determined from the wound at either the entrance or the exit. It would be "merely guesswork." Dr. M. C. Barkwell had said that no one could tell the caliber from the bullet hole and he did not agree with Lacey's contention otherwise. Of the four physicians the defense had presented, Dr. George Johnston had admitted that all possibilities in this area were conjectural, depending upon many varying circumstances. The defense witness, Dr. William F. Lewis, had even admitted that under certain circumstances a soft-nosed .30 caliber bullet could make a wound as large as three-eighths of an inch. Walter Stoll showed that Dr. John Conway had acknowledged in his inquest testimony that "of course" the bloated condition of the body made a difference in the condition of the holes caused by the bullet. And Dr. W. A. Burgess had conceded that often very large projectiles made very small wounds and very small projectiles made large wounds.[48]

During the presentation of evidence, Lacey had elicited from Victor Miller that the firearms owned by the men within the family were all .30 caliber.[49] This was another problem with Lacey's assertion that Willie Nickell was shot with a large-bore rifle. If so, neither Victor Miller nor Gus Miller could have been the shooter, at least using their own guns.

Lacey then took a "dramatic" step, which, according to the *Cheyenne Daily Leader*, was done "with the finesse of an able pleader and adroit general." He picked up the clothes that Peter Bergerson had examined (and declared contained holes made by a .30 caliber bullet). The lawyer placed a .38

caliber bullet on the bullet holes in the fabric and showed how the bullet went into the holes "with ease." Said the *Daily Leader,* "This undoubtedly went a long way toward convincing the jury that the holes were not made by a .30 calibre bullet if the testimony of Mr. Bergersen [*sic*] was to be believed that these holes proved the size of the projectile."[50]

Addressing the blue sweater and all the events associated with it, Lacey set out Horn's version and those of witnesses supporting him, ignoring the testimony of two deputies that Horn had said quite different things to them.[51] By such a presentation, Lacey did just what Stoll had referred to in his initial argument: that the defense wanted the jury to accept a proposition (and reject a contrary one) simply because Horn said it was so.

The state, noted Lacey, had insisted that Horn rode into Laramie on Thursday, July 18, 1901, based upon the testimony of Irwin and Titus, while the defense claimed that Horn was in the field and did not ride into Laramie until Saturday, July 20. "Many witnesses," Lacey said, swore that "Horn did not ride into Laramie on the 18th, but took the route through the Bosler ranch and into Laramie on the 20th." Lacey told the jury that either they must believe Irwin and Titus or that "all the other witnesses and the book of the livery stable lies." Taking a harsher tack toward Irwin than had Burke, Lacey said that Irwin "had a grudge against Horn and wanted to see Horn downed."[52] "Can you say," asked Lacey of the jury, "that you have not a reasonable doubt as to the theory of the prosecution"?[53] The problem with this argument, however, was that contrary to Lacey's statement, *no* witnesses had testified that Horn did *not* ride into Laramie on July 18. The Bosler witnesses only said they had seen Horn on July 20. The livery stable book did lend support to the defense contention, but the evidence from that document was not compelling.

Lacey repeated Burke's argument about Otto Plaga, saying that given the ten men who said Plaga's testimony could be believed and only five men who said otherwise, there could be no doubt that "Horn was too far away from the scene of the crime at the time it occurred to have committed that crime." Completing his speech "just as the whistles announced noon," Lacey summed up all the evidence for and against the defendant, "showing how that evidence all went to prove his innocence and not his guilt. Not only did it create a reasonable doubt but it practically established the fact that Tom Horn could not [have] commit[ed] the crime with which he stands charged."[54]

Then came that terrible time for Tom Horn when the only speaker remaining was Walter Stoll. "I am not so much afraid of the evidence, so much as Stoll," Horn had admitted to a friend. That expression, said the *Cheyenne Daily Leader,* "admits the ability of the man, his insistent combativeness, his shrewdness and above all, his peerless oratory carrying with it the power to sway the minds of men, to stir their emotions, and thus to raise up in their brains a conviction of the guilt of the defendant beyond a reasonable doubt and to a moral certainty."[55]

CHAPTER TWENTY-TWO

Stoll's Last Words

When word got out that Walter Stoll would again speak to the jury, people flocked to the courtroom. The *Denver Post* said that people stood in line waiting to get seats for more than half an hour before the doors of the courtroom were opened. "And when the word was given to admit them the rush was terrific. People fought for seats and filled the stairs and windows of the little room." This was to be "Stoll's masterpiece," and, the *Post* noted, "the crowd was not disappointed."[1]

A "pen sketch" of Stoll described him as an average, middle-aged man, a little overweight—nowhere near the physical specimen of Tom Horn, for example. Despite an indifferent appearance, however, Stoll soon became very notable indeed. "He stood in front of the jury never at rest, and constantly his impressive voice hurled denunciation at Horn, explaining the philosophy of the evidence to the jury, oblivious, apparently, to everyone else."[2]

Stoll began this rebuttal, his final argument before the jury, as many attorneys do, by first addressing vexing points the defense had made in its argument but intending to move to broader themes wrapping up the prosecution's case. Stoll declared that the case had two parties: one seeking the truth, and the other, the defense, that sought to instill doubt in the minds of the jurors. The defense had introduced immaterial matters into the case, Stoll said—the mention of "an aged mother and three sisters," for example. Referring to another case in which "immaterial" matters had been introduced, but instead of an "aged mother," Stoll said, it was a "sick wife," and the upshot was that a minority of three jurors convinced nine jurors not to convict, but then the freed defendant soon "snuffed out the life of an aged father and husband."[3]

The defense had also referred to size-six shoe prints found near the scene. But, said Stoll, "That is entirely extraneous to the case and proves nothing." "There may have been 10 men who wore a No. 6 shoe." Many people, he implied, had wandered over the scene of the murder.[4] Besides, Stoll added, the tracks near the body were made by Willie Nickell himself. "Is it not a waste of time and an insult to your intelligence," said Stoll, "to ask you to say that Willie Nickell made no tracks, but they were made by an imaginary enemy? And why do they say this? Just to save the neck of this self-confessed murderer."[5]

Still another extraneous matter forwarded by the defense was the contention that the testimony of witnesses who saw Horn both at Laramie and Bosler somehow strengthened the alibi statements of Otto Plaga. "We don't deny that Horn reached the Bosler ranch on the morning of July 20th," Stoll countered, "but we claim that Horn, previous to that, was in Laramie." "Is there any logic in the statement that because Horn was at the Bosler ranch on the 20th he could not have been in Laramie on the 18th, and yet that is what the defense would ask you to believe."[6]

Stoll was vexed by Lacey's frequent assertions that many components of the state's case had not been proven beyond a reasonable doubt and that this showed how weak the prosecution's case was, that indeed it was the basis for an acquittal. This was not the law, Stoll said. "There are but three material allegations in the information which must be proved beyond a reasonable doubt. All of the facts in the case need not be proved by even a preponderance of evidence, but only that the jury be convinced that the boy was killed, the murder occurred in Laramie County and that the defendant committed that murder."[7] In other words, each of the items of evidence did not have to be proven beyond a reasonable doubt, so long as the evidence in total persuaded the jury beyond a reasonable doubt that Tom Horn had murdered Willie Nickell.

Walter Stoll made a "terrible denunciation" of Tom Horn when he compared the story told by Horn against the evidence of other witnesses. Horn's story, he said, in many material facts "contradicted the testimony of a dozen others." Stoll pleaded with the jurors: "I ask you in the name of your firesides and your children, in the name of your God, to scrutinize the testimony of Tom Horn as you do that of the other witnesses. Horn has been contradicted by the testimony of almost every other witness and in the light of that evidence his testimony must fall. Remember that he is a man on trial for his life and every fibre of his being cries out for mercy that is not due."[8]

Saying that Horn had been contradicted by the testimony of almost every other witness was an overstatement. But it was true that many people had testified contrary to Horn, including Joe LeFors, E. D. Titus, Frank Irwin, George Powell, George Matlock, Sheriff E. J. Smalley and Deputy Sheriff R. A. Proctor, and the three Denver men, Roy Campbell, Frank Mulock, and Robert G. Cowsley.

"Everybody must be disbelieved and Horn must always be believed," said Stoll. "It is the same old story when able and anxious counsel are defending a criminal. God help this country if its officers under oath cannot be believed. And God help this country when the word of a criminal is to be taken in preference to the word of its officers."

When Stoll noted George Powell's saying there were grass roots on the sweater left at Powell's shoe store in Laramie by a man resembling Horn, defense attorney Burke interrupted: "That was not the testimony, Mr. Stoll." Stoll turned to Burke and thundered out: "It was the testimony, sir. He said it looked like grass roots. We say a thing looks white, because it is white. We say a thing looks black, because it is black. If that was not the evidence, . . . tell me so and we will look it up in the records." "For a full minute," reported the *Daily Leader,* "Mr. Stoll waited, but his challenge was not accepted." Resuming his argument, Stoll continued: "The defense has made the contention, gentlemen of the jury, that this case rests entirely upon circumstantial evidence. That conclusion," he told the jurors, "is erroneous. There was an eye witness to the crime and that eye witness confessed every detail of the awful deed to Joe LeFors. Who else but an eye witness could have told every incident surrounding the murder of that young boy with such startling accuracy and correctness, the one who had witnessed the terrible deed"?[9]

With this statement, Stoll completed three hours of argument, and the court was recessed until the next morning.

The morning of Friday, October 24, 1902, was cold and bitter. "It is a dull, dark day," described one reporter. "A cold wind is twisting from the trees in the court yard the few remaining leaves. There is no fire in the room, and although the windows are closed the women, scores of them, standing up, wear their wraps; Kels Nickell is shivering as if he had the ague. The wind shakes the windows and snow is in prospect. There is one voice filling the room, a dominant thrilling voice, that of the prosecutor."[10]

Stoll resumed his argument with comments about the nature of the crime and its possible commission by the Miller brothers. "Whoever committed this crime committed a dastardly deed." Referring to the Miller boys, he said, "No child could have committed it. It was the work of a cold-blooded and heartless murderer."

Stoll then spoke of how Horn had told LeFors about running barefoot after Willie Nickell, but he said Horn had not necessarily been barefoot and would have had on stockings or moccasins—nevertheless intending to leave no trail.[11] He spoke of "men steeped with criminality, and with damnable instincts and who are well acquainted with methods of covering up their tracks. Therefore, it was no uncommon thing for this man to have said that he ran across the ground barefooted. The leaden missiles of death were fired by an expert; an expert in shooting; expert in shooting game—human game. A boy could not have made those shots. Who was it who said it was the best shot I ever made?"[12]

Reporters noted how the prosecutor's argument upset Mrs. Nickell. "His frequent reference to her dead boy caused her to sob pitifully, and she held a handkerchief to her eyes all the time."[13] The victim's mother was not the only person affected by Stoll's comments. The *Denver Post* reported that "there were dim eyes in the jury box several times."[14]

"Where is the motive in this case?" Stoll asked the jury, hauling up the question the defense had thrown at him. Pulling up the stenographer's report of Horn's confession to LeFors, Stoll said, "Here it is." "This is what he says: 'I shot him to keep him from going to the house and raising a h[ell] of a commotion.'" "The murderer was in that draw waiting to kill Kels Nickell, the father; the boy recognized him, started to the house to warn his father. That's motive enough. What more do you want?" Stoll then referred to how "the kid rode upon him" and added, "The whole defense of the prisoner rests on the skill of his counsel."[15]

As for the trouble Frank Irwin had had with Horn, Stoll said: "Thank God here and there in that country is a man who is not afraid of a coward and yet the defense asks you to throw away God's immutable law because Horn's neck is in danger." Of the confession, Stoll said: "Had not Horn's confession been heard by witnesses he would have denied it, but that is impossible and so he says I did not mean it." Stoll ridiculed the defense claim that he, Stoll, had said that a confession is only made when "the gravity of a crime overwhelms the offender." "Admissions have been made time and again when the offender is under the influence of the intoxicating cup." Stoll said that the plea of the defense that Horn's confession was only "a josh" was the "last straw of a drowning man," and he referred to Horn's previous record, reading to the jury the letter Horn wrote to LeFors in which he said: "I don't care how big or bad they are, I broke up the Brown's Hole gang." And, Stoll added, "Horn also said that he got $2100 for three men killed and one shot at five times. Who were the three men? Powell, Lewis, and Willie Nickell. He said it was a josh. But in considering this you must remember the character of the man who said it."[16]

Stoll's final comments, referred to by the press as a "sublime peroration," spoke to the jury's duty:

> When the matter gets to the court [Judge Scott,] the court will do its duty; when it gets to the Supreme Court, the supreme court will do its duty, and when it gets to the governor, the governor will do his duty; all these officers, one and all, will do their duty, but you must do yours. . . .
>
> In all countries and in all climes the safety of society has demanded the stern and inexorable enforcement of these provisions ["Whoso sheddeth man's blood by man shall his blood be shed"]. Religion, philosophy and common experience for ages have declared that [all men] have each and all an inalienable right to their allotted course, unmolested and unharmed by the dagger of the highwayman or the bullet of the cowardly assassin.
>
> Gentlemen of the jury, the oath which you have taken, and that oath which is registered before the throne of eternal justice and in the minds of your fellow citizens, simply required you to do your duty, and that duty we submit requires at your hands a verdict of murder in the first degree.
>
> Do not think for a minute, gentlemen, that you can escape the consequences of not doing your duty. Duty fulfilled remains with us for all time as a consolation; duty violated remains with us for all time as a remorse. Our conscience appeals to us and will not be stilled. There is no ocean wide enough to enable us to flee from it; there is no mountain high enough to shut it out from our mental vision; there is no valley deep enough to hedge us about and protect us from its approach. It whispers in our ears in the

silence of the darkest night, and its voice will not be stilled amid the din of our busiest day. It will go with you as you leave this jury box, and it will remain with you during the balance of your lives, and in the land of the great beyond it will stand at your side as a vision of joy, or a spectre of woe while eternity rolls its endless rounds. Gentlemen, the people of this county and the officers of this county, at vast expense and under great and overwhelming difficulties, have done their duty. It now remains for you to do yours.[17]

At this point, "amid hushed silence," the court delivered a few final instructions, and the jurors "slowly marched to their jury room." As the *Cheyenne Daily Leader* reported, "Their faces were subjected to the keenest scrutiny by Horn and the attorneys on both sides as they left the room, but their impassive faces threw no light on their possible verdict."[18]

The audience emptied out of the courtroom almost immediately, but Tom Horn, Sheriff Smalley, reporters, attorneys, and the judge remained for about another half hour, until noon, waiting to see if the jury would render an immediate verdict (if so, it almost surely would have meant an acquittal). No such verdict was forthcoming, however, and the people in the courtroom dispersed.[19]

Reporters covering the case rendered their own verdict, however, on the final argument of Walter Stoll. The *Denver Post* termed it "one of the cleverest delivered in a Wyoming court."[20] Stoll's hometown newspaper, the *Daily Leader*, said the prosecutor "closed his masterly arraignment of the accused and spoke the last word in his effort to convict the man suspected of the dastardly crime which has been committed." "It was Stoll's masterpiece. The Horn case is his masterpiece." What Stoll was seeking, explained the *Leader*, was the "cessation of the long series of unpunished crimes" committed in Laramie County. Arrayed against him had been "four of the best attorneys in the state and from the beginning to end every point, every step, had been hotly contested." Stoll was completely committed to the conviction of Tom Horn, however, because if he could secure it, Horn's "conviction will have a widespread influence in putting a stop to the promiscuous taking of human life."[21]

The *Denver Times* said, "The jury is of the best sort for a case of this kind. All but two are cowmen and familiar with all the conditions of the case." But there was a concern, added the *Times*, because "these men have known

Horn personally or by reputation for years and may unconsciously let their opinions formed from such acquaintance enter into the rendering of a verdict."The *Times* concluded, "It is because of this and the fact that one or two of Horn's friends are on the jury that a disagreement [hung jury] is predicted. It is a common report that one man on the jury said before being drawn that nothing could induce him to vote for [Horn's conviction], and there are three who, judging from thirteen days' careful scrutiny, would never vote against him."[22]

Despite high praise for Stoll's masterly performance, the consensus seemed to be that Horn would go free. "Stoll has worked hard to destroy the object of Lacey's arguments, but the quiet, clear explanation of the defense has done its work," concluded the *Denver Times*. "Few look for conviction. Nearly all agree that Lacey's alibi is a strong one and will stand a bold assault."[23] Many observers repeated this thought. Three days earlier the *Cheyenne Daily Leader* had predicted a hung jury despite Stoll's strong showing. There was "no more encouraging outlook than a hung jury," said the paper. "That is the opinion of the majority of the people who have listened attentively to the evidence as adduced from the witness stand." What had been "said and reiterated" was that Horn was guilty of the crime but he would never hang because there was too much money back of him.[24] But the trial had affected Horn's reputation: "Tom Horn is no more the debonair criminal and splendid assassin in the eyes of worshipers of this type of heroes. He may be guilty, but he is now the coward villain, admitting, as he has, by his own confession on the witness stand, that he is a miserable braggart, a monumental liar, or else a man with a soul steeped in guilty crime, seeking to save a worthless life by the pitiable excuse that he lied to a friend."[25]

All the speculation about the jury's probable actions quickly became moot. At twenty minutes past four that Friday afternoon, the bailiff heard "a voice calling from above." The voice was the foreman of the jury, saying, "We have arrived at a verdict."[26]

CHAPTER TWENTY-THREE

The Verdict

When the jury foreman summoned the bailiff, the courtroom was nearly empty. Only five or six people were there, but the news "spread like wild-fire," and before long the Cheyenne district courtroom overflowed with spectators. "It was just 4:30 o'clock when the jury filed into the court room," reported the *Cheyenne Daily Leader.* "A dead silence followed their arrival and it was with anxious face that the prisoner scrutinized the face of each juryman as he solemnly took his seat."[1]

The attorneys may have had a good idea what the verdict was before the jury members were even seated. No newspaper reports describe the jurors' behavior as they entered the courtroom, except one. The *Denver Post* noted that Homer Payne, Tom Horn's friend, "glanced swiftly at Horn, then back to the court." If the jury was not otherwise looking at Horn and his attorneys, it was a bad sign for Horn. Those who have watched juries bring in verdicts know there are strong signs indicating how a jury has decided.[2] If the jurors look away from the defendant and his lawyers, a conviction is probable. If they look at the defendant and his lawyers, and even smile at them, they have most likely voted to acquit.

Still, nobody would know for sure until the verdict was read. A jury's rendering of a verdict is always dramatic, but when the charge is a capital offense and the defendant's life is at stake, the suspense creates a tension so intense that it can be hard to breathe. Moving directly to the matter at hand, Judge Scott asked:

"Gentlemen, have you arrived at a verdict?"

"We have, your honor."

Reporting on the moment, the *Daily Leader* wrote:

> Amidst breathless silence, so profound the dropping of a pin could
> have been heard in the court room, the bailiff took the small piece
> of paper upon which was written the words that to Tom Horn
> meant life or death.
>
> It was a supreme moment, a moment which was the great
> crisis in the life of Tom Horn, when Clerk Fisher slowly opened
> the verdict and began to read.
>
> "We, the jury, empaneled in the above entitled case, do find
> the defendant, Tom Horn, guilty of murder in the first degree, as
> charged in the information."
>
> It was all over. The last word in the famous case had been
> uttered and Prosecuting Attorney W. R. Stoll had won the greatest
> triumph in his entire career.[3]

Tom Horn "listened with his face intently fixed on the speaker, as the
fatal words were read. Not by a single move, not even by the winking
of an eye, did that grand stoic depart from the demeanor he had displayed
throughout this eventful trial. He even smiled to a friend as he was led
back to his cell, a condemned murderer."[4]

Walter Stoll was not present in the courtroom when the verdict was
rendered. He was sick and in bed when the jury came in. The defense attorneys were present, however, and the *Laramie Boomerang* said they were "visibly
disappointed. Only this morning they had expressed themselves confident
of winning and the verdict comes as a shock to them."[5] As with Stoll, Joe
LeFors was not present, despite the "graphic description" by Denver newspapers of a face-to-face meeting between LeFors and Horn right after
the verdict came in. Supposedly, LeFors was in the courtroom "with a gun
ready to kill Horn if he was declared innocent." The *Cheyenne Daily Leader*
reported, however, that LeFors was not in the courtroom when the verdict
was read, and he was "justly indignant." "You can say for the sake of these
enterprising reporters," said LeFors, "that when the verdict of the jury was
read I was in my office writing letters, and was not even at the court house
during the afternoon. Tom Horn is safe so far as I am concerned. I have
no ill will against the man."[6]

Among the members of the Nickell family, only young Freddie was
in the courtroom when the verdict was pronounced. Hearing it read, he

"darted from the room and ran at breakneck speed to his home, several blocks away, where he notified his mother." When Mrs. Nickell heard the news, she collapsed.[7]

Jurors interviewed afterward about their deliberations were generally consistent, though with some variations. Two members of the jury told the *Daily Leader* that the first ballot was eleven to one for conviction, although another version had the first vote ten to two.[8] There was some variance also regarding how many jurors initially voted for first-degree murder. According to the *Denver Post,* the first vote taken showed eight jurors believing that Horn was guilty of first-degree murder, but the *Rocky Mountain News* referred to nine jurors.[9]

Regardless of the exact details, the overall pattern of jury deliberation was clear. The jury started with a solid majority in favor of conviction of first-degree murder and two or three jurors who voted for second-degree murder. There was no reasonable basis for second-degree murder, and the majority jurors apparently quickly convinced those who voted for it to switch to first-degree murder. Then the remaining one or two jurors, including Homer Payne, held out for a while, but finally the vote was unanimous for first-degree murder.

Two jurors who spoke to the *Cheyenne Daily Leader* said Tom Horn's own testimony had convicted him. "There might have been some doubt as to the facts," said one juror, "but when Horn told his story on the stand he signed his own death sentence. His story was too palpably false to be believed, too contradictory."[10] Homer Payne said, "It was hard to go against a man I have known and liked. But what could I do. The question was too hard to be dodged." Echoing Stoll's exhortation, Payne added: "I did my duty." Indeed, it was said that "every man on the jury looked as if he felt he had done his duty. All were glad to get off and agreed that they had had a most tedious time."[11] Remarkably, after the verdict came in, Payne went with Otto Plaga and some other cowboys of the Iron Mountain area and "took in" the town of Cheyenne.[12] Still another juror, F. F. Simon, a man thought to have been leaning in favor of Horn, said it had been the confession that swung the jury, that the confession had determined Horn's guilt.[13]

The verdict should not have been a surprise. The jurors knew Tom Horn and knew his reputation. While their knowledge might have helped Horn at the beginning because of sympathy toward him in the ranch community, that knowledge may well have worked against him in the end. Horn's testimony about his deep sensitivity to LeFors's feelings, which might be wounded if Horn did not admit to killing Willie Nickell, just did not jibe with the Tom Horn known to the ranching community, a man so grim and ruthless that he struck terror in the hearts of people throughout southeastern Wyoming. Horn said he did not understand why he would have such a reputation, but the jury knew exactly why. Even Horn's friend Payne had to admit that "the question was too hard to be dodged," with Payne asking the forlorn question, "What was I to do?" Years later, one of Tom Horn's lawyers commented on the remarkable fact that six men, whom Horn had said would be good jurors for him, actually were selected as jurors but still voted Horn guilty of first-degree murder.[14]

Once the jurors rejected Tom Horn's story about the confession being a josh, Horn was in deep trouble. As indicated by some of the jurors' comments, if all Horn's statement were made in earnest, it was a complete admission of Horn's guilt of first-degree murder, and the inability of the prosecution to present a fully persuasive set of facts aside from the confession was not that significant. The jury obviously did not give much weight to the Plaga alibi or the contention that the killing bullets were not .30 caliber. No juror made any reference to these issues, so vigorously contested during the trial.

In a bizarre postscript, Horn supposedly told his attorneys that he had in fact been lying in wait near the fatal gate but to kill Kels Nickell. Then, Horn said, he had heard a shot and Victor Miller came running up to him, saying that he had just killed Willie Nickell using his .30-30. Why Horn would think such a story might help him is hard to fathom. By this latest tale, Horn admitted that he was at the scene of the murder on the morning of July 18, 1901 (and obviously not where Otto Plaga said he was that morning), and that Willie Nickell had been killed by a .30 caliber bullet, not by bullets of a size between three-eights of an inch and forty-five-hundredths of an inch.[15]

The newspapers reported other of Horn's comments as well. He was asked about whether he had taken his counsel into his "entire confidence," and Horn said, "Oh, I conducted my own case. They [his attorneys] did what I told them to. They ain't to blame."[16]

Horn's attorneys had put up "a splendid fight," said the *Denver Post,* but the odds were too great. "There was never the kind of feeling between Lacey and Burke and Horn as should exist between a defendant and his attorneys." The social gulf between Horn and his lawyers was too great. Horn himself was responsible for his own conviction, it was said, because he talked too much when he was on the stand. Horn's attorneys reportedly were saying something very similar: that Horn had made a fool of himself by his talk when Stoll cross-examined him.[17] More than that, Stoll's going through each and every question and answer between LeFors and Horn, with Horn giving his spin to each one, undercut defense attempts to paint Horn as a drunken dupe to a conniving Joe LeFors. Each of the jurors could see that Horn was actively involved in the conversation, sometimes even exuberantly engaged. In one telling piece of dialogue from the confession, LeFors actually did ask a leading question of Horn—"How about the shells, did you carry them away"? Horn's response was not a numb acquiescence, but a bold declaration: "You bet your God damn life I did."[18] All Horn's extensive, volunteered comments about what a clever and determined assassin he was, juxtaposed with his lame reconstructions on the stand, truly seemed a signing of his own death sentence.

The verdict in the Horn case was the subject of intense interest in Cheyenne, Laramie, and seemingly all over the state of Wyoming and beyond. "That Horn had been condemned" was the sole topic of discussion over the city, the *Denver Post* reported. "Men gathered on street corners and talked the case over. Not only in the hotels, restaurants and saloons, but in every home the verdict was the only thing talked about, and the case was tried and re-tried."[19] Noting the great importance Albany County citizens attached to the Horn trial, the *Laramie Boomerang* told its readers that the news of the conviction "caused a great sensation" because very few expected such a verdict.[20]

Response to the verdict can be summarized in one word: jubilation. Under the headline "Dawn of a New Era," the *Cheyenne Daily Leader* said: "A deep sense of relief; a feeling akin to joy, mingled with pride went over this community yesterday evening when the verdict of the jury in the Tom Horn case was announced. It was a result merely that ninety-nine people out of a hundred hoped for . . . but few expected. They seemed to think almost universally that justice would be foiled." Explaining why people might lack faith in the court system, the newspaper cited the assassinations of Lewis and Powell and the failure of the grand jury to indict Horn, as well as other cases where there had been a "miscarriage of justice." Since Horn had confessed to the "terrible secret of the assassinations," "there has been a dark cloud over the county and we might almost say that it rested upon the state." Indeed, said the *Leader,* as the time for the Horn trial approached, "a corps of newspaper correspondents and picture makers began to hover over us to depict the moral turpitude of the state." The whole state of Wyoming was "under trial before the world." Just think, said the *Leader,* what would have been said if Horn had been acquitted. Thus, Tom Horn's conviction marked "a new era." "The time has passed when men can with impunity make contracts for the assassination of their neighbors.[21]

The *Leader* expressed gratitude "to the twelve men who stood the ordeal of a two weeks trial and came forth with their righteous and just verdict." Referring to Walter Stoll's "faithful and brilliant labor" it added, "He seemed to realize that a great and solemn duty had been imposed upon him and most grandly did he discharge it."[22]

The *Denver Post* also reported a "sentiment of gratification" within Cheyenne because the sentence meant that "the reign of Tom Horn, cattle detective, boasting slayer of men, and the all around bad man of the Wyoming range, is ended." And such sentiment was all the stronger because "few had believed a conviction would be secured."[23] Even Stoll had been unsure of the result, the *Denver Times* said, and lost several nights sleep worrying about it. Stoll issued a statement saying he was delighted with the result as it "means much for the future development of Wyoming." Such events as the assassination of Willie Nickell "have a tendency to lower the moral character of the community in which they occur." "The tendency is to degrade the people in this locality. They gradually become cowards. The greatest difficulty I had to overcome was the abject fear entertained by so many citizens. There was only once in a while a man who had not lost his moral courage."[24]

Perhaps the *Denver Post* offered the most dramatic expression of feelings about the Horn conviction when on the top center of its front page, it published an illustration of a blindfolded female figure of justice. In her right hand she holds a long, lethal sword, and with her left arm she holds by the throat a small, frightened figure labeled "Hired Assassin," an obvious depiction of Tom Horn. Groveling at Lady Justice's feet is a cattle baron, who is pushing a bag of money at her, which she is ignoring. Captioned "Dawn in Wyoming!," the cartoon shows a rising sun in the background.[25]

Meanwhile, defense attorneys said they had started work on an appeal, beginning with a motion for new trial, which would be filed the following Monday (October 27). "We have not given up our fight for the life of Tom Horn," said one of the defense attorneys, "and hope to save him yet." An appeal hardly surprised Walter Stoll. "Of course they will appeal," he said, but Stoll had to be brimming with confidence, given the almost universal praise for his performance (the *Daily Leader* referred to Stoll as the "most congratulated man in Cheyenne" and the *Denver Post* published a large drawing of Stoll on its front page with the caption "The Hero of the Hour"), and he certainly did not seem alarmed by the actions announced by the defense. Some even assumed that the motion for new trial would be quickly denied.[26]

The covering newspapers also urged authorities to go after Horn's employers. The *Denver Post* had sounded this theme even before the verdict. Afterward the *Post* headlined a story "The Hirer of Horn is Next to Suffer," with a sub-headline stating: "The Finale of the Wyoming Drama Will Be Complete and the Conviction of Horn Is Only the Beginning for the Punishment for the Employment of Assassins." The *Denver Times* headline read "Horn Convicted and State Will Prosecute Employers," and the newspaper said that Stoll would now proceed against the men accused of hiring and paying Horn.[27] The newspapers, however, were going beyond what the prosecutor had actually said. The *Denver Post* admitted that Stoll himself was "not talking on future developments in the case," which was probably because he was well aware that the ability to go after the employers would depend on Tom Horn's cooperation, and that remained to be seen. Still, all this talk must have made George Prentiss and his cohorts exceedingly nervous.[28]

CHAPTER TWENTY-FOUR

The Motion for New Trial

The first step in an appeal to the Wyoming Supreme Court in 1902 was the filing of a motion for new trial. In filing the motion, Tom Horn's defense attorneys detailed all the errors they asserted had been committed in *State v. Horn*. The defense declared that together they constituted grounds to give Horn a new trial.

The attorneys wasted no time filing the motion, doing so on October 27, the Monday following the Friday on which Horn was convicted. It must have made for a grueling weekend for the defense attorneys and their employees. The forty-seven-page document set out seventy rulings by Judge Scott that might be considered erroneous.[1]

Of the first forty-six points, all but two related to questions asked of witnesses. The defense complained about Scott's rulings when Kels Nickell was on the stand, saying that the judge had erred when he refused to allow the defense to pursue the subject of trouble between Nickell and James Miller or questions about the guns the Miller boys carried.[2] The defense also maintained that not letting A. F. Whitman testify to all the disputes between Kels Nickell and his neighbors was in error.[3]

The defense asserted that prosecutor Stoll had improperly been allowed to impeach his own witness, Dr. Amos Barber, when Stoll confronted Barber with his long and inconsistent statements at the preliminary hearing and Barber's testimony before the coroner's jury.[4] The defense also asserted that the district court had erred when it allowed two incompetent and irrelevant questions to the publisher of the *Laramie Republican* asking when an article about the death of Willie Nickell had first appeared in the newspaper.[5]

Four defense complaints related to Laramie County sheriff's deputy Pete Warlamount's testimony.[6] John Lacey had asked Warlamount what he had learned in his investigation of Horn's riding into Laramie after the death of Willie Nickell, but Judge Scott had refused to allow the question because it sought Warlamount's testimony about statements made by people not before the court (hearsay). The defense also complained about Warlamount's testimony that he had received a .30-30 cartridge from Freddie Nickell. During the trial the defense had contended that this testimony was "remote."[7]

The defense wrote at length about restrictions upon John Lacey's questioning of Victor Miller. Lacey had tried to elaborate on the troubles between Victor and Willie Nickell, but Judge Scott's rulings had cut him off.[8] The defense also did not like the rulings allowing statements of the two Laramie shoemakers, Matlock and Powell, about the blue sweater, the tepid identification of Horn, and of the substance on the sweater (that it "resembled blood very much").[9]

The defense said that the district judge had also ruled incorrectly when he decided that defense attorney Burke's questions about a bullet striking Willie Nickell at right angles were improper redirect examination (having been fully addressed in the direct examination) of Dr. George Johnston.[10]

The defense had a long list of complaints about Joe LeFors's testimony, especially LeFors's rebuttal testimony. Horn had testified that LeFors had proposed that he and Horn go in together to pin the Nickell murder on some innocent person in order to obtain the reward money. The defense said that Judge Scott had erred when he let LeFors contradict Horn's statement.[11] The defense team also complained about LeFors's testimony in which he told of Horn saying that his shots at Kels Nickell might have turned out differently had the sun not been shining on the sights of his gun, that Nickell had run and yelled "like a Comanche Indian," and that Horn knew a man on the coroner's jury who would tell him everything that happened there.[12] The defense objected to LeFors's testimony that Horn was "perfectly sincere" when they conversed and that he, LeFors, could see no joshing.[13] And the defense stated that it had been error to allow Walter Stoll to read into evidence the contents of two letters, one written on January 7, 1902 by Horn to LeFors (wherein Horn said, "I will get the men sure for I have never let a cow thief get away from me unless he just got up and jumped clean out of the country"), and the other of the same date to LeFors from W. D. Smith, who discussed the arrangements for Horn in Montana.[14] The testimony by LeFors was especially objectionable to the defense because it brought in evidence of Horn's bad acts that were not the subject of charges against Horn.

The defense also made several isolated objections relating to the admission of evidence, including the reading to Duncan Clark of a part of the coroner's inquest official report, the reading of a portion of the *Denver Post* to Dr. W. L. Davis (who had treated Horn for his broken jaw in Denver), Judge Scott's refusal to allow Robert Stockton to testify to the general moral character of the Denver witness Frank Mulock, and Stoll's handing to Charles H. Miller (proprietor of the Elkhorn stable) a July 17, 1901, copy of the *Laramie Republican*.[15] These kinds of contentions by the defense were unlikely to be considered error by the Wyoming Supreme Court, but given the requirement of listing all possible items of error before the court would address them, many complaints were standard objections, made just to preserve the possibility that they might later prove of interest to the state supreme court judges.

The defense said that a number of objects should not have been allowed into evidence, including Dr. Lewis's measuring tape, a measuring scale showing the division of an inch into sixty-four parts, and Horn's Winchester rifle. The defense objected to Judge Scott's allowing the prosecution's challenge for cause of a George P. Knight, a "man of strong views."[16]

With the exception of a short list of concluding items, all the remaining defense complaints were to jury instructions forwarded by the prosecution that Judge Scott had accepted or instructions forwarded by the defense that Scott had disallowed. Scott had accepted prosecution instructions regarding first-degree and second-degree murder, intent, the consideration by the jury of bias by witnesses, impeachment, confessions, corroboration of confessions, alibis, the burden of proof of the prosecution, and an explanation of reasonable doubt.[17] Scott had refused the proposed instructions of the defense as to the caliber of the bullets that killed Willie Nickell, reasonable doubt, circumstantial evidence, and one instruction urging extreme caution with confessions.[18] The remaining assignments of error were catchalls, including the statements that the verdict was contrary to the evidence, contrary to law, not sustained by sufficient evidence, and contrary to instructions, and finally that Walter Stoll, in his final argument, had made improper statements.[19]

Accompanying the motion for new trial was an affidavit filed by defense attorneys Lacey, Burke, Matson, and Kennedy describing portions of Stoll's final argument. They objected to Stoll's saying that Horn was not an ordinary man but a man of "criminal mind and instincts," Stoll's reference to the duties of the prosecution, the court, the supreme court and the governor, and Stoll's description of a criminal defendant who was acquitted but then killed a family of six.[20]

In a few days, the defense filed a supplemental motion for new trial, claiming misconduct and "irregularity in the proceedings of the jury." They attached affidavits of Greta Rohde, a waitress at the Inter Ocean Hotel (where the jurors had gone to lunch), of Homer Payne, and of J. Emerson Smith, a *Denver Post* reporter.[21] Rohde swore that during the trial, when the jury was staying and eating at the Inter Ocean, she had heard comments while the jury was in the dining room. The comments were from people sitting at a table "adjoining" the jurors' table, to the effect that three men on the jury would not vote to convict because they were friends of Horn's, and that a man would be more apt to tell the truth drunk than sober. Homer Payne said that during jury deliberations he had heard comments from other jurors that any mistake made in the trial proceedings would be corrected by the Wyoming Supreme Court. Payne also said he had heard remarks that he was a friend of Horn's and that the jury would probably hang. These remarks gave him the impression, Payne said, that people thought he had been "bought or fixed" by the defense. In his affidavit, J. Emerson Smith said that he had heard people at the Inter Ocean make comments similar to what Rohde and Payne reported, adding that these people were speaking so loudly that the jury could have easily overheard. Smith also said he had heard similar remarks when the jury was passing through the rotunda of the hotel. At one point, he said, the bailiff, John Reese, "protested to the manager of the hotel, Mr. J. H. Fullerton, in regard to a conversation overheard by the said Bailiff while sitting at the same table with said jurors, which conversation was in relation to the same case."

The prosecution quickly responded to the defense presentation, forwarding a series of counter-affidavits. Charles Tolson, a juror who was a porter from Cheyenne, swore that he had occupied the same seat whenever the jury ate, which was directly across the table from Homer Payne and nearer to other persons in the dining room. He said that he had paid close attention to these other people but had not heard the kinds of comments

Payne and Smith referred to. After five ballots, he said, the vote was ten for first-degree murder and two (Howard B. Thomas, a ranchman who resided near LaGrange, and Homer Payne) for acquittal. The jurors had then engaged in a discussion in which Thomas and Payne said they were voting for acquittal because they saw the confession as a "josh," but after a full discussion of the surrounding circumstances, the two holdouts had changed their minds and joined in the vote for first-degree murder. During all the deliberations, Tolson said, these two jurors made no mention of pressure from outside parties.[22]

In another affidavit, juror James E. Barnes, a butcher from Cheyenne, also denied having heard any conversation of the kind Payne spoke of. Barnes affirmed juror Tolson's description of the discussion just before all twelve jurors voted for first-degree murder, and he added that the jurors had gone over every point in evidence "and each . . . was explained and gone over in detail." At this point in the deliberations, Payne and Thomas had then gone by themselves to an area near a window and conversed. Barnes said that he had not heard what they said, but when they came back to the group, Thomas had stated, "Gentlemen, do not think we are not men," and then he had suggested another ballot. The new ballot had resulted in the unanimous determination of first-degree murder.

The state also presented affidavits from both of the bailiffs in charge of the jury during the trial. One, John H. Reese, said at all recesses the bailiffs were admonished to not permit the jurors "to converse with any one or any one with the jurors." All the meals were eaten at the Inter Ocean Hotel, Reese said, and the jurors were set apart from all patrons, with a bailiff stationed at each end of their table. The jurors had not mingled with hotel guests, and every precaution had been taken to prevent contact with the jurors. The only time anyone had attempted to speak to one of the jurors was when an intoxicated man had tried to advance toward one of the jurors who was an old friend, but he was pushed away without making contact. Saying he had read the affidavits of Payne and Smith, Reese said he had not heard any of the comments referred to by these two men, and if such a conversation had taken place he "could not have failed to have heard it." Reese supported Tolson's and Barnes's statements that they were nearer to restaurant patrons than were Payne and Thomas, and he said jurors never were in the rotunda of the hotel. Reese contradicted Smith's comment that he (Reese) had protested to the hotel manager about a conversation. Reese said he had "never on any occasion whatever protested to the hotel manager" or to anyone else about any conversation overheard by him. Once, Reese stated, he had asked three persons connected with the defense to "occupy seats further away from the jury," but that request had been made in an abundance of caution and not "upon the ground of any misconduct of such persons whatever."[23]

In his affidavit, George Proctor, the other bailiff, said much the same things as Reese. He emphasized that every precaution had been taken to keep people away from the jurors and that the man who wanted to say "how do you do" did not even succeed in shaking hands with his juror friend. Proctor said he had never heard Reese "raise any protest to the manager of the Hotel" while the jurors were eating their meals.[24]

The prosecution also offered two additional short affidavits. In one, George S. Walker said he had met Homer Payne the evening of the verdict, and Payne had said that "he had known Horn for a long time and felt sorry for him but he thought he was guilty and had to do it." J. Emerson Smith, the same *Denver Post* reporter who had provided an affidavit to the defense, gave one to the prosecution as well. Smith said he had interviewed Payne on the evening of October 24, 1902, after the verdict was announced, and Payne had told him, "It was hard to go against a man I have known and liked. But what could I do? The question was too hard to be dodged. I did my duty."[25]

Walter Stoll submitted the longest counter-affidavit for the prosecution, one of six pages.[26] This vigorous response was understandable, since the defense attacks on Stoll's final argument not only might support a reversal of Horn's conviction, but any prosecuting attorney would be sensitive to assertions that he treated a criminal defendant unfairly, inviting a jury to abrogate its responsibility. In his affidavit, Stoll said that the defense attorneys' affidavit was "in some respects substantially incorrect" and that in others his statements had been taken out of context.

Stoll said the statement that Horn was not an ordinary man but an "extraordinary" man with "criminal instincts" was used only at the conclusion of the prosecutor's comments about the evidence Horn gave on the stand and related to Horn's "appearance and demeanor while testifying, and the unreasonableness of his story together with the fact of his being contradicted on material matters by other credible and reliable testimony." Stoll said that his arguments to the jury had been in reply to the defense contention that only the statements of Horn should be credited, an invitation by the defense not to follow the instructions of the trial judge regarding scrutiny of the testimony. Stoll therefore had told the jury that they needed to carefully weigh Horn's testimony and scrutinize it, treating it as they would other evidence. None of this was a declaration, said Stoll, that if the jurors made an error, the governor or the supreme court would correct it.

Stoll also said that his comments about freeing a defendant on a too-strict application of rules relating to circumstantial evidence was in response to Mr. Burke's long and earnest argument calling the jurors' attention to "three or four instances" showing "how little reliability could be placed upon circumstantial evidence." Stoll said his response had been to emphasize to the jury that they ought to "conscientiously consider all of the evidence relating to the different facts in the case, and not to ruthlessly throw aside the evidence of other witnesses and accept simply the evidence of the defendant as to such facts."

Stoll concluded his affidavit by saying that Horn's defense attorneys had never during the trial called the attention of the court to an asserted impropriety. They had never sought to have the court admonish the prosecutor that his "line of argument" was improper. They had never requested that the court instruct the jury with regard to any of Stoll's arguments. And never had any instruction or suggestion been made to him about the impropriety of any argument.

The prosecution completed its November 8 presentation of affidavits with two short statements from Stoll's co-counsel, Clyde Watts and H. Waldo Moore. Both men said that they had read Stoll's affidavit, that they had been present during all the events commented upon, and that Stoll's sworn statements were accurate.[27]

The defense promptly responded on November 10, 1902, with "counter-counter-affidavits" from three men. All said substantially the same thing, that they watched the jury come to dinner on several occasions and that the jury members had all passed through the rotunda of the Inter Ocean Hotel. These three affidavits were the final ones submitted in connection with the defense's motion for new trial, and the court officials were no doubt relieved that the affidavit caravan had at last concluded.[28] The final affidavits were filed even after the arguments before Judge Scott on the motion for new trial had begun. Those arguments started on Saturday, November 8, 1902, and the defense led off with an all-day speech by T. F. Burke.

Arguments relating to a motion for new trial are usually an empty exercise, although the notoriety of the Horn case gave them more significance than they would normally have had. Any attorney appearing before a judge after a long trial, however, knows that the sitting judge is highly unlikely to grant a new trial. All participants in any sensational case are fully aware of the great public interest. So, from the beginning, the lawyers are apt to make abler presentations and the judge to weigh decisions especially carefully. A sitting judge has already thought through in depth the knotty problems being presented in the arguments for a new trial. More than this, a judge in 1902 Wyoming, when judges were nominated by political parties and chosen in competitive elections, was highly unlikely to declare that he had made some grievous error compelling a county, because of his blunder, to again undertake the substantial expense of a new trial (said to be $30,000 in Horn's case, an immense sum in 1902).[29] Some newspapers openly predicted that a motion for new trial would not be granted.[30] Still, none of the attorneys wanted to appear as if he were not taking seriously an important motion in the Horn case.

At eleven o'clock on that Saturday morning, Burke began by saying, "My client is deeply thankful that the time has come when the feeling against the crime cannot effect [sic] the interests of the man accused of the offense." Burke spoke then for the rest of the day, not closing until 5:30 P.M. Addressing primarily the evidence introduced at the trial, he seemed especially vexed that prosecution witnesses had been allowed to testify that Horn was sincere when he made his confession.[31]

If Horn was "deeply thankful," as his lawyer asserted, it was a well-concealed emotion. Horn did not seem to care much. The *Cheyenne Daily Leader* described Horn as "listless and dispirited, taking but little interest in the proceedings. His face is decidedly paler than during the trial, he rarely smiles, and his face is pinched, and drawn with dark circles under the eyes." The paper noted that Horn was "wearing a pair of new tan shoes which give a jaunty air to his make-up, incongruous with his careworn features."[32] Horn had been so despondent since the verdict that a deputy sheriff asked him what the matter was when he was put back in his cell. The wind had been blowing hard in Cheyenne, not uncommonly, and Horn told the deputy: "It's the wind, I guess. It makes me nervous."[33]

Stoll gave his presentation on Monday, November 10, and he too spoke all day. Unlike Stoll's soaring rhetoric in his final argument, these comments were more prosaic, "being of a technical nature regarding the evidence in the case and the law as applicable to the admissibility or inadmissibility of the evidence." Disappointed, the *Daily Leader* stated that "nothing of interest developed during the day."[34]

Stoll had a cold on Tuesday, November 11, and so could not attend court. It was, therefore, November 12 when John Lacey made the final argument on the motion for new trial. Lacey spoke most of the morning, not concluding until 11:30. Lacey's argument was said to be "able and telling," and afterward Lacey said he "felt confident of securing a new trial." Judge Scott declared he would take the matter under advisement and would announce his decision "as speedily as possible."[35]

That announcement proved to be speedy indeed. Upon returning from the noon recess, Scott declared that he was ready to state his decision. A group of spectators had hung around the courthouse all day waiting for the judge's decision, and these people no doubt comprised the small audience in the courtroom when Scott convened court at 2:10 P.M.[36]

The judge did not go into the usual preliminaries of opening court but instead "plunged at once into his decision." After careful consideration of the materials before him, Scott concluded, "There was no irregularity in the care of the jury, and nothing which could have preclude[d] the jury from giving the defendant a fair trial." "There was no misconduct on the part of the prosecuting attorney. There was at the time no mention made of any . . . impropriety in the address of the counsel for the state by the counsel for the defense." Speaking directly to Lacey, Scott said: "Judge Lacey, when the jury was filing out, you stepped to the bench and said . . . you desired to except to the argument of the counsel for the state. The court told you that in order to do so you must return to your table and make your exception so that the counsel for the state might know. No exception was taken." Scott closed by saying, "I cannot find any error prejudicial to the defendant. The motion for a new trial for the defendant is overruled."

Horn became "white as marble," when he realized what the ruling of the court would be, but then "straightened back and assumed his wonted stolidity." Judge Scott moved immediately to the sentencing, which he announced "is as unpleasant to the court as it is unwelcome to the attorneys for the defense." Scott had never sentenced a man to death before, and the *Wyoming Tribune* spoke of how his voice "trembled as he commenced to speak, and he was deeply moved."

The *Tribune* wrote: "Horn arose almost as with a spring and took two steps toward the bench, then stopped and straightened like a grenadier. His head was tilted high on a rigid neck, his chest protruded and his heels were together like those of a soldier. His hands were clasped behind his back, and where the fingers gripped white spots spread. He tried to keep his eyes on those of the judge, but failed, and several times glanced hurriedly aside. The only other sign of emotion was a constant swallowing."[37]

Judge Scott asked Horn if he had anything to say before judgment was pronounced. Horn answered, "In a clear tone and without a quiver," "I don't think I have[,] sir." Then Scott sentenced Horn to be executed on the ninth day of January 1903, between the hours of 9:00 A.M. and 3:00 P.M., being "taken by the sheriff of Laramie county to a place prepared by him convenient to the jail and there hanged by the neck until you are dead." After the judge's pronouncement, Horn "remained erect, motionless, staring through a window to the judge's left." He stood like that for about half a minute, when Judge Scott looked at him and said, "That is all." Horn then rushed from the courtroom, so quickly it seemed it might be a "bolt for liberty," but Horn stopped at the bottom of a staircase. He tried to enter the sheriff's office but found the door was locked. "I am locked out, Mr. Sheriff," said Horn.[38]

Taken back to his cell to await execution, Horn was placed in a kind of isolation, not even allowed his "accustomed exercise" or allowed to go to "the court house yard to cut into strips hides of cattle with which to make the wonderful products of his genius as a braider."[39]

CHAPTER TWENTY-FIVE

A New Era

While attorneys and the court were caught up in the motion for new trial, the public continued to buzz about the Horn verdict. People in Wyoming were elated by the Horn verdict. Said *Bill Barlow's Budget* of Douglas, Wyoming, "The recording angel set down more expressions of thanks to Deity than were ever before credited to Wyoming." Public opinion, the paper continued, had long ago decided that "Willie Nickell was shot in the back by the man on trial at Cheyenne; that he was a black-hearted, cowardly assassin, whose hands reeked with the blood of more than one victim." He deserved to hang, said the *Budget,* but would he? Given all the money pledged to defeat any prosecution, "what wonder that the wisest shook their heads and predicted an acquittal, or at best a disagreement." "But Wyoming has grown—grown stronger, better and nobler. A 'gun' rampant on a field of $20 weasel-skins no longer suffices for a state seal. An honest judge and an honest jury have waded patiently through a slough of testimony and a maze of oratorical efforts calculated to mystify and mislead, and Tom Horn has reached the end of his rope at last."[1] Other Wyoming newspapers concurred. The *Laramie Republican* and the *Cheyenne Leader* both ran the *Budget* editorial.[2]

The *Denver Post's* Polly Pry, to no one's surprise, strongly approved the conviction, saying: "Wyoming has awakened. She has put out her fair hand upon the plague spot in her domain—and more, she has spoken in no uncertain voice—the spot must be removed. There are to be no more licensed killers in her beautiful kingdom. No more children are to be murdered for the gratification of any man's vengeance—if she can help it." The *Wyoming Derrick* expressed its concurrence, filling most of its front page with Pry's long story.[3] Pry's articles carried weight in Wyoming because the *Denver Post* was following, not leading Wyoming public opinion, expressing thoughts to which Pry had been led by Wyoming people.[4]

Other Wyoming papers concurred. "The verdict struck a popular chord here in Wyoming, and throughout the Rocky Mountain region for that matter," announced the *Wyoming Industrial Journal,* "for crime in this State had gone unpunished for so many years that people were beginning to be ashamed of the fact that they resided in the commonwealth. But we can now lift our heads once more and say to the world, Paid assassins and their employers will no longer be tolerated in Wyoming."[5] The *Saratoga Sun* spoke of the "great wave of relief" that swept over Wyoming with news of the verdict.[6] And the *Wheatland World* explained why Wyoming's people viewed the case with such deep significance:

> The great mass of the people of Laramie County, and of the state, regard the verdict as a righteous one, and will only be satisfied when Horn has paid the extreme penalty which the law provides for the punishment of crime. The Horn case at no time was considered in the light of an ordinary murder. There were principles involved which made it of vital importance, not alone to the people of the county but as well to those of the entire state. The fact that it was generally believed that Horn was a hired assassin, that his business was to kill at so much per head, that he had become bold in this calling until he could repeatedly boast of his deeds, caused people to stand aghast at the revelation and to seriously inquire if these things were to continue and were to be acknowledged in a public manner as a necessary plank in the Wyoming Decalogue. People reasoned, too, that if Horn could kill one, two or three men for hire and go unpunished he could ply his calling to a much further extent, that if Horn could do these things others could be found to enter the same field—that the taking of human life on the Wyoming ranges would become a mere matter of pay.
>
> But these things are not to be . . . and a new era has been ushered in, when the gun will not be an accepted means of adjusting personal grievances.[7]

Meanwhile, the opposing sides in *State v. Horn* lobbed salvos at each other, as if the trial was still continuing. In a newspaper interview, John Lacey announced that he had "positive evidence" of the killer of Willie Nickell (referring to a confession), and it was not Tom Horn. "We tried to bring out this matter on the trial," Lacey said, "but the court would not permit the testimony to be introduced."[8] The claim was inaccurate. At no time during the trial did Lacey offer into evidence a purported confession from a third party. More than that, his statement was contrary to Wyoming law. The law was clearly established in 1902 that while evidence showing only a motive to commit murder was inadmissible, actual evidence showing that a victim was killed by someone other than the defendant was admissible. Lacey was too good an attorney to believe the accuracy of his comment, so perhaps the defense attorney had a tactical reason for not submitting his alleged proof during the trial. Lacey also asserted that Tom Horn had not been of sound mind since he had returned from Cuba some years before. He was not legally insane, said Lacey, but his mind was so affected that he would "admit the commission of any crime imputed to him."[9]

In the same issue as Lacey's comments, the *Cheyenne Daily Leader* reported the prosecution as saying that the state had evidence "which proves most conclusively that Horn told the truth when he said that he killed Powell and Lewis." If Horn should somehow avoid punishment for the killing of Willie Nickell, therefore, he would be arrested for the murder of Powell and Lewis. "The man who received the money for these killings and paid that money over to Tom Horn is known to the authorities." Allegedly, a partial payment had been made in the amount of $250, consisting of two hundred-dollar bills, two twenty-dollar bills and one ten-dollar bill. The go-between was said to be living in Cheyenne and was even a candidate for office as a Democrat. The public was never given the name of this person, but he could only have been George Prentiss, the man Joe LeFors talked with on the train from Bosler to Laramie in November 1901.[10] Many people in Cheyenne must have noticed this article, even if Prentiss did not. In a town of fourteen thousand people, there seems little doubt that Prentiss and the people who used him to pay Horn would become aware of the article. And each had to have known that he was vulnerable to a charge of being an accessory before the fact of first-degree murder (which carried the same penalty as committing the murder itself).[11] The phrase "sweating blood" comes to mind.

Indeed, several newspapers still spoke of the importance of prosecuting the men who had hired Horn, an idea voiced even before his conviction. In October, when evidence was still being heard in the trial court, Polly Pry wrote a provocative article titled, "When Is 5 Cents Worth $12,000?" She spoke of the facts that Tom Horn, when arrested, had only had five cents to his name, but that within three days, $12,000 had been forwarded by John Coble, and probably other cattlemen, for the payment of talented lawyers to defend him. Pry asked rhetorically: "Why is the protection of Tom Horn worth $12,000 to Mr. Coble and his associates?" "What crime have these wealthy gentlemen committed, aided or abetted, of which Horn is cognizant, that they should seek, not alone by their money, but by their all-pervading influence, to defeat the ends of justice and to again turn an unnatural and terrible monster loose among their people?" She concluded that these men were only trying to protect themselves and that they should be prosecuted as vigorously as Horn had been, and she declared: "The conviction of Tom Horn should be followed by the arrest, the prosecution, the conviction and the punishment of the men who instigated his crimes."[12]

Horn's conviction certainly did not diminish Polly Pry's ardor. In her article reprinted in the *Wyoming Derrick* after the conviction, Pry hit particularly hard the theme of going after those who hired Horn. She referred to "that black-hearted fiend who sent him forth on his mission of death," concluding that a conviction of the procurer of Willie Nickell's murder would be "a warning that neither the hirer nor the hired, who traffic in human life[,] can ever again find a foothold in Wyoming: A protest against any discrimination between the criminal rich and the criminal poor, and a promise that equal justice shall be given to all alike."[13] Another newspaper, noting the diminishment of Horn's "indomitable spirit," openly predicted that Horn would inevitably break down, making "a full confession before he walks up the steps of the gallows."[14]

Two more unusual stories arose just after Tom Horn's conviction. The first related to Homer Payne, Horn's friend on the jury who finally voted to convict him. Payne had a sweetheart from Chugwater, and he had proposed to her just before the trial. Based on a newspaper description, Payne was "a blue-eyed, high cheeked, muscular young cattleman" who could attract a pretty young woman. If Payne had strong feelings toward his sweetheart, she appeared to have strong feelings about him too because, rather than wait for his time on the jury to be completed, she did her best to

get a letter to him, sending it to the courthouse, where the bailiff inter-
cepted and delivered it instead to Judge Scott. Seeing that the letter had no
nefarious purpose, the judge "could not find it in his heart to deny the
happiness the letter contained for Payne," so he handed the letter to him.
The jury verdict was rendered on Friday, the couple obtained a license on
Saturday, and they were married Saturday evening.[15]

The second story relates to public comments about a "delivery," meaning, in 1902, either the hostile seizure of a prisoner by, for example, a
lynch mob, or an escape by a prisoner, either by himself or with the aid
of allies.[16] The *Cheyenne Daily Leader*'s discussion of fear of a "delivery" was
a reminder that Tom Horn still had fervent supporters. During his trial,
Horn's friends had secreted rifles throughout the courthouse. This came
to light because a few days after the trial a reporter watched two men go
into the courthouse carrying nothing and then each emerge with a rifle.
When asked, they had apparently asserted that in the event of an acquittal
they were determined to protect Horn and get him out of town. The presence of rifles in the courthouse could also have aided in an escape if an
opportunity had arisen.[17] In fact, it was concern for Horn's delivery that
seemed to occupy everyone even as his lawyers labored mightily over an
appeal of Herculean dimensions.

CHAPTER TWENTY-SIX

Escape

Tom Horn sat in his jail cell throughout most of 1903, but the time of his stay was hardly placid. Events throughout Wyoming kept people continuously stirred.

Wyoming was a violent place in 1903. In February, Ben Minnick, a young sheepman (barely twenty), was grazing his brother's sheep in an area of the southern Big Horn Basin said to be within an 1897 deadline imposed by local cattlemen. This grazing was perceived as a capital offense by these cattlemen, and a gunman came after Ben's brother, William. The gunman shot Ben in the back but then apologized when he learned that his victim was not William Minnick. Little good it did Ben, who died that night.[1]

Oddly enough, the Minnick murder indirectly affected Tom Horn, in a way nobody could have anticipated then. It all began when a man named Jim McCloud was eventually arrested for the murder. Big Horn County authorities were never able to develop sufficient evidence against McCloud for the murder of Ben Minnick, but they did send him to Cheyenne on charges pending against him in Laramie County.[2]

Shortly after Minnick's murder, on May 23, 1903, an eastern Wyoming lynch mob killed a prisoner. "Diamond Slim" Clifton had been charged with the murder of a young, well-liked couple in Weston County, and thirty-five cowboys hit the Weston County jail and took Clifton to a high railroad bridge near Newcastle, where a noose was placed about his neck and he was pushed off the bridge. The long fall decapitated Clifton.[3]

On July 19, 1903, a lynch mob hit the Big Horn County jail in Basin, Wyoming. They shot up the jail, killing a deputy sheriff and two men convicted of murder awaiting appeal. The mob was incensed by the delays in carrying out the execution of the two convicted men.[4] The actions of the Basin mob were not widely criticized in Wyoming. The *Laramie Boomerang* carried an article, the gist of which was that the cause of the recent lynch mob actions was the unacceptable delays by the courts, and that until Wyoming received "a thorough waking up," lynchings would continue.[5] When Big Horn County tried to bring to justice the perpetrators of the raid on the jail, the effort fell apart after the first trial. Intimidated witnesses failed to support the state's case, and all charges against eight men indicted for the raid were dismissed.[6] The Wyoming attorney general felt compelled to declare to the public that the Wyoming courts were not to blame for the recent lynchings. He pointed out a fact, ominous to Tom Horn, that in the history of Wyoming there had never been a reversal by the supreme court of a first-degree murder conviction.[7]

From the beginning of January 1903, the public groused about "the law's delays."[8] The *Laramie Boomerang* reprinted an editorial from the *Cody Enterprise* complaining bitterly about how the delays in the Horn case were "altogether at variance with the principles of justice," because "many months will elapse before sentence is carried into execution." The *Enterprise* complained that Big Horn County (in which Cody was located in 1903) "also has had a convicted murderer loafing in the county jail, protected by the law's technicalities, for over a year." The Cody newspaper noted, presciently, that mob violence was frequently "incited by these tedious and apparently unnecessary delays."[9] The *Wheatland World* also grumbled about the law's delays, citing favorably an article from the *Buffalo Bulletin* that said that by the time the Wyoming Supreme Court passed on the Horn appeal, "there will be people in the state who will be declaring what a great pity it was that poor Willie Nickell stubbed his toe while running and fell, striking his head on a stone and knocking his brains out."[10]

Horn was not bothered by the slow progress of his case. Very early it became evident that it would be at least eight months before the appeal process was completed.[11] And during that time a stay of execution would be granted, given the undeniable reality that without a stay there would be no point to an appeal.[12] These developments were said to help Horn's spirits, as he realized that he would still have close to a year to live (counting delays after the appeal) even if the appeal was lost. Horn was supposedly "in the best of spirits" and laughed and joked with his jailers when served a turkey dinner. He was said to believe that the actual granting of the stay of execution "meant his ultimate freedom," and it was reported that the stay made him "jocular and a wit."[13] Then again, perhaps the reports of Horn's good mood were slanted to reflect a prevalent attitude of Wyoming people in 1903 that prisoners not promptly executed were enjoying themselves in jail.

The public's demand for swift and sure punishment was understandable in the early twentieth century. Wyoming county jails were notoriously lacking in security, which made them highly susceptible to escape by determined men. Part of the problem was that Wyoming counties were poor and small, not usually holding many prisoners, and the jailers were not experienced. Cheyenne had better facilities than most communities in Wyoming and more experienced men, but it was still a small, rural outpost.

From January 1903, there were several plots and rumors of plots to free Horn. The first plot was apparently unearthed by the *Wyoming Tribune,* and the Cheyenne daily did not hesitate to compliment itself. The *Tribune's* January 21, 1903 issue presented as its top headline the declaration: "The Tribune Has Averted Most Daring Jail Delivery Ever Attempted in the West." Beneath this headline was a series of other headlines covering most of the top half of the first page of the paper:

SENSATIONAL PLOT TO DELIVER
TOM HORN FROM COUNTY JAIL

ONE OF THE BOLDEST AND MOST DARING SCHEMES EVER CONCOCTED
IN CRIMINAL HISTORY. A TRUE BUT ALMOST INCREDULOUS STORY

UNAIDED THE TRIBUNE UNEARTHS THE PLAN

correspondence from horn to his confederates
obtained by the tribune. every detail arranged.
five sticks of dynamite to be used in
blowing out wall of jail and everything in readiness
for horn's escape, signal last night that plot is complete."

The plot had begun, said the *Wyoming Tribune,* when a man named Herr was arrested for the false charge of the theft of a saddle. He readily confessed to the crime and was sentenced to sixty days in the Laramie County jail (the same facility that held Tom Horn). However, Herr went to jail, the *Tribune* said, "not because he was guilty of the theft of a saddle, but because he was the tool through which the plotters expected to communicate with Tom Horn."[14]

The idea was that Horn would slip detailed instructions to Herr for delivery to Horn's friends. And that is what was done. Herr obtained papers with such instructions (on the back of a letter and on toilet paper) and took them to Bosler. But somehow—the *Tribune* is vague about this— Herr suddenly became "overcome with the fear of punishment" and decided to "voluntarily reveal the details of the dark plot" to the *Tribune*. Herr then apparently slipped away from Cheyenne.

The details of the plot, though certainly complex, were hardly vague. Horn's friends were to explode five sticks of "giant powder" (dynamite) and blow in the east wall of the Laramie County jail during Horn's exercise period. Horn would run through the hole to a saddled horse (complete with six-shooter, clothing, and food), and then ride off into the night. He would then wait a week and come to Bosler. As the plan proceeded, signals were to be given to Horn by placement of a snowball and a stepping-stone.[15]

It is not clear why the plot did not go forward, but it is certain that the *Wyoming Tribune* was the proud possessor of the back of an envelope and some toilet paper containing long instructions seeming to facilitate an escape. Unfortunately, the *Wyoming Tribune's* crowing about its journalistic coup offended the *Cheyenne Daily Leader,* and the *Leader* looked for every possible hole in the *Tribune* story. The *Leader* wrote a short, dismissive editorial saying that there had been all sorts of tales about plots by Horn and that none of them had proved to be valid.[16] The *Leader* also ran a story in the same issue stating that the plot had been entirely undertaken by Horn and that Horn's friends knew nothing of the plot, and setting out the numerous errors it had detected in the *Tribune* report.[17] Other newspapers showed their skepticism. For example, the *Natrona County Tribune* wrote, "If there was any real danger of Horn making his escape," then "the people of Laramie County could do no better than to call on the Natrona County's vigilant committee for assistance."[18] That committee had lynched Charles Francis Woodard in May 1902 for the murder of the Natrona County sheriff.[19]

This skepticism was unfortunate, because there were several plots by Horn, and the sneering of the *Daily Leader* and other newspapers perhaps caused Cheyenne people to overlook the full dangers of an escape. In all the bickering between newspapers some salient facts almost got lost. The handwriting on the papers in the *Wyoming Tribune's* possession, addressing a myriad of details relating to an escape, was almost certainly Horn's, and both Walter Stoll, the prosecutor, and E. J. Smalley, the sheriff, believed there had been a plot.[20]

In only few days a new sensation arose over another plot for Tom Horn to evade justice, although this one did not entail escape. House Bill no. 100 came before the judiciary committee of the Wyoming statehouse, the chairman of which was R. N. Matson, who had been one of Horn's attorneys. The bill would abolish capital punishment in Wyoming and it would be retroactive. This retroactive provision would save Horn from the gallows, and its presence led to great suspicion about Representative Matson's motivation in forwarding the bill. It was later observed by the *Daily Leader* that the proposed legislation was "cleverly drawn" so that the key part, the provision that would have spared Tom Horn the death penalty, was slipped in at the very end.[21]

No one paid close attention to the provisions of this bill until George Walker, a correspondent for the *Denver Republican and Post,* was tipped off about the retroactivity provision, and his newspaper ran a story that "exposed the scheme."[22] Then a real furor erupted, as the public realized that this new legislation might mean that Horn could only be sentenced to life imprisonment, and that he might possibly be freed.[23] The uproar led the legislature to quickly kill the offending bill by a "strong vote in committee of the whole." This was not an issue that was going to quietly fade away, however, and Matson made the situation worse by his responses.[24]

Only two days after the *Post's* story, a long resolution was submitted to the house censuring Mr. George Walker because his reports were said to be "an affront upon the dignity and honor and integrity of the gentlemen assailed, as well as the whole house." Some representatives opposed the resolution, saying there was nothing false about the reports. During the debate, Representative Richard Hardman asked the chairman of the judiciary committee to stand, and when Matson arose, Hardman shouted: "Are you one of the attorneys for Tom Horn?" When Matson admitted he was, "the chamber was very quiet." Nevertheless, a member made a motion to pass the resolution and the motion carried.[25]

Harsh comments and criticism followed. The *Cheyenne Daily Leader* pointedly observed that the censure was passed at the "urgent appeal of Mr. Matson who threatened to resign if such action was not taken in his vindication. It would have been interesting to see what would have happened if his bluff had been called."[26] In other articles, the *Leader* pointed out that House Bill no. 100 had become famous, being "the subject of sensational dispatches to Denver," the subject of "warm debate in the house," and "the cause of resolutions of explanation and censure being introduced in that body." The *Leader* also commented that despite the censure of George Walker, it was admitted by all the parties that "his exposure helped to protect the passage of an infamous piece of legislation."[27]

The comments of other Wyoming newspapers joining in the chorus of criticism of House Bill no. 100 showed that citizens throughout the state strongly objected to this proposed new law. The legislature finally withdrew its censure of Walker.[28]

Taking a more balanced view, the *Buffalo Voice* observed meanwhile that violent events throughout Wyoming constituted a statement about progress (or lack of it) in the state. "The rustler wars—the bandits—the killers of the infamous Tom Horn stripe and the bitter conflict between cattlemen and sheepmen over the occupation of the ranges," said the *Voice,* are the things which have given Wyoming a reputation far from envious—a shame to the sisterhood of states."[29]

Tom Horn's own behavior spurred public agitation. In early August 1903, the *Denver Post* reported that Horn had made several plots to escape and said that they had all involved assaulting the jailer, R. A. Proctor. For one reason or another, Horn and a co-conspirator, an inmate named P. D. Shepardson, were never able to pull off their plans. The plots had been revealed by three men resident in the jail as witnesses but not as defendants. These three had heard "the startling details" of the plots.[30]

Before the people of Cheyenne had hardly digested news of these planned escapes, however, the real thing happened: Tom Horn broke out of the Laramie County jail.

Horn's cell sat atop all the other cells in the jail, with one exception. There was one other elevated cell adjacent to Horn's, in which Jim McCloud had been placed. Both cells were reached by means of a narrow corridor, and a mechanical device was employed to open their doors (both cells were opened at the same time). Each day, the jailer, Proctor, brought a medicine prescribed for McCloud's "dyspepsia."[31] Shortly after eight o'clock on Sunday morning, August 9, 1903, Proctor climbed a set of stairs, carrying McCloud's medicine to him. He found the two prisoners, Horn and McCloud, outside their cells, seated on a small bench placed in the corridor.

Proctor unlocked the door to the corridor and opened it five or six inches to hand McCloud the medicine. Just at that moment the "strong, powerful desperadoes" threw themselves against the door and a "terrible struggle ensued."[32] Proctor fought so hard that he almost threw McCloud to the ground below, but just at that time Horn wrapped his hands around the jailer's neck, choking Proctor, who gave in to save his life.

Horn and McCloud bound Proctor with a window rope and then led him back to the ground floor and into the sheriff's office. There the two prisoners found a .30-40 Winchester (overlooking five .30–30s inside a cabinet) but with only a few cartridges. The men demanded that Proctor produce more .30-40 shells. Proctor had been thinking of a way to get to his Belgian automatic pistol inside a safe and he immediately told Horn and McCloud that ammunition was in the safe. He was commanded to open the safe. Proctor fumbled with the combination and said he could not open the safe with his hands tied. His hands were untied, but Proctor continued to fumble, and McCloud lost patience. He pointed the rifle at the jailer, saying, "Open that door, you son of a bitch, or I will blow your brains out."[33] The door was then quickly opened and as it was swinging out, Proctor told McCloud to get a key out of an adjacent desk. McCloud lowered the rifle and turned toward the desk. Just at that moment Proctor reached into the safe, seized his pistol, and turned it toward the prisoners, but Horn had been watching Proctor closely and leaped on him. Once again there was a desperate struggle, this time for some ten minutes, as the men rolled over and over. Once again, Proctor, though considerably smaller than his adversary, put up a long fight. The officer managed to get off a couple of rounds (one bullet grazing McCloud's leg), but other deputies apparently did not hear the shots. As the fight continued, however, Deputy Sheriff Leslie Snow happened to come upon the scene. Opening the door to the sheriff's office he found himself staring at the muzzle of a .30-40 rifle held by McCloud. Snow slammed the door before McCloud acted, and he ran off, shooting his pistol in the air. McCloud realized that this alarm meant that if he was to escape he should take advantage of his opportunity immediately. So, while Horn was still wrestling with Proctor, McCloud reentered the jail and found a way out to the jail yard.

Horn and Proctor continued to fight over the pistol, a struggle that ensued for another five or six minutes, until Horn finally obtained such a strong grip on it that the prisoner could twist Proctor's hand so that it threatened to break. Proctor finally gave in, telling Horn that if he would let go, he would give Horn the gun. Horn did relax, but in that moment Proctor managed to engage the safety on the pistol, a safety with an unusual mechanism.

Proctor then released the pistol, and the instant Horn possessed it, as the *Cheyenne Daily Leader* dramatically reported, "With a baleful gleam in his eye, evidencing his hatred for all officers of the law and his lack of every element which goes to make up a man, he turned on the unarmed jailor and leveled the gun on him, [and] tried to pull the trigger."[34] But the pistol did not fire, and Horn could not make it work. Only Proctor's engagement of the safety on the pistol had saved his life. Seeing that he could not use the pistol against Proctor, Horn turned and ran out the door toward the stable. But no horse was available (unknown to him, McCloud had just taken the last horse from the stable) and so Horn went back across the front of the jail and crossed Ferguson Street to an alley.

In the meantime, McCloud was trying to make good his escape. Having entered the jail yard, he had gone directly to the stable, where he'd found a buckskin horse. Without bothering to saddle it, he had thrown a bridle over its head and was beginning to lead it away. Just then Sheriff Smalley, who lived adjacent to the jail, stepped out of his house and heard someone yell that prisoners had broken out. Told by someone that a horse was coming out of the stable, Smalley ran toward it, saw McCloud, drew his gun, and fired a shot. The horse started to pitch and plunge, and McCloud abandoned the animal, running westward up an alley. Smalley then ran back to his office to get a rifle, and McCloud ran through the alley and turned north onto Eddy Street. Here he was confronted by Pat Hennessy, a mail clerk armed with a double-barreled shotgun. (It seems that the majority of the many men chasing the escaped prisoners that Sunday morning had guns close at hand.) McCloud thought fast, however, and blurted out, "Tom Horn has broken jail. Have you seen him running this way?" Hennessy then asked, "Which way did he go?"—whereupon McCloud apparently muttered something like "thataway" and hurried by Hennessy and into another alley between Twentieth and Twenty-First Streets.

The prisoner ran about a block to a house where he leaped over a fence and entered a shed or barn at the rear. A girl employed at the house saw him enter. At this opportune moment, Sergeant Oscar Lamm of Company E, Wyoming National Guard, appeared on the scene with a militia rifle, as did police officer John Nolan. Lamm then raised his rifle and declared, evidently in a loud voice: "There he is, I can kill him now." McCloud heard

Lamm and immediately called out, "I surrender. Don't shoot me." McCloud was told to come out but still feared being shot, so he first stuck an arm out. After no shot was fired, the escapee emerged.[35] McCloud's immediate fear was of being lynched, and he "begged piteously," saying, "Don't let them kill me."[36] He was said to be greatly relieved after being taken back to the jail.

As McCloud's short-lived flight played out, Horn was having a similar experience. As he reached the jail yard he heard Sheriff Smalley's shots at McCloud and so moved away from them, going toward the front of the courthouse, "passing out into the sidewalk in plain view of a half a hundred people," and then ran north.[37] A man from Colorado, who was later described as "an engineer from a merry-go-round," one O. M. Aldrich (also referred to as "Eldrich"), heard shooting and grabbed his pistol, walked across the street, and stood opposite the jail. Just at that moment, Tom Horn came around the corner. Aldrich identified Horn only as a fugitive, took a quick shot at him, and started running after Horn. At first Horn fled, but then he turned and tried to fire back at Aldrich. Once again the Belgian pistol would not fire, and so Horn turned and started to run again as Aldrich fired another shot at him. Horn jumped a fence just before reaching Capitol Avenue, crossing a yard and then again leaping a fence and reaching Twentieth Street. Aldrich was then close behind Horn and fired once more, this time "the bullet ploughing a furrow across Horn's scalp on top of his head."[38] Horn dropped to the ground. He tried one more time to fire the pistol he was carrying, and one more time the gun refused to cooperate. Aldrich, together with Robert LaFontaine, another mail clerk who had just come upon the scene, jumped on Horn and started wrestling him. Aldrich used his gun to beat Horn on the back of his head, causing extensive bleeding. Exhausted now, Horn was quickly overpowered. Three officers, Smalley, Snow, Proctor, then came onto the scene, and this small group started walking Horn back to the jail. On the way, Snow tried to hit Horn with his rifle, and another peace officer deflected the blow, suffering a broken wrist bone as a result. Some men in a following crowd talked lynching— cries of "Rope!" and "Hang him!" were made—but "no overt act was committed." McCloud reached the jail about the same time as did Horn and "considerable talk of lynching" continued. The officers ordered the growing crowd back, however, and the prisoners were then deposited in their cells.[39]

In the middle of this commotion, Kels Nickell showed up and started to harangue the crowd, making "inflammatory utterances" and talking wildly.[40]

Nickell quickly shut up, however, when Sheriff Smalley threatened to put him in the same cell as Horn if he did not quiet down.[41]

All the sensational events that Sunday morning in August 1903 took place in downtown Cheyenne, and the wonder is that no bystanders were hurt. Deputy Snow had taken a shot at a man he believed was Horn but was actually a man named T. F. Durbin, who was hurrying toward the excitement. A woman who resided at the corner of Capitol Avenue and Twentieth Street had nearly been shot in the head by Aldrich when he fired at Horn.[42] And when rifles were being distributed to militiamen at an arsenal, one had "prematurely discharged" while being taken out of a rack—the bullet was fired into the ceiling.[43]

Of course, there were comments throughout the state about the events of August 9, 1903. Most newspapers had high praise for the quick thinking and bravery of the jailor, R. A. Proctor, but the *Laramie Boomerang* observed that Proctor, despite all the warnings given by Horn's plans and attempts to escape earlier, had given two desperate men a "palpable opening to escape."[44] It was also noted that for almost two weeks a "fine bay horse, equipped with a cowboy saddle" had been tied near the jail, but was taken away after dark. Surprisingly, on August 10, the horse was not at what had become its customary station.[45] And it was surprising too that apparently no one from the sheriff's office had gone to look at the horse and check it out. Newspapers continued the talk of lynching, but the general opinion seemed to be that the attempted escape had firmed people's determination to hang Horn legally.[46] The one concrete good to come out of the brief escape of Horn and McCloud was that Wyoming legislators resolved to reintroduce bills to conduct all executions at the state penitentiary. Such an act had been voted down in the previous legislature, but the reintroduced act would pass in 1905.[47]

Aldrich was considered a hero, although he had not even known it was Horn he was chasing. In fact, many of the prisoners' pursuers did not know whom they were chasing. Horn and McCloud bore a "striking resemblance," so that the men who captured McCloud thought they had caught Horn.[48]

Perhaps the most remarkable episode in the whole event was an interview of Horn by a *Denver Post* reporter after the jailbreak. Horn admitted that the *Post*'s stories about escape plans had been accurate and wanted to know how the *Post* had gotten that information. Horn also admitted that he would have killed Proctor and others had the safety on Proctor's pistol not prevented him from firing it. Proctor, who was part of this interview, said he bore no grudge against Horn, and, indeed, the two men talked as respectful combatants. Horn said that Proctor could beat "any two men I have ever seen," and he said he had no idea that Proctor could hold up him and McCloud as he did. "Well, you won out," Horn said to Proctor, "and you deserve all the credit you can get, for you certainly put up a magnificent fight and against big odds."[49]

The jailbreak, however exciting and all-consuming for a few days, was soon eclipsed by another big event. Eleven days after Tom Horn enjoyed his brief taste of freedom, the Wyoming Supreme Court heard oral arguments in his appeal.

CHAPTER TWENTY-SEVEN

The Appeal to the Wyoming Supreme Court

The appeal in the biggest trial in Wyoming's history was expected to drag on as much of the case had, but the Wyoming Supreme Court resolved to promptly complete the court's duties in this most contentious case and quickly played out its role.

An appeal to the Wyoming Supreme Court in 1903 consisted of three parts. The first was the writing of briefs. The appellant (Tom Horn, the party bringing the appeal) filed a brief, through his lawyers, and then the appellee (the state) responded. The purpose of the briefs was to demonstrate to the members of the court, by citing relevant precedent and other authority tied to the facts of the case, that the court should or should not reverse the decision of the district court. The second part of an appeal was oral argument, wherein lawyers appeared before the court and argued why their clients' points of view should be accepted. And the third and last part was the issuance of a written opinion.[1]

Oral arguments in the Horn case were scheduled for August 20, 1903. Both sides had submitted long and exhaustively detailed briefs and were preparing for an epic oral argument battle. An August 19, 1903, article from the *Cheyenne Daily Leader* spoke of beginning skirmishes in the Wyoming state library where "as high as 400 books have been taken out at a time," mentioning that "the tables in the supreme court room are being piled several feet high with legal authorities."[2]

An appeal to the Wyoming Supreme Court in 1903 was an especially demanding exercise, because Wyoming had virtually no controlling precedent.

"Controlling precedent" refers to earlier cases decided by the court wherein the circumstances were so close to the instant case that those earlier cases would resolve the case at hand. Since statehood in 1890, however, the Wyoming Supreme Court had decided only a few hundred cases and the court had rarely addressed comparable points.[3] So lawyers (and judges when rendering decisions) had to scour the case law of every state in the union to determine a majority rule or one otherwise appropriate for Wyoming. The exercise was arduous.[4] The combatants in the Horn case were hardworking, aggressive attorneys, however. They were as determined as any lawyers in Wyoming, and they certainly did not shrink from their duties.

The court convened at 11:00 A.M., Thursday, August 20, and each side was allotted six hours, with all arguments to be completed by Saturday afternoon, August 22. T. F. Burke led the Horn team, followed by R. N. Matson (Representative Matson, the one at the heart of the storm over House Bill no. 100). The state would follow with Wyoming Attorney General J. A. Van Orsdel and then Walter Stoll. John Lacey would make the final statement for the defense.[5]

Burke repeated the arguments he made before the district court, saying that the only evidence tying Horn to the crime was the "so-called" confession but that this confession had been merely a "josh" when Horn and LeFors were telling tall tales and when Horn was intoxicated.[6]

During the oral arguments, the supreme court room, "well filled with spectators," probably included some lawyers who rooted for Tom Horn.[7] If so, from their viewpoint, and judging from the way his remarks were reported in the newspapers, Burke's opening argument, usually the best the appellant has to offer, could have been stronger. For the court to decide for Horn on such an argument, it would have to disregard all the evidence contrary to what Burke contended. That is, it would have to disregard the evidence from LeFors, Snow, Ohnhaus, and several others, not to mention Horn himself—tending to show that Horn was not so intoxicated that all his statements should be disregarded and that the confession had not been a "josh." Indeed, under Burke's argument, the court would have to resolve that the jury had no reasonable basis to do anything but just push aside all evidence contrary to Horn's declarations. Based on remarks in the written opinion of the case, however, it appears that the defense arguments were presented effectively and did catch the attention of the court.

Burke's second argument was that LeFors had obtained the confession by flattery and upon the assumption that Horn was guilty. Burke said that Horn had not disputed the assumption because at the time LeFors was trying to get Horn a position in Montana "with the Nickell killing as a recommendation."[8] The problem for Burke was that this argument had no factual basis in the record. Horn never testified at the trial that he had gone along with LeFors because he wanted to protect his job prospects. And appellate courts may only consider what was placed in the record in earlier proceedings.

Burke also again insisted that all the circumstances were inconsistent with guilt when the confession was interpreted as a josh. That meant, Burke said, that the state's interpretation was contrary with nearly all the circumstances as proven. Hence, declared Burke, the verdict was not consistent with the evidence. Burke also argued against the instructions given relating to confessions, and against the restrictions on testimony relating to hard feelings between the Miller and Nickell families.[9]

There are no indications from the newspaper reports that any of the justices asked questions. Most appellate lawyers grow uneasy when a court sits silently during oral arguments. It can mean that the members of the court are already in full agreement with a lawyer's argument and have nothing more to add. Or it can mean that the members of the court have already firmly made up their minds against the lawyer's positions, and the lawyer is not challenging any of what they have already resolved in their minds.

Then again, perhaps there were questions but they were not reported. The full proceedings in the appeal in *Horn v. State* were not set out by the Cheyenne newspapers, and the papers saw the arguments as "technical" and not of great interest to their readers. The *Wyoming Tribune,* however, did carry a long report of Walter Stoll's comments to the court. Stoll spent a good deal of time making court members thoroughly aware of the evidence presented to the jury, including, especially, all the maps and photographs of the area around the famous gate where Willie Nickell was shot. Stoll also addressed at length the three Denver witnesses presented by the prosecution, responding to statements that attorney Burke had made. And Stoll was said to "set out to prove that outside of the Denver testimony and the confession made to Joe LeFors, there would still be sufficient evidence of the guilt of Horn."[10]

The supreme court took the case under advisement. It was predicted that it would be at least three months before a decision was rendered.[11] In only a week, however, after an interview with a member of the Wyoming Supreme Court, the *Daily Leader* announced to its readers that "all three of the supreme judges have been devoting almost their entire time to the consideration of this case to the exclusion of other cases pending for months." The court wanted to arrive at a speedy decision, the Cheyenne daily said, because of "the recent lynchings in Wyoming, the blame for which has been attributed to the laws which give the defendant one year in which to perfect an appeal." Because of this work by the judges, the *Leader* reported, the decision would almost surely be issued on September 23, 1903. The supreme court judge did caution, however, that since hundreds of pages of testimony had to be read and hundreds of legal authorities reviewed, not to mention the writing of the decision, which was a huge task alone, it was possible that the judges would not be able to complete their decision by then.[12] In a later release to the press, a supreme court member denied that the court had assured that a decision would be rendered by September 23, nor could they, and this judge particularly expressed his displeasure with the idea that the actions of lynch mobs would affect the pace of making decisions.[13] It was not specifically addressed, but the Wyoming Supreme Court surely did not agree that the recent lynchings were the fault of the law giving a year to perfect an appeal (as opposed to, say, the fault of the members of the lynch mob). Still, despite their denials, it is understandable why lynch mobs may have influenced the members of the court to quickly complete the Horn case. So long as the case lingered and there was doubt about Horn's fate, the risk for an attempted lynching would remain. The supreme court members were probably well aware of the attempt to move all executions to the state penitentiary in Rawlins in order to negate the lynching problem in the future, and they could have felt that once the Horn situation was resolved Cheyenne would never again have to fear a lynch mob.

The Wyoming Supreme Court convened on September 21, did not then issue an opinion in *Horn v. State,* but did tell newsmen that the court hoped to be able to announce an opinion on September 30, although there was still an immense amount of work remaining.[14] Shortly after 10:00 A.M. on September 30, the court convened in a courtroom containing a "large number of spectators" and the attorneys for the parties. A state supreme court hearing is normally lightly attended by the public. Apparently the crowd was drawn by the expectation that the Horn decision would be presented. The crowd would not be disappointed.

Justice Charles Potter immediately began reading the court's decision in *Horn v. State.* He read from a tall stack of papers and continued reading for the next two hours. The decision was the longest in the history of the court, eighty-seven pages in the Wyoming Reports, and the court seemed to address every contention of Horn's lawyers.[15]

Potter read a passage from the first page of the opinion, which is probably unique in Wyoming jurisprudence, wherein the court praised the attorneys' presentations to the court:

> It is contended with much earnestness that the verdict is not supported by sufficient evidence. This proposition was presented in brief and upon oral argument with unusual skill, and the same is true of the manner of presentation of the other side of the question by counsel for the State. Indeed, on the whole case the arguments both for the plaintiff in error and the State were not only able and instructive, but displayed immense labor and research, and it is doubtful, to say the least, if in any criminal case this court has ever listened to more able or learned arguments.[16]

The Supreme Court of Wyoming, like most appellate courts, rarely says anything about the quality of the work of the attorneys before it, and so this statement is extraordinary, a declaration of praise as high as lawyers have ever received from the court.[17] Perhaps the members of the court considered the political influence of people on both sides of this controversial case, but a safer action would have been to say nothing. The statement more likely reflects a genuine appreciation for the attorneys' fine work.

The court reviewed all the facts before the jury, including a full presentation of the circumstances surrounding the July 18, 1901, killing of Willie Nickell. Justice Potter also set out at length all the details relating to the confession and virtually every statement in that confession. The court particularly noted that Horn had admitted making all the statements attributed to him, and that while he had been drinking some, he also admitted that he had known what he was saying, although Horn also had said this whole conversation was a "josh." The court observed that there was a split in the evidence relating to Horn's sobriety.[18]

The opinion recited all the facts that tended to connect Horn with the crime "independent of that confession," addressing Horn's presence in the neighborhood, conflicting evidence about Horn's presence in Laramie on July 18, and the asserted statement by Horn to LeFors that Horn had shot at Kels Nickell seventeen days after the boy was killed. The opinion also referred to the fact that Kels Nickell was the only person in the Iron Mountain neighborhood who had sheep and said, "It is a matter so notorious that the jury might have considered it that more or less enmity between cattle and sheep owners is frequently the result where cattle and sheep are kept in the same locality." And, the court said, Horn himself acknowledged that he had been watching the Nickell sheep.[19]

Then the court went to the heart of the legal question when "sufficiency of the evidence" was challenged: "We are not permitted under the law to substitute our judgment for that of the jury upon the facts." The opinion pointed out that the jury actually saw and heard the witnesses and was the sole judge of their credibility. So, where "there is evidence upon which a verdict might reasonably be founded," an appellate court would "refuse to intercede."[20]

In one permutation or another, this is the universal rule of all appellate courts, necessarily so. The members of the Wyoming Supreme Court were not in the courtroom when Tom Horn was examined and cross-examined. They did not look him in the eye as he testified. They did not hear the tone of his voice, the hesitations he may have made, the anxiety he may have exhibited (or the calmness), or a hundred other signs of body language that tell other people whether a person is lying or telling the truth. So an appellate court has no choice but to limit its review of the jury's determinations to whether there was evidence upon which a verdict of guilt might reasonably be founded. It is still a big obstacle for the prosecution to get over, when highly skilled opponents are attacking every bit of evidence presented, and especially given the high barrier of reasonable doubt, but an appellate court's decision is not and normally cannot be a final and definitive pronouncement of the sufficiency of the evidence.

The supreme court concluded that after carefully examining all the testimony, it was constrained to hold that the verdict in the case was supported by the testimony. The court acknowledged that there was evidence that the circumstances did not accord with Horn's statement, but there was also directly opposite evidence showing it was. When addressing the issue over the caliber of the fatal bullets, the court's comments showed how successful Stoll's cross-examination had been. The court referred to "what the jury may have believed to be the uncertainty of the expert opinions," and it said that "we do not think the evidence is to be construed as pointing so positively to the contrary that we should hold the jury unwarranted in that conclusion."[21]

The court discussed the prosecution's theory that Horn had come to Laramie on July 18, 1901, immediately following the killing of Willie Nickell. The defense had apparently dwelt at length upon the evidence inconsistent with this theory (it was probably the prosecution's weakest point of evidence), causing the supreme court to address the issue. The opinion of the court, however, was that if Horn had not gone into Laramie, the jurors "may have believed that he remained in the immediate or comparative vicinity of the crime, screening himself from observation until Saturday [July 20]. It was not essential to their verdict that it should be found beyond a reasonable doubt that the prisoner rode to Laramie on the day of the crime."[22] The court observed that another factor supporting the jury's determination was that they had before them "such facts as indicated quite strongly that the accused had some object in observing the Nickell ranch or property, and that he would be concerned in preventing a commotion that might be caused if his presence should be noted." The court's overall conclusion: "On the entire case we find ourselves unable to say that the evidence was insufficient, and that for such reason the court ought to have granted a new trial, and erred in not doing so."[23]

The supreme court addressed another point apparently strongly pushed by Horn's legal team, that one of the Denver witnesses was impeached, and that, besides, Horn had a broken jaw at the time he was supposed to have made statements. But the court said that the evidence was admissible (although it may have been flawed) and the jury could consider it for what it was worth. More significantly, the court said that even if all the Denver testimony was disregarded, "we would not feel justified in reversing the case."[24]

The court addressed the Tom Horn confession and the ways it should be considered. The defense wanted an instruction that confessions were "a doubtful piece of evidence and should be acted upon by the jury with great caution," and they insisted that Judge Scott's failure to present this instruction to the jury was erroneous. The supreme court discussed this rule forwarded by the defense and cited a great deal of authority about it. The court said that such an instruction was normally only given when the proof of the confession was wobbly—where, for example, someone had overheard statements by an accused and was repeating them later from memory. Here, however, the defendant himself had admitted the accuracy of every word, and the confession was not given when he was under arrest (or even publicly accused of a crime); his statements could not have been misinterpreted. Horn's only contention was that he had been intoxicated and under such influence was joshing. But the court pointed out that the jury had received an instruction forwarded by the defense that they should not consider Horn's statement if they were "idle vaporings or part of a mere contest in telling yarns." And the jury was also told that they were the judges of the effect of alcohol upon Horn's statements "to such an extent as to render his statements unreliable." The court concluded: "It thus appears that all the law upon this subject applicable to the case was given. We think the request [by the defense for its instruction about confessions] was properly refused."[25]

The defense had vigorously challenged the rulings by the trial court that questions about trouble between Willie Nickell and the Millers not be allowed. The supreme court sustained the ruling of the trial court on this point, saying that the questions were improper because nothing in Victor Miller's testimony had been elicited about trouble with Willie Nickell, and cross-examination was limited to matters raised in the direct examination. Victor Miller had only testified to the presence of Horn at the Miller ranch.[26]

As well as questions to Victor, however, the defense had presented the testimony of "one Whitman," A. F. Whitman, who would have spoken about feuds between two or three immediate neighbors of the Nickell family. The defense insisted that when the prosecution was trying to secure a conviction by circumstantial evidence, testimony was admissible to show that another person may have committed the crime. But the court responded that the defense was stating the rule too broadly, and it cited several cases from other jurisdictions in which the rule was limited to the ability of a defendant in a criminal case to establish his own innocence by showing that someone else actually *was,* not just *may have been,* the guilty party. Evidence of mere threats was held to be inadmissible, having no legal tendency to establish the innocence of the defendant. Here, the supreme court said, the proposed evidence of the defense was *not* "connected with an offer to show overt facts" or even an opportunity on a third party's part to have perpetrated the crime. All the defense had been offering was to show a possible motive on the part of someone other than Tom Horn, and the court said that such evidence was not competent and was appropriately disallowed.[27]

The Wyoming Supreme Court had little problem with the defense contention that Walter Stoll had acted improperly when he asked Dr. Barber about his earlier testimony. The court noted that "it is evident from the record that the prosecutor was surprised at the testimony of the witness," and under the circumstances it had been proper to question the doctor about his former testimony "to lay the foundation for contradicting him." So it was too with regard to the ruling allowing into evidence a .30-30 cartridge found by Fred Nickell. The court observed that there was a possible connection to the line of Horn's flight and, in any event, though the cartridge may not have been strong evidence, it was still admissible. The jury "were doubtless capable of determining the weight to be given" to the evidence.[28] The court also brushed aside the complaint of the defense about the admission of the January 7, 1902, letter from Horn to LeFors and the letter of Smith "of Montana" to LeFors regarding the employment of Horn in Montana, not regarding these letters as prejudicial. "We are inclined to the view that they were admissible to explain the circumstances under which the conversation with LaFors [sic] occurred."[29]

Identifying it as "one of the most vital and serious questions in the case," the supreme court spent most of its time on a question that arose from the testimony by Joe LeFors about Tom Horn's admissions indicating he was the one who had shot at Kels Nickell in early August 1901, seventeen days after Willie Nickell's killing. LeFors had testified about conversations between Horn and himself before the January 1902 confession by Horn. The court noted that there was a connection between the killing and the assault upon Kels Nickell, in that the killing of Willie Nickell was said by Horn to have been undertaken to prevent Willie from going home and making a big commotion and thus alerting his father to danger. In other words, there was evidence indicating that Kels Nickell was the primary target and that Willie had been shot to prevent him from interfering with Horn's stalking of Kels.[30]

The defense had strongly objected to the whole series of questions about the later shots at Kels Nickell, saying that this was simply an attempt to smear Horn by showing that he had an evil character. And there certainly was a well-established tenet of law that a defendant should be convicted only upon evidence of the guilt of the crime of which he was charged. The supreme court pointed out, however, that this rule was not absolute and that there were situations in which guilt of another offense might show guilt of the charged offense. The court quoted a New York decision which contained a statement applicable to the Horn case: "Evidence is then permitted to show that the person was the person who committed the other crime, because in so doing, under the circumstances, and from the connection of the prisoner with the other crime, the evidence of his guilt of the other crime is direct evidence of his guilt of the crime for which he is on trial."[31]

In addition, said the court, there were a number of exceptions to the general rule forbidding evidence of other crimes, including to establish motive, intent, the absence of mistake, a common scheme, or the identity of the person charged. And in this case there was an issue as to the identity of the defendant as the party who shot Willie Nickell, and the question of Horn's motive for killing Willie Nickell was also at issue. Said the court: "Such proof [that Horn had fired at Kels Nickell] would have tended to establish both the identity of the defendant as the party guilty of the crime charged and his motive in the commission of that crime."[32] The court did not mention it, but a "common scheme" to all the murders with which Horn was associated was firing a rifle from ambush.

The defense, from the beginning, had complained bitterly about LeFors and Snow being allowed to testify about Horn's sincerity when he was talking to LeFors. This was an odd posture, however, because it had long been the rule that statements of certain kinds of observations—such as speed, temper, anger, fear, pleasure, or excitement—would be permitted to a witness. The theory was that human beings make some judgments for which the source of the opinion is difficult or impossible to quantify and describe, and so, as a matter of necessity, a shorthand statement of opinion would be allowed. And that's exactly what the supreme court ruled. An opinion that Horn was sincere fell easily within the ambit of the general rule.[33]

The defense had not liked the instruction given to the jury about the burden of proof. That instruction stated that there were only three overall "material allegations" that the prosecution had to prove beyond a reasonable doubt—essentially that Willie Nickell had been killed, that he had purposely been killed by the defendant, and that the killing had taken place in Laramie County, Wyoming. The supreme court ruled against the defense, saying: "It is not true that the prosecution is bound to establish beyond a reasonable doubt every minor circumstance given in proof as tending to establish the main or ultimate fact essential to conviction. If that were the law all that a defendant would be required to accomplish to secure an acquittal would be to throw a reasonable doubt by his proof upon the truth of some slight circumstance entering into the evidence for the State."[34]

The defense also complained that their submitted instruction was not given which said that the state, in order to prove its circumstantial evidence case, had to show facts that were "absolutely incompatible" with anything but the innocence of the accused. The court first noted that though circumstantial evidence was involved, so was the confession, and so this case was not solely a circumstantial evidence case. But the key problem with the defendant's submitted instruction was the phrase "absolutely incompatible." Guilt must be established, said the court, beyond a reasonable doubt, not beyond all doubt.[35]

The defense had complained of what they termed prosecutor Stoll's "misconduct" in his final argument. The supreme court recited the affidavits presented before the trial court on this point, both by the defense and the prosecution, and discussed legal authority. The fact that the defense had not objected at the time Stoll was arguing stuck in the craws of the court members. They seemed to feel that the defense was gaming the system by not objecting, but still wanting to preserve the ability to use the complaint to obtain a new trial. "But we are convinced that the chance for mistrials ought not to be encouraged by a rule permitting counsel to remain silent in the presence of prejudicial misconduct of an adversary in an argument, and afterward, should an adverse verdict be returned, obtain a new trial on that ground. We think it a salutary requirement as a condition to review in an appellate court of such an objection that it be presented first to the trial court at the time of the occurrence of the misconduct."[36]

The final point the supreme court addressed was the set of allegations saying that the jury had been improperly influenced and pressured. The court members did not buy it. The opinion discussed great conflict in the evidence of what had allegedly been done to influence the jury and observed that the district court had ruled that there was no prejudice to the defendant. The court concluded: "It is evident to our minds that such a condition of affairs is not set forth as to justify our interference with the finding of the [trial] court in that respect. It is not clear to us that there is any reasonable ground to presume that the verdict was influenced by the remarks said to have been made by others."[37]

Having addressed all the points raised in the appeal, the court provided a final comment about the case, probably meant to be read by the citizens of Wyoming:

> The several objections urged have now been considered. The case is not only important in view of the character of the crime, and the penalty imposed upon it by law, but because of the unusual

and peculiar features presented by the facts, and the legal propositions involved in its determination. A case of this kind always demands the most patient, studious and impartial consideration; and we think that this court has never underrated the responsibility resting upon an appellate tribunal of last resort, especially where the life or liberty of a citizen is in question. In the case at bar, in view of the earnestness of counsel both in relation to the facts and the law, and their apparent feeling that the verdict was to some extent influenced by public clamor, we have endeavored, by a close scrutiny of the record, to ascertain whether there was disclosed anything to reasonably indicate that the accused had not been afforded a fair and impartial trial. The objections to the rulings of the court have received our most careful consideration; a very large number of authorities have been consulted, in addition to those cited in this opinion; and it has all resulted in convincing our minds that the record furnishes no justification for a reversal of the case. It seems to have been ably and dispassionately tried. We are, therefore, of the opinion that the judgment should be and same will be affirmed.

Only one item remained to be addressed by the court: "And now this court appoints Friday, the 20th day of November, in the year of our Lord 1903, for the execution of the sentence pronounced by the court below."[38]

CHAPTER TWENTY-EIGHT

Clemency?

The Wyoming Supreme Court decision in *Horn v. State* was greeted with approval throughout the state. The *Wyoming Tribune* reported that those in the courtroom were "warm in their admiration" for "the evident pains" the court had taken "to sift every question to its logical answer."[1] The *Laramie Boomerang* said the decision spoke well "for the courts of Wyoming." In the face of "all sorts of pressure exerted on behalf of Horn, they never wavered a hair from the strict path of duty." Human life, the *Boomerang* said, "is held as highly in Wyoming as anywhere and . . . man cannot murder and escape the penalty."[2] Said the *Wheatland World:* "The verdict at the time was generally approved by the public and the decision of the supreme court will have an equally hearty approval on the part of the great majority of the people of the state." The paper added: "Horn's conviction was no doubt wholly due to LeFors' clever work and to the magnificent efforts which Prosecuting Attorney Stoll made in the trial of the case."[3]

The *Wyoming Tribune* noted that professional murderers were losing their caste in Wyoming and expressed hope Wyoming's reputation would change as a result:

> The professional murderer is not only losing his standing, but is losing his head.
>
> Public sentiment is taking a bracing tonic and there is something doing in the courts of the state.
>
> The murderer is no longer a hero, but an outcast and a felon.

These are good, healthy symptoms, and if we continue to cultivate them Wyoming will soon stand in a different light before the world.[4]

Sitting in his jail cell, Tom Horn as yet knew nothing of the court's decision and the responses to it. None of his lawyers visited Horn for days after the supreme court decision was handed down, and Sheriff Smalley, though he certainly knew of the decision, concluded that since he had not been officially notified, he did not see it as "imperative on him to notify Horn."[5] Finally, ten days after the appellate decision, Horn's lawyers visited their client to tell him of his fate.[6]

The next step and only remaining recourse for Horn was to apply to the governor for a commutation of his sentence to life imprisonment.[7] The governor was Fenimore Chatterton. Forty-three years old, Governor Chatterton had practiced law in Cheyenne and then run for Wyoming secretary of state in 1898. He had been elected twice, but during his second term Governor DeForest Richards had died, thus elevating Chatterton to acting governor.[8]

There was no doubt that Tom Horn's defense team would move aggressively to push Governor Chatterton to grant clemency. T. F. Burke announced that he had possession of an affidavit from Ollie Whitman.[9] Whitman swore that Victor Miller had confessed to him that he had killed Willie Nickell. The *Denver Post* reported that pressure would be put on Governor Chatterton, trying to convince him that he would be a "dead duck politically" if he did not commute Horn's sentence. If Chatterton did commute Horn's sentence, he might be offered the Republican nomination for governor in the upcoming election and, in five years, perhaps be nominated to run for a seat in the U.S. Senate.[10]

Like the *Post*, the *Laramie Boomerang* was highly skeptical of big cattlemen trying to save Horn. A *Boomerang* story referred to the Ollie Whitman affidavit as "fake" and said that Horn was "as slippery as an eel" and may yet "cheat the gallows."[11]

The *Boomerang* article referred to John Coble, the big cattlemen and close friend of Tom Horn, as well as John Lacey, the attorney for the Union Pacific (surely the biggest client any Wyoming lawyer could hope to represent) and "one of the cleverest lawyers in the state." It said that Coble was working hard to get more money for Horn's lawyers so they could file more papers in the district court and supreme court and "create a fund for lobbyists" to influence Governor Chatterton. Coble was said to have a stack of letters "a foot high" asking for clemency, and the *Boomerang* predicted that the "leading cattle barons will also be asked to bring their influence to bear upon Wyoming's young governor."[12] An alibi would be presented to Chatterton that was to have been submitted at the trial, but, the *Boomerang* stated, the defense had held back because the prosecution had such strong contrary evidence. Besides, the defense had been confident that four jurymen were with them and so "they did not care to take chances of having their alibi and affidavit shown upon their true light before the jury." As well, the Plaga alibi had been so completely disproven ("Horn himself proving it false") that Horn's attorneys decided to save other alibi evidence for a later time if that became necessary.[13]

The *Boomerang* asked the rhetorical question whether Whitman's affidavit and other alibi evidence would have weight with Governor Chatterton. Answering its own question, the *Boomerang* concluded that they should not. All this evidence had been in the hands of the defense before the trial began, and "that was the time to spring them and not wait until the accused man is approaching the gallows." Whitman's affidavit must be discounted, the paper said, because Glendolene Kimmel's testimony at the coroner's inquest had completely exonerated the Millers. Kimmell was Horn's sweetheart (again, an overstatement) and loved him, said the *Boomerang,* and therefore would have said anything to exonerate him if she could have.[14]

The *Boomerang* article spoke of the enticements of office supposedly being offered to Chatterton and declared how strongly the people of Wyoming felt that Tom Horn was guilty of the murder of Willie Nickell and others. Further, Wyoming citizens believed Horn to have been fairly tried and convicted and they would look to Chatterton to do his duty. "If he fails," said the *Boomerang,* "then the wrath of the entire state will be heaped upon his head, and he will be as dead as the proverbial herring." Horn's attorneys and friends, it was stated, "are moving heaven and earth to defeat the ends of justice," but they would fail "unless Gov. Chatterton permits himself to be misled. And the people of Wyoming are praying that the Wyoming executive will not allow the false promises of a few men, whose prestige died with the conviction of Tom Horn, to lead him away from his plain duty."[15]

Thus framed, the battle lines were set, but when Horn's attorneys fired the first salvo, it still shocked the people of Wyoming and shook their

confidence. On Saturday, October 31, at 3:00 P.M., papers were presented to Governor Chatterton. They were surprising and dramatic. A
Wyoming Tribune sub-headline read: "A Startling Array of Affidavits Presented to Governor Chatterton Tending to Show that Tom Horn Is an
Innocent Man."[16]

The presentation to Chatterton was made in his office at a kind of
hearing. T. F. Burke, T. B. Kennedy, and John Lacey appeared on Horn's
behalf. John Coble, Harry Windsor, and Glendolene Kimmell were also
present in support of Horn. For the state, Attorney General Van Orsdel
appeared, and Kels Nickell was present.[17]

Burke made the presentation to Chatterton, saying his team would be
presenting evidence that pointed "with unerring accuracy" to the guilt
of Victor Miller (while asserting that none of the evidence of the guilt
of Miller could have been presented before the district court). The "sensation of the day" was an affidavit from Miss Kimmell, which Burke read
aloud to the governor. Kimmell swore that on three different occasions
she had heard a conversation implicating Victor Miller in the killing of
Willie Nickell. Reciting the conversations in great detail, Kimmell said
they had been between Victor and his father, James, and contained admissions by Victor of his guilt. Later she had told James Miller that she had
overheard the conversations between him and Victor, and she had told him
that if he tried to pin the crime on Horn or another innocent person, she
would "tell all" about what she had heard. Miller had supposedly broken
down, saying that they would not try to incriminate any innocent person.
According to Miss Kimmell, a few days later James Miller had told her
that Victor and Willie had met accidentally, had "resumed their old quarrel," and that Victor had then shot and killed Willie. Kimmell added that
on October 10, 1901, Victor himself had confessed to the crime, saying
that on the morning of July 18 he had met Willie, "renewed their former
quarrel, quickly came to blows and, having his gun, . . . shot and killed
him."[18] She finished the affidavit by saying that it was likely that Horn had
just been telling yarns when he confessed to Joe LeFors. Kimmell also said
that she had made two efforts in October 1901 to see Walter Stoll but on
each occasion "was unable to see him."[19]

Other affidavits also provided sensational information. John (Jack) Martin
swore that Joe LeFors had told him that Jim Miller had obtained a $500
loan for the purpose of buying off LeFors, to keep the detective from pursuing an investigation against Miller. Frank Mulock, one of the Denver

witnesses, said by affidavit that since his testimony he had learned that the man he saw the night of September 30, 1901, was not Horn but another man who looked a lot like Horn (but who could not be found). Peter Anderson said he had been the bartender in Denver when Horn supposedly bragged about shooting Willie Nickell, but he had never heard anything of this sort. An Iron Mountain woman, Lillie Graham, said that she had heard James Miller swear to avenge the death of his son Frank, accidentally killed in 1900 by a gun "Miller was carrying through his fear of Nickell." And deputy sheriff Peter Warlamount swore that Kels Nickell had told him he had recognized James Miller and one of his sons the day that Nickell was fired at five times.[20] These last two affidavits were consistent with earlier information and were most probably correct.

The newspaper story about the expected testimony of Ollie Whitman proved to be accurate. Whitman swore that at a June 1902 dance, "he noticed Victor Miller's nervousness and by questioning him, Victor told him that he had killed Willie Nickell because his father told him to and that his father shot five times at Kels Nickell a week later." Whitman further swore that Victor had told him that "he was secreted behind a rock; that he shot at Willie and then 'pulled out.'" Interestingly, the affidavit had been in the hands of the defense for almost a year; it was sworn to in December 1902.[21] The *Cheyenne Daily Leader* noted that Whitman's version of the alleged confession by Victor Miller was inconsistent with that of Miss Kimmell. According to Kimmell, Victor and Willie had confronted one another, but according to Whitman, Victor had been concealed, fired from ambush, and then fled the scene.[22]

Attorney General Van Orsdel "asked for time in which to procure counter affidavits and examine the testimony introduced before he cross examined the witnesses." Governor Chatterton announced that he would take the case under advisement and later announce his decision. Chatterton also said that he wanted to see Miss Kimmell in private, and in fact he "interrogated her at considerable length [without witnesses] regarding many matters brought out in her evidence."[23] The *Laramie Weekly Boomerang* reported that the little schoolteacher "does not look good" and doubted that she made a favorable impression on the governor.[24]

The covering newspapers took the presentation of Tom Horn's lawyers seriously, stating that if true it meant that Horn had needlessly suffered "all of the horrors of long imprisonment, the trial and the imposition of the death penalty." The people of Wyoming also took the new evidence of the defense seriously. The *Laramie Boomerang* reported, "The remarkable new evidence in the case of Tom Horn laid before Governor Chatterton on Saturday is on everyone's lips here, and heated discussions about the reliability of the evidence are frequent."[25]

The *Cheyenne Daily Leader* noted that Miss Kimmell's statements were problematic. If true, she knew all the time that Willie Nickell's real killer was Victor Miller "yet abetted in the effort of that person to escape punishment for his crime and permitted Tom Horn to be sentenced to hang. If not true, then she is guilty of perjury."[26] Walter Stoll believed the latter and filed perjury charges against Glendolene Kimmell.[27] Stoll had watched Miss Kimmell testify at the coroner's inquest, declaring earnestly that she remembered with "the utmost distinctness" that Jim Miller and his sons Gus and Victor were all at breakfast between seven and seven thirty on the morning of July 18, 1902. To later be presented with a pronouncement that all this was a lie, one kept from him until after a long and arduous trial, followed by a monumental appeal, no doubt infuriated Stoll. He probably felt that Kimmell was trying to manipulate the criminal justice system, and no prosecuting attorney is ever amused by such effrontery. When Kimmell was arraigned, John Coble was one of two men providing a bond for her. The *Cheyenne Daily Leader* article reporting the perjury charge also noted that another hearing was scheduled before Governor Chatterton, at which the state would present its side. The importance of Kimmell's evidence was underlined in another statement by the *Leader,* that "if the state can prove perjury on the part of Miss Kimmell, it will absolutely remove Tom Horn's last chance for his life."[28]

On November 12 the prosecution submitted its case countering all the evidence submitted by the defense, and it packed a wallop. As the *Wyoming Tribune* declared in headlines, the prosecution came up with a "strong rebuttal," in which every point made by the defense was "vigorously attacked."[29] Walter Stoll began his presentation by "opening a voluminous stack of affidavits." They started with a statement from a Mrs. Simpson of Laramie, swearing that she had seen Tom Horn in Laramie on July 19, 1902 (a day after Willie Nickell was shot). Another Laramie resident, James Daugherty, said he had seen Horn in Laramie on July 18, 19, and 20. On July 18, the day Willie was killed, said Daugherty, he saw Horn ride into Laramie about eleven o'clock in the morning and afterward saw him in the Wyoming, a saloon that was supposedly Horn's Laramie headquarters. Horn wore a sweater and was covered with dust, said Daugherty, "showing that he

had just come in from a long horseback ride."[30] The prosecution also
presented the affidavit of Van Guilford, a man from Laramie who swore
that Horn had come into his shop several weeks before the Willie Nickell
killing and bought a sweater from him. "Voluminous" correspondence with
a "Professor Haynes" was presented "in regard to examinations made on
the sweater admitted into evidence at the trial to determine whether the
stains were made of human blood." Stoll had earlier stated that although
a report had not arrived in time for the trial, examination of the sweater
had shown it to contain human blood.

Walter Stoll presented an affidavit with a letter from Frank Mulock
sent to him from Denver after the conviction. In the letter Mulock congratulated Stoll and said that he had other evidence corroborating what
he had testified to. In the letter Mulock also said that he had spoken to
Roberts, the bartender at the Scandinavian Hotel, and Roberts had told
him that the check Horn presented was from J. C. Coble for $200.[31]

A particularly effective affidavit addressing the charge by John (Jack)
Martin that Jim Miller had been loaned $500 to pay off Joe LeFors showed
that the loan was for $600 from "Riner & Schnitzer" but that the entire
amount loaned to Miller was paid to "various merchants and business-
men."[32] The *Laramie Boomerang* said that the charge that LeFors had been
bribed was "completely shattered" by the evidence demonstrating a direct
link between $600 loaned to Miller by Riner and Schnitzer of Chey-
enne and checks showing bills paid "about town."[33]

The prosecution also went after Jack Martin. M. N. Grant, Laramie justice
of the peace, swore that Martin's reputation for truth was bad. Joe LeFors,
besides denying completely any assertions of a bribe, swore that Martin
had been involved in criminal conduct, and Frank Irwin and Charles Settelle
said that Martin claimed to have been a member of the infamous Younger
gang. Three other men, S. C. Downey, Frank H. Eggleston, and George E.
Eggleston, submitted affidavits that declared that Martin had a bad reputation for veracity.

The defense immediately countered all these affidavits with several of
their own. E. J. Bell, Ora Haley, E. A. Williams, W. H. Frazne, N. Boswell,
John W. Connor, A. Whitehouse, and R. H. Homer all declared that
Martin had a good reputation. At least some of these men were probably
big cattlemen (Ora Haley certainly was). The basis for their knowledge
about Martin was that they had employed him in years past.[34]

Prosecutor Stoll presented two affidavits considered a "sensation," those of Chris Lund and Charles Fletcher. Lund swore he had seen Horn "a short time after the killing near the scene of the crime." Fletcher's statement was even stronger. He said that he had been an eyewitness to the crime, seeing "Horn fire the shots which killed the boy." Stoll explained that he had this evidence in hand at the time of the trial, but Fletcher was then in a Colorado prison for the theft of a calf and Stoll could not verify Fletcher's statements. Stoll had therefore declined to call him as a witness, but thereafter he was able to verify "nearly every one of the statements made by Fletcher." Stoll acknowledged that Lund was "in his dotage," and his testimony would not be relied upon as heavily as that of other witnesses.[35]

Fletcher and Lund were obviously not ideal witnesses, and Stoll's comments reveal a great deal about this affidavit exercise before Governor Chatterton. Whenever a big case is prepared involving dozens of witnesses (such as the Horn case), some prospective witnesses are shaky. For any of a hundred reasons an attorney may choose not to call a witness. Paramount is that a jury may not believe the witness, may even see the attempt to sway them by the testimony of a shaky, shady witness as being dishonest with them. Thus, an ill-chosen witness may taint the entire presentation. For this reason great care must be given to witness selection. When the case was presented to the Horn jury, both Stoll and Lacey undoubtedly chose not to use certain witnesses. The expected testimony of Glendolene Kimmell might very well have tempted John Lacey to put her on the stand, but envisioning what Stoll might have done to her on cross-examination would have made Lacey cringe. All those contradictory statements by Kimmell in the coroner's inquest would have been grist for Stoll's mill. And the testimony of John Coble could have been worse. Stoll would have loved to cross-examine the man said to have facilitated Horn's assassinations. And so too with some potential prosecution witnesses such as Lund and Fletcher. Lacey could have had a field day. The whole exercise before Governor Chatterton smacks of the resurrection of potential witnesses deemed too dangerous to use at the trial. In the proceeding before Chatterton, however, each side could trot out abandoned witnesses and usually not fear cross-examination.

Walter Stoll then went after the most dangerous witness against his case, Glendolene Kimmell. Stoll told Governor Chatterton that Kimmell had

spoken to him upon leaving Cheyenne and that "she then made no reference to having important evidence or information regarding the case of
Tom Horn." Stoll added that he had written a number of letters to Kimmell at Kansas City, but she had answered none. Stoll also read the affidavit
of attorney W. B. Ross, who had gone to Kansas City to induce Kimmell
to come to Cheyenne and "testify to what she knew to be the truth."[36]
Ross said she had showed a reluctance to appear and had many questions.
She had said nothing about Victor Miller having confessed to her that he
had killed Willie Nickell.[37]

Stoll offered an affidavit of H. A. Mendenhall, sheriff of Wyandotte
County, Kansas, in which Mendenhall swore that on September 18, 1902
(just before the Horn trial began), he had interviewed Kimmell about
the Tom Horn case. He said that she had told him that a certain person
asserted to be the perpetrator of a crime for which Horn was charged
(Mendenhall could not remember the name) was, in fact, innocent, and
that Horn was guilty of the crime. She had said she was willing to return to
Cheyenne to testify. Mendenhall had so notified Laramie County sheriff
E. J. Smalley and sought further instruction and rail fare. Mendenhall had
spoken again with Kimmell and she had again indicated her willingness to
go to Cheyenne. But three days later, before Sheriff Smalley acted, Miss
Kimmell backed out. Mendenhall had explained to her that the witness
fees and mileage would work out to more than her pay in Kansas City,
but she had replied: "But suppose the other fellows would give you more
than that, what would you do?"[38]

Stoll presented other affidavits, including those from Gus, Victor, and
James Miller vigorously denying the charges of confessions. Victor further
said that Neil Clark, the present foreman of the Coble ranch, and Charles
Irwin, the former foreman, at some date had taken him "behind the barn"
and suggested that he come in and confess to the murder of Willie Nickell,
saying that officers were then on the way to his home to arrest him. Victor
said he had told Clark and Irwin that he was not guilty of the crime and
intended to return to his home even if there were a dozen officers waiting
for him there. In rebuttal, John Lacey presented affidavits from Clark and
Irwin qualifying their statements made to Victor Miller "by saying that they
told Victor and the family that if Victor were really innocent they would
certainly not expect him to make a confession."[39]

Other odds-and-ends affidavits were presented to Governor Chatterton, and Burke and Lacey made other arguments, but the presentation of

evidence to the governor was essentially complete by Thursday, November 12. It did not take the governor long to act. At three thirty the afternoon of Saturday, November 14, Chatterton announced his decision, and it began ominously for Tom Horn.

Chatterton said that he had been asked "to set aside the findings of a jury of twelve good men and true and to reverse the judgment of the supreme court rendered in said case on appeal from the judgment" of the district court. Personally opposed to the death penalty, Chatterton said he nonetheless had to abide by state law. He did not believe the commutation or pardon power was given to a governor to reverse the judgments of courts, the *Daily Leader* reported, "unless, in his best judgment from competent evidence adduced[,] and by competent evidence I mean such as could be introduced on behalf of the defendant at the trial court, he believes a wrong otherwise irreparable has been committed."[40]

Governor Chatterton wrote that in addition to all the evidence presented to him he had interviewed "many persons" connected to the case and thereby gained much evidence not shown in the record. He said that as a general principle of law, a "confession of guilt supported by the corpus delicti [the substantial fact that a crime has been committed] is sufficient to sustain a verdict," and he said that these had been "conclusively established" in the trial of the case. But the defense had asserted, first, that the confession was a "josh," and, second, that stenographer Ohnhaus's notes had been "doctored."[41]

Regarding the stenographic notes, Chatterton said that he and his secretary, Jesse Knight, had obtained the original notes and read them over. The governor said that Knight could read these notes (apparently having training), and after a close review they had concluded that "every stenographic sign checked with the evidence; there was nothing left out, and there were no interlineations." The confession, was therefore not doctored but was "honestly reported."[42]

The governor also addressed the "Denver evidence." He concluded that the affidavits presented by the defense were inconsistent and "not worthy of consideration," but more than that, he said the supreme court had deemed the Denver evidence presented in the trial not to be a factor, because even if it were all discarded there was ample evidence to support the jury's verdict.[43]

The defense had accused Joe LeFors of taking a bribe to leave Jim Miller alone, but the governor concluded that the bribe accusation was completely rebutted by the evidence showing the disposition of all the monies loaned to Miller. And the governor noted that the assault upon LeFors was misplaced: "Had LeFors not testified at all, there would have been sufficient evidence to support the verdict."[44]

The affidavit of Ollie Whitman, wherein he asserted that Victor Miller had confessed to having shot Willie Nickell, seemed to be major plus for the defense. Governor Chatterton, however, was distinctly unimpressed both by the affidavit and by Whitman's testimony apparently presented to the governor as part of the proceedings. Chatterton said first that the defense had the Whitman information prior to the trial and made a tactical decision not to present Whitman's testimony even though he was present at the trial. "The failure to do so can only be accounted for upon the ground that the evidence was either not considered admissible, reliable or sufficient." More than this, said the governor, Whitman's statements were highly questionable. Chatterton indicated that Whitman suffered from low intelligence and from comprehension problems because of deafness, so much so that the affidavit appeared to have been "manufactured," a statement "put into the young man's mind by others." Said the governor: "On cross-examination by myself, the young man contradicted a part of the affidavit and many things others had told me he would substantiate. I cannot believe the affidavit is a truthful statement of actual fact." It was later revealed that Whitman had been the victim of a blow on the head, which caused him to act "queerly" and made him "subject to violent outbursts of temper."[45]

The most significant evidence presented to Chatterton had been the statements of Glendolene Kimmell. The governor declared: "If the Kimmell affidavit is true, it is all that is required, and Tom Horn should be pardoned." The defense, however, knew of the Kimmell statements even before the term of court in which Horn was convicted, the governor observed, but chose not to forward it. Chatterton rejected the idea that the Wyoming courts were powerless to act, however, saying, "It is never too late for the courts to do justice." He concluded: "If the facts set forth in this affidavit were true, they should have been presented to the court." To the governor, however, the issue still came down to whether the presented facts were true.[46]

The Kimmell affidavit was so crucial to Governor Chatterton, so basic to his "mind and conscience," that he had checked "every statement in the affidavit with every other statement in it and with all the evidence in the coroner's inquest in the trial of the case, with Miss Kimmell's correspondence with the attorneys and every circumstance surrounding the case in its entirety." The governor said that it would be too burdensome to set out all the details of his investigation but stated that one sample would suffice. Chatterton had been struck by an October 5, 1903, letter to Coble, in which Kimmell had written: "Now that matters have reached their present plight, I strongly hope that you will have faith in me to let me put some of my 'theories to the test.'" Immediately thereafter, the October 13 affidavit of Miss Kimmell had been submitted. Based on his investigations, confirmed by Sheriff Mendenhall's affidavit (showing Kimmell's sharply inconsistent statements), the governor did not believe the statements made in the Kimmell affidavit. "My investigations lead me to believe that Miss Kimmell, at this stage of the proceedings, was willing to present 'theories' to save Horn, intending after the commutation of Horn's sentence, to exonerate Victor Miller of the imputation cast upon him by her affidavit."[47]

"For these reasons," the governor concluded, "and with more regret than I can express, I do not believe that law and justice would be served by the interposition of Executive clemency." The consequences of the governor's determination were clear and stark. As the *Cheyenne Daily Leader* put it, "Death now stares Tom Horn in the face with no barrier between." Tom Horn would hang in six days, on Friday, November 20.[48]

CHAPTER TWENTY-NINE

Tom Horn Hangs

The *Cheyenne Daily Leader* story announcing that Governor Chatterton had refused clemency also addressed the one remaining possible impediment to Tom Horn's execution in six days: "There is absolutely no hope for [Horn] unless his friends deliver him from the hands of the authorities, and this, it is thought, will be impossible for them to accomplish."[1]

A "delivery" was essential if Horn were to survive. While in government hands, even if he were not to be executed for killing Willie Nickell, he would probably be executed for killing other men. Colorado authorities had charged Horn with the murders of Matt Rash and Isom Dart. They had turned up an eyewitness, a young man who had come forward after Horn's Wyoming arrest.[2] And Horn's comments to LeFors had not been confined to the Brown's Hole killings. Horn had made even more extensive comments about the 1895 killings of Lewis and Powell. If need be, Wyoming authorities were prepared to charge Horn with those killings.[3]

For some time the Laramie County authorities had been taking steps to prevent a delivery by Tom Horn's friends (and to keep any lynch mob at bay). After the August 10 jailbreak the precautions of sheriff's deputies were greatly increased. Horn had been receiving liberties, in the form of moving outside his cell and even running for a mile daily along the jail corridors, but these were all stopped, and he was allowed no visitors.[4] Still, it was said that Horn's "confidence in escaping remains supreme" because of promises "made to him by friends in whom he places implicit confidence." The promises were allegedly made because "he is said to know enough about them to cause them no end of trouble were he to talk."[5] If Horn was truly convinced that he would escape, his confidence must have been severely shaken by the actions of the Laramie County authorities in October 1903. They set up a Gatling gun in the jail.

The Laramie County sheriff went to military officials at Fort D.A. Russell and not only obtained a Gatling gun but the services of a Sergeant Mahon, a man said to have "a reputation for bravery and coolness," who was "an expert gunner of the United States Army."[6] The Gatling gun was brought into the jail about October 13, and it was set atop the lower tier of cells, just ten feet from the two on the upper tier, one of which contained Horn, the other of which held Jim McCloud. The gun commanded a field of fire that covered "all points from which an attack on the jail might be made."

The Gatling gun could fire 250 .30-30 rounds per minute, and every night Sergeant Mahon assumed his position next to the gun. He was on furlough for sixty days, engaged by the sheriff until Horn was executed. Sheriff Smalley said that he did not expect an attack but that several sources had warned him of plans to free Horn (newspapers were just then reporting a plot out of Routt County, Colorado), and so he was acting upon the theory that the best way to prevent an attack was "to take such precautions as to make the failure of the attack almost certain."[7]

At first after Horn was convicted, there was much discussion about going after those who had hired him. As the months dragged on, however, and Horn refused to talk to the authorities, it became evident that even if Horn's employers could not deliver him, he would not give them up. Still, to the very end, speculation continued that Horn might talk. It was noted, though, that any statement that Horn might make would have limited usefulness, because it would need to be corroborated.[8]

Horn's demeanor in November 1903 was said to be remarkably calm. It was written, "[He] continues to eat and sleep well, and is not at all nervous over his impending doom."[9] But Horn was not as placid as he sometimes appeared. In October he wrote letters to two witnesses asking them both to contact John Coble and to let the authorities know that they (the witnesses) had committed perjury against him—although no doubt under the influence of the prosecuting attorney and the deputy U.S. marshal (LeFors). One letter was sent to a Denver witness and another to Charles Ohnhaus, the stenographer. To Ohnhaus, Horn wrote that both he and Ohnhaus knew that his notes had been "doctored to convict me."[10] Horn

also complained about the role of newspapers, saying that they had preju-
diced people against him.[11] The witnesses did not recant.

The *Cheyenne Daily Leader* reported Horn's reaction when, on Tuesday,
November 17, he was given a copy of the newspaper containing Governor Chatterton's decision against him. The *Leader* said that Horn took
the paper to his cell, read the whole decision without comment, "then
calmly turned to the other news features and read them with apparently
as much interest as [he] had the news of his fate." The newspaper said it
appeared that Horn was less moved by the story about his impending
execution "than any other man about the courthouse." Said the *Leader:*
"Knowing that he must go into the presence of his maker before the week
is out, he is able to joke and laugh, to accept foul as he would fair fortune,
to utterly conceal the conflict that must be occurring in his soul." The
Leader concluded by noting that a few minutes after Horn received the
news of Governor Chatterton's decision, "the death watch was placed."[12]

On Wednesday, November 18, Horn was visited by evangelists. He was
willing to see them but refused to pray with them. Horn had very little
contact with his family, although he had a brother in Boulder, Colorado.
On this second to last day of his life, however, Horn did dispose of his
personal effects. He gave all of them to his close friend John Coble, another
indication that he would not say anything to the authorities about his
employers. Most notably, he gave Coble a history of his life, handwritten
in four books of about 125 pages each. The *Laramie Boomerang* referred to
Horn's writing as a "novel" and said he had been writing it in jail since
December the previous year.[13] Horn continued to show wonderful nerve,
it was reported, so much so that Sheriff Smalley and his deputies talked of it.[14]

Horn was visited on Thursday, November 19, by Reverend Ira D. Williams, who later would insist that Horn had confessed to him that he had
killed Willie Nickell.[15] About four o'clock that afternoon, an architect
and carpenters were admitted to the jail and immediately began to build a
scaffold to bear the mechanism of the gallows. Their work was noisy as they
drove large spikes to hold timbers in place, "while the trap doors were raised
and lowered many times and slammed in a careless manner to see if they
would work regularly." Horn could not have failed to hear all this, and the
Laramie Boomerang said that "Horn's nerves yesterday afternoon were put to
the severest test, but he never so much as flinched." The hanging mechanism was one designed by architect J. P. Julien so that when Horn stepped
on a trapdoor his own weight would open a valve leading to a vessel of

water. After about a minute, weight within the vessel would jerk a plug holding the trap door, and Horn, it was written, "will shoot down into eternity." In essence, Tom Horn would hang himself.[16]

At 4:15 P.M. that Thursday afternoon, Governor Chatterton issued orders to his adjutant general "to take charge of the situation and place an adequate force of troops on duty at and near the county court house, and keep the soldiers there until after the execution." The soldiers took their responsibility seriously, challenging anyone who passed too close to the courthouse, and if they did, they were "brought to a standstill by the stentorian command of a militia man to halt." No persons were allowed to pass by the sidewalk next to the courthouse; all were compelled to cross the street. Said the *Laramie Boomerang,* "On every side of the building blue clothed sentries pace their beats, loaded guns in their hand. Everyone, no matter whom, is halted, and made to state his business." As well, "In addition to the militiamen, nearly every window of the court house is occupied by a guard and as anyone approaches he is covered with shotguns from these vantage points."[17]

Despite all this activity, which Horn must have noticed, that evening he thought he was going to go free. Horn had supposedly been informed by his friends (how was not known) that they would "set him free and that all of the armed guards in Laramie County cannot stop them." Horn told this to McCloud, who told it to other prisoners, and one of them told the jail authorities.[18] When the sun rose the next morning, however, Horn was still in his cell, and there had been no efforts to free him. It was Friday, November 20, 1903, the day scheduled for Horn's execution.

The day was "dull and cloudy, with a chilly wind blowing from the northwest."[19] People were up early. At 7:00 A.M., a delegation of Horn's friends made a final, "vivid and earnest" appeal for Governor Chatterton to at least put off the execution for a few days. The governor was said to have listened "quite respectfully" but then said: "There is no use, gentlemen: This execution must take place at the time set by the law. I will not interfere. My decision is absolute and final."[20]

John Coble was apparently among the delegation before Governor Chatterton, and he promptly went to Horn's jail cell and was admitted. Coble said a tearful goodbye to Horn, and Horn told Coble that he had written a letter to be given to Charlie Irwin for delivery to Coble after the execution.[21]

Also up early that morning were soldiers. The *Laramie Republican* said: "At 9 o'clock this morning the number of militiamen had been greatly increased, and thereafter until the hanging was over, a complete cordon surrounded the court house square and held back the curious crowd of spectators."[22]

Horn had slept well. He woke early, however, and started writing letters to his friends. Horn ate a hearty breakfast but was anxious to get back to his writing. He asked the deputy clearing away the breakfast dishes how much time he had left. It was then about nine, and the deputy said that Horn had at least another hour. Horn replied that he "could do a good deal in that time." A few minutes before 10:00 A.M., Dr. G. C. Rafter, apparently an Episcopal clergyman, entered Horn's cell, and for the next half-hour Horn and the pastor engaged in an "earnest conversation."[23]

A 1903 photograph of the Laramie County jail shows it to be a large and unusually tall structure. Horn's scaffold was erected within the jail itself, in its northeast corner, only a few feet from Horn's cell. At about 10:45 A.M., visitors were admitted into the jail. They saw Horn in his cell, lying on his cot while smoking a cigar, "looking as cool and unconcerned as if he was spending his moments in ease."[24] Deputy Proctor came to the cell, and Horn arose and started out but then turned "as though to see if he had left anything behind." He was dressed in a "red and white striped negligee shirt, open at the neck, a corduroy vest, dark trousers and low slippers." When Horn emerged from the door, Proctor told him that the Irwin brothers were there and wanted to sing a song for him. It was a favorite of Horn's, a religious song titled "Life's Railway to Heaven."[25]

Horn listened intently to the Irwins' song and then gave Charlie Irwin the letters he had been writing. Irwin asked Horn whether he had made a confession to "the preacher," apparently referring to Ira Williams. "No," said Horn, in a loud and clear voice.[26] Horn made no statement about the Nickell case.

The deputies put straps about Horn's wrists and thighs, while he moved around to accommodate them. During this grim interlude, Horn was talking to those around him and laughing at his own jokes. Led to the scaffold, he walked in a firm manner and viewed the scaffold construction with curiosity. A black cap was placed over Horn's head, "shutting out from his eyes forever the light of day." Still, as the *Laramie Boomerang* said, Horn "treated the whole matter as a joke, and met death with Spartan fortitude." Even after the hood was placed over Horn's head, he continued to banter. He said to one of the deputies, "I understand you are a married man," and upon being told that the deputy was, Horn replied in a jesting tone,

"Well, treat her right, and I hope you live happily." Horn was then lifted onto the trap, and Horn said to the men lifting him, "Ain't getting nervous[,] are you?" Horn then laughed audibly.[27]

When Horn was placed on the trap, silence descended. The only thing that people could hear was the dripping of liquid, as water started to pour from a balance tank. Horn was as "motionless as stone," with "his figure drawn to his full height and his hands clenched tightly." He made no sound. The water continued to flow for another thirty-five seconds, a time said to be "the longest that any of those who witnessed the execution will ever pass."[28]

Suddenly Horn's body dropped through the trap "like a stone" and "stopped with a jerk at the end of the rope." The head and shoulders showed above the trap and the body swung slowly from side to side, but there was no other movement. Horn had apparently been killed instantly. The spectators (about thirty people, including the sheriffs of Wyoming and a few of Horn's friends) immediately started leaving the building, and physicians took over. Horn's body was left to hang for several minutes, and then it was cut down, and Horn was pronounced dead. The body was turned over to Deputy Sheriff Ed Sperry, of Boulder, Colorado. Sperry was to return the body to Boulder where Horn's brother, Charles, would bury him.[29]

For all Tom Horn's apparent equanimity on the day of his death, he had suffered torment in the months awaiting his execution. The body taken to Boulder, Colorado, was not the 204 pounds of muscle that graced Horn before his trial but that of a man weighing about 155 pounds. Horn had lost fifty pounds. Sheriff's deputies had not taken into account Horn's great weight loss, and the fall had almost decapitated him.[30]

Still, Horn's demeanor was remarkable. He seemed determined not to let those who brought him to this moment gain the satisfaction of watching him whine or grovel. The poise and courage with which Horn went to his death calls up Malcolm's famous line from *King Lear:* "Nothing in his life became him like the leaving it."[31]

Epilogue

The people of Wyoming saw the trial, conviction, and execution of Tom Horn as a declaration that Wyoming was determined to stop the control of the state by a small faction of murderous cattle barons. Since the 1880s Wyoming citizens had watched the killings by big cattlemen on the range, including the atrocious lynching of a woman, Ellen Watson. The worst episode was the 1892 Johnson County War, in which cattlemen arrogated to themselves the power to execute seventy men who had displeased them. At the polls in November 1892, Wyoming people had unequivocally declared their disapproval of the bullying and terrorizing by rich cattlemen, but it was not enough to stop the brutality. Some of the big ranchers simply moved to a different solution: hiring a paid assassin. This they found in the person of Tom Horn. Laramie County residents had noted that no action had followed the killing of William Lewis and Fred Powell in 1895. They had also witnessed the killing of two men in the Brown's Hole country of Colorado, again followed by no action. Even if they had not heard it themselves, they had heard of Horn bragging in Cheyenne and Laramie bars about how he had a corner on the market of killing men. And they seethed.[1]

When a strong case was made against Horn for gunning down a fourteen-year-old boy, and Wyomingites watched high-priced lawyers rush to Horn's aid, they seethed. They deeply believed that Horn was the instrument to oppress every little man in the state and that the big cattlemen would get away with a killing yet again. When Horn drew a remarkably favorable trial jury composed of fellow cattlemen, their worst fears seemed confirmed:

Wyoming would forever remain the bastion of a brutal gang of cattle barons, men who exercised the ultimate power to override the laws of the state and pronounce life or death.

So it was no surprise that people all over Wyoming were jubilant when Tom Horn was convicted and his conviction upheld. He had become a symbol, the living embodiment of big cattlemen's reign of terror. The citizens of Wyoming believed that if Wyoming was ever to join the community of states in which the government was truly of the people and by the people, Tom Horn must die.

People throughout Wyoming expressed strong feelings about the fate of Tom Horn. The *Laramie Republican* offered one of the most cogent statements:

> After many years of patient effort the people of Wyoming have risen above the methods of the anarchist and have proved their ability to enforce the law against murder. Tom Horn has paid the extreme penalty fixed by the statutes for the crime of cold-blooded assassination. The mandate of the courts has been fulfilled. . . .
>
> For many years it has been openly stated that Horn was the hired assassin of certain interests; that when a man was marked by the men who paid him[,] his death soon followed. This practice might have continued on for years had not a mistake been made and a boy killed instead of a man. . . .
>
> Through their courts the people of Wyoming have spoken. Now let the criminals take warning.[2]

Even more trenchant were the comments of the Green River *Wyoming Star*, which noted, after Tom Horn hanged: "The killing of Willie Nickell has been avenged and justice is triumphant. No event in the history of Wyoming could do more to restore the confidence in the courts and uphold them in the administration of the law."[3]

Popular prejudice ran against Tom Horn when he was tried; it usually does when a person is charged with a heinous crime. Prejudice in the larger community does not automatically translate to prejudice within a courtroom, however. The solution to such prejudice is not to declare that a murderer must be freed because by his actions he has offended so many people. By such reasoning the worse the atrocity the more likely a killer will go free. Instead, the law, even in 1902, built in safeguards. One was the right to hire skilled attorneys. Another was to ask for a change of venue. (Horn's attorneys did not do so because they knew that Laramie County offered their client the best chance for acquittal.) A third was the jury selection. The skill of Horn's lawyers, at least in part, assured a sympathetic jury for Horn.

The well-paid defense attorneys hired for Tom Horn were reputed to be the best in Wyoming. They were, indeed, remarkably resourceful, hard-working, and innovative in their efforts on Horn's behalf. If those attorneys had not been opposed by a lawyer of Walter Stoll's caliber, they probably would have won the case. But every time Horn's high-priced lawyers for-warded a seemingly unbeatable defense, Walter Stoll, the part-time prose-cutor paid only $125 per month, found a hidden key showing that the defense's evidence was not what it appeared to be.[4] Stoll's high skill made the trial come down to Horn's credibility—whether he was telling the truth when he declared he had just been joshing in his discussion with Joe LeFors. This issue should have greatly favored Horn. He was given full opportunity to tell his story, and he did so over the course of two days. The jury, however, consisting of men who knew Tom Horn well, had no doubt that he was telling them lies. As jurors stated later, Horn convicted himself. Even his good friend, Homer Payne, the man who held out to the last, finally had to do his duty because he thought Horn was guilty. This was Walter Stoll's supreme accomplishment, that he convinced twelve men, many of whom were sympathetic to Tom Horn, to simply do their duty.

All this is not to say that the strong public feelings against Horn had no effect on the Horn trial. The presiding judge, Richard Scott, an elected official, had shown in the Johnson County War cases that his decisions could be influenced by powerful cattlemen. Judge Scott was surely aware, however, that the case was of intense public interest and that the public at large strongly believed Horn should be convicted. Governor Chatterton too was fully aware of the attitudes toward Horn. Both men seemed to take positions that lawyers do when their actions are under scrutiny. They were conservative and carefully balanced in their determinations. Neither wanted to see himself painted as a crony of big cattlemen.

Following the execution, stories began to circulate that Tom Horn had not actually died but had been spirited away to another place. Sixteen minutes after he was hung, however, two physicians confirmed that Horn was dead. Then a few close friends viewed the body and after it was taken to a funeral home, coroner Thomas Murray impaneled a jury on the spot,

which found that "the deceased, Tom Horn, came to his death by hanging, said hanging having been inflicted by the sheriff of Laramie County
in the execution of a sentence of death."[5] There can be no doubt that Tom
Horn was executed on November 20, 1903.

Despite Horn's ignominious death, a small segment of Wyoming people
continued to support him and what he had represented. John Coble
mourned the death of his friend and tried to honor his memory, even to
the point of publishing Horn's autobiography (including other writings
by Horn and his friends). In 1904, Coble had Horn's handwritten pages
prepared into manuscript form by Glendolene Kimmell. They were printed
and bound, and beginning in April the book was sold through various
public outlets.[6]

Why Coble would think these writings would do anything but support
the jury's verdict against Horn and, in another sense, the verdict of Wyoming citizens against Horn, is hard to guess. Perhaps Coble truly believed
the made-up stories Horn told about himself, but Horn's written record
has allowed a thorough evaluation of the autobiography and shown it to
be fable in great part. Larry D. Ball, in his recent biography, a complete
treatment of Horn's life, shows throughout how contrived and inaccurate
so many statements from Horn's autobiography are.[7]

Coble even published Horn's last two letters to him, ones that did no
service to Horn's memory. Horn came up with a new story about the
killing of Willie Nickell, a far different tale than he told at the coroner's
inquest, at the trial, or after the trial. In it, Horn said Jim Miller had asked
him to come to his ranch to talk to Miller and Billy McDonald. Miller and
McDonald supposedly proposed to Horn that he come in with them to
"wipe up the whole Nickell outfit." Horn said he refused to have anything to do with them and that he was not interested "in any way." Horn's
tone was far different from his statements about Kels Nickell to a reporter
in October 1901, when Horn blasted Nickell because Nickell said he
"intended to keep [sheep] there no matter what people said or thought"
and further commented: "There is no man who is big bad good or tough
enough to bring sheep into a cattle country."[8] Horn did not explain why he
had declined to reveal such exculpatory evidence in earlier proceedings.

In the letters, Horn changed completely what he testified to repeatedly
at the trial: that every statement set out in the transcribed confession was
accurate and understood, comments he would have made even if he knew
law officers were present. Rather, in the November 17, 1903, letter to Coble,

Horn wrote: "The notes read at the trial were not the original notes at all. Everything of an incriminating nature read of those notes was manufactured and put in."[9] In a November 20 letter, Horn declared that Ohnhaus, LeFors, and Snow were all swearing to lies to fit the case, and that he, Horn, had made no admissions.[10] Horn apparently abandoned his position that everything he told LeFors was a "josh."

Also included in the Horn autobiography was a long statement from Glendolene Myrtle Kimmell, which helps explain Kimmell's erratic behavior at the time of the clemency proceedings before Governor Chatterton. She spoke of how strongly attracted she was to "the frontier type" and also how she had been "doomed to disappointment" until she met Tom Horn at the Miller ranch on July 15, 1901, "a man," she said, "who embodied the characteristics, the experiences and the code of the old frontiersman." She went on at great length about Horn's character and physique, saying, for example, that he was a "man of action" "built in perfect proportion to his height—broad-shouldered, deep-chested, full hipped. Without an ounce of superfluous flesh upon him and with muscles of steel, he could perform feats of strength which were the admiration and despair of other men."[11] Apparently caught up in a romanticism about Horn and the Wyoming of 1901, Kimmell's evaluation of Horn and the case against him stand in marked contrast to the clear-eyed assessments she gave at the coroner's inquest.

In a "closing word" for the Horn autobiography, Coble shows how deeply committed he was to his friend. He excoriated the press, which he said had hatched "brood after brood of lies, harmless or harmful as they may be, with or without consequences, but lies just the same, deliberately manufactured and circulated." Coble also railed against the public officials involved in the case, referring to men puffed up with "their little brief authority" who "besmirched their trust and stooped to odious means for their selfish ends." Coble added: "If it be true that 'kings play chess with nations for pawns,' then it is as true that Wyoming politicians play the game of justice with human souls for pawns, and, I may add, with Cowardice as referee."[12]

Coble's emotion can be understood. He was deeply partisan about the trial and execution of his good friend. But that emotion cannot be accorded credence. Coble's assessments were a flight from reality. Much as Horn and his close supporters might rail about the confession to LeFors, that it was a "josh" (first position), that it was manufactured (later position), and that the execution of Tom Horn was solely a product of the lies and dishonesty of the press and politicians (last position), two points should be noted about Horn's confession. One is that although John Coble may have passionately believed Horn to be an innocent man, many other cattlemen were not so convinced. People from Iron Mountain, those who were in the best position to know the truth (and who, by and large, refused to assist the prosecution), did not even bother to assert Horn's innocence when speaking to the press during the trial. They declared, among other things, that the "annihilation" of Kels Nickell would have been a "benefit to the community," and they added that the killing of Willie Nickell had just been an unfortunate mistake.[13] As well, W. C. Irvine, a leader of the 1892 Johnson County invaders and a past president of the Wyoming Stockgrowers Association, said Horn was a man who "killed without feeling or compunction," adding that "in the line of his business he had killed many men." Irvine also said that after the failure of the invasion, Horn had been the instrument for "secret individual killing." Irvine, probably referring primarily to John Coble, noted that some people who knew Horn well believed him not to be guilty of the killing of Willie Nickell. Irvine nevertheless praised Horn's "honorable trait" of not "peaching" (informing) on accomplices and employees "to the great relief of many very respectable citizens of the West."[14]

The second point is that Horn's confession to LeFors was only one of many confessions Horn made to many different people. Besides bragging to people in bars around Cheyenne and the three men from Denver who testified at the trial, Horn had confessed complicity to murders to Mr. and Mrs. Fred Bell.[15] He had confessed to the murder of Willie Nickell to two Denver women, including Elizabeth Sims (whose testimony was not used because of her "bad reputation"—she was probably a prostitute).[16] And he had testified to the killings of Rash and Dart to fellow detective Charlie Siringo.[17] Horn had even confessed that he would have killed the jailer, Proctor, if he could have operated the Belgian pistol taken from the sheriff's office.[18]

The unavoidable reality is that Tom Horn was a deeply insecure man who relished the notoriety of being a feared and dreaded assassin to boost his self-esteem—sadly not uncommon among men who commit heinous crimes. The nobility of his demeanor at the time of his execution obscured these facts, but Horn was both of these men, the one who could calmly stare death in the face without blinking and the one who could callously gun down another man.

Even in Horn's time, there were those, other than big cattlemen and the Iron Mountain enemies of Kels Nickell, who idolized him. During the trial, numbers of young boys managed to filter clandestinely into the courtroom to watch the proceedings. They saw Horn, as one reporter put it, "greater than the hero of any dime novel ever written." When Judge Scott recognized their presence he quickly had them removed.[19]

But Tom Horn was not a hero. He had some interesting and appealing features to his character, but his one overriding deficiency was a big hole in the center of his soul, the inability to feel and understand the suffering of another human being. Horn could not have understood the deep grief of Willie Nickell's family.

John Coble would surely have said that the Nickell family's grief for the death of Willie Nickell had nothing to do with Tom Horn. They were certainly connected, however. It is undeniable that Horn's death came about because of Willie Nickell's death. Coble was said to be so over-come with grief when Horn was executed that as he walked to his hotel he had to be supported by friends, a problem made worse because Coble was unwell. During that time, he was also at loggerheads with his business partner, Frank Bosler, brought on at least partly by indebtedness incurred because of Coble's support of Horn.[20] In 1904, Coble sued Bosler, saying that in the dissolution of their partnership, Coble had not received his fair share. He won a settlement, but these legal difficulties probably added to Coble's unhappiness with life.

Other disputes relating to Horn continued. In a 1905 case, two promi-nent cattlemen were accused of reneging on a promise to contribute to Horn's defense. Despite newspaper speculation that "some of the mysteries of the Horn case may be explained," no public disclosures came out of the lawsuit.[21] Things did not go well for Coble after he split with Bosler. He tried ranching on his own but was not successful and drifted to Elko, Nevada in 1914. There, "despondent over financial failure," Coble com-mitted suicide, shooting himself while in the lobby of a local hotel.[22]

John Coble was not alone in lamenting Horn's death. Miss Kimmell mourned the passing of her frontier man of action. Soon after the trial and execution, Kimmell moved to the Denver area, remained there for a year or two, and then returned to Missouri. She had not had to stay in Wyoming, because Walter Stoll had dropped the perjury charges against her for the simple reason that it turned out that for a statement to constitute perjury it had to be presented to a court of law. A presentation to a governor did not count.[23] Kimmell never married, perhaps because she felt no other man measured up to Tom Horn. In 1919 she moved to Atascadero, California, where she lived with her mother, and she died there in 1949 at age seventy.[24]

Other people associated with Tom Horn's trial defense fared better in life. John Lacey had a long and distinguished career as a Wyoming lawyer. He continued to practice law in Cheyenne and was remarkably active. He appeared in sixty-two cases before the Wyoming Supreme Court, the last two of which were in 1933, when Lacey turned eighty-five. In one, Lacey participated in oral argument.[25] He died in 1936 and is buried in the Lakeview Cemetery in Cheyenne.[26]

Governor Fenimore Chatterton also practiced law for a remarkably long time, although doing so may not have been his first choice. The people of Wyoming strongly approved of the way Chatterton had handled the Horn case, but in 1904 they did not decide who would be the Republican nominee for governor. The party bosses did, and the biggest boss of all was Senator Francis E. Warren.[27] Even before the Horn case, Chatterton had deeply offended Warren, and one newspaper even referred to Warren's "virulent hostility" to Chatterton.[28] In 1893, Chatterton had helped keep Warren out of the U.S. Senate, and Warren was not the kind of man to forgive and forget.[29] In 1904, Chatterton was interested in the nomination for governor, and, as the acting governor, seemed a logical choice, but the Republican Party nominated B. B. Brooks instead.[30] Wyoming Democrats criticized the Republicans, especially Francis E. Warren, for their shabby treatment of Chatterton.[31] Chatterton continued practicing law in Cheyenne and retired in 1932. He remained in Cheyenne until his death in 1958. As with John Lacey, he is buried in the Lakeview Cemetery in Cheyenne.[32]

Walter Stoll ran for Laramie County attorney again in 1904, but when caught up in a very close election against W. B. Ross, the final canvass showed Ross ahead by twenty-two votes, about 0.5 percent of all the votes counted.[33] Stoll had received threatening letters even before the election, but after the initial results were announced, he received taunting letters, including one from Denver, Colorado (which Stoll believed came from Glendolene Kimmell). The Denver letter contained one message, apparently in blood, referring to Stoll's defeat, and a calling card from "Tom Horn," also apparently in blood.[34]

A recount was made, and at one point the press reported that Stoll would certainly win, because the recount showed a gain of 240 votes. But then Judge Richard Scott, presiding over the challenge to Ross's apparent victory, decided that the records were so confused that he could not rule to overturn the initial count.[35] Ross was declared the winner.

Like John Lacey and Fenimore Chatterton, Walter Stoll continued to practice law, although his remaining time as an attorney was much shorter than Chatterton or Lacey. For all his remaining days, however, Stoll was referred to as the man who had gained a conviction against Tom Horn. That mention was included in an embarrassing March 10, 1906, story announcing that Stoll's wife Bertha had filed suit against him for divorce on the grounds of drunkenness and extreme cruelty. Mrs. Stoll alleged that her husband "attacked, slapped and drove from their home women friends who were visiting her."[36] Mrs. Stoll apparently dropped the case, however, because she was still with her husband five years later when he suffered a heart attack and died on June 2, 1911.[37]

Stoll fascinates because of his brilliance as an attorney, but he was also a distinct eccentric. The *Laramie Republican* caught some of this when it wrote: "In the death of Attorney Walter R. Stoll of Cheyenne, Wyoming lost a brilliant and unique character. His life was positively without parallel. No rule applied to him. He disregarded all law, human and divine. He was not the victim of any particular habit but seemed to be at the mercy of all habits. In his professional career he had few peers in the state. His mind was a never-ending source of wonder to friend and foe."[38]

Joe LeFors, the detective who provided Stoll with the evidence that made Tom Horn's conviction possible (and who received the thousand-dollar reward from the Laramie County commissioners for information leading to the arrest and conviction of the murderer of Willie Nickell), continued to act as a detective throughout Wyoming with much success.[39] In 1906, LeFors was credited with trapping 150 gamblers in Big Horn County. LeFors received reward money for his excellent work in the 1909 case of *State v. Brink,* which arose out of the Spring Creek Raid.[40] His fine detective work was much commented upon and admired. In a 1909 story, the *Cheyenne State Leader* referred to LeFors as a "frontier Sherlock Holmes."[41] In January 1915, the *Park County Enterprise* remarked: "Joe LeFors is a stock detective, who established his right to fame by solving many a range mystery, most prominent among them was the capture and conviction of Tom Horn, who was sent to the gallows."[42] LeFors retired in Buffalo, wrote a book titled *Wyoming Peace Officer,* and died in 1940.[43]

The Kels Nickell family first moved to Lake Creek (north of Saratoga) in 1904 and then, in 1909, to Encampment.[44] Kels Nickell died in Kelechawa, Kentucky (where he had gone for medical treatment), on October 13, 1929, and he is buried in the family plot in Cheyenne.[45]

The conviction and execution of Tom Horn, potent symbols though they may have been, did not stop all extralegal violence in Wyoming. Willie Nickell may have been the first Wyoming male to die in clashes between sheep and cattle interests, but he was hardly the last. For years after the execution of Horn, cattlemen waged war on sheepmen throughout the state. It took another judge and another jury in 1909 to finally stop the killing by organized groups. Following the Big Horn County conviction of Herb Brink for his part in the April 1909 Spring Creek Raid, five men were sent to prison and that punishment stopped the killing in sheep raids in Wyoming. The *Wyoming Tribune,* a Cheyenne daily, noted the connection between the cases against Herb Brink and Tom Horn, saying, "The legal execution of Tom Horn sounded the death knell to range war and promiscuous killing in Laramie County. The Tribune trusts Big Horn County will never again be called upon to answer for such a crime."[46] Even after 1909, however, there were lynchings, apparently spontaneous, of African-American men, although 1920 was the last year for such a killing.[47]

Wyoming, during the late nineteenth and early twentieth century, was faced with a gargantuan problem with vigilantism in all its forms. A culture had grown up from the 1880s and 1890s that fostered extralegal action. This culture was not unique to Wyoming, although the details of violence varied greatly from state to state. Yet the problem for each began with a concept of democracy declaring that the people could seize the reins if the government failed them, followed by lonely societies in which men sometimes had to become a law unto themselves, and then followed, in the mountain West, by a cattle industry whose self-interest fostered vigilantism. And so, law-abiding citizens in Wyoming watched a parade of lynchings, raids, and assassinations, all done in the name of good but producing a violent society capped by atrocities. Throughout it all, decent people wanted the lawful authorities to gain the upper hand, first to suppress criminal lawlessness and then to suppress lawlessness by people ordinarily law-abiding. The first blow was struck by Johnson County when it vanquished the invaders who came to lethally chastise its citizens. The second was against the remaining defiant cattlemen and their murderous agent, Tom Horn. The last was against cattlemen bent on expelling sheepmen. Horn's case involved both the murderous arrogance of big cattlemen and the struggle between all cattlemen and all sheepmen. It was a bitter and long struggle for the people of Wyoming, but they succeeded at last. Tom Horn's conviction and execution were essential to the final triumph of the forces of law and order.

Notes

CHAPTER 1

1. See "Over in the Hills," *Laramie Republican,* May 11, 1900, 2.

2. The oldest child, Julia, was married to T. F. Cook, and the second child, Kels Nickell, Jr., was away at school in Kentucky. The remaining children were William (Willie), Fred, Beatrix, Catherine, Maggie, Ida, and Harlan, all of whom were still at home in 1901. See Polly Pry, "Career of Kels Nickell," *Denver Post,* March 2, 1902, 13; Dennie Trimble Nickell, "The Story of the Nickell Family," in "In Wyoming," Tom Horn biography file, Wyoming State Archives; Joint Centennial Committee of Saratoga and Encampment, Wyoming, *Saratoga and Encampment, Wyoming: An Album of Family Histories* (Woodlands, Tex.: Portfolio Publishing, 1989), 341, 342. See also Larry D. Ball, *Tom Horn in Life and Legend* (Norman: University of Oklahoma Press, 2014), 171.

3. This narrative directly follows the testimony at coroner's inquest immediately following the death of Willie Nickell. See coroner's inquest transcript, July 20, 1901, Wyoming State Archives, Cheyenne (hereafter CIT), 1, 9, 16, 18, 19, 21, 22, 23, 24; trial transcript, *State v. Horn,* October 10, 1903, Wyoming Archives (hereafter TT), 53 (testimony of Kels Nickell). See also TT, 23 (testimony of G. W. Zorn, civil engineer). I visited the scene on July 19, 2011 (the road, fence, and gate are extant), and what I viewed is incorporated in my narrative. I have assumed that the 2011 setting was not substantially different from that in 1901, except for vegetation situated differently. The differences in the location of ponderosa pines would affect the lines of sight to the gate.

4. Regarding Willie's clothing, see CIT, 380 (testimony of Mary Nickell, Willie's mother). J. A. B. Apperson examined the scene when he went there with Kels Nickell the morning of July 19, and he reported that Willie had opened the wire gate, had led his horse through, and had then been shot when he proceeded to close the gate (CIT, 22, 23). It is equally likely, however, that Willie had closed the gate and resumed his journey

but then saw whatever alarmed him, came back to the gate, and was reopening it when he was shot. Cattle moving through during the following twenty-four hours obliterated all the tracks from Willie's horse and those of anyone else, so neither sequence of events can be established or ruled out, at least by the tracks.

When lawman Joe LeFors would later ask Tom Horn why Willie Nickell had been killed, Horn said, "Well, I suppose a man was in that [the draw that comes into the main creek below Nickell's house], and the kid came riding up on him from this way, and suppose the kid started to run for the house, and the fellow headed him off at the gate and killed him to keep him from going to the house and raising a hell of a commotion. That is the way I think it occurred" (Krakel, *The Saga of Tom Horn,* 51). Although the on-the-ground facts make it as likely that Willie Nickell was killed while closing the fence as that he was killed while opening it, the Horn statement swings the balance toward Willie going through the fence, running into his assailant, fleeing back to the gate, and being shot while opening the gate.

5. This description follows testimony at the coroner's inquest into the death of Willie Nickell and incorporates my interview of Aubrey D. Wills, M.D., of Basin, Wyoming. The testimony shows that Willie was shot twice while standing at a wire gate and hit by bullets that struck under his left arm. The bullets described the same trajectory through his body, but one was six to eight inches below the other. Dr. Wills, who was a battalion surgeon in Vietnam and treated gunshot wounds, read the inquest testimony of three physicians who conducted what they termed an autopsy on the body of Willie Nickell (CIT, 4<n>9), and he concluded that the boy was standing at the gate, probably opening it, with his arms raised (otherwise the bullet would have gone through his left arm), when the first bullet hit him in the left side. It proceeded slightly downward, then exited at the sternum in the center of the chest. This wound probably put Willie into deep shock, and he stayed frozen at the gate. The second shot entered just below the first, entering directly below the armpit, again proceeding slightly downward, through the viscera, and probably the aorta, coming out just above the right hip. The identical plane of the two shots indicates they were made from the same place. A bullet through the aorta creates the same effect as one directly through the heart: it produces a surge of adrenalin and causes the victim to run and then collapse. Dr. Wills concluded that either of the wounds would have been fatal, but the second was the more devastating. Not only did it smash through Willie's intestines, but a shot through the aorta would have created massive hemorrhaging, causing the loss of most of the body's blood within minutes. It is impossible to know exactly when Willie Nickell died, but given his severe wounds, he could not have lived long. Aubrey Daryll Wills, interview with the author, Orchard Bench, Wyoming, December 5, 2010. See also the trial testimony of Dr. Amos Barber, TT, 85. Regarding the distance Willie ran, see the trial testimony of J. A. B. Apperson, TT, 66.

6. CIT, 21 (testimony of J. A. B. Apperson).

7. TT, 50, 54 (testimony of Mary Nickell); CIT, 5, 11 (testimony of J. A. B. Apperson).

8. CIT, 21, 22; TT, 48, 56 (testimony of Kels Nickell), 73 (testimony of J. A. B. Apperson).

9. CIT, 9, 21–23.

10. TT, 67, 68.

11. See CIT, 24, where Apperson testified that he had previously looked around the area but not carefully.

12. TT, 50.

13. CIT, 22, 24; TT, 54, 55, 61, 62, 74, 75, 81, 82.

14. CIT, 24; TT, 56.

15. CIT, 27. There was no trouble between the Nickells and Mrs. Miller. They had always been friends, according to Gus Miller, the oldest boy in the Miller family (CIT, 50).

16. CIT, 2, 3 (testimony of Joseph E. Reed).

17. CIT, 26.

CHAPTER 2

1. Larry D. Ball, *Tom Horn in Life and Legend* (Norman: University of Oklahoma Press, 2014), 264, 265. The Nickell ranch was in Laramie County in 1901.

2. See Wyoming Revised Statutes, 1899, § 1173; coroner's inquest transcript (hereafter CIT), 1; Ball, *Tom Horn,* 264. Regarding the reference to Peter Warlamount, I have used the spelling "Warlamount" herein rather than another spelling encountered, "Warlaumont," because "Warlamount" is uniformly used in the trial transcript (*State v. Horn*).

3. The coroner's inquest statutes are still on the books; see §§ 7–4-201 to 210, Wyo. Stat. Ann. (LexisNexis 2011). The most recent use of a coroner's inquest in Wyoming appears to be in the unusual Natrona County murder case of *State v. Humphrey.* Charges were first brought against Rita Ann Humphrey in 1980 but dismissed for lack of evidence the same year. Charges were refiled in 2004. See *State v. Humphrey,* 2005 WY 131, 120 P.3d 1027 and *Humphrey v. State,* 2008 WY 67, 185 P.3d 1276. After the charges were refiled, a coroner's inquest was convened in the case. Mrs. Humphrey was convicted of second-degree murder. Michael Blonigen, the Natrona County district attorney who prosecuted this case states that, to his knowledge, this use of the coroner's jury has been the only one in Natrona County in the last thirty years. Author's interview of Michael A. Blonigen, July 19, 2012.

The Wyoming Supreme Court did not refer to the coroner's jury in its two *Humphrey* opinions. The most recent reference in Wyoming Supreme Court opinions to the holding of a coroner's inquest is in the case of *Kimbley v. City of Green River,* 663 P.2d 871 (Wyo. 1983). In the earlier case of *Rarigosa v. State,* 562 P.2d 1000 (Wyo. 1977), the defendant complained about the failure to convene a coroner's inquest, but the Wyoming Supreme Court stated that there was no requirement that this be done. Another recent reference to the holding of a coroner's inquest is in the case of *Opie v. State,* 422 P.2d 84 (Wyo. 1967). Prior to the *Opie* case, references to coroner's inquest proceedings are common.

4. See §§ 1172–78, Wyo. R. S., 1899.

5. CIT, 1.

6. Ibid., 2, 3.

7. Ibid., 3; Willie Nickell was fourteen in July 1901 and Fred was ten, so Catherine was about twelve.

8. All the population figures come from the 1900 census. See T. A. Larson, *History of Wyoming* (Lincoln: University of Nebraska Press, 1965), 295; Bill O'Neal, *Cheyenne: A Biography of the "Magic City" of the Plains* (Austin, Tex.: Eakin Press, 2006), 313.

9. O'Neal, *Cheyenne,* 3, 23, 36.

10. Ibid., 301.

11. Ibid., 24, 184, 185, 303, 306, 316, 319.

12. "Asks Vengeance," *Cheyenne Daily Leader,* July 22, 1901, 4; Ball, *Tom Horn,* 265.

13. "Asks Vengeance," *Cheyenne Daily Leader,* July 22, 1901, 4. See also "At the Grave of Willie Nickell," *Cheyenne Daily Leader,* November 6, 1903, 3; Ball, *Tom Horn,* 266, 491n8.

14. "Walter R. Stoll," *Sun Annual* (Cheyenne), November 1, 1892.

15. Ibid. Lacey and Van Devanter were brothers-in-law and partners in the firm of Lacey & Van Devanter. For a discussion of Van Devanter, see John W. Davis, *Wyoming Range War: The Infamous Invasion of Johnson County* (Norman: University of Oklahoma Press, 2010), 197, 198.

16. Stoll served two terms as the Laramie County attorney from 1886 to 1890 and then was reelected in 1900. See *Graphic* (Douglas, Wyoming), July 11, 1891, 1; *Wyoming Tribune* (Cheyenne), November 23, 1900, 4.

17. Davis, *Wyoming Range War,* 232.

18. See *Graphic* (Douglas, Wyoming), July 11, 1891, 1, in which Stoll is praised profusely because of his exceptional work in the Fillebrown murder case. See also "Abstract of Oil Lands," *Wyoming Tribune* (Cheyenne), February 11, 1900, 4; "Water Right Contest," *Wyoming Tribune,* May 20, 1900, 4; "Sued for $7,500," *Wyoming Tribune,* September 21, 1900, 4.

19. Regarding Stoll's skills as an orator, see *Wyoming Tribune,* December 12, 1900, 4; *Cheyenne Daily Leader,* August 20, 1902, 4; "Local News," *Graphic* (Douglas, Wyoming), July 11, 1891, 2. See "Prosecution Rests," *Laramie Boomerang,* October 16, 1902, 1, regarding Stoll's reputation as a cross-examiner.

20. Larson, *History of Wyoming,* 266; Davis, *Wyoming Range War,* 132.

21. See Davis, *Wyoming Range War,* 132–36, 276.

22. CIT, 4.

23. Ibid., 4–7; trial transcript, *State v. Horn,* October 10, 1903, Wyoming Archives (hereafter TT), 420.

24. CIT, 4–6.

25. Ibid.

26. Ibid., 5.

27. Ibid., 6.

28. Ibid., 7.

29. Ibid., 7–9.

30. Ibid., 8.

31. Ibid., 9.

32. Ibid., 9, 10. In the inquest, Apperson testified that the distance from the gate to the place Willie collapsed was 135 feet. He must have concluded that this was in error, because at the trial, he testified that the distance was about sixty-six feet (TT, 66).

33. CIT, 11, 27, 31.

34. Ibid., 11, 16.

35. Ibid., 13–15.

36. Ibid., 13, 14.

37. Ibid., 15–17; TT, 53.

38. CIT, 16.

39. Ibid., 16, 17.

40. Ibid., 18, 19.

41. Ibid., 20.

42. Ibid., 22, 23. See also TT, 75.

43. CIT, 23, 24.

44. Ibid., 21, 22.

45. Ibid., 24, 25.

CHAPTER 3

1. See Wyoming Revised Statutes (1899), § 4950.

2. Coroner's inquest transcript, July 20, 1901, Wyoming State Archives, Cheyenne (hereafter CIT), 27.

3. Ibid., 27. When Nickell said that Miller "snapped it at him," I assume that Nickell meant that Miller was carrying a shotgun with an exposed hammer and was pulling that hammer back and forth.

4. "Court News," *Wyoming Tribune* (Cheyenne), June 23, 1900, 4.

5. Larry D. Ball, *Tom Horn in Life and Legend* (Norman: University of Oklahoma Press, 2014), 264.

6. Ibid.

7. CIT, 48, 29, 71, 72. See also §§ 7–3–502, 503 and 505, Wyo. Stat. Ann. (Lexis-Nexis 2011).

8. "Tried for Stabbing," *Cheyenne Sun,* August 9, 1890, 4.

9. "The Sybille Cases," *Laramie Boomerang,* May 3, 1894, 11.

10. "A Shooting Affray," *Wyoming Tribune* (Cheyenne), March 20, 1900, 4. See also *Wyoming Tribune* (Cheyenne), March 27, 1900.

11. CIT, 28, 29.

12. Ibid., 29.

13. Ibid.

14. Ibid., 30.

15. Ibid., 31.

16. Ibid., 32.

17. Ibid., 39, 40.

18. Ibid., 40.

19. Ibid.

20. *Rocky Mountain News,* September 18, 1895; see also the discussion in Ball, *Tom Horn,* 174–84.

21. CIT, 41.

22. *Cheyenne Daily Leader,* July 23, 1901, 4.

23. "Asks Vengeance," *Cheyenne Daily Leader,* July 22, 1901, 4.

24. Dennie Trimble Nickell, "Who Were Tom Horn's Victims?," in "In Wyoming," 23, Tom Horn biography file, Wyoming State Archives; regarding Nickell's efforts as a homesteader, see "Wyoming Products," *Daily Leader,* October 19, 1883, 4; "Throughout

Wyoming," *Laramie Boomerang,* October 4, 1897, 6; "Over in the Hills," *Laramie Republican,* May 11, 1900, 2.

25. CIT, 45. The "station" Miller referred to was no doubt the railroad station at the village of Iron Mountain. People in that area typically boarded the train at Iron Mountain.

26. Ibid., 46.

27. Ibid., 48, 49.

28. Ibid., 49–51.

29. Ibid., 51.

30. Ibid., 52, 53.

31. Ibid., 53, 55. By "magazine gun," Stoll was referring to rifles such as Winchester 1895 lever actions, which hold several shells in a magazine, ejecting a spent shell and replacing it with a live shell when the lever mechanism is operated. Repeating rifles of this kind were popular and were manufactured for and used by the general public after the end of the Civil War.

32. Ibid., 59. Another consideration is that a bullet fired from a cartridge with smokeless powder will likely create a sonic crack and one with black powder will probably not, at least after traveling through the air a short while.

33. Ibid., 58, 59.

34. Ibid., 60, 61.

35. Ibid., 60–62.

36. Ibid., 62.

37. Ibid., 63, 64.

38. Ibid., 67, 68.

39. Ibid., 132.

40. Ibid., 134.

41. The testimony of Harley Axford is found at CIT, 69–74, 77.

CHAPTER 4

1. *Cheyenne Daily Leader,* July 23, 1901, 4.

2. Coroner's inquest transcript, July 20, 1901, Wyoming State Archives, Cheyenne (hereafter CIT), 80.

3. Ibid., 81, 96, 97.

4. Ibid., 88, 89.

5. Ibid., 81–83, 96.

6. Ibid., 90, 95.

7. Ibid., 84, 85.

8. Ibid., 86.

9. Ibid., 87, 88.

10. Ibid., 91, 92, 94, 95.

11. Ibid., 93.

12. Ibid., 97.

13. "Cold Blooded Murder," *Wheatland (Wyo.) World,* July 26, 1901.

14. CIT, 98–100.

15. Ibid., 104.

16. Ibid., 105.

17. John W. Davis, *A Vast Amount of Trouble: A History of the Spring Creek Raid* (Niwot: University Press of Colorado, 1993), 153.

18. CIT, 105.

19. Ibid., 111.

20. See chapter 8 about the fascination of newspapers with Miss Kimmell.

21. CIT, 94.

22. Ibid., 106–9.

23. Ibid., 109, 110.

24. Ibid., 110.

25. Ibid., 111–13; Chip Carlson, *Tom Horn: Blood on the Moon: Dark History of the Murderous Cattle Detective* (Glendo, Wyo.: High Plains Press, 2001), 99.

26. CIT, 114, 115.

27. Ibid., 116.

28. Ibid., 119, 120. Axford may also have been perceived as an enemy by Miller because Axford ran about 150 sheep. See "Trial of Tom Horn, Alleged Professional Man-killer, for Murder of a Boy, Begins," *Denver Times,* October 10, 1902, 1.

29. CIT, 118.

30. When Eva testified at the trial in October 1902, she was said to be eighteen, so she was probably seventeen in July 1901. Ibid., 123–25.

31. Ibid., 125, 126.

32. Ibid., 127, 128.

33. Ibid., 129.

34. Ibid., 130.

35. Ibid., 136.

36. Ibid., 139, 140.

37. "More Evidence," *Cheyenne Daily Leader,* July 23, 1901, 4.

CHAPTER 5

1. "Extermination of Entire Family," *Cheyenne Daily Leader,* August 5, 1901, 4.

2. Ibid. The reference to "magazine guns" is to firearms such as Winchester, Savage, or Marlin lever-action rifles.

3. Ibid.

4. Ibid.; "Under 6,000 Bonds," *Cheyenne Daily Leader,* August 9, 1901, 1; "A Human Target," *Wheatland (Wyo.) World,* August 9, 1901, 1.

5. Coroner's inquest transcript, July 20, 1901, Wyoming State Archives, Cheyenne (hereafter CIT), 278–80.

6. Ibid., 246, 253, 259, 280, 281.

7. Ibid., 245, 246.

8. Ibid., 249, 250, 330.

9. Ibid., 377.

10. Ibid., 220.

11. Ibid., 329, 330 (testimony of Joe Reed); ibid., 272, 274 (testimony of Gus Miller).

12. Ibid., 215 (testimony of William McDonald); ibid., 397 (testimony of Minnie Chambers); ibid., 399 (testimony of Anne Nolan). For Victor Miller's testimony, see ibid., 260–78.

13. Ibid., 304–6.

14. Ibid., 312.

15. Ibid., 333.

16. Ibid., 303. West's Annotated California Code of Civil Procedure, § 1880, shows the earlier position (before uniform rules of evidence were adopted such as Wyoming Rules of Evidence, patterned after the Federal Rules of Evidence) regarding the competence of children to testify, indicating that children under the age of ten are not competent "who appear incapable of receiving just impressions of the facts respecting which they are examined, or of relating them truly."

17. CIT, 332.

18. Ibid., 181–93 (testimony of Dora Miller); ibid., 348, 349 (testimony of James Miller); ibid., 356, 357 (testimony of Glendolene Kimmell); ibid., 260, 272–74, 347 (testimony of Victor Miller).

19. Ibid., 199, 202 (testimony of Mary McDonald); ibid., 329, 330 (testimony of Joe Reed); ibid., 317 (regarding the arrival time of Dorman and Stein).

20. Ibid., 199.

21. Ibid., 318.

22. Ibid., 317.

23. Ibid., 383–85.

24. Ibid., 341–44.

25. Ibid., 164, 171 (testimony of John Scroder). Scroder, the man who brought the sheep up from Colorado, said he began working for Kels Nickell on May 9, 1901.

26. Bill O'Neal, *Cattlemen vs. Sheepherders: Five Decades of Violence in the West, 1880–1920* (Austin, Tex.: Eakin Press, 1989), provides an excellent compilation of the mayhem caused by sheep raids in the western United States in the late nineteenth and early twentieth century. See especially the tables at pages 15 and 16.

27. See page 46 and chapter two of John W. Davis, *A Vast Amount of Trouble: A History of the Spring Creek Raid.* (Niwot: University Press of Colorado, 1993).

28. CIT, 171, 172.

29. See, for example, the testimony of Louis Dorman (ibid., 321), Diedrick George (ibid., 394), and A. F. Whitman (ibid., 139).

30. Davis, *A Vast Amount of Trouble,* 101, referring to the testimony of W. W. Early.

31. CIT, 392, 393; Davis, *A Vast Amount of Trouble,* 12, 13. See also Edward Norris Wentworth, *America's Sheep Trails: History, Personalities* (Ames: Iowa State College Press, 1948).

32. With regard to the grasshopper comment, see the testimony of Diedrick George (CIT, 394, 395); with regard to the comments about "every damned son of a bitch," see the testimony of Tom Horn (ibid., 290, 291).

33. See Davis, *A Vast Amount of Trouble,* 11.

34. CIT, 277.

35. Ibid., 298 (testimony of Julia Cook); ibid., 148 (testimony of Biango Vingenjo); ibid., 149.

36. Ibid., 150.

37. Ibid., 152.

38. See the testimony of James Miller (ibid., 351, 352) and the testimony of Glendolene Kimmell (ibid., 358–60).

39. Ibid., 351, 352.

40. Ibid., 352.

41. Ibid., 351, 352 (testimony of James Miller); ibid., 150 (testimony of Vingenjo Biango).

42. Ibid., 150, 151.

43. Ibid., 151.

44. Ibid., 153.

45. Ibid., 153–56.

46. Ibid., 153.

47. Ibid., 334, 335.

48. Joe LeFors, *Wyoming Peace Officer: An Autobiography* (Laramie, Wyo.: Laramie Printing Company, 1953), 133, 134.

49. CIT, 327, 328.

50. Ibid., 338, 339.

51. Ibid., 322, 323.

CHAPTER 6

1. "A Denver Tough Breaks Tom Horns Jaw with a Cane," *Laramie Boomerang,* October 8, 1901, 1.

2. Tom Horn, *Life of Tom Horn, Government Scout and Interpreter* (Norman: University of Oklahoma Press, 1964), 8, 9.

3. Larry D. Ball, *Tom Horn in Life and Legend* (Norman: University of Oklahoma Press, 2014), 41, 42.

4. Ibid., 44.

5. Ibid., 60–71.

6. Horn, *Life of Tom Horn,* 267–79; Jay Monaghan, *Tom Horn: Last of the Bad Men* (Lincoln: University of Nebraska Press, 1997), 54, 55.

7. Ball, *Tom Horn,* 113, 114; Horn, *Life of Tom Horn,* 213.

8. Ball, *Life of Tom Horn,* 142. Horn stated that he came to Wyoming in 1894, which is almost certainly wrong. Horn, *Life of Tom Horn,* 225. The May 1892 arrival is established by the February 22, 1914, letter of W. C. Irvine to Charles Penrose, box 1, Penrose Papers, American Heritage Center, University of Wyoming. Irvine was one of the leaders of the 1892 Johnson County invasion (which was complete by April 13, when the invaders were taken into custody by the U.S. Army) and so had full knowledge of the facts, with no incentive to misrepresent.

9. Ball, *Tom Horn,* 161–66; *Wyoming State Tribune,* November 20, 1903, 1.

10. A partial list of those killed: Ellen Watson and Jimmy Averill in July 1889; Tom Waggoner in June 1891; John N. Tisdale and Orley Jones in December 1981; Nate Champion and Nick Ray in April 1892; Dab Burch and Jack Bedford, in fall of 1892. See John W. Davis, *Wyoming Range War: The Infamous Invasion of Johnson County* (Norman: University

of Oklahoma Press, 2010), 73–75, 95, 108, 111, 149, 154, 269, 270. Regarding the "radical element," see Ball, *Tom Horn,* 168–70.

11. Ball, *Tom Horn,* 168–72.

12. See Dean F. Krakel, *The Saga of Tom Horn: The Story of a Cattleman's War* (Cheyenne, Wyo.: Powder River Publishers, 1954), 5, 6.

13. Ball, *Tom Horn,* 174, 175.

14. Ibid., 176–78.

15. Ibid., 177. See also "It Is Mostly Hearsay," *Laramie Boomerang,* October 3, 1895, 1.

16. Ball, *Tom Horn,* 178; LeFors, *Wyoming Peace Officer: An Autobiography* (Laramie, Wyo.: Laramie Printing Company, 1953), 133.

17. Ball, *Tom Horn,* 189, 190.

18. Chip Carlson, *Tom Horn: Blood on the Moon: Dark History of the Murderous Cattle Detective* (Glendo, Wyo.: High Plains Press, 2001), 81–85.

19. Ball, *Tom Horn,* 201–12.

20. Ibid., 218–19. Wilcox lies just north of Rock River, Wyoming.

21. Carlson, *Tom Horn,* 99; coroner's inquest transcript, July 20, 1901, Wyoming State Archives, Cheyenne (hereafter CIT), 111–12.

22. "The U. P. Robbers," *Laramie Republican,* January 30, 1900, 4.

23. See "Train Robbery Story a Fake," *Buffalo Bulletin,* February 1, 1900, 2; "Killed in their Tracks," *Weekly Boomerang* (Laramie), February 1, 1900, 1.

24. Ball, *Tom Horn,* 223–28.

25. "Tom Horn's Battle with Outlaws," *Wyoming Derrick* (Casper), February 15, 1900, 1.

26. Ball, *Tom Horn,* 227, 228. It is hard to know how Horn or a supporter came up with the rank of colonel for Horn. In all his dealings with the U.S. Army in Arizona and Cuba, he never served in a position carrying a rank.

27. Ball, *Tom Horn,* 230–33.

28. Regarding the barroom brawl in Baggs in the fall of 1900, see Ball, *Tom Horn,* 235–36.

29. "A Rustler Chief," *Wyoming Tribune* (Cheyenne), November 18, 1900, 4. Regarding the *Tribune's* editorial stances and the distortions printed by the Cheyenne newspapers in 1892, see Davis, *Wyoming Range War,* 68 and chapter 16.

30. Ball, *Tom Horn,* 252–54.

31. Ball, *Tom Horn,* 258, 259; "Albany County Boys," *Laramie Boomerang,* September 1, 1901, 1.

32. See "Tom Horn Confesses," *Cheyenne Daily Leader,* January 23, 1902, 3; "Horn Loses Nerve," *Cheyenne Daily Leader,* February 20, 1902, 2.

33. "Fiercest Ordeal in Tom Horn's Life—Says His Confession Was a Josh," *Denver Post,* October 18, 1902, 1.

34. CIT, 283, 284.

35. Ibid., 285, 286.

36. Ibid., 287, 288.

37. Ibid., 289, 290.

38. Ibid., 291, 292. The misspelling of "Plaga" may have been a mistake by the reporter.

39. Ibid., 292–94.

40. Ibid., 295, 296.

41. Ibid., 369, 370.

42. Ibid., 370, 371.

43. Ibid., 371, 372.

44. Ibid., 373.

45. Ibid., 362, 368.

46. Ibid., 375, 376.

47. See Ball, *Tom Horn,* 270.

48. See LeFors, *Wyoming Peace Officer,* 1, 2, 3–6, 17–19. At pages 3–6, LeFors describes a time in 1878 when his family was captured by Comanche warriors, and only the calm control of his father saved them from being scalped or killed. This was a lesson LeFors took to heart, as shown by his description of a tense chase by Indian warriors.

49. Ibid., 16, 45–51.

50. Ibid., 59, 60, chapter 9. See also Chip Carlson, *Joe LeFors: "I Slickered Tom Horn": The History of the Texas Cowboy Turned Montana-Wyoming Lawman, a Sequel* (Cheyenne, Wyo.: Beartooth Corral, 1995), chapter 7.

51. See Carlson, *Joe LeFors,* chapter 12; John W. Davis, *A Vast Amount of Trouble: A History of the Spring Creek Raid* (Niwot: University Press of Colorado, 1993), 81. The movie *Butch Cassidy and the Sundance Kid* had a catchy line about LeFors's doggedness as a tracker. "Who are those guys?" referred to a posse relentlessly led by LeFors.

52. LeFors, *Wyoming Peace Officer,* 116, 121, 131, 134, 135.

53. CIT, 402.

54. LeFors, *Wyoming Peace Officer,* 131, 132.

55. Ibid., 133.

56. CIT, 402–404.

57. Ibid., 402, 403.

58. Clay was a rancher "who often provided accommodations for Horn while in the service of the big ranchers." Ball, *Tom Horn,* 271.

59. See CIT, 214, 326–27, 193–94, 341.

60. "Mystery Unsolved," *Cheyenne Daily Leader,* August 15, 1901, 4.

61. "The statement of Nickell's that he recognized the Millers as the parties who did the shooting is not given much weight, as the officers recognize the prejudice which exists between the parties" ("A Human Target," *Wheatland (Wyo.) World,* August 9, 1901).

62. See CIT, 365, 366.

63. "Mystery Unsolved," *Cheyenne Daily Leader,* August 15, 1901, 4. I found no later newspaper stories indicating that a suit was actually filed.

64. "Jury's Verdict," *Cheyenne Daily Leader,* December 27, 1901, 2.

CHAPTER 7

1. *Cheyenne Daily Leader,* January 14, 1902, 4. As the reader will note, the *Cheyenne Daily Leader* is frequently referred to regarding 1902 events. This is because the paper was active and involved and generally provided well-informed reporting to its readers. The *Wyoming Tribune,* another daily Cheyenne newspaper, which might have provided a good contrast to the stories in the *Daily Leader,* is unfortunately not extant for 1902.

2. "Arrest of Tom Horn, Detective," *Laramie Boomerang,* January 14, 1902, 1.

3. Ibid.

4. "Short Items," *Cheyenne Daily Leader,* January 14, 1902, 4.

5. "Should Investigate," *Cheyenne Daily Leader,* January 15, 1902, 2.

6. See "The Latest News Boiled Down," *Cody Enterprise,* January 16, 1902, 2; "Tom Horn Arrested," *Saratoga (Wyo.) Sun,* January 16, 1902, 1; "State News Items," *Newcastle News-Journal,* January 17, 1902, 1; "Tom Horn Arrested," *Wheatland (Wyo.) World,* January 17, 1902, 1; "From over the State," *Buffalo Voice,* January 18, 1902, 3.

7. "From Over the State," *Buffalo Voice,* January 18, 1902, 3.

8. "A Strong Case Against Horn," *Laramie Boomerang,* January 15, 1901, 1. Even though Bob Burnett was mentioned in this article about Horn's past, apparently because he was killed in the Iron Mountain area and seemed to have been a victim of an assassination, another man (George Black) was tried and hanged for the murder.

9. "The Horn Case," *Cheyenne Daily Leader,* January 18, 1901, 4; "$6,000 for Defense," *Cheyenne Daily Leader,* January 21, 1901, 1.

10. I used Morgan Friedman's online inflation calculator (http://www.westegg.com /inflation), which seemed well-tied to reliable inflation indicators. It should be remembered, however, that inflation does not rise at the same rate for all goods and services. Legal services may be relatively more or less expensive in 2012 compared to 1902, and a superstar attorney has always been able to command a premium fee. Still, from my practice of law in Wyoming since 1968 and being familiar with Wyoming attorneys' charges going back to 1892, my impression is that the 2012 cost of attorneys' services are generally comparable to those in 1902, but somewhat higher on an inflation-adjusted basis. In other words, my impression is that a consumer of legal services could obtain more time and quality work from an attorney in 1902 than in 2012 for the same cost after adjusting for inflation. Either way, $6,000 could buy a lot of legal work in 1902, and $157,000 could buy a lot of legal work in 2012.

11. "The Horn Hearing," *Cheyenne Daily Leader,* January 22, 1901, 4.

12. "Tom Horn Confesses," *Cheyenne Daily Leader,* January 23, 1902, 3.

13. See trial transcript, *State v. Horn,* October 10, 1903, Wyoming Archives, 87.

14. Ibid.

15. "Conflicting Evidence Presented at the Trial of Tom Horn," *Saratoga (Wyo.) Sun,* January 30, 1902, 2.

16. Ibid.; "Complete Story of Tom Horn's Admissions," *Cheyenne Daily Leader,* January 24, 1902, 2, 4.

17. "Tom Horn Confesses," *Cheyenne Daily Leader,* January 23, 1902, 3.

18. Ibid.

19. The following discussion of the presentation at the preliminary hearing, including details of the Horn confession, the testimony of Joe LeFors and Charles Ohnhaus, and the effort to obtain bail for Horn, is taken from "Complete Story of Tom Horn's Admissions," *Cheyenne Daily Leader,* January 24, 1902, 2, 4, except as augmented by other cited newspaper articles.

20. See *Cheyenne Daily Leader,* January 22, 1902, 4. The *Leader* referred to the magistrate hearing the case as "Judge Samuel Becker," but Becker was probably a justice of the peace.

CHAPTER 8

1. LeFors, *Wyoming Peace Officer: An Autobiography* (Laramie, Wyo.: Laramie Printing Company, 1953), 131–34.

2. Ibid., 134, 135. In his book, LeFors, apparently relying on his memory, referred to Corson as "Carson."

3. "LaFors Tells How He Trapped Tom Horn," *Cheyenne Daily Leader,* January 25, 1902, 4; LeFors, *Wyoming Peace Officer,* 136; trial transcript, *State v. Horn,* October 10, 1903, Wyoming Archives (hearafter TT), 707–709.

4. "LaFors Tells How He Trapped Tom Horn," *Cheyenne Daily Leader,* January 25, 1902, 4.

5. LeFors, *Wyoming Peace Officer,* 136, 137.

6. Ibid., 137.

7. "A Denver Tough Breaks Tom Horns Jaw with a Cane," *Laramie Boomerang,* October 8, 1901, 1; "How It Happened," *Cheyenne Daily Leader,* October 9, 1901, 3; "Tom Horn Tells Newspaper Man All about It," *Laramie Boomerang,* October 11, 1901, 1; "Denver Testimony Worthless in Defense of Tom Horn," *Denver Post,* October 17, 1902, 1; TT, 529, 530.

8. "Nickell Will Leave," *Laramie Boomerang,* October 4, 1901, 1; "Tom Horn Tells Newspaper Man All about It," *Laramie Boomerang,* October 11, 1901, 1; "Sold His Ranch," *Laramie Boomerang,* October 14, 1901, 8.

9. "A Denver Tough Breaks Tom Horns Jaw with a Cane," *Laramie Boomerang,* October 8, 1901, 1.

10. "Proceedings of the Horn Trial at Cheyenne," *Denver Post,* October 11, 1902, 1; Larry Ball, *Tom Horn in Life and Legend* (Norman: University of Oklahoma Press, 2014), 99, 121; "Horn's Father a Fugitive," *Cheyenne Daily Leader,* August 19, 1903, 4.

11. "Tom Horn Tells Newspaper Man All about It," *Laramie Boomerang,* October 11, 1901, 1.

12. "Sold His Ranch," *Semi-Weekly Boomerang* (Laramie), October 14, 1901, 8.

13. Ball, *Tom Horn,* 284.

14. "LaFors Tells How He Trapped Tom Horn," *Cheyenne Daily Leader,* January 25, 1902, 4.

15. LeFors, *Wyoming Peace Officer,* 137; Ball, *Tom Horn,* 284. As Larry Ball shows, LeFors thought that Prentiss was with Coble's ranch, but he probably was a Swan Cattle Company employee.

16. LeFors, *Wyoming Peace Officer,* 137.

17. Ibid., 137, 138.

18. Ibid., 138. Prentiss may have been referring to the killings of Rash and Dart in Colorado, rather than to those of Lewis and Powell. At that time (late 1901), it was widely assumed in southeastern Wyoming that Horn had killed Lewis and Powell, but Horn's connection to the Rash and Dart killings was not as well recognized.

19. LeFors, *Wyoming Peace Officer,* 138.

20. Ibid. The sequence of the letters from Montana is confusing. As Larry Ball observes, "The precise sequence of communications between Horn, LeFors and the potential Montana employers is difficult to unravel." Ball, *Tom Horn,* 285.

21. January 1, 1902, letter from Tom Horn to Joe LeFors, reprinted in LeFors, *Wyoming Peace Officer*, 190, 191.

22. January 7, 1902, letter from Tom Horn to Joe LeFors, and January 7, 1902 letter from W. D. Smith to Joe LeFors, reprinted in LeFors, *Wyoming Peace Officer*, 191, 192.

23. See Ball, *Tom Horn*, 287, 288. Ball makes the point that although Joe LeFors in his autobiography seemed to claim that he was primarily responsible for the arrangements for the confession of Tom Horn (LeFors, *Wyoming Peace Officer*, 138, 139), that is inconsistent with a contemporary newspaper report ("$1,000 Reward," *Cheyenne Daily Leader*, October 27, 1902, 4). This makes sense. A prosecuting attorney has the ultimate control of a criminal case, having the responsibility to present a convincing set of facts. An experienced and highly competent prosecutor like Stoll would normally direct the peace officers working on the case to supply evidence that the attorney knows is usable and persuasive in court. Regarding the drink at the Inter Ocean Hotel the morning on January 12, 1902, see TT, 400, 404, 408.

24. "Arrest of Tom Horn, Detective," *Laramie Boomerang*, January 14, 1902; LeFors, *Wyoming Peace Officer*, 145.

25. Ball, *Tom Horn*, 313.

26. "Court House Notes," *Cheyenne Daily Leader*, February 11, 1902.

27. "Strict Guard," *Cheyenne Daily Leader*, January 14, 1902, 4.

28. Ibid.; "Horn's Brother," *Cheyenne Daily Leader*, January 25, 1902, 2; *Cheyenne Daily Leader*, March 29, 1903, 3.

29. *Semi-Weekly Boomerang* (Laramie), February 3, 1902, 7.

30. "Horn Gets Outing," *Cheyenne Daily Leader*, June 11, 1902, 4; "Horn Growing Nervous," *Semi-Weekly Boomerang* (Laramie), February 24, 1902, 5; "Horn Losing Nerve," *Cheyenne Daily Leader*, February 20, 1902, 2.

31. "Court House News," *Cheyenne Daily Leader*, April 25, 1902, 3.

32. "Court House Notes," *Cheyenne Daily Leader*, February 13, 1902, 2; *Weekly Boomerang* (Laramie) April 3, 1902, 6.

33. "Short Items," *Cheyenne Daily Leader*, October 13, 1902, 3.

34. "A Word of Caution," *Cheyenne Daily Leader*, January 30, 1902, 2.

35. *Cheyenne Daily Leader*, March 13, 1902, 3.

36. "Sensational Charge Made," *Cheyenne Daily Leader*, March 13, 1902, 4.

37. "Working on Horn Case," *Weekly Boomerang* (Laramie), March 27, 1902, 7.

38. Regarding the general anger of the public against Horn, see "Proceedings of the Horn Trial at Cheyenne," *Denver Post*, October 11, 2013, 1, wherein the *Post* stated that after the revelations from the published confession to LeFors, the feeling against Horn is "very bitter, especially in Cheyenne," and indicated that if there was no conviction, Horn would be lynched.

39. "Bill Barrow," *Cheyenne Daily Leader*, January 31, 1902, 2; "Bill Barrow on Tom Horn," *Sheridan Post*, February 6, 1902, 2.

40. "Horn Warned by His Sweetheart," *Cheyenne Daily Leader*, January 27, 1902, 4. See also "Tragedy and Love," *Laramie Boomerang*, January 30, 1902, 1.

41. Ball, *Tom Horn*, 275; "Lacey Pleads for Horn in a Deserted Courtroom," *Denver Times*, October 23, 1902, 1.

42. "Tom Horn Confesses," *Wyoming Derrick*, January 30, 1902, 1; "Did Horn Kill Them?," *Cheyenne Daily Leader*, January 31, 1902, 4; "Makes Grave Charges," *Cheyenne Daily Leader*, February 3, 1902, 4.

43. "Northwest Notes," *Wyoming Press* (Evanston, Wyo.), March 3, 1902, 2; "Colorado Wants Horn," *Weekly Boomerang* (Laramie), March 3, 1902, 8.

44. See "The Latest News Boiled Down," *Cody Enterprise*, January 30, 1902, 2; "Tom Horn Confesses," *Wyoming Derrick* (Casper), January 30, 1902, 1; *Sheridan Post*, January 30, 1902, 2; "Chickens Will Come Home to Roost," *Buffalo Voice,* February 1, 1902, 2; *Wyoming Industrial Journal* (Cheyenne), February 1, 1902, 246; "Sundance Cattlemen Fear Tom Horn," *Laramie Republican*, February 10, 1902, 1.

45. "Chickens Will Come Home to Roost," *Buffalo Voice*, February 1, 1902, 2. See also *Laramie Boomerang*, February 6, 1902, 4, which reprinted the piece from the *Buffalo Voice*.

46. Regarding the true identity of Polly Pry, see "Polly Pry," Wikipedia, http://en.wikipedia.org/wiki/Polly_Pry.

47. All the stories referred to are found in the *Denver Post*, March 2, 1902, 1, 13.

48. In my *Wyoming Range War: The Infamous Invasion of Johnson County* (Norman: University of Oklahoma Press, 2010), 269–70, I list ten people whom big cattlemen and their agents had killed by March 1893. There were probably others.

49. See "More Trouble," *Cheyenne Daily Leader*, February 3, 1902, 2; "Jury Law Held to be Constitutional," *Cheyenne Daily Leader*, September 4, 1902, 6.

50. "A Needed Change," *Wheatland (Wyo.) World*, May 30, 1902, 2; "Get One Year," *Cheyenne Daily Leader*, September 4, 1902, 3. Several county attorneys followed Stoll's lead and postponed trials pending a decision of the Wyoming Supreme Court. See *Wheatland (Wyo.) World*, September 19, 1902, 2.

51. June 1, 1902, letter from Tom Horn to Duncan Clark, in possession of the author (courtesy of Dale Leatham of Casper, Wyoming).

52. "Jury Law Held to be Constitutional," *Cheyenne Daily Leader*, September 12, 1902, 6.

53. See "Tom Horn Trial Begins at Cheyenne," *Denver Post*, October 10, 1902, 1. During my legal career, I have practiced law in many courtrooms built in the late nineteenth and early twentieth centuries, which could be described much as the Laramie County courtroom where the Horn trial was held.

54. "Reflections of Sauntering Silas," *Sheridan Post*, September 25, 1902, 3.

55. "Strong Evidence Against Horn," *Wheatland (Wyo.) World*, October 3, 1902, 1.

56. See, for example, "Wyoming News," *Crook County Monitor*, September 26, 1902, 1; "Horn Trial," *Cheyenne Daily Leader*, September 22, 1902, 4; "From over the State," *Buffalo Voice*, September 27, 1902, 2; "New Jury List," *Laramie Boomerang*, September 24, 1902, 1.

57. "Iron Mountain Friends of Tom Horn Standing by Him Nobly," *Denver Times*, October 4, 1902, 7. The attitudes of Iron Mountain ranch people were remarkably similar to those of cattle people in the Big Horn Basin when five cattlemen were charged with the 1909 Spring Creek murder of three sheepmen. See John W. Davis, *A Vast Amount of Trouble: A History of the Spring Creek Raid* (Niwot: University Press of Colorado, 1993), especially 59, 140, 238.

58. "More Interesting Testimony," *Laramie Boomerang*, October 14, 1902, 1.

59. "Horn Trial," *Cheyenne Daily Leader*, September 22, 1902, 4.

60. "A Black Life Awaits a Fair Trial," *Denver Post*, October 7, 1902, 16A.

61. "Men Called for the Jury to Try Horn," *Denver Republican*, September 24, 1902, 8.

62. T. Blake Kennedy memoir by T. Blake Kennedy, box 1, folder 6, p. 206, T. Blake Kennedy Papers, 1892–1957, collection no. 405, American Heritage Center, Laramie, Wyoming.

63. See "A Black Life Awaits a Fair Trial," *Denver Post*, October 7, 1902, 16A.

64. "A Huge Hoax," *Cheyenne Daily Leader*, October 7, 1902, 3.

65. "More Jurors," *Cheyenne Daily Leader*, October 9, 1902, 4.

66. "Slumbering Passion in Horn Case Breaks Out," *Denver Post*, October 9, 1902, 2. See also "Assaults Juror," *Cheyenne Daily Leader*, October 10, 1902, 4.

CHAPTER 9

1. "The Horn Case," *Laramie Boomerang*, October 11, 1902, 1; "Horn on Trial for His Life," *Cheyenne Daily Leader*, October 10, 1902, 4.

2. "Tom Horn Case," *Laramie Boomerang*, October 10, 1902, 1.

3. "Horn on Trial for his Life," *Cheyenne Daily Leader*, October 10, 1902, 4. These tables were probably like those I used in trials in the old courtrooms in Basin, Buffalo, Cody, and Sheridan, Wyoming. They were large, muscular pieces of furniture that could easily accommodate six people.

4. See "Correspondent's [*sic*] Arrive," *Cheyenne Daily Leader*, October 9, 1902, 3; "A Huge Hoax," *Cheyenne Daily Leader*, October 7, 1902, 3. Each of the listed Denver newspapers carried long stories at different times in the trial, the *Denver Post* virtually every day. See, for example, "Tom Horn Trial Begins at Cheyenne," *Denver Post*, October 10, 1902, 1.

5. See John W. Davis, *Wyoming Range War: The Infamous Invasion of Johnson County* (Norman: University of Oklahoma Press, 2010), 213, 214.

6. "Only the Jury Now Stand Between Horn and Gallows," *Denver Post*, October 24, 1902, 5.

7. "Attorneys for Horn Say Last Words in His Defense," *Cheyenne Daily Leader*, October 23, 1902, 4.

8. Van Pelt, *Capital Characters of Old Cheyenne*, 158, 167

9. "Tom Horn Trial Begins at Cheyenne," *Denver Post*, October 10, 1902, 1.

10. Ibid.

11. Ibid.

12. "Trial of Tom Horn, Alleged Professional Man-Killer, for Murder of a Boy, Begins," *Denver Times*, October 11, 1902, 1, 5.

13. "Tom Horn Trial Begins at Cheyenne," *Denver Post*, October 10, 1902, 1.

14. Ibid.

15. "Horn on Trial for His Life, "*Cheyenne Daily Leader*, October 10, 1902, 4.

16. Ibid.

17. Ibid.

18. "Tom Horn Trial Begins at Cheyenne," *Denver Post*, October 10, 1902, 1.

19. "Horn on Trial for His Life," *Cheyenne Daily Leader*, October 10, 1902, 4.

20. "The Horn Jury," *Cheyenne Daily Leader*, October 25, 1902, 6. The *Denver Republican* described the jury as including ten ranchmen, rather than nine. See "Jury Selected and Accepted, Each with a Challenge Left," *Denver Republican*, October 11, 1902, 12. The *Denver Post* referred to "H. W. Yoder," and the *Cheyenne Daily Leader* to "H. M. Yoder"; the "H. M." was apparently in error because the *Daily Leader* also referred to Yoder as "H. W."

21. T. Blake Kennedy memoir by T. Blake Kennedy, box 1, folder 6, pp. 205, 206, T. Blake Kennedy Papers, 1892–1957, collection no. 405, American Heritage Center, Laramie, Wyoming.

22. "Six Ballots Taken," *Cheyenne Daily Leader*, October 27, 1902, 4. It is hard to know why Stoll did not use a peremptory challenge against Payne. A good guess is that he had to use his challenges against potential jurors he feared even more.

23. "Tom Horn Case is Progressing," *Laramie Boomerang*, October 13, 1902, 1.

24. "Horn on Trial for his Life," *Cheyenne Daily Leader*, October 10, 1902, 4; "Tom Horn Trial Begins at Cheyenne," *Denver Post*, October 10, 1902, 1.

25. See "Introduction of Testimony Begins," *Cheyenne Daily Leader*, October 11, 1902, 1. Stoll's statement was consistent with legal rules: the opening is referred to as a "statement" and the closing as an "argument."

26. Ibid., 4; "Proceedings of the Horn Trial at Cheyenne," *Denver Post*, October 11, 1902, 1, 3. "Jury Selected the First Day," *Denver Republican*, October 11, 1902, has a particularly good recitation of Stoll's opening statement.

27. *Cheyenne Daily Leader*, October 11, 1902.

28. Ibid.

29. "Tom Horn Case," *Laramie Boomerang*, October 11, 1902, 1.

30. "Trial of Tom Horn Begins in Cheyenne," *Denver Times*, October 10, 1902, 1, 4. The identity of the "politician and lawmaker of Wyoming" was never revealed.

CHAPTER 10

1. Regarding the weather: "Tom Horn Case Is Progressing," *Laramie Boomerang*, October 12, 1902, 1. Regarding the courtroom: "Introduction of Testimony Begins," *Cheyenne Daily Leader*, October 11, 1902, 4.

2. Trial transcript, *State v. Horn,* October 10, 1903, Wyoming Archives (hereafter TT), 1, 2, 10.

3. Ibid., 10–12.

4. Ibid., 25–28; "Tom Horn Case Is Progressing," *Laramie Boomerang,* October 12, 1902, 1.

5. TT, 1, 2.

6. Ibid., 5, 6; "Tom Horn Case Is Progressing," *Laramie Boomerang,* October 12, 1902, 1.

7. TT, 12–17.

8. "Introduction of Testimony Begins," *Cheyenne Daily Leader,* October 11, 1902, 4.

9. Coroner's inquest transcript (herafter CIT), 287, 288.

10. TT, 29. See also the testimony of James Mathewson, editor of the *Laramie Republican* (TT, 143, 144).

11. Ibid., 29.

12. Ibid., 30–32.

13. Ibid., 33.

14. Ibid., 33–36.

15. Ibid., 36, 37, 43.

16. "The Horn Trial," *Denver Post,* October 12, 1902, 1.

17. TT, 49–51.

18. See "The Horn Trial," *Denver Post,* October 12, 1902, 1; "Introduction of Testimony Begins," *Cheyenne Daily Leader,* October 11, 1902, 4.

19. TT, 56, 57.

20. Ibid., 57.

21. By 1902, the Wyoming Supreme Court had created only a tiny amount of binding precedent (that is, cases in the same jurisdiction showing what had been decided in similar cases), and so the evaluation of this question had to come from opinions of other jurisdictions. That is exactly what the Wyoming Supreme Court did in the case of *Horn v. State,* 12 Wyo. 80, 73 Pac. 705 (Wyo. 1903), Horn's appeal, when it addressed the question at length at pp. 127–33.

22. TT, 61.

23. "The Horn Trial," *Denver Post,* October 12, 1902, 1.

24. "Proceedings of the Horn Trial at Cheyenne," *Denver Post,* 1, 3.

25. TT, 63–68.

26. Ibid., 68. See also CIT, 23. Stoll and Apperson apparently believed that all these tracks were made by Willie Nickell, but that was not then specifically stated.

27. TT, 68.

28. The cross-examination of Apperson is reported at TT, 68–75.

29. Ibid., 77–82.

30. Ibid., 80–82.

31. See John W. Davis, *Wyoming Range War: The Infamous Invasion of Johnson County* (Norman: University of Oklahoma Press, 2010), chapter 19 (227–46, especially 245).

32. TT, 83, 84; "The Horn Trial," *Denver Post,* October 12, 1902, 1.

33. TT, 85, 86.

34. Ibid., 87.

35. Ibid., 87, 88. The transcript contains errors and shortcomings in punctuation, and this excerpt is presented as it appears.

36. Ibid., 88.

37. See "Tom Horn Trial," *Denver Post* October 13, 1902, 1.

38. TT, 90.

39. Ibid., 92 and 82(II). The numbering in the trial transcript is messed up. After page 92, it goes back to 82, which I am indicating by adding a "II" at the end of the number.

40. See "Horn Lawyers 'Tip Their Hand,'" *Denver Republican,* October 12, 1902, 10. Interestingly, a juror asked Dr. Barber a question. During the time I've practiced law (since 1968), and until about 2000, this was not done. See TT, 83(II).

41. "Tom Horn Case Is Progressing," *Laramie Boomerang,* October 12, 1902, 1.

42. "Tom Horn's Life or Death the Question of the Hour," *Denver Post*, October 13, 1902, 1.

43. "Tom Horn Case Is Progressing," *Laramie Boomerang*, October 13, 1902, 1.

CHAPTER 11

1. Regarding the "bullet" inspections, testimony was presented by H. Waldo Moore (trial transcript, *State v. Horn,* October 10, 1903, Wyoming Archives (hereafter TT), beginning at page 84), and J. A. B. Apperson (TT, beginning at page 85). Sheriff Cook's testimony begins at page 86 of the trial transcript; the discussion about seeing Horn is found at page 87; the statements regarding the horse left by Horn are at pages 86 and 87; T. F. Cook's testimony begins at page 88.

2. TT, 94.

3. "Will Tom Horn's Sweetheart Turn State's Evidence?," *Cheyenne Daily Leader*, October 13, 1902, 4.

4. "Tom Horn's Life or Death the Question of the Hour," *Denver Post,* October 13, 1902, 1. See also "Alibi for Horn," *Cheyenne Daily Leader,* October 13, 1902, 4.

5. TT, 96, 97; "Alibi for Horn," *Cheyenne Daily Leader,* October 13, 1902, 4.

6. TT, 100, 101; "Alibi for Horn," *Cheyenne Daily Leader,* October 13, 1902, 4.

7. TT, 116.

8. "Tom Horn's Life or Death the Question of the Hour," *Denver Post,* October 13, 1902, 1.

9. TT, 102.

10. Ibid., 104, 105.

11. Ibid., 105–107.

12. Ibid., 108, 109.

13. Ibid., 111–13.

14. Ibid., 113.

15. "Tom Horn's Life or Death the Question of the Hour," *Denver Post,* October 13, 1902, 1.

16. TT, 116–20; "Tom Horn's Life or Death the Question of the Hour," *Denver Post,* October 13, 1902, 1.

17. TT, 121–43; "The Horn Trial," *Cheyenne Daily Leader,* October 13, 1902, 1, 4.

18. "Will Tom Horn's Sweetheart Turn State's Evidence?," *Cheyenne Daily Leader,* October 13, 1902, 4.

19. "Expert on Bullet Wounds on Horn Case," *Denver Post,* October 15, 1902, 6.

20. "Experts Think Bullets Were of Small Caliber," *Denver Republican,* October 14, 1902, 2.

21. "Will Tom Horn's Sweetheart Turn State's Evidence?," *Cheyenne Daily Leader,* October 13, 1902, 4.

22. TT, 143, 144.

23. Ibid., 144, 145. This testimony was never followed up on, probably meaning that the prosecution hoped to use it in conjunction with other evidence but the other evidence fell through.

24. Ibid., 146, 147.

25. Ibid., 148–50.

26. Ibid., 152, 153.

27. Ibid., 154.

28. Ibid., 155, 156.

29. Ibid., 158, 159.

30. Ibid., 159–66.

31. Ibid., 169–73, especially 171.

32. "Forging Strong Chain of Evidence around Tom Horn," *Cheyenne Daily Leader*, October 14, 1902, 4; TT, 173–75.

33. TT, 176–78.

34. "Will Tom Horn's Sweetheart Turn State's Evidence?," *Cheyenne Daily Leader*, October 13, 1902, 4.

35. Ibid.

36. Ibid.

37. "Will Tom Horn's Sweetheart Turn State's Evidence?," *Cheyenne Daily Leader*, October 13, 1902, 4; "Horn Trial Notes," *Cheyenne Daily Leader*, October 13, 1902, 1.

38. "Alibi for Horn," *Cheyenne Daily Leader*, October 13, 1902, 4. Regarding the Frontier Days 1901 competition: "Albany County Boys," *Laramie Boomerang*, September 1, 1901, 1. It is hard to know the source of the cited information in the news stories in the *Leader* and the *Denver Post*. Much of it proved inaccurate. "Will Tom Horn's Sweetheart Turn State's Evidence?," *Cheyenne Daily Leader*, October 13, 1902, refers to "facts ascertained," but then says that the prosecution, when asked about the possibility of Miss Kimmell's testifying, "appeared very reticent." The same article refers to George Matlock's arriving by train; it appears that reporters caught wind of his arrival and asked him questions. "Alibi for Horn," *Cheyenne Daily Leader*, October 13, 1902, 4, states that Otto Plaga would provide an alibi but indicates that Horn's attorneys "have not offered to satisfy public curiosity in this regard." "Tom Horn's Life or Death the Question of the Hour," *Denver Post*, October 13, 1902, 1 ("Developments of the Most Sensational Character Expected by the Watchers of the Now Famous Trial") refers to information by "an agent of the prosecution," which could be any Laramie County law enforcement officer or the employee of any prosecuting attorney. It appears that the Horn case was of such intense public interest that reporters sought every leak they could obtain. Given the number of people involved in the case, some loose statements would inevitably be made and prompt a frenzy by the press.

39. "Tom Horn's Life or Death the Question of the Hour," *Denver Post*, October 13, 1902, 1.

40. Ibid.

41. "Forging Strong Chain of Evidence around Tom Horn," *Cheyenne Daily Leader*, October 14, 1902, 4.

CHAPTER 12

1. "Forging Strong Chain of Evidence around Tom Horn," *Cheyenne Daily Leader*, October 14, 1902, 4.

2. Ibid.

3. Trial transcript, *State v. Horn,* October 10, 1903, Wyoming Archives (hereafter TT), 179–82.

4. Ibid., 199–202.

5. Ibid. (testimony of Kels Nickell); ibid., 202 (testimony of Mrs. Kels Nickell); ibid., 254 (testimony of Peter Warlamount).

6. Ibid., 183–86.

7. Ibid., 186–89.

8. See John W. Davis, *A Vast Amount of Trouble: A History of the Spring Creek Raid* (Niwot: University Press of Colorado, 1993), 176, 177.

9. TT, 189, 190.

10. Ibid., 190.

11. Ibid., 192–97.

12. "The Horn Trial," *Cheyenne Daily Leader,* October 14, 1902, 1; "The Tom Horn Trial Crisis—LaFors Now on the Stand," *Denver Post,* October 15, 1902, 3.

13. TT, 212–16, 218.

14. Ibid., 230.

15. Ibid., 230–34, 242.

16. Ibid., 235–45, especially 245, regarding the "hot words." See the *Denver Republican,* October 14, 1902, 3. The *Republican* refers to the cross-examination of Irwin by "Judge Lacey," but the trial transcript indicates that the cross-examination was undertaken by Burke (234).

17. TT, 245.

18. Ibid., 221, 222.

19. Ibid., 222, 223, 228, *CIT,* 285.

20. Ibid., 223, 227, 229.

21. Ibid., 247.

22. Ibid., 248, 249.

23. Ibid., 251, 252.

24. Ibid., 252, 253.

25. Ibid., 255, 256.

26. "The Horn Trial," *Cheyenne Daily Leader,* October 14, 1902, 1 ("When Did Horn Arrive").

27. TT, 256, 257.

28. Ibid., 259–261 (four pages, including one without a page number).

29. "Tom Horn Trial Crisis—LeFors on the Stand," *Denver Post,* October 15, 1902, 1, 3; See also "The Horn Trial," *Cheyenne Daily Leader,* October 14, 1902, 1 ("When Did Horn Arrive").

30. TT, 266.

31. Ibid., 267.

32. Ibid., 267, 268.

33. Ibid., 268, 270.

34. Ibid., 270–72.

35. Ibid., 273, 274.

36. Ibid., 275.

37. "Network of Evidence," *Laramie Boomerang,* October 15, 1902, 1, 4.

38. TT, 276.

39. Ibid., 274, 301, 303.

40. Ibid., 303.

41. Ibid., 278.

42. Ibid., 278, 279.

43. Ibid., 279.

44. Ibid., 280.

45. Ibid., 281, 282.

46. See "Tom Horn Tells Newspaper Man All About It," *Laramie Boomerang,* October 11, 1902, 1.

47. "Miss Kimmell Has Not Been Subpoenaed," *Denver Republican,* October 14, 1902, 2.

48. TT, 282, with exhibit no. 27.

49. *Cheyenne Daily Leader,* October 14, 1902.

CHAPTER 13

1. "A Minstrel Appears at Tom Horn Trial and Fiddles Merrily, "*Denver Post,* October 16, 1902, 5. See also photograph of "Dr. Moore and his fiddle," *Denver Post,* October 3, 1902, 3.

2. "The Eagerly Curious yet Secretive Crowd at Trial," *Denver Post,* October 15, 1902, 9.

3. Ibid. See also "Tom Horn Trial Crisis—La Fors on the Stand," *Denver Post,* October 15, 1902, 1.

4. "The Eagerly Curious yet Secretive Crowd at Trial," *Denver Post,* October 15, 1902, 9.

5. "Short Items," *Cheyenne Daily Leader,* October 15, 1902, 3.

6. "Was Horn Boasting When He Made His Confession?," *Cheyenne Daily Leader,* October 15, 1902, 4.

7. Trial transcript, *State v. Horn,* October 10, 1903, Wyoming Archives (hereafter TT), 382.

8. Ibid., 284.

9. Ibid., 284, 285.

10. Ibid., 285, 286.

11. Ibid., 287, 288.

12. Ibid., 290.

13. Ibid., 291.

14. Ibid., 291, 292.

15. Ibid., 293, 296. The pagination of the trial transcript here jumps from 293 to 296.

16. Ibid., 318a (which follows 324).

17. Ibid., 319a.

18. Ibid., 321a.

19. Ibid., 324a.

20. Ibid., 324a, 325a.

21. "Tom Horn Trial Crisis—La Fors on the Stand," *Denver Post*, October 15, 1902, 1. The scar on Horn's neck was a result of a barroom brawl in Baggs, Wyoming, in the fall of 1900. See Larry D. Ball, *Tom Horn in Life and Legend* (Norman: University of Oklahoma Press, 2014), 235–36.

22. TT, 229, 230, 309, 318.

23. Ibid., 304.

24. It should be remembered that this trial took place far before the revolution in the Earl Warren Supreme Court during the 1950s and 1960s that excluded confessions unless certain conditions were closely followed (*Miranda v. Arizona*) and that excluded evidence improperly obtained (*Mapp v. Ohio*). See also "Horn His Own Nemesis," *Denver Post*, October 16, 1902, 16, in which a Denver attorney is quoted as saying, "There is no doubt the Horn confession is admissible." The same article provides a string of legal cases ruling that a confession was admissible even though obtained by officers through deception.

25. TT, 305.

26. Ibid., 306–16. A modern attorney would handle this common situation similarly, using a more suggestive form until the opposing attorney challenges the tactic.

27. Ibid., 305–309.

28. Ibid., 310–17. Regarding the January 1, 1902, letter, see ibid., 313, 314, exhibit no. 32.

29. Ibid., 317.

30. Ibid., 318–24.

31. "Tom Horn's Defense Opens," *Denver Post,* October 16, 1902, 1, 3.

32. "Was Horn Boasting When He Made His Confession?," *Cheyenne Daily Leader*, October 15, 1902, 4.

33. TT, 309, 325–31.

34. Ibid., 332, 334.

35. This office is extant, located on the Lincoln Highway (Sixteenth Street), the main east–west thoroughfare through Cheyenne, in the second floor of the Commercial Building. It is open to the public during regular business hours.

36. TT, 332, 334, 335. See also the recounting of Ohnhaus's testimony at the preliminary hearing, in "Complete Story of Tom Horn's Admissions," *Cheyenne Daily Leader*, January 24, 1902, 2.

37. The entire verbatim conversation was read into the record (TT, 335–41).

38. TT, 336, 337.

39. Ibid., 336.

40. Ibid.

41. Ibid.

42. Ibid., 336, 337.

43. Ibid., 337, 338.

44. Ibid., 338.

45. Ibid.

46. Ibid., 338, 339.

47. Ibid., 338, 339.

48. Ibid., 339.

49. Ibid., 340.

50. Ibid., 340, 341.

51. Ibid., 341.

52. Ibid.

53. Ibid., 342.

54. Ibid., 343.

55. Ibid., 344.

56. *Cheyenne Daily Leader*, October 16, 1902, 2 (first column).

57. "State Rests in Horn Case; Sensation Doesn't Appear," *Denver Republican*, October 16, 1902, 1, 2.

58. "State's Case," *Cheyenne Daily Leader*, October 16, 1902, 4.

59. "Was Horn Boasting When He Made His Confession?," *Cheyenne Daily Leader*, October 15, 1902, 4.

60. "State's Case," *Cheyenne Daily Leader*, October 16, 1902, 4; "How Horn Was Trapped," *Cheyenne Daily Leader*, October 16, 1902, 3.

CHAPTER 14

1. "Prosecution Rests," *Laramie Boomerang,* October 16, 1902, 1.

2. "Tom Horn's Defense Opens," *Denver Post,* October 16, 1, 3.

3. Trial transcript, *State v. Horn,* October 10, 1903, Wyoming Archives (hereafter TT), 400, 401.

4. Ibid., 401–404.

5. Ibid., 404, 405.

6. Ibid., 405–407.

7. Ibid., 408, 409.

8. "Tom Horn's Defense Opens," *Denver Post,* October 16, 1902, 1.

9. Instruction 9, page 10, of the instructions to the jury in *State v. Horn,* records of the Laramie County Clerk of Court (docket 4, no. 58). This instruction was not challenged by the defense before the Wyoming Supreme Court; the defense apparently had no legal authority showing that the instruction was erroneous.

10. "Volgoque veritas iam attributa vino est." Pliny the book Elder, *Naturalis Historia,* book 14, 141. Sayings to this effect did not begin with Pliny and are found in many cultures.

11. "Denver Testimony Worthless in Defense of Tom Horn and Coble's Effort Was in Vain," *Denver Post,* October 17, 1902, 1, 3.

12. TT, 410.

13. Ibid., 413, 414.

14. Ibid., 414, 415.

15. Ibid., 415, 416.

16. Ibid., 416, 417.

17. Ibid., 417, 418.

18. Ibid., 419.

19. See "Fiercest Ordeal in Tom Horn's Life—Says His Confession Was a Josh," *Denver Post,* October 18, 1902, 1. A sub-headline reads: "Horn's Examination Quietly Conducted."

20. TT, 419.

21. The .30-30 Winchester was introduced by Winchester in 1895 and was considered revolutionary because it fired a small but relatively fast round, the first American small-bore cartridge specially designed for smokeless powder. See F. C. Barnes, F. C., *Cartridges of the World,* 6th ed., ed. Ken Warner (Northbrook, Ill.: DBI Books, 1989). It shot a 150-grain bullet at 2,380 feet per second, which compares to 1,330 feet per second for a 405-grain .45–70, a standard black powder round. Philip B. Sharpe, *The Rifle in America* (Mountain Brook, Ala.: Odysseus Editions, 1938), 614, 616. In 1957, when I first shopped for a deer rifle (at age fourteen), while the .30-30 was considered old-fashioned, it was still a popular round and a viable option.

22. TT, 425.

23. Ibid., 426, 427.

24. Ibid., 423, 424.

25. Ibid., 436.

26. Ibid., 437, 438.

27. "Defense Begins Fight for Life of Tom Horn," *Cheyenne Daily Leader,* October 16, 1902, 4.

28. "Was Tom Horn Drunk When He Made His Confession?," *Denver Times,* October 16, 1902, 1, 7.

29. "Defense Begins Fight for Life of Tom Horn," *Cheyenne Daily Leader,* October 16, 1902, 4.

30. "Denver Testimony Worthless in Defense of Tom Horn and Coble's Effort Was in Vain," *Denver Post,* October 17, 1902, 1, 3.

31. TT, 441, 442.

32. Ibid., 443–47.

33. Ibid., 448.

34. Ibid., 448–51.

35. Ibid., 452.

36. Ibid., 453–55.

37. Ibid., 456.

38. Ibid., 457.

39. "Defense Takes a Hand," *Laramie Boomerang,* October 17, 1902, 1.

40. Ibid.; TT, 489; coroner's inquest transcript, 7. As well, although John Lacey was careful in his questions to limit Conway's affirmation of Dr. Barber's work to the stated *facts,* Stoll showed that he had actually agreed that Barber's report expressed his *conclusions* (TT, 495; coroner's inquest transcript, 7).

41. "Denver Testimony Worthless in Defense of Tom Horn and Coble's Effort Was in Vain, "*Denver Post,* October 17, 1902, 1, 3.

42. Ibid., 1.

43. "Defense Takes a Hand," *Laramie Boomerang,* October 17, 1902, 1.

CHAPTER 15

1. "Tom Horn's Defense Opens (Horn's Demeanor)," *Denver Post,* December 16, 1902, 1.

2. Trial transcript, *State v. Horn,* October 10, 1903, Wyoming Archives (hereafter TT), 511–16.

3. Ibid., 517.

4. Ibid., 519, 521.

5. Ibid., 524, 525.

6. "Denver Testimony Worthless in Defense of Tom Horn and Coble's Effort Was in Vain," *Denver Post,* October 17, 1902, 1.

7. Ibid.

8. TT, 528–30.

9. Ibid., 531.

10. Ibid., 532.

11. Ibid., 290.

12. Ibid., 280.

13. TT, 532–34.

14. Ibid., 665 (testimony of Tom Horn).

15. "Denver Testimony Worthless in Defense of Tom Horn and Coble's Effort Was in Vain," *Denver Post,* October 17, 1902, 1.

16. TT, 255, 256.

17. Ibid., 537.

18. Ibid., 538.

19. Ibid., 539.

20. "Tom Horn Testifies," *Laramie Boomerang,* October 18, 1902, 1.

21. TT, 546.

22. Ibid., 148, 555.

23. Ibid., 551–54.

24. Ibid., 555.

25. Ibid., 556.

26. Ibid., 557, 558.

27. Ibid., 560.

28. Ibid., 561.

29. Under modern rules, an attorney may ordinarily not testify to contested issues other than such things as establishing authentication for a document. See "Rules of Professional Conduct for Attorneys at Law," Wyoming Court Rules Annotated, Rule 3.7.

I visited the scene in July 2011 and apparently it has not changed much in 110 years, though trees certainly have fallen since 1901 and have grown up in different places. My impression—to which I would *not* testify if representing one of the parties to a case—is that the ground where the murder took place is, in fact, rough and rocky, and still has quite a bit of cactus. But if a man was careful, he could make his way across the ground barefoot without injury. It would be imprudent to run across such ground, however.

30. TT, 563, 564, 566.

31. Ibid., 557, 558.

32. "Defense Closes in Horn Case," *Denver Times*, October 20, 1902, 1; "Defense Rests in Horn's Trial," *Denver Post*, October 20, 1902, 1.

33. "Albany County Boys," *Laramie Boomerang*, September 1, 1901, 1.

34. TT, 569, 570.

35. Ibid., 571, 572.

36. Ibid., 575, 576.

37. "Tom Horn Tells His Own Story," *Denver Republican*, October 18, 1902, 3.

38. "Fiercest Ordeal in Tom Horn's Life," *Denver Post*, October 18, 1902, 3 (sub-headline: "Horn Has Friends").

39. TT, 583, 584.

40. Ibid., 585, 586.

41. Ibid., 594.

42. "Fight in the Yards," *Cheyenne Daily Leader*, October 15, 1902, 1. This article identified the assaulted man as A. F. Whitman, but later articles would seem to indicate that the assaulted man was A. F. Whitman's son "Ollie" Whitman. See chapter 28, note 9.

43. Coroner's inquest transcript, 139.

44. "Fiercest Ordeal in Tom Horn's Life—Says His Confession Was a Josh," *Denver Post*, October 18, 1902, 1.

45. "Horn Takes Stand in his Own Behalf," *Cheyenne Daily Leader*, October 18, 1902, 2.

CHAPTER 16

1. "Fiercest Ordeal in Tom Horn's Life—His Confession Was a Josh," *Denver Post, October 18, 1902, 1.

2. "Horn Takes Stand in His Own Behalf," *Cheyenne Daily Leader*, October 18, 1902, 1.

3. Trial transcript, *State v. Horn,* October 10, 1903, Wyoming Archives (hereafter TT), 595, 596.

4. Ibid., 596–98.

5. Ibid., 598, 599.

6. "Alibi for Tom Horn," *Rocky Mountain News,* October 18, 1902, 1, 8.

7. TT, 600.

8. Ibid., 600, 601.

9. Ibid., 601, 602.

10. The modern spelling of this small stream is "Sybille," but the name usually appears in the transcript as "Sabylle." Ibid., 604a.

11. Ibid., 634.

12. Ibid., 605a. Horn was most probably referring to the Coble ranch near Bosler, which is about forty-five miles (as the crow flies) southwest of Chugwater.

13. Ibid., 606a, 607a.

14. Ibid., 608a.

15. Ibid., 608a, 609a.

16. Ibid., 602.

17. Ibid., 603, 604.

18. Ibid., 604.

19. Ibid., 605.

20. Ibid., 605, 606.

21. Ibid., 607, 608.

22. Ibid., 608.

23. "Horn Takes Stand In His Own Behalf," *Cheyenne Daily Leader,* October 18, 1902, 2.

24. "Tom Horn Tells His Own Story," *Denver Republican*, October 18, 1902.

25. Ibid., 23.

26. "Alibi for Tom Horn," *Rocky Mountain News,* October 18, 1902, .

27. "Horn Swears He Never Slew a Man, That His Stories Were All Lies, and He Told Them to Amuse," *Denver Post,* October 19, 1902, 1, 2.

28. "Horn Takes Stand in His Own Behalf," *Cheyenne Daily Leader,* October 18, 1902, 2; "Today He Is Being Cross-Examined by the Prosecution and Faces the Assault with Only His Wits to Protect Him," *Denver Post,* October 19, 1902, 1.

CHAPTER 17

1. "Fiercest Ordeal in Tom Horn's Life—Says His Confession Was a 'Josh,'" *Denver Post,* October 18, 1902, 1. See also "Tom Horn Placed under Severe Cross Examination," *Cheyenne Daily Leader,* October 18, 1902, 45).

2. "Tom Horn is Firm," *Laramie Boomerang,* October 19, 1902, 1.

3. Trial transcript, *State v. Horn,* October 10, 1903, Wyoming Archives (hereafter TT), 608, 609.

4. Ibid., 610, 611.

5. "Horn Swears That His Confession Was a Joke," *Rocky Mountain News,* October 19, 1902, 1.

6. "Fiercest Ordeal in Tom Horn's Life—Says His Confession Was a 'Josh,'" *Denver Post,* October 18, 1902, 1.

7. Ibid.

8. TT, 612, 613.

9. Ibid., 613.

10. Ibid., 614.

11. "Tom Horn Placed under Severe Cross Examination," *Cheyenne Daily Leader,* October 18, 1902, 4.

12. "Fiercest Ordeal in Tom Horn's Life—Says His Confession Was a 'Josh,'" *Denver Post,* October 18, 1902, 1.

13. TT, 614.

14. Ibid., 614–21.

15. Ibid., 622, 623.

16. Ibid., 624–27.

17. Ibid., 628–31.

18. Ibid., 632–34. The "Colcord place" appears to be about a mile due east of the Nickell ranch.

19. Ibid., 635–40. Regarding the reference to the Waechter and Allen places, see ibid., 645.

20. Ibid., 640–43. Horn does not distinguish between the Otto Plaga place and the Earnest Plaga place but was probably referring to Earnest, because his land was closer to Moore and Hencke, being further north.

21. Ibid., 650–54.

22. "Tom Horn Placed under Severe Cross Examination," *Cheyenne Daily Leader,* October 18, 1902, 4.

23. TT, 633; coroner's inquest transcript, 285.

24. "Tom Horn Tripped on the Stand," *Denver Republican,* October 19, 1902, 5. See also "Horn Swears That He Never Slew a Man, That His Stories Were All Lies, and He Told Them to Amuse," *Denver Post,* October 19, 1902, 2.

25. TT, 657, 658, 661.

26. Ibid., 661.

27. Ibid., 661–63.

28. Ibid., 663.

29. Ibid., 664.

30. Ibid., 666, 667.

31. Ibid., 667.

32. Ibid., 668.

33. "Horn Case Closing," *Weekly Boomerang* (Laramie), October 23, 1902, 2.

CHAPTER 18

1. Trial transcript, *State v. Horn,* October 10, 1903, Wyoming Archives (hereafter TT), 669.

2. Ibid., 669, 670.

3. Ibid., 670.

4. T. Blake Kennedy memoir by T. Blake Kennedy, box 1, folder 6, p. 207, T. Blake Kennedy Papers, 1892–1957, collection no. 405, American Heritage Center, Laramie, Wyoming.

5. "Tom Horn Placed under Severe Cross Examination," *Cheyenne Daily Leader,* October 18, 1902, 4.

6. TT, 670, 671.

7. Ibid., 671, 672.

8. Ibid., 672, 673.

9. Ibid., 673, 674.

10. Ibid., 674, 675.

11. Ibid., 675, 676.

12. Ibid., 675–77.

13. Ibid., 680.

14. Ibid., 681.

15. Ibid., 681, 682.

16. Ibid., 682, 683.

17. Ibid., 685, 686.

18. Ibid., 687.

19. Ibid.

20. Ibid., 691.

21. Ibid., 693, 694.

22. Ibid., 695, 696.

23. Ibid., 696, 697.

24. Ibid., 697, 698.

25. Ibid., 693, 700. See also "Tom Horn Tripped on the Stand," *Denver Republican*, October 19, 1902, 1, wherein it is stated that Horn "knew at the time that LeFors was trying to connect him with the murder of Willie Nickell."

26. TT, 698.

27. Ibid., 699.

28. Ibid.

29. Ibid., 699, 700.

30. Ibid., 700, 701.

31. "Horn Swears That His Confession Was a Joke," *Rocky Mountain News,* October 19, 1902, 1.

32. "Talked Too Much," *Cheyenne Daily Leader*, October 20, 1902, 1.

33. "Tom Horn Tripped on the Stand," *Denver Republican,* October 19, 1902, 1.

34. "Horn Swears He Never Slew a Man, That His Stories Were All Lies, and He Told Them to Amuse," *Denver Post,* October 19, 1902, 1.

35. "Tom Horn Is Firm," *Laramie Boomerang,* October 19, 1902, 1.

36. See instruction 5 of the instructions to jury, *State v. Horn,* docket 4, no. 58, records of the clerk of the Laramie County (Wyoming) District Court.

CHAPTER 19

1. Trial transcript, *State v. Horn,* October 10, 1903, Wyoming Archives (hereafter TT), 704a, 705a. The transcript runs from 702 to 710 and then reverts to 702. Someone, presumably the court reporter, apparently went back and added an "a" to the original pages 702 to 710.

2. Ibid.

3. Ibid., 705a, 706a.

4. Ibid., 707a–709a.

5. During my tenure as chairman of the Wyoming Bar Association's Civil Pattern Jury Instruction Committee (1995–2003), the committee considered instructions to accommodate new rules allowing and encouraging juror participation, including asking questions. So I was surprised to read this question by a juror—apparently done in a routine way—a hundred years before our new reform.

6. TT, 709a, 710a.

7. Ibid., 710a.

8. "Evidence in the Horn Case Is All In," *Cheyenne Daily Leader,* October 20, 1902, 4.

9. Ibid.

10. TT, 702, 703. No explanation was given why "Colonel Bell" was demoted to "Major Bell."

11. TT, 703.

12. Ibid., 705–707.

13. Ibid.

14. The reference to the law books being brought in by a "porter" is from "Defense Closes in Horn Case," *Denver Times,* October 20, 1901, 1. All other quotes in this paragraph are from "Evidence in the Horn Case Is All In," *Cheyenne Daily Leader,* October 20, 1902, 4.

15. TT, 707; "Evidence in the Horn Case Is All In," *Cheyenne Daily Leader,* October 20, 1902, 4.

16. Ibid., 707, 708.

17. Ibid., 708–10.

18. Ibid., 710.

19. Ibid., 712.

20. Ibid., 713.

21. Ibid., 713, 714.

22. Ibid., 715, 716.

23. Ibid., 716, 717.

24. Ibid., 717.

25. Ibid., 718.

26. Ibid., 718, 719.

27. "State Rests in Horn Case; Sensation Doesn't Appear," *Denver Republican* October 16, 1902, 2.

28. TT, 720, 721.

29. Ibid., 722.

30. Ibid.

31. TT, 723.

32. "Evidence in the Horn Case is All In," *Cheyenne Daily Leader,* October 20, 1902, 4.

33. "Defense Rests in Horn's Trial," *Denver Post,* October 20, 1902, 7.

34. TT, 724–37.

35. Ibid., 730–33.

36. "Close to a Verdict," *Rocky Mountain News,* October 21, 1902, 1.

37. Ibid.

38. TT, 737.

CHAPTER 20

1. For a discussion of the arguments in the dramatic Big Horn County, Wyoming, case that arose out of the 1909 Spring Creek sheep raid, see Davis, *A Vast Amount of Trouble: A History of the Spring Creek Raid* (Niwot: University Press of Colorado, 1993), 220–24. Oratory was not confined to the courtroom. Perhaps the best known orator of this time

was William Jennings Bryan, Democratic candidate for the presidency in 1896 and 1900 (referred to as the "Boy Orator of the Platte"). See Paulo E. Colleta, *William Jennings Bryan,* vol. 1, *Political Evangelist, 1860–1908* (Lincoln: University of Nebraska Press, 1964).

2. "Pleading for Life and Liberty of Tom Horn," *Cheyenne Daily Leader,* October 22, 1902, 4.

3. "Stoll Arraigns Tom Horn as Slayer of Murdered Boy," *Cheyenne Daily Leader,* October 21, 1902, 4.

4. Ibid.

5. "Tom Horn Verdict on Thursday," *Denver Post,* October 21, 1902, 8.

6. Instructions 1 and 2 of the instructions to the jury in *State v. Horn,* records of the Laramie County Clerk of Court (docket 4, no. 58).

7. Instructions 5 (weight and credibility), 6–7 (impeachment), and 8 (disregard of entire testimony) of the instructions to the jury in *State v. Horn,* records of the Laramie County Clerk of Court (docket 4, no. 58).

8. Instruction 9 of the instructions to the jury in *State v. Horn,* records of the Laramie County Clerk of Court (docket 4, no. 58).

9. "Tom Horn Shrinks When Riddled with Fire of Hard Facts," *Rocky Mountain News,* October 22, 1902, 3.

10. Instruction 10 of the instructions to the jury in *State v. Horn,* records of the Laramie County Clerk of Court (docket 4, no. 58). This instruction also applied to the admissions testified to by the three men from Denver—Campbell, Mulock, and Cowsley.

11. Instruction 11–13 of the instructions to the jury in *State v. Horn,* records of the Laramie County Clerk of Court (docket 4, no. 58).

12. Defense instructions 1 and 2 of the instructions to the jury in *State v. Horn,* records of the Laramie County Clerk of Court (docket 4, no. 58).

13. Defense instructions 3–7, 13, 15 of the instructions to the jury in *State v. Horn,* records of the Laramie County Clerk of Court (docket 4, no. 58).

14. Defense instructions 8–12 of the instructions to the jury in *State v. Horn,* records of the Laramie County Clerk of Court (docket 4, no. 58).

15. Instruction Given by Court, instructions to the jury in *State v. Horn,* records of the Laramie County Clerk of Court (docket 4, no. 58).

16. "Tom Horn Verdict on Thursday," *Denver Post,* October 21, 1902, 8.

17. "Stoll Arraigns Tom Horn as Slayer of Murdered Boy," *Cheyenne Daily Leader,* October 21, 1902, 1.

18. "Tom Horn Shrinks When Riddled with Fire of Hard Facts," *Rocky Mountain News,* October 22, 1902, 1.

19. "Arguments Begin," *Cheyenne Daily Leader,* October 21, 1902, 4.

20. "The Horn Jury is Instructed," *Denver Post,* October 21, 1902, 1.

21. "Summing Up in the Tom Horn Trial," *Denver Times,* October 21, 1902, 10.

22. "Stoll Arraigns Tom Horn as Slayer of Murdered Boy," *Cheyenne Daily Leader,* October 21, 1902, 4.

23. The source of this paragraph is "Tom Horn Arraigns Tom Horn as Slayer of Murdered Boy," *Cheyenne Daily Leader,* October 21, 1902, 4, except for the comment about the testimony of ranchmen being better than that of the expert testimony, which is found in "Attorney Stoll Begins His Address," *Denver Post,* October 21, 1902, 8.

24. "Horn's Trip," *Cheyenne Daily Leader*, October 21, 1902, 4; "The Horn Trial," *Cheyenne Daily Leader*, October 21, 1902, 1.

25. "The Horn Jury Is Instructed," *Denver Post*, October 21, 1902, 1.

26. "Afternoon Session," *Cheyenne Daily Leader*, October 21, 1902, 4.

27. Ibid.

28. "Tom Horn Shrinks When Riddled with Fire of Hard Facts," *Rocky Mountain News*, October 22, 1902, 1.

29. Ibid.

30. Ibid.

31. "Pleading for Life and Liberty of Tom Horn," *Cheyenne Daily Leader*, October 22, 1902, 4. During my time as a criminal defense attorney and as a prosecutor (briefly, while serving in the U.S. Army Judge Advocate General's Corps), I noted the strong propensity of criminal defendants to confess. I don't agree that they "invariably" do so, but it was surprising how many confessions were elicited even after a Miranda warning telling of the consequences.

32. Ibid.

33. "Tears and Sighs Mark the Day—It Was a Most Pathetic Scene When Stoll Spoke to Jury," *Denver Post*, October 22, 1902, 1.

34. Ibid.

35. "Tom Horn Shrinks when Riddled with Fire of Hard Facts," *Rocky Mountain News*, October 22, 1902, 3.

36. Ibid.

37. "Tears and Sighs Mark the Day—It Was a Most Pathetic Scene When Stoll Spoke to Jury," *Denver Post,* October 22, 1902, 1.

38. "Tom Horn Shrinks when Riddled with Fire of Hard Facts," *Rocky Mountain News,* October 22, 1902, 3.

CHAPTER 21

1. "Pleading for Life and Liberty of Tom Horn," *Cheyenne Daily Leader,* October 22, 1902, 4; "Horn Had Motive, Says Prosecution," *Denver Post,* October 22, 1902, 1. In my opinion, it is unlikely Mr. Stoll made this arrangement for any ulterior purpose.

2. "Powerful Speeches," *Laramie Boomerang,* October 23, 1902, 1.

3. "'Horn Had Motive,' Says Prosecution," *Denver Post,* October 22, 1902, 1.

4. "Pleading for Life and Liberty of Tom Horn," *Cheyenne Daily Leader,* October 22, 1902, 4.

5. "'Horn Had Motive,' Says Prosecution," *Denver Post,* October 22, 1902, 1.

6. "Pleading for Life and Liberty of Tom Horn," *Cheyenne Daily Leader,* October 22, 1902, 4.

7. "'Horn Had Motive,' Says Prosecution," *Denver Post,* October 22, 1902, 1.

8. Ibid.

9. "Pleading for Life and Liberty of Tom Horn," *Cheyenne Daily Leader,* October 22, 1902, 4.

10. See the discussion herein at chapter 8.

11. Ibid.

12. For the testimony of Campbell, see chapter 12 herein, and for that of Mulock and Cowsley, see chapter 13.

13. See chapter 15 herein.

14. "'Horn Had Motive,' Says Prosecution," *Denver Post,* October 22, 1902, 1.

15. See "Lacey Pleads for Horn in a Deserted Courtroom," *Denver Times*, October 23, 1902, 1; "Powerful Speeches," *Laramie Boomerang,* October 23, 1902, 1.

16. For the testimony of Tom Horn regarding his drinking the day he spoke to Joe LeFors, see chapters 17 and 18 herein.

17. "'Horn Had Motive,' Says Prosecution," *Denver Post,* October 22, 1902, 1.

18. "The Horn Trial," *Cheyenne Daily Leader,* October 22, 1902, 1; "'Horn Had Motive,' Says Prosecution," *Denver Post,* October 22, 1902, 1, 10. The *Post* article is the source of the discussion about Burke's sarcasm and ridicule.

19. "The Horn Trial," *Cheyenne Daily Leader*, October 22, 1902, 1.

20. Ibid.

21. "'Horn Had Motive,' Says Prosecution," *Denver Post*, October 22, 1902, 1, 10.

22. "The Horn Trial," *Cheyenne Daily Leader,* October 22, 1902, 1.

23. Ibid.

24. Regarding the testimony of Jim Miller, Victor Miller, Gus Miller, Eva Miller, and Glendolene Kimmell at the coroner's inquest, see chapters 3–5 herein. "The Horn Trial," *Cheyenne Daily Leader,* October 22, 1902, 1.

25. "Attorneys for Horn Say Last Words for His Defense," *Cheyenne Daily Leader*, October 23, 1902, 4.

26. "Lacey Pleads for Horn in a Deserted Courtroom," *Denver Times*, October 23, 1902, 1.

27. "The Miller Boy Accused of Slaying Willie Nickell by Horn's Chief Counsel," *Denver Post*, October 23, 1902, 1.

28. "Lacey Pleads for Horn in a Deserted Courtroom," *Denver Times*, October 23, 1902, 1.

29. "Attorneys for Horn Say Last Word in His Defense," *Cheyenne Daily Leader*, October 23, 1902, 4.

30. Ibid.

31. Ibid.

32. Regarding the references to instructions, see "Lacey Pleads for Horn in a Deserted Courtroom," *Denver Times*, October 23, 1902, 1. As to the remaining statements, see "Attorneys for Horn Say Last Word in His Defense," *Cheyenne Daily Leader*, October 23, 1902, 4.

33. "Attorneys for Horn Say Last Word in His Defense," *Cheyenne Daily Leader*, October 23, 1902, 4.

34. Ibid.

35. See the discussion of John Apperson's testimony in chapter 10 herein.

36. Today if an attorney is perceived as trying to persuade a jury not to follow a judge's ruling of law, an objection would probably be sustained, although it may be that under 1902 practice and custom, broader latitude was given in final argument than is true in 2016. "Lacey Pleads for Horn in a Deserted Courtroom," *Denver Times*, October 23, 1902, 1.

37. "The Miller Boy Accused of Slaying Willie Nickell by Horn's Chief Counsel," *Denver Post*, October 23, 1902, 1.

38. "Attorneys for Horn Say Last Word in His Defense," *Cheyenne Daily Leader*, October 23, 1902.

39. "The Miller Boy Accused of Killing Willie Nickell by Horn's Chief Counsel," *Denver Post*, October 23, 1902, 1.

40. The quoted language is found in "Attorneys for Horn Say Last Word in His Defense," *Cheyenne Daily Leader*, October 23, 1902, 4, except for the statement that "all the answers were in reply to leading questions," which comes from "Lacey Pleads for Horn in a Deserted Courtroom," *Denver Times*, October 23, 1902, 1.

41. See chapter 13 herein.

42. "Lacey Pleads for Horn in a Deserted Courtroom," *Denver Times*, October 23, 1902, 1.

43. "The Miller Boy Accused of Slaying Willie Nickell by Horn's Chief Counsel," *Denver Post*, October 23, 1902. The one draw is to the south.

44. "The Miller Boy Accused of Slaying Willie Nickell by Horn's Chief Counsel," *Denver Post*, October 23, 1902.

45. "Attorneys for Horn Say Last Words in His Defense," *Cheyenne Daily Leader*, October 23, 1902, 4.

46. This statement is based on the fact that sunrise in Cheyenne, Wyoming, on July 18, 2014 occurred at 4:42 A.M. MST (5:42 A.M. MDT). I assume that it becomes light approximately one-half hour before sunrise. Records of the National Weather Service Forecast Office, Cheyenne, Wyoming.

47. "The Miller Boy Accused of Slaying Willie Nickell by Horn's Chief Counsel," *Denver Post*, October 23, 1902, 1.

48. For the trial testimony of Dr. Barber, see chapter 10 herein; for the testimony of Drs. Maynard, Desmond, and Barkwell, see chapter 11; for the testimony of Dr. Lewis, see chapter 14; for the testimony of Dr. Burgess, see chapter 15.

49. Trial transcript, *State v. Horn*, October 10, 1903, Wyoming Archives, 190.

50. "The Horn Trial," *Cheyenne Daily Leader*, October 23, 1902, 1.

51. Ibid.

52. "Lacey Pleads for Horn in a Deserted Courtroom," *Denver Times*, October 23, 1902, 1.

53. "The Horn Trial," *Cheyenne Daily Leader*, October 23, 1902, 1.

54. Ibid. The reference to the whistles "announcing" noon comes from "The Miller Boy Is Accused of Slaying Willie Nickell by Horn's Chief Counsel," *Denver Post*, October 23, 1902, 1, 3.

55. "The Horn Trial," *Cheyenne Daily Leader*, October 23, 1902, 1.

CHAPTER 22

1. "Only the Jury Now Stands between Horn and Gallows," *Denver Post*, October 24, 1902, 5.

2. Ibid.

3. Ibid.

4. "The Horn Trial," *Cheyenne Daily Leader*, October 23, 1902, 1.

5. "Only the Jury Now Stands between Horn and Gallows," *Denver Post*, October 24, 1902, 1.

6. "The Horn Trial," *Cheyenne Daily Leader*, October 23, 1902, 1.

7. Ibid.

8. "Tom Horn's Fate Hangs Trembling at the Balance," *Cheyenne Daily Leader*, October 24, 1902, 4.

9. "Only the Jury Now Stands Between Horn and Gallows," *Denver Post*, October 24, 1902, 5.

10. Ibid., 1.

11. Ibid. Stoll may not have had a problem with the jury on this issue. The assertions by the defense that it was impossible to go barefoot over the ground near the gate had already been met by skepticism by at least one of the participants. One witness, who was apparently waiting outside the courtroom, commented: "Why my babies go barefoot every summer over just such ground. I could not keep their shoes on them after the ground and the water in the creek got warm." "Tom Horn Shrinks When Riddled with Fire of Hard Facts," *Rocky Mountain News*, October 22, 1902, 2. The reference to "stockings or moccasins" comes from "Horn Case Goes to Jury," *Denver Times*, October 24, 1902, 1.

12. "Only the Jury Now Stands between Horn and Gallows," *Denver Post*, October 24, 1902, 1.

13. "Horn Case Goes to Jury," *Denver Times*, October 24, 1902, 1.

14. "Only the Jury Now Stands between Horn and Gallows," *Denver Post*, October 24, 1902, 1.

15. Ibid.

16. Ibid.

17. "Tom's Horn's Fate Lies Trembling in the Balance," *Cheyenne Daily Leader*, October 24, 1902, 4. The *Denver Post* also carried a large segment of this "peroration." See "Only the Jury Now Stands between Horn and Gallows," *Denver Post*, October 24, 1902, 1. It was the *Cheyenne Daily Leader* that referred to Stoll's last words as a "sublime peroration."

18. "Tom Horn's Fate Hangs Trembling in the Balance," *Cheyenne Daily Leader*, October 24, 1902, 4.

19. Ibid.

20. "Only the Jury Now Stands between Horn and Gallows," *Denver Post*, October 24, 1902, 1.

21. "A Hung Jury," *Cheyenne Daily Leader*, October 24, 1902, 4.

22. "Horn Case Goes to Jury," *Denver Times*, October 24, 1902, 1.

23. Ibid.

24. "Stoll Arraigns Tom Horn as Slayer of Murdered Boy," *Cheyenne Daily Leader*, October 21, 1902, 4. See also "Close to a Verdict," *Rocky Mountain News*, October 21, 1902, 1.

25. "A Lost Reputation," *Cheyenne Daily Leader*, October 21, 1902, 4.

26. "Horn Guilty," *Cheyenne Daily Leader*, October 25, 4.

CHAPTER 23

1. "Horn Guilty," *Cheyenne Daily Leader,* October 24, 1902, 4.

2. Quotation from "Judge Scott Showed Emotion," *Denver Post,* October 25, 1902, 3.

3. "Horn Guilty," *Cheyenne Daily Leader,* October 245, 1902, 4.

4. Ibid.

5. "Stoll Prostrated," *Laramie Boomerang,* October 25, 1902, 1.

6. "LeFors Indignant," *Cheyenne Daily Leader,* October 25, 1902, 1.

7. "The Hirer of Horn Is Next to Suffer," *Denver Post* October 25, 1902, 1.

8. "Convicted Himself," *Cheyenne Daily Leader,* October 25, 1902, 1; "Six Ballots Taken," *Denver Post,* October 24, 1902, 1.

9. "Six Ballots Taken," *Denver Post,* October 25, 1902, 1; "Tom Horn Is Guilty," *Rocky Mountain News,* October 25, 1902, 1.

10. "Convicted Himself," *Cheyenne Daily Leader,* October 24, 1902, 1.

11. "Tom Horn Is Guilty," *Rocky Mountain News,* October 25, 1902, 2.

12. "Six Ballots Taken," *Denver Post,* October 25, 1902, 1.

13. "Horn Convicted and State Will Prosecute Employers," *Denver Times* October 25, 1902, 1.

14. T. Blake Kennedy memoir by T. Blake Kennedy, box 1, folder 6, pp. 206, 208, T. Blake Kennedy Papers, 1892–1957, collection no. 405, American Heritage Center, Laramie, Wyoming. See also the discussion in chapter 9, herein.

15. "The Hirer of Horn is Next to Suffer," *Denver Post,* October 25, 1902, 1.

16. "Tom Horn Talks," *Denver Post,* October 25, 1902, 3.

17. "The Fears of the People Were Great," *Denver Post,* October 25, 1902, 3.

18. Trial transcript, *State v. Horn,* October 10, 1903, Wyoming Archives, 339.

19. "The Fears of the People Were Great," *Denver Post,* October 25, 1902, 3.

20. "Guilty of Murder in the First Degree," *Laramie Boomerang,* October 25, 1902, 1. Laramie is the seat of Albany County and by the far the largest town in the county.

21. "Dawn of a New Era," *Cheyenne Daily Leader,* October 25, 1902, 2.

22. Ibid.

23. "Cheyenne Is Glad," *Denver Post,* October 25, 1902, 3.

24. "Horn Convicted and State Will Prosecute Employers," *Denver Times,* October 25, 1902, 1, 3.

25. "The Hirer of Horn Is Next to Suffer," *Denver Post,* October 26, 1902, 1.

26. "New Trial," *Cheyenne Daily Leader,* October 25, 1902, 1; "The Hirer of Horn Is Next to Suffer," *Denver Post,* October 25, 1902, 1.

27. "The Hirer of Horn Is Next to Suffer," *Denver Post,* October 25, 1902, 1; "Horn Convicted and State Will Prosecute Employers," *Denver Times,* October 25, 1902, 1. For the earlier statement about going after Horn's employers, see Polly Pry, "When Is 5 Cents Worth $12,000?," *Denver Post,* October 20, 1902, 1.

28. "Tomorrow Horn's Doom," *Denver Post,* October 27, 1902, 1. Regarding George Prentiss, see the discussion in chapter 8 herein.

CHAPTER 24

1. Motion for New Trial, *State v. Horn,* docket 4, no. 58, records of the Clerk of the Laramie County (Wyoming) District Court.

2. Ibid., paragraphs 1–4.

3. Ibid., paragraphs 27, 28.

4. Ibid., paragraphs 5, 11.

5. Ibid., paragraphs 6, 7; trial transcript, *State v. Horn*, October 10, 1903, Wyoming Archives (hereafter TT), 143, 144.

6. The Motion for New Trial referred to Warlamount several times and in each case used the spelling "Warlaumont." As noted earlier, however, since the uniform spelling in the trial transcript of this deputy sheriff's name was "Warlamount," that is the spelling used throughout this book.

7. Motion for New Trial, paragraphs 8, 9, 17, 18; TT, 254.

8. Ibid., paragraphs 12–16.

9. Ibid., paragraphs 19–21.

10. Ibid., paragraphs 24, 25; TT, 439.

11. Ibid., paragraphs 34–37.

12. Ibid., paragraphs 38–42.

13. Ibid., paragraphs 43–46.

14. Ibid., paragraphs 22, 23.

15. Ibid., paragraphs 10, 26, 29, 30.

16. Ibid., paragraphs 31–33, 47. Regarding Knight, see the discussion in chapter 9.

17. Ibid., paragraphs 48–61 (except for 53, which seems to have been omitted).

18. Ibid., paragraphs 62–65.

19. Ibid., paragraphs 66–70. The probable reason for this long litany of asserted errors in the Motion for New Trial was that under Wyoming appellate rules (Rule 13, especially), the defense could not raise a point as error on appeal unless it had asserted it in a motion for new trial. See *Conradt v. Leber*, 78 Pac. 1, 13 Wyo. 99 (Wyo. 1904) and *Bank of Chadron v. Anderson*, 53 Pac. 280, 7 Wyo. 441 (Wyo. 1898).

20. Exhibit A, Motion for New Trial.

21. See Supplemental Motion for New Trial, with attached affidavits of Greta Rohde, Homer Payne, and J. Emerson Smith, *State v. Horn*, docket 4, no. 58, records of the Laramie County Clerk of Court.

22. The discussion relating to Tolson and Barnes (following) comes from the affidavits of Tolson and Barnes submitted on November 8, 1902, by the prosecution in *State v. Horn*.

23. Affidavit of John H. Reese in response to defendant's Supplemental Motion for New Trial, *State v. Horn*.

24. Affidavit of George A. Proctor in response to defendant's supplemental motion for new trial, *State v. Horn*.

25. Affidavits of George S. Walker and J. Emerson Smith in response to Defendant's Supplemental Motion for New Trial, *State v. Horn*. In his affidavit, other than providing his name, Walker does not further identify himself or explain how he came to speak to Payne.

26. See the affidavit of Walter R. Stoll, submitted on November 7, 1902, in response to Defendant's Supplemental Motion for New Trial, *State v. Horn*. The ensuing discussion directly follows this affidavit.

27. See the affidavits of Clyde M. Watts and H. Waldo Moore, submitted on November 7, 1902, in response to Defendant's Supplemental Motion for New Trial, *State v. Horn*.

28. See the affidavits of George A. Johnson, Henry Altman, and W. E. Brooks, Jr., relating to Defendant's Supplemental Motion for New Trial, *State v. Horn*.

29. "Horn Trial Costs Money," *Wyoming Tribune* (Cheyenne), May 13, 1903, 4.

30. See "Argue Motion for a New Trial," *Cheyenne Daily Leader*, November 8, 1902, 4; *Bill Barlow's Budget* (Douglas, Wyo.), October 29, 1902, 1. The *Daily Leader* pointed out that the defense had already ordered the very expensive transcript of the trial, only needed if a motion for new trial was denied.

31. "Argue Motion for New Trial," *Cheyenne Daily Leader*, November 8, 2014, 4. Regarding Burke's five thirty closing time, see also "Pleading for Horn," *Laramie Boomerang*, November 9, 1902, 1; "Tom Horn Convicted," *Saratoga (Wyo.) Sun*, October 30, 1902, 1.

32. "Argue Motion for New Trial," *Cheyenne Daily Leader*, November 8, 2014, 4.

33. "Horn Has Lost Hope," *Denver Post*, October 28, 1902, 3.

34. "Stoll Argues," *Cheyenne Daily Leader*, November 10, 1902, 4.

35. "The Horn Case," *Laramie Boomerang*, November 12, 1902, 1.

36. The following discussion of Judge Scott's ruling comes from "To Hang January 9," *Wheatland (Wyo.) World*, November 14, 1902, 2. This article, in turn, was taken from the *Wyoming Tribune* (the Cheyenne daily). The *Wyoming Tribune* articles about the Horn trial are not available, except as they were reprinted by other newspapers, as here. This is unfortunate because, if this story is any indication, the *Tribune's* writings about the trial were first-rate, filled with cogent detail.

37. "To Hang January 9," *Wheatland (Wyo.) World*, November 14, 1902, 2, citing the *Wyoming Tribune*.

38. Ibid.

39. "Condemned Felon," *Cheyenne Daily Leader*, November 13, 1902, 4.

CHAPTER 25

1. *Bill Barlow's Budget* (Douglas, Wyo.), October 29, 1902, 1.

2. "Horn Comment," *Laramie Republican*, November 3, 1902, 2; *Cheyenne Daily Leader*, October 31, 1902, 2.

3. "Tom Horn Found Guilty," *Wyoming Derrick* (Casper), October 31, 1902, 1.

4. Regarding Polly Pry, see chapter 8 herein.

5. *Wyoming Industrial Journal* (Cheyenne), November 1, 1902, 120.

6. "Tom Horn Convicted," *Saratoga (Wyo.) Sun*, October 30, 1902, 1.

7. "The Horn Conviction," *Wheatland (Wyo.) World*, October 31, 1902, 1.

8. "Has Confession," *Cheyenne Daily Leader*, October 30, 1902, 4.

9. Regarding the Wyoming rule as to evidence showing another person to be the real killer, see the discussion in chapter 10 herein, especially note 21.

10. "Horn Was Slayer of Powell and Lewis," *Cheyenne Daily Leader*, October 30, 1902, 3. See the discussion in chapter 10 herein. Other information emerged later against Horn, including evidence undercutting Horn's statement that he was one hundred miles away when Powell was shot. See "Horn's Wild Ride," *Sheridan Post*, November 27, 1902, 3.

11. Revised Statutes of Wyoming, 1899, § 5160.

12. "When Is 5 Cents Worth $12,000?," *Denver Post*, October 20, 1902, 1.

13. "Tom Horn Found Guilty," *Wyoming Derrick* (Casper), October 30, 1902, 1.

14. "Tom Horn Convicted," *Saratoga (Wyo.) Sun*, October 30, 1902, 1.

15. "Horn Has Lost Hope," *Denver Post*, October 28, 1902, 3.

16. See, for example, ibid.

17. "Guns For Horn," *Cheyenne Daily Leader*, October 20, 1902, 4.

CHAPTER 26

1. John W. Davis, *Goodbye, Judge Lynch: The End of a Lawless Era in Wyoming's Big Horn Basin* (Norman: University of Oklahoma Press, 2005), 85.

2. Ibid., 98.

3. Ibid., 106.

4. See ibid., chapter 7.

5. "Cattlemen Are to Blame," *Laramie Boomerang*, July 25, 1903.

6. See Davis, *Goodbye, Judge Lynch*, 108–16.

7. "Courts Not to Blame," *Cheyenne Daily Leader*, August 3, 1903, 3.

8. In 1903, Shakespeare's writings were widely known and appreciated and this phrase ("the law's delays"), based on a line from Prince Hamlet's "To be or not to be" soliloquy, was frequently cited. It was a justification given for suicide.

9. "Notorious Delays," *Laramie Boomerang*, January 8, 1903, 2, citing the *Cody Enterprise*.

10. "This and That," *Wheatland (Wyo.) World*, January 16, 1903, 2, citing the *Buffalo Bulletin*.

11. "Eight Months," *Cheyenne Daily Leader*, December 18, 1902, 3.

12. See "Respite Granted Tom Horn," *Laramie Boomerang*, January 3, 1903, 1.

13. "Horn Is Happy," *Cheyenne Daily Leader*, January 2, 1903, 3.

14. "The Tribune Has Averted Most Daring Jail Delivery Ever Attempted in the West," *Wyoming Tribune* (Cheyenne), January 21, 1903, 1.

15. Ibid.

16. "Other Tales," *Cheyenne Daily Leader*, January 22, 1903, 3.

17. "Plot Was Horn's," *Cheyenne Daily Leader*, July 22, 1903, 3.

18. "Tom Horn Plans to Break Jail," *Natrona County Tribune*, January 22, 1903, 1. See also "Short Items," *Cheyenne Daily Leader*, January 28, 1903, 3, citing a comment made in the *Sheridan Post*.

19. Davis, *Goodbye, Judge Lynch*, 106.

20. "Story Absolutely Genuine," *Wyoming Tribune* (Cheyenne), January 25, 1903, 1; "A Sensation," *Wyoming Tribune*, January 22, 1903, 4.

21. "History of Bill No. 100," *Cheyenne Daily Leader*, February 10, 1903, 3.

22. "Walker Vindicated," *Cheyenne Daily Leader*, February 12, 1902, 2.

23. "May Free Horn," *Cheyenne Daily Leader*, February 7, 1903, 1.

24. "Measure Killed," *Cheyenne Daily Leader*, February 7, 1903, 1.

25. "House Censures," *Cheyenne Daily Leader*, February 9, 1902, 4.

26. "Give Walker a Hearing," *Cheyenne Daily Leader*, February 9, 1903, 2.

27. "History of Bill No. 100," *Cheyenne Daily Leader*, February 10, 1903, 3; "Walker Vindicated," *Cheyenne Daily Leader*, February 12, 1903, 2.

28. See *Laramie Boomerang*, February 10, 1993, 2; *Bill Barlow's Budget* (Douglas, Wyo.), February 18, 1902, 1; "Northwest Notes," *Rock Springs (Wyo.) Miner*, February 12, 1903, 2; "Editorial Correspondence," *Saratoga (Wyo.) Sun*, February 12, 1903, 2; "Vote of Censure Is Erased," *Laramie Boomerang*, February 15, 1902, 1.

29. "The State's Disgrace," *Buffalo (Wyo.) Voice*, February 14, 1903, 4.

30. "Horn Hatches a New Plot," *Laramie Boomerang*, August 4, 1903, 1.

31. The two Cheyenne dailies carried long and detailed stories about this jailbreak, and, unless otherwise indicated, this discussion about the escape comes from "Horn and McCloud Make Desperate Attempt to Escape from Jail," *Cheyenne Daily Leader*, August 10, 1903, 1, and "Spectacular Escape and Capture," *Wyoming Tribune* (Cheyenne), August 10, 1903, 1.

32. The quotes are taken from "Horn and McCloud Make Desperate Attempt to Escape from Jail," *Cheyenne Daily Leader*, August 10, 1903, 1.

33. Ibid.

34. Ibid.

35. Ibid.

36. Ibid.

37. Ibid.

38. Ibid.

39. Ibid. See also "Spectacular Escape and Capture," *Wyoming Tribune* (Cheyenne), August 10, 1903, 4.

40. "Spectacular Escape and Capture," *Wyoming Tribune* (Cheyenne), August 10, 1903, 4.

41. "Horn's Brief, Blasted Liberty: It Was Picturesque and Fast, but So Fleeting and Foolish," *Denver Post*, August 10, 1903, 1.

42. "Short Items," *Cheyenne Daily Leader*, August 11, 1903, 3.

43. Quote from "Spectacular Escape and Capture," *Wyoming Tribune* (Cheyenne), August 10, 1903, 4.

44. "The Escape of Tom Horn," *Laramie Boomerang*, August 11, 1903, 2. See also "Citizens Were Cool," *Wyoming Tribune*, August 10, 1903, 4.

45. "Horn's Brief, Blasted Liberty: It Was Picturesque and Fast, but So Fleeting and Foolish," *Denver Post*, August 10, 1903, 1; "Strange Horse," *Wyoming Tribune* (Cheyenne), August 11, 1903, 4.

46. "Viewed from the Outside," *Laramie Boomerang*, August 13, 1903, 2; "Law Is Too Slow," *Natrona County Tribune*, August 13, 1903, 4; "Crumbs of Comfort," *Cheyenne Daily Leader*, August 10, 1903, 2.

47. "Prevent Escapes," *Cheyenne Daily Leader*, October 19, 1903, 3; (Wyoming) Laws 1905, chap. 11, §4.

48. "Spectacular Escape and Capture," *Wyoming Tribune* (Cheyenne), August 10, 1903, 4.

49. "Horn's Liberty was Picturesque, but Very Fleeting," *Denver Post*, August 10, 1903, 1, 3.

CHAPTER 27

1. The essential components of an appeal have not changed since 1902. Appellate briefs are followed by oral arguments, which in turn are followed by a decision from the court. For an overview of the current practices before the Wyoming Supreme Court, see John W. Davis, "The Insider's Guide to the Wyoming Supreme Court," in Appellate Practice Compendium, vol. 2, ed. Dana Livingston (Chicago: American Bar Association, Judicial Division, 2014), chapter 66 (1421–33).

2. "Working on Horn Case," *Cheyenne Daily Leader,* August 19, 1903, 3. Regarding the extensive topics addressed in the briefs, see *Horn v. State,* 12 Wyo. 80, 73 Pac. 705 (Wyo. 1903), at pp. 86–103, as long a citation of legal points as any I recall in an early Wyoming Supreme Court case. The citation of the points of each party was discontinued in the 1950s, I believe.

3. I went through six of the first eleven books of the Wyoming Reports and found they contained an average of thirty-four cases. Extrapolating that would mean a total of 374 cases decided before *Horn v. State.*

4. When I first started practicing law in Wyoming, in 1968, this was still so. In most instances there was no determinative Wyoming law. Later in my career, maybe in the last twenty years, that changed. Now there are usually Wyoming decisions that apply directly to a case.

5. See "Fight for Horn's Life," *Cheyenne Daily Leader,* August 20, 1903, 3. Regarding the argument times allotted and the overall length of the arguments, see "Court Says Keffer Must Hang," *Wyoming Tribune* (Cheyenne), August 20, 1903, 1.

6. "Fight for Horn's Life," *Cheyenne Daily Leader,* October 20, 1903, 3.

7. Ibid.

8. Ibid.

9. Ibid.

10. "The State Opens," *Wyoming Tribune,* August 21, 1903, 4.

11. "Supreme Court Decisions," *Saratoga (Wyo.) Sun,* August 27, 1903, 1.

12. "Horn to Hang," *Cheyenne Daily Leader,* August 30, 1902, 4.

13. "Supreme Court Cannot Hurry," *Laramie Boomerang,* September 1, 1903, 1.

14. "No Decision," *Wyoming Tribune,* September 21, 1903, 4.

15. "Tom Horn to Hang," *Wyoming Tribune,* September 30, 1903, 1. See also *Horn v. State,* 12 Wyo. 80–167. The defense apparently abandoned many of its contentions in the motion for new trial before the trial court. The listed contentions in *Horn v. State* (86–94) do not include several earlier raised.

16. *Horn v. State,* 103.

17. I have not reviewed all cases decided by the Wyoming Supreme Court, but believe I know the court's opinions well. Since beginning law school in 1965, I have read hundreds of opinions of the court, and since I entered the bar in 1968 have engaged in an active appellate practice. I have never seen a comparable statement in any opinion of the court. In the early days, when *Horn v. State* was decided, the court sometimes made perfunctory statements, such as generally referring to the able work of the attorneys for both sides, but nothing like this one. In recent years the court has not even made such perfunctory statements.

18. *Horn v. State*, 106–15.

19. Ibid., 116–20.

20. Ibid., 120, 121.

21. Ibid., 121, 122.

22. Ibid., 122.

23. Ibid., 123.

24. Ibid., 124.

25. Ibid., 126, 127.

26. Ibid., 128.

27. Ibid., 129–33.

28. Ibid., 135, 136.

29. Ibid., 137.

30. Ibid., 137–47.

31. Ibid., 145.

32. Ibid., 146.

33. Ibid., 148–52. For the very similar modern rule, see Rule 701, Wyoming Rules of Evidence.

34. *Horn v. State,* 153. This commonsense rule is still the law in Wyoming. See *Sanchez v. State,* 751 P.2d 1300, 1306 (Wyo. 1988); *Jones v. State,* 228 P.3d 867, 870 (Wyo. 2010).

35. *Horn v. State,* 156–58.

36. Ibid., 158–64.

37. Ibid., 164–66.

38. Ibid., 167.

CHAPTER 28

1. "Tom Horn to Hang," *Wyoming Tribune,* September 30, 1903, 1.

2. "The Tom Horn Case," *Laramie Boomerang,* October 1, 1903, 2.

3. "Tom Horn to Hang," *Wheatland (Wyo.) World,* October 2, 1903, 2. See also "Tom Horn to Hang," *Rock Springs (Wyo.) Miner,* October 1, 1903, 1.

4. "Professional Murderers Losing Caste," *Wyoming Tribune* (Cheyenne), October 1, 1903, 2.

5. "Courthouse Notes," *Wyoming Tribune* (Cheyenne), October 1, 1903, 5. The *Tribune* reported on October 7, 1903, that Horn was still "in ignorance of his fate." "Magic City Gossip," *Wyoming Tribune* (Cheyenne), October 7, 1903, 7.

6. "Tom Horn Had Learned His Fate," *Laramie Boomerang,* October 13, 1903, 2.

7. "Still Has Friends," *Wyoming Tribune* (Cheyenne), October 7, 1903, 4; "Tom Horn to Hang," *Rock Springs (Wyo.) Miner,* October 1, 1903, 1.

8. T. A. Larson, *History of Wyoming* (Lincoln: University of Nebraska Pressm 1965), 315, 374. Chatterton is buried at the Lakeview Cemetery, Cheyenne.

9. Ollie Whitman was the son of A. F. Whitman, the man at whose home a lynching of Kels Nickell was planned. Ollie was probably the man badly beaten by Nickell in March 1903. See "Cheyenne Man Slain by Kansas City Thugs," *Cheyenne Daily Leader,* July 22, 1907, 1; chapter 15, note 42, herein. See also "Other Affidavits," *Wyoming Tribune* (Chey-

enne), October 31, 1903, 8; "Nickell Will Be Charged with Aggravated Assault," *Semi-Weekly Boomerang* (Laramie), March 26, 1903, 6.

10. "Still Has Friends," *Wyoming Tribune* (Cheyenne), October 7, 1903, 4, citing an article in the *Denver Post* from the previous day.

11. "Horn May Cheat Gallows," *Laramie Boomerang,* October 8, 1903, 4.

12. Ibid. Chatterton was born on July 21, 1860, and in November 1903, was forty-three. Perhaps Horn's supporters saw him as someone they could intimidate.

13. "Horn May Cheat Gallows," *Laramie Boomerang,* October 8, 1903, 4.

14. Ibid.

15. Ibid.

16. "Miss Glendolene Kimmell Swears Victor Miller Confessed Killing Willie Nickell," *Wyoming Tribune* (Cheyenne), October 31, 1903, 1.

17. Ibid. If the governor's office was in the same room I first visited in the mid 1970s, then it was a large room but not nearly the size of the typical courtroom used by a Wyoming district court.

18. "Horn's Fate Hangs on Woman's Words," *Cheyenne Daily Leader,* November 1, 1903, 3.

19. "Miss Glendolene Kimmell Swears Victor Miller Confessed Killing Willie Nickell," *Wyoming Tribune,* October 31, 1903, 1, 8.

20. Ibid.

21. Ibid.

22. "Horn's Fate Hangs on Woman's Words," *Cheyenne Daily Leader,* November 1, 1903, 3. See also "Will Reply on Thursday," *Wyoming Tribune* (Cheyenne), November 2, 1903, 4.

23. "Horn's Fate Hangs on Woman's Words," *Cheyenne Daily Leader,* November 1, 1903, 3; "Will Reply on Thursday," *Wyoming Tribune* (Cheyenne), November 2, 1903, 4.

24. "Governor to Decide Soon," *Weekly Boomerang* (Laramie), November 5, 1903, 1.

25. "Governor Will Take His Time," *Laramie Boomerang,* November 3, 1903, 1.

26. See "Horn's Fate Hangs on Woman's Words," *Cheyenne Daily Leader,* November 1, 1903, 3; "Miss Glendolene Kimmell Swears Victor Miller Confessed Killing Willie Nickell," *Wyoming Tribune* (Cheyenne), October 31, 1903, 1, 8.

27. "Alleged Perjury," *Cheyenne Daily Leader,* November 4, 1903, 4.

28. Ibid.

29. "Prosecution Comes up with Strong Rebuttal," *Wyoming Tribune* (Cheyenne), November 12, 1903, 1.

30. Ibid.; "More of Horn Affidavits," *Laramie Boomerang,* November 14, 1903, 1.

31. "Prosecution Comes up with Strong Rebuttal," *Wyoming Tribune* (Cheyenne), November 12, 1903, 1.

32. Ibid.

33. "More of Horn Affidavits," *Laramie Boomerang,* November 14, 1902, 1.

34. "Prosecution Comes up with Strong Rebuttal," *Wyoming Tribune* (Cheyenne), November 12, 1903, 1. Connor had apparently been a mayor of Laramie, and Bell was apparently a Laramie promoter and landowner. See Larson, *History of Wyoming,* 205, 362.

35. "Prosecution Comes up with Strong Rebuttal," *Wyoming Tribune* (Cheyenne), November 12, 1903, 1; "More of Horn Affidavits," *Laramie Boomerang,* November 14, 1902, 1.

36. "Prosecution Comes up with Strong Rebuttal," *Wyoming Tribune* (Cheyenne), November 12, 1903, 1.

37. "More of Horn Affidavits," *Laramie Boomerang*, November 14, 1903, 1.

38. "From Kansas," *Wyoming Tribune* (Cheyenne), November 14, 1903, 5. It is not clear whether Stoll offered the Mendenhall affidavit at the November 12 proceeding before Governor Chatterton, but, if not, it was done shortly thereafter.

39. "Prosecution Comes up with Strong Rebuttal," *Wyoming Tribune* (Cheyenne), November 11, 1903, 4.

40. "Governor Refuses Clemency and Horn Will Be Hanged," *Cheyenne Daily Leader*, November 15, 1903, 4. This article seems to set out verbatim the ruling of Governor Chatterton, and therefore I've relied on it heavily.

41. Ibid.

42. Ibid.

43. Ibid.

44. Ibid.

45. Ibid.; "Cheyenne Man Slain by Kansas City Thugs," *Cheyenne Daily Leader*, June 22, 1907, 1. As the headline indicated, Ollie Whitman was murdered in Kansas City in 1907.

46. "Governor Refuses Clemency and Horn Will Be Hanged," *Cheyenne Daily Leader*, November 15, 1903, 4.

47. Ibid.

48. Ibid.

CHAPTER 29

1. "Governor Refuses Clemency and Horn Will be Hanged," *Cheyenne Daily Leader*, November 15, 1903, 4.

2. See "Other Crimes of Tom Horn," *Buffalo Voice*, December 27, 1902, 1; "Horn Killed Rustler," *Wyoming Derrick*, December 18, 1902, 1.

3. "Horn Was Slayer of Powell and Lewis," *Cheyenne Daily Leader*, October 30, 1902, 3. See also "Horn's Wild Ride," *Cheyenne Daily Leader*, November 27, 1902, 3.

4. "Horn and McCloud Attempt Escape" ("No More Chances,") *Cheyenne Daily Leader*, August 10, 1903, 4; "Wyoming Briefs," *Wheatland (Wyo.) World*, August 21, 1903, 4; "Court House Notes," *Wyoming Tribune* (Cheyenne), September 4, 1903, 4. The reports on Horn's incarceration after his conviction are inconsistent, with earlier ones indicating that Horn's privileges had been curtailed earlier.

5. "Another Plot Is Suspected," *Laramie Boomerang*, August 25, 1903, 1.

6. This paragraph is based on "Gatling Gun in the Jail," *Rock Springs (Wyo.) Miner*, October 19, 1903, 1. The story was said to be taken from the Cheyenne *Leader*, but the only Gatling gun story I found in the *Leader*, seemingly identical to the October 19, 1903, *Miner* story, was not published until October 24, 1903 (p. 4). The story apparently earlier ran in the *Leader*, for which few issues from 1903 are available.

7. "Gatling Gun in the Jail," *Rock Springs (Wyo.) Miner*, October 19, 1903, 1. See also "Another Tom Horn Story," *Semi-Weekly Boomerang* (Laramie) October 26, 1903, 4.

8. See "Will Remain Secret," *Laramie Boomerang*, October 15, 1903, 1; "Horn Shows Great Nerve," *Laramie Boomerang*, November 17, 1903, 1.

9. "Horn Shows Great Nerve," *Laramie Boomerang,* November 17, 1903, 1.

10. "Tom Horn Writes Appeal," *Laramie Boomerang,* October 20, 1903, 1; "Horn's Letter to Ohnhaus," *Laramie Boomerang,* October 29, 1903, 1.

11. "Horn Shows Great Nerve," *Laramie Boomerang,* November 17, 1903, 1.

12. "Horn as Indifferent as Ever," *Laramie Boomerang,* November 18, 1903, 1, quoting the *Cheyenne Daily Leader.* It is not clear from the *Leader* article whether reporters interviewed Horn in his jail cell, but it seems unlikely. Sheriff's deputies probably provided the information for the story.

13. "A Novel by Tom Horn," *Laramie Boomerang,* October 30, 1903, 1. So much of the writing was fiction that perhaps referring to it as a novel was appropriate.

14. "Evangelists Visit Horn," *Laramie Boomerang,* November 18, 1903, 1.

15. See "Affidavit of Tom Horn's Confession," *Laramie Boomerang,* November 24, 1903, 2, wherein the *Boomerang* printed an affidavit of Reverend Williams saying that "Horn admitted he was a guilty man."

16. "Many Soldiers at the Jail," *Laramie Boomerang,* November 20, 1903, 1; "Horn Will Be His Own Executioner," *Laramie Boomerang,* October 6, 1903, 2. No source was given for Horn's demeanor while workmen built the scaffold.

17. "Many Soldiers at the Jail," *Laramie Boomerang,* November 20, 1903, 1.

18. Ibid.

19. "Execution of Tom Horn," *Laramie Boomerang,* November 21, 1903, 1. In the following discussion I principally used three articles from Wyoming newspapers, which were remarkably consistent, but also contained their own perspective: "Many Soldiers at the Jail," *Laramie Boomerang,* November 20, 1903, 1; "Tom Horn Hanged at Cheyenne at 11:08 A.M.," *Laramie Republican,* November 20, 1903; *Wyoming Tribune* (Cheyenne), "Tom Horn the Noted Desperado Dies on the Gallows," November 20, 1903, 1.

20. "Tom Horn Hanged at Cheyenne at 11:08 A.M.," *Laramie Republican,* November 20, 1903, 1.

21. Ibid.; "Emotional Farewell to Coble," *Laramie Boomerang,* November 22, 1903, 1.

22. "Emotional Farewell to Coble," *Laramie Boomerang,* November 22, 1903, 1.

23. Larry D. Ball, *Tom Horn in Life and Legend* (Norman: University of Oklahoma Press, 2014), 301 (November 20, 1903, photo of jail); "Tom Horn the Noted Desperado Dies on the Gallows," *Wyoming Tribune* (Cheyenne), November 20, 1903, 1.

24. "Tom Horn Hanged at Cheyenne at 11:08 A.M.," *Laramie Republican,* November 20, 1903, 1.

25. "Tom Horn the Noted Desperado Dies on the Gallows," *Wyoming Tribune* (Cheyenne), November 20, 1903, 1. This song was recorded by Patsy Cline, a beautiful rendition performed with "power and authority," as noted in a pamphlet accompanying *The Patsy Cline Collection* (MCA Records, 1991).

26. "Tom Horn Hanged at Cheyenne at 11:08 A.M.," *Laramie Republican,* November 20, 1903, 1.

27. "Execution of Tom Horn," *Laramie Boomerang,* November 21, 1903, 1.

28. "Tom Horn Hanged at Cheyenne at 11:08 A.M.," *Laramie Republican,* November 20, 1903, 1; "Tom Horn the Noted Desperado Dies on the Gallows," *Wyoming Tribune* (Cheyenne), November 20, 1903, 1.

29. "Tom Horn Hanged at Cheyenne at 11:08 A.M.," *Laramie Republican*, November 20, 1903, 1; "Tom Horn the Noted Desperado Dies on the Gallows," *Wyoming Tribune* (Cheyenne), November 20, 1903, 1. Regarding the crowd, see "Horn and Mortensen Executed," *Wyoming Press* (Evanston, Wyo.), November 21, 1903, 1. Peter Mortensen was a man executed in Salt Lake City (not far from Evanston, Wyoming) the same day Horn was executed in Cheyenne.

30. Ball, *Tom Horn*, 410, 420, 422.

31. William Shakespeare, *King Lear*, act 1, scene 4.

EPILOGUE

1. For samples of Wyoming people's opinions of Tom Horn and his execution, as expressed in Wyoming newspapers, see "Sagebrush Philosophy Done into Some Scintillating Solecisms," *Bill Barlow's Budget* (Douglas, Wyo.), November 25, 1903, 1; "The True Remedy Applied," *Laramie Boomerang,* November 22, 1903, 2 (citing the *Cheyenne Leader*); "The Career of Tom Horn," *Semi-Weekly Boomerang* (Laramie), November 23, 1903, 2; *Saratoga Sun,* November 26, 1903, 1, first column. Regarding Horn's bragging in both Cheyenne and Laramie bars, see Larry D. Ball, *Tom Horn in Life and Legend* (Norman: University of Oklahoma Press, 2014), 185.

2. "The Law Supreme," *Laramie Republican,* November 20, 1903, 2.

3. "Tom Horn Hung," *Wyoming Star* (Green River, Wyo.), November 20, 1903, 1.

4. Regarding Walter Stoll's salary, see "Horn Convicted and State Will Prosecute Employers," *Denver Times,* October 25, 1902; "Tom Horn Is Guilty," *Rocky Mountain News,* October 25, 1902, 2.

5. Ball, *Tom Horn,* 421.

6. "The Life of Tom Horn," *Laramie Boomerang,* April 6, 1904, 1. See also "Life of Tom Horn," *Wyoming Tribune* (Cheyenne), May 3, 1904, 1; "The Life of Tom Horn," *Laramie Boomerang,* April 6, 1904, 1; ad for the Horn autobiography, *Wyoming Tribune (Cheyenne),* May 7, 1904, 2. Regarding the involvement of Miss Kimmell, see Ball, *Tom Horn,* 428.

7. Ball, *Tom Horn.*

8. Ibid., 240, 241 (Tom Horn letter to John C. Coble, esquire, November 20, 1903).

9. Tom Horn, *Life of Tom Horn, Government Scout and Interpreter* (Norman: University of Oklahoma Press, 1964), 238, 239 (Tom Horn letter to John C. Coble, esquire, November 17, 1903).

10. Ibid., 240, 241 (Tom Horn letter to John C. Coble, esquire, November 20, 1903).

11. Ibid., *Life of Tom Horn,* 244–64 (April 12, 1904, statement).

12. Ibid., *Life of Tom Horn,* 270–72 (March 1, 1903, closing word).

13. "Iron Mountain Friends of Tom Horn Standing by Him Nobly," *Denver Times*, October 4, 1902, 7.

14. Charles B. Penrose, *The Rustler Business* (Buffalo, Wyo.: Jim Gatchell Memorial Museum Press, 2007), 37. It is not clear whether Penrose was directly quoting Irvine or not. Regardless, I believe the thoughts expressed originated with Irvine.

15. "Was Missing Man Murdered by Horn?," *Cheyenne Daily Leader*, October 29, 1902, 3.

16. "To Ferret Out Hirers of Murderer Tom Horn" ("Another Confession"), *Cheyenne Daily Leader*, October 27, 1902, 4.

17. Ball, *Tom Horn*, 242. See also Charles A. Siringo, *Two Evil Isms: Pinkertonism and Anarchism* (Chicago: C. A. Siringo, 1915), 46–47. Regarding further admissions, see Ball, *Tom Horn*, 431.

18. See chapter 26 herein.

19. "Children Drawn to Tom Horn Trial," *Denver Post*, October 19, 1902, 4; "Horn Swears That His Confession Was a Joke," *Rocky Mountain News*, October 19, 1902, 1.

20. Ball, *Tom Horn*, 326, 429.

21. Ibid., 428–30.

22. Ibid., 430; "Discouraged Coble Kills Himself in Hotel Lobby," *Wyoming Tribune* (Cheyenne), December 4, 1914, 1.

23. "Miss Kimmell Is Quite Safe," *Weekly Boomerang* (Cheyenne), December 10, 1903, 1; "Glendolene Kimmell Is Now Free," *Laramie Boomerang*, December 18, 1903, 2.

24. Carol L. Bowers, "School Bells and Winchesters: The Sad Saga of Glendolene Myrtle Kimmel," *Annals of Wyoming* 73, no. 1 (Winter 2001), 30, 31.

25. My Casemaker Legal Research program shows John W. Lacey as the attorney for one party or another in sixty-two cases decided by the Wyoming Supreme Court, including *Utah Construction Company v. State Highway Commission*, 45 Wyo. 403, 19 P.2d 951 (Wyo. 1933) and *Moshannon National Bank v. Iron Mountain Ranch Co.*, 45 Wyo. 265, 18 P.2d 623 (Wyo. 1933). In the *Utah Construction* case, Lacey is stated to have been one of the attorneys who submitted a brief and who argued before the court. In *Moshannon National Bank*, Lacey was listed as an attorney who submitted a brief.

26. "John Wesley Lacey," Find a Grave, http://www.findagrave.com/ (which shows a photograph of Lacey's gravestone).

27. See, for example, comments about Chatterton in *Grand Encampment Herald*, November 20, 1903, 4; "Honorable and Successful Career," *Wyoming Tribune* (Cheyenne), May 4, 1904, 2; "Thanksgiving," *Rock Springs Miner*, November 26, 1903, 2.

28. "Political Campaign of Marked Interest," *Laramie Boomerang*, November 2, 1904, 1.

29. T. A. Larson, *History of Wyoming* (Lincoln: University of Nebraska Press, 1965), 317.

30. Ibid., 314.

31. "Dictation by Dissatisfied," *Semi-Weekly Boomerang* (Laramie), September 19, 1904, 2; "Speech of Mr. Osborne," *Semi-Weekly Boomerang* (Laramie), September 7, 1904, 3.

32. State Biography File, Wyoming State Archives; Find a Grave, http://www.findagrave.com/. Like John Lacey's, Fenimore Chatterton's name is found listed as participating counsel in cases before the Wyoming Supreme Court, although only twice, compared to Lacey's sixty-two times. The last one was in 1929, *Weaver v. Public Service Commission of Wyoming*, 40 Wyo. 462, 278 Pac. 542 (Wyo. 1929).

33. "Contest Is Filed," *Wyoming Tribune* (Cheyenne), December 23, 1904, 1.

34. "The Horn Case Still Lives," *Semi-Weekly Boomerang* (Laramie), December 1, 1904, 1.

35. "240 in Lead," *Wyoming Tribune* (Cheyenne), May 19, 1905, 1; "Ross Elected," *Wyoming Tribune* (Cheyenne), September 1, 1905, 5.

36. "Society Woman Seeks Divorce," *Semi-Weekly Boomerang* (Laramie), March 20, 1906, 3.

37. "Attorney Stoll Dies Very Suddenly," *Cheyenne State Leader*, June 2, 1911, 1.

38. "Walter R. Stoll," *Laramie Republican*, June 4, 1911, 2.

39. "Horn Reward Paid," *Laramie Boomerang*, October 10, 1903, 2.

40. "Joe LeFors Cleverly Traps 150 Gamblers," *Wyoming Tribune* (Cheyenne), April 9, 1906, 4; John W. Davis, *A Vast Amount of Trouble: A History of the Spring Creek Raid* (Niwot: University Press of Colorado, 1993), 82, 239.

41. See "LaFors: A Type of Westerner," *Cheyenne State Leader*, September 15, 1909, 2.

42. "Governor Carey's Last Act," *Casper Daily Press*, January 6, 1915, 2 (quoting the *Park County Enterprise*).

43. Davis, *A Vast Amount of Trouble*, 263.

44. "Kels Nickell Buys a Ranch on the Platte," *Weekly Boomerang* (Laramie), June 15, 1904, 1. Thereafter there are several references in area newspapers showing the Nickell family in Encampment, including one from the *Encampment Echo*, June 14, 1928, saying that Mrs. Fred Nickell had moved to Saratoga and that Fred was still employed at the Parco Refinery. See also *Encampment Echo*, September 18, 1924.

45. Joint Centennial Committee of Saratoga and Encampment, Wyoming, *Saratoga and Encampment, Wyoming: An Album of Family Histories* (Woodlands, Tex.: Portfolio Publishing, 1989), 341, 342.

46. "The Conviction of Herbert Brink," *Wyoming Tribune* (Cheyenne), November 12, 1909, 4.

47. Todd Guenther, "The List of Good Negroes: African American Lynchings in the Equality State," *Annals of Wyoming* 81 (Spring 2009), 2–33.

Bibliography

ABBREVIATIONS

CIT. Coroner's inquest transcript, July 20, 1901, Wyoming State Archives, Cheyenne.
TT. Trial transcript, *State v. Horn,* October 10, 1903, Wyoming Archives.

ARCHIVES AND PUBLIC RECORDS

American Heritage Center, University of Wyoming, Laramie.
Kennedy (T. Blake) Papers.
Penrose (Charles B.) Papers.
Clerk of the Laramie County (Wyoming) District Court. Records.
Wyoming State Archives, Cheyenne.

BOOKS AND ARTICLES

Ball, Larry D. *Tom Horn in Life and Legend.* Norman: University of Oklahoma Press, 2014.
Barnes, F. C. *Cartridges of the World.* 6th ed. Edited by Ken Warner. Northbrook, Ill.: DBI Books, 1989.
Bowers, Carol L. "School Bells and Winchesters: The Sad Saga of Glendolene Myrtle Kimmell." *Annals of Wyoming* 73, no. 1 (Winter 2001): 14<n>32.
Carlson, Chip. *Tom Horn: Blood on the Moon: Dark History of the Murderous Cattle Detective.* Glendo, Wyo.: High Plains Press, 2001.
————. *Joe LeFors: "I Slickered Tom Horn": The History of the Texas Cowboy Turned Montana-Wyoming Lawman, a Sequel.* Cheyenne, Wyo.: Beartooth Corral, 1995.
Colleta, Paulo E. *William Jennings Bryan,* vol. 1, *Political Evangelist, 1860–1908.* Lincoln: University of Nebraska Press, 1964.

Davis, John W. *Goodbye, Judge Lynch: The End of a Lawless Era in Wyoming's Big Horn Basin.* Norman: University of Oklahoma Press, 2005.

———. "The Insider's Guide to the Wyoming Supreme Court." In *Appellate Practice Compendium*, vol. 2. Edited by Dana Livingston, chapter 66 (1421–33). Chicago: American Bar Association, Judicial Division, 2014.

———. *A Vast Amount of Trouble: A History of the Spring Creek Raid.* Niwot: University Press of Colorado, 1993.

———. *Wyoming Range War: The Infamous Invasion of Johnson County.* Norman: University of Oklahoma Press, 2010.

Guenther, Todd. "The List of Good Negroes: African American Lynchings in the Equality State." *Annals of Wyoming* 81 (Spring 2009): 2–33.

Horn, Tom. *Life of Tom Horn, Government Scout and Interpreter.* Norman: University of Oklahoma Press, 1964.

Joint Centennial Committee of Saratoga and Encampment, Wyoming. *Saratoga and Encampment, Wyoming: An Album of Family Histories.* Woodlands, Tex.: Portfolio Publishing, 1989.

Krakel, Dean F. *The Saga of Tom Horn: The Story of a Cattleman's War.* Cheyenne, Wyo.: Powder River Publishers, 1954.

Larson, T. A., *History of Wyoming.* Lincoln: University of Nebraska Press, 1965.

LeFors, Joe. *Wyoming Peace Officer: An Autobiography.* Laramie, Wyo.: Laramie Printing Company, 1953.

Monaghan, Jay. *Tom Horn: Last of the Bad Men.* Lincoln: University of Nebraska Press, 1997.

O'Neal, Bill. *Cheyenne: A Biography of the "Magic City" of the Plains.* Austin, Tex.: Eakin Press, 2006.

———. *Cattlemen vs. Sheepherders: Five Decades of Violence in the West, 1880–1920.* Austin, Tex.: Eakin Press, 1989.

Penrose, Charles B. *The Rustler Business.* Buffalo, Wyo.: Jim Gatchell Memorial Museum Press, 2007.

Sharpe, Philip B., *The Rifle in America.* New York: W. Morrow, 1938.

Siringo, Charles A. *Two Evil Isms: Pinkertonism and Anarchism.* Chicago: C. A. Siringo, 1915.

Van Pelt, Lori. *Capital Characters of Old Cheyenne.* Glendo, Wyo.: High Plains Press, 2006.

Wentworth, Edward Norris. *America's Sheep Trails: History, Personalities.* Ames: Iowa State College Press, 1948.

COURT REPORTERS AND STATUTE BOOKS

Pacific Reports (West Publishing).

West's Annotated California Code of Civil Procedure.

Wyoming Court Rules Annotated.

Wyoming Reports.

Wyoming Revised Statutes, 1899.

Wyoming Statutes Annotated.

NEWSPAPERS

Bill Barlow's Budget (Douglas, Wyo.)
Buffalo (Wyo.) Bulletin
Buffalo (Wyo.) Voice
Casper Daily Press
Cheyenne Daily Leader
Cheyenne State Leader
Cheyenne Sun
Cody Enterprise
Crook County Monitor
Denver Post
Denver Republican
Denver Times
Encampment (Wyo.) Echo
Grand Encampment Herald (Encampment, Wyo.)
Graphic (Douglas, Wyo.)
Laramie Boomerang
Laramie Republican
Natrona County Tribune
Newcastle (Wyo.) News-Journal
Park County Enterprise
Rock Springs (Wyo.) Miner
Rocky Mountain News (Denver)
Saratoga (Wyo.) Sun
Semi-Weekly Boomerang (Laramie)
Sheridan Post
Sun Annual (Cheyenne)
Weekly Boomerang (Laramie)
Wheatland (Wyo.) World
Wyoming Derrick (Casper)
Wyoming Industrial Journal (Cheyenne)
Wyoming Press (Evanston, Wyo.)
Wyoming Star (Green River, Wyo.)
Wyoming Tribune (Cheyenne)

Afterword

Over the past twenty-two years, I've written four books looking at the problems with law and order in early Wyoming. With *The Trial of Tom Horn* I feel I've finally addressed all the important legal events in the long and difficult pathway to a mature society in the Cowboy State. The sudden opening of virtually all the lands in the northern half of the Territory of Wyoming, with no regulations or restrictions, was an open invitation to conflict, and conflict followed. Ambitious men flooded into northern Wyoming in 1879 and created large cattle ranches almost overnight in areas completely void of law enforcement. A powerful culture of extralegal violence grew up. The strong survived by becoming a law unto themselves. The result, however, was a thirty-year struggle to wrest back the control of Wyoming from these willful cattle barons. It took the heroic efforts of men such as Walter Stoll to finally place society's ultimate power in the hands of lawfully constituted authorities.

To a historian, the fortuitous thing about the big, violent events of a very young Wyoming is that the ensuing trials were so well documented. That's especially true of the Tom Horn murder case, which is replete with primary material, from the long transcripts of the coroner's inquest and the trial, to the court files and the excellent coverage of newspapers. As I worked on this book, I felt that it was a story that practically told itself, so long as I was diligent and not too obtrusive.

I was also lucky in that I had two published authors to consult with, Larry Ball and Chip Carlson. While I was writing this work, Larry published his thorough biography of Tom Horn. Time and again I found that he had addressed a point I might otherwise have been forced to spend hours on. The availability of Larry's biography allowed me to focus on the trial itself, and as a lawyer, that's what I wanted to do. I also found Chip Carlson to be a great resource, a good man to use as a sounding board. Chip has lived the saga of Tom Horn and has an excellent command of the events of Horn's life. It was a fascinating exercise to visit the scene of the murder of Willie Nickell with Chip (and others) and listen to his thoughts about it. I didn't always agree with Chip, but I always had to respect his knowledge and very much appreciated his help.

I should explain my dedication of this book to Dr. David Freeman. I met Dave in the fall of 1964, when we each arrived at the New Hampton School in New Hampton, New Hampshire. Both of us had just received our bachelor degrees, and both of us had waited too long to get into professional schools. So we each decided to teach for a year, Dave courses in history and I in mathematics.

Dave was impressive. He was a brilliant scholar (magna cum laude, Harvard) and a really decent, enjoyable guy. He was thoroughly urban, having grown up in eastern Massachusetts, while I was a small-town kid from a remote corner of Wyoming. Although polar opposites of the American spectrum, we took to each other immediately and enjoyed a strong friendship through the school year. Then we went our separate ways: I headed back west to the University of Wyoming College of Law and Dave went to the Harvard University School of Medicine. Forty years later I found myself wondering how Dave was doing and I found him. When my wife and I traveled through Lexington, Massachusetts, in 2005, Dave and I met and talked all about what we'd done with our lives since New Hampton. It was one of the best conversations of my life. We kept in contact, and in 2011 my wife and I stayed with Dave and his wife, Amanda (both physicians) in their beautiful Queen Anne house in Newton Centre, Massachusetts. We had a great time running all over the Boston area. The plan was that the next year we would host the Freemans in Wyoming, showing them our very different lives in a very different place.

Dave became a fan of my writing. He was especially taken by *Wyoming Range War* and gave me a marvelous review of the book. I treasured his perceptive comments. As I got into this latest book about Tom Horn, Dave and I discussed it in some detail, and again I very much appreciated his insight.

We scheduled the time for the Freemans' trip to Wyoming for early August 2012. In June we made plans for excursions, ranging from the Big Horn Basin to Yellowstone and the Tetons. I know Dave was excited about the trip because one of his sons later told me so. But I never got to show Wyoming to Dave and Amanda. On July 8, 2012, Dave died of a heart attack. It was a shock and I felt robbed of our resurrected friendship. It seemed only fitting to dedicate this book to him.

It's often said that the writing of a book is a collaborative effort, and this is not a cliché. I'll get most of the credit if the book does well, but I've had some great help on this one. As usual, it starts with my excellent editor, Chuck Rankin. It's been a privilege to work with him through the years and this time was no exception. And, as always, the Wyoming people I dealt with were helpful and friendly. Candy Moulton stood out, though, as she responded to my routine request for information about an Encampment family by furnishing research worthy of a master's thesis. Though he is not from Wyoming, I especially appreciated the help of C. J. Backus, a Denver researcher who did an excellent job navigating old Denver newspapers. Along these lines, I used a lot of photos and illustrations from the *Denver Post*. Consent for their use was not required (because they go back so far), but the *Denver Post* was so intimately involved in the Tom Horn story, and their photos and illustrations are such a special contribution, that I feel I should extend my thanks. Bob Stottler, the curator at the Washakie Museum, in Worland, Wyoming, was very helpful with the first chapters of the book (which I found especially difficult), reading them and making good suggestions to address some of the deficiencies. Finally, my wife, Celia, as usual, helped with everything.

Index